Lineberger Memorial

Library

Given In Honor Of

_____

Lutheran Theological Southern Seminary   Columbia, S. C.

The NEW ENCYCLOPEDIA *of* SOUTHERN CULTURE

VOLUME 24 : RACE

Volumes in

The New Encyclopedia of Southern Culture

are:

The NEW

ENCYCLOPEDIA *of* SOUTHERN CULTURE

CHARLES REAGAN WILSON General Editor

JAMES G. THOMAS JR. Managing Editor

ANN J. ABADIE Associate Editor

VOLUME 24

Race

THOMAS C. HOLT & LAURIE B. GREEN

Volume Editors

Sponsored by

THE CENTER FOR THE STUDY OF SOUTHERN CULTURE

at the University of Mississippi

THE UNIVERSITY OF NORTH CAROLINA PRESS

Chapel Hill

This book was published with the
assistance of the Anniversary Endowment Fund
of the University of North Carolina Press.

Designed by Richard Hendel
Set in Minion types by Tseng Information Systems, Inc.
Manufactured in the United States of America
The paper in this book meets the guidelines for permanence and durability
of the Committee on Production Guidelines for Book Longevity of the
Council on Library Resources.
The University of North Carolina Press has been a member
of the Green Press Initiative since 2003.
Library of Congress Cataloging-in-Publication Data
Race / Thomas C. Holt and Laurie B. Green, volume editors.
p. cm. — (The new encyclopedia of Southern culture; v. 24)
"Published with the assistance of the Anniversary Endowment
Fund of the University of North Carolina Press"
"Sponsored by The Center for the Study of Southern Culture at the
University of Mississippi."
Includes bibliographical references and index.
ISBN 978-1-4696-0722-1 (alk. paper) —
ISBN 978-1-4696-0723-8 (pbk.: alk. paper)
1. African Americans—Southern States—Encyclopedias. 2. Hispanic
Americans—Southern States—Encyclopedias. 3. Asian Americans—
Southern States—Encyclopedias. 4. Southern States—Race relations—
Encyclopedias. 5. Southern States—Ethnic relations—Encyclopedias.
6. Southern States—Social conditions—Encyclopedias. I. Holt,
Thomas C. II. Green, Laurie B. III. University of Mississippi.
Center for the Study of Southern Culture. IV. Series.
F209 .N47 2006 vol. 24
[F216.2]
975.003 s—dc22
2012473092
The *Encyclopedia of Southern Culture*, sponsored by the Center for
the Study of Southern Culture at the University of Mississippi, was
published by the University of North Carolina Press in 1989.
cloth   17 16 15 14 13   5 4 3 2 1
paper   17 16 15 14 13   5 4 3 2 1

Tell about the South. What's it like there.

What do they do there. Why do they live there.

Why do they live at all.

WILLIAM FAULKNER

Absalom, Absalom!

CONTENTS

GENERAL INTRODUCTION

In 1989 years of planning and hard work came to fruition when the University of North Carolina Press joined the Center for the Study of Southern Culture at the University of Mississippi to publish the *Encyclopedia of Southern Culture*. While all those involved in writing, reviewing, editing, and producing the volume believed it would be received as a vital contribution to our understanding of the American South, no one could have anticipated fully the widespread acclaim it would receive from reviewers and other commentators. But the *Encyclopedia* was indeed celebrated, not only by scholars but also by popular audiences with a deep, abiding interest in the region. At a time when some people talked of the "vanishing South," the book helped remind a national audience that the region was alive and well, and it has continued to shape national perceptions of the South through the work of its many users—journalists, scholars, teachers, students, and general readers.

As the introduction to the *Encyclopedia* noted, its conceptualization and organization reflected a cultural approach to the South. It highlighted such issues as the core zones and margins of southern culture, the boundaries where "the South" overlapped with other cultures, the role of history in contemporary culture, and the centrality of regional consciousness, symbolism, and mythology. By 1989 scholars had moved beyond the idea of cultures as real, tangible entities, viewing them instead as abstractions. The *Encyclopedia*'s editors and contributors thus included a full range of social indicators, trait groupings, literary concepts, and historical evidence typically used in regional studies, carefully working to address the distinctive and characteristic traits that made the American South a particular place. The introduction to the *Encyclopedia* concluded that the fundamental uniqueness of southern culture was reflected in the volume's composite portrait of the South. We asked contributors to consider aspects that were unique to the region but also those that suggested its internal diversity. The volume was not a reference book of southern history, which explained something of the design of entries. There were fewer essays on colonial and antebellum history than on the postbellum and modern periods, befitting our conception of the volume as one trying not only to chart the cultural landscape of the South but also to illuminate the contemporary era.

When C. Vann Woodward reviewed the *Encyclopedia* in the *New York Review of Books*, he concluded his review by noting "the continued liveliness of interest in the South and its seeming inexhaustibility as a field of study." Research on the South, he wrote, furnishes "proof of the value of the *Encyclopedia* as a scholarly undertaking as well as suggesting future needs for revision or supplement to keep up with ongoing scholarship." The two decades since the publication of the *Encyclopedia of Southern Culture* have certainly suggested that Woodward was correct. The American South has undergone significant changes that make for a different context for the study of the region. The South has undergone social, economic, political, intellectual, and literary transformations, creating the need for a new edition of the *Encyclopedia* that will remain relevant to a changing region. Globalization has become a major issue, seen in the South through the appearance of Japanese automobile factories, Hispanic workers who have immigrated from Latin America or Cuba, and a new prominence for Asian and Middle Eastern religions that were hardly present in the 1980s South. The African American return migration to the South, which started in the 1970s, dramatically increased in the 1990s, as countless books simultaneously appeared asserting powerfully the claims of African Americans as formative influences on southern culture. Politically, southerners from both parties have played crucial leadership roles in national politics, and the Republican Party has dominated a near-solid South in national elections. Meanwhile, new forms of music, like hip-hop, have emerged with distinct southern expressions, and the term "dirty South" has taken on new musical meanings not thought of in 1989. New genres of writing by creative southerners, such as gay and lesbian literature and "white trash" writing, extend the southern literary tradition.

Meanwhile, as Woodward foresaw, scholars have continued their engagement with the history and culture of the South since the publication of the *Encyclopedia*, raising new scholarly issues and opening new areas of study. Historians have moved beyond their earlier preoccupation with social history to write new cultural history as well. They have used the categories of race, social class, and gender to illuminate the diversity of the South, rather than a unified "mind of the South." Previously underexplored areas within the field of southern historical studies, such as the colonial era, are now seen as formative periods of the region's character, with the South's positioning within a larger Atlantic world a productive new area of study. Cultural memory has become a major topic in the exploration of how the social construction of "the South" benefited some social groups and exploited others. Scholars in many disciplines have made the southern identity a major topic, and they have used a variety of methodologies to suggest what that identity has meant to different social groups. Literary critics have adapted cultural theories to the South and have raised the issue of postsouthern literature to a major category of concern as well as exploring the links between the literature of the American South and that of the Caribbean. Anthropologists have used different theoretical formulations from literary critics, providing models for their fieldwork in southern communities. In the past 30 years anthropologists have set increasing numbers of their ethnographic studies in the South, with many of them now exploring topics specifically linked to southern cultural issues. Scholars now place the Native American story, from prehistory to the contemporary era, as a central part of southern history. Comparative and interdisciplinary approaches to the South have encouraged scholars to look at such issues as the borders and boundaries of the South, specific places and spaces with distinct identities within the American South, and the global and transnational Souths, linking the American South with many formerly colonial societies around the world.

The first edition of the *Encyclopedia of Southern Culture* anticipated many of these approaches and indeed stimulated the growth of Southern Studies as a distinct interdisciplinary field. The Center for the Study of Southern Culture has worked for more than three decades to encourage research and teaching about the American South. Its academic programs have produced graduates who have gone on to write interdisciplinary studies of the South, while others have staffed the cultural institutions of the region and in turn encouraged those institutions to document and present the South's culture to broad public audiences. The center's conferences and publications have continued its long tradition of promoting understanding of the history, literature, and music of the South, with new initiatives focused on southern foodways, the future of the South, and the global Souths, expressing the center's mission to bring the best current scholarship to broad public audiences. Its documentary studies projects build oral and visual archives, and the New Directions in Southern Studies book series, published by the University of North Carolina Press, offers an important venue for innovative scholarship.

Since the *Encyclopedia of Southern Culture* appeared, the field of Southern Studies has dramatically developed, with an extensive network now of academic and research institutions whose projects focus specifically on the interdisciplinary study of the South. The Center for the Study of the American South at the University of North Carolina at Chapel Hill, led by Director Jocelyn Neal and Associate Director and *Encyclopedia* coeditor William Ferris, publishes the lively journal *Southern Cultures* and is now at the organizational center of many other Southern Studies projects. The Institute for Southern Studies at the University of South Carolina, the Southern Intellectual History Circle, the Society for the Study of Southern Literature, the Southern Studies Forum of the European American Studies Association, Emory University's SouthernSpaces.org, and the South Atlantic Humanities Center (at the Virginia Foundation for the Humanities, the University of Virginia, and Virginia Polytechnic Institute and State University) express the recent expansion of interest in regional study.

Observers of the American South have had much to absorb, given the rapid pace of recent change. The institutional framework for studying the South is broader and deeper than ever, yet the relationship between the older verities of regional study and new realities remains unclear. Given the extent of changes in the American South and in Southern Studies since the publication of the *Encyclopedia of Southern Culture*, the need for a new edition of that work is clear. Therefore, the Center for the Study of Southern Culture has once again joined the University of North Carolina Press to produce *The New Encyclopedia of Southern Culture*. As readers of the original edition will quickly see, *The New Encyclopedia* follows many of the scholarly principles and editorial conventions established in the original, but with one key difference; rather than being published in a single hardback volume, *The New Encyclopedia* is presented in a series of shorter individual volumes that build on the 24 original subject categories used in the *Encyclopedia* and adapt them to new scholarly developments. Some earlier *Encyclopedia* categories have been reconceptualized in light of new academic interests. For example, the subject section originally titled "Women's Life" is reconceived as a new volume, *Gender*, and the original "Black Life" section is more broadly interpreted as a volume on race. These changes reflect new analytical concerns that place the study of women and blacks in broader cultural systems, reflecting the emergence of, among other topics, the study of male culture and of whiteness. Both volumes draw as well from the rich recent scholarship on women's life and black life. In addition, topics with some thematic coherence are combined in a volume, such as *Law and Politics* and *Agriculture and Industry*. One new topic, *Foodways*, is the basis of a separate volume, reflecting its new prominence in the interdisciplinary study of southern culture.

Numerous individual topical volumes together make up *The New Encyclopedia of Southern Culture* and extend the reach of the reference work to wider audiences. This approach should enhance the use of the *Encyclopedia* in academic courses and is intended to be convenient for readers with more focused interests within the larger context of southern culture. Readers will have handy access to one-volume, authoritative, and comprehensive scholarly treatments of the major areas of southern culture.

We have been fortunate that, in nearly all cases, subject consultants who offered crucial direction in shaping the topical sections for the original edition have agreed to join us in this new endeavor as volume editors. When new volume editors have been added, we have again looked for respected figures who can provide not only their own expertise but also strong networks of scholars to help develop relevant lists of topics and to serve as contributors in their areas. The reputations of all our volume editors as leading scholars in their areas encouraged the contributions of other scholars and added to *The New Encyclopedia*'s authority as a reference work.

The New Encyclopedia of Southern Culture builds on the strengths of articles in the original edition in several ways. For many existing articles, original authors agreed to update their contributions with new interpretations and theoretical perspectives, current statistics, new bibliographies, or simple factual developments that needed to be included. If the original contributor was unable to update an article, the editorial staff added new material or sent it to another scholar for assessment. In some cases, the general editor and volume editors selected a new contributor if an article seemed particularly dated and new work indicated the need for a fresh perspective. And importantly, where new developments have warranted treatment of topics not addressed in the original edition, volume editors have commissioned entirely new essays and articles that are published here for the first time.

The American South embodies a powerful historical and mythical presence, both a complex environmental and geographic landscape and a place of the imagination. Changes in the region's contemporary socioeconomic realities and new developments in scholarship have been incorporated in the conceptualization and approach of *The New Encyclopedia of Southern Culture*. Anthropologist Clifford Geertz has spoken of culture as context, and this encyclopedia looks at the American South as a complex place that has served as the context for cultural expression. This volume provides information and perspective on the diversity of cultures in a geographic and imaginative place with a long history and distinctive character.

The *Encyclopedia of Southern Culture* was produced through major grants from the Program for Research Tools and Reference Works of the National Endowment for the Humanities, the Ford Foundation, the Atlantic-Richfield Foundation, and the Mary Doyle Trust. We are grateful as well to the College of Liberal Arts at the University of Mississippi for support and to the individual donors to the Center for the Study of Southern Culture who have directly or indirectly supported work on *The New Encyclopedia of Southern Culture*. We thank the volume editors for their ideas in reimagining their subjects and the contributors of articles for their work in extending the usefulness of the book in new ways. We acknowledge the support and contributions of the faculty and staff at the Center for the Study of Southern Culture. Finally, we want especially to honor the work of William Ferris and Mary Hart on the *Encyclopedia of Southern Culture*. Bill, the founding director of the Center for the Study of Southern Culture, was coeditor, and his good work recruiting authors, editing text, selecting images, and publicizing the volume among a wide network of people was, of course, invaluable. Despite the many changes in the new encyclopedia, Bill's influence remains. Mary "Sue" Hart was also an invaluable member of the original encyclopedia team, bringing the careful and precise eye of the librarian, and an iconoclastic spirit, to our work.

INTRODUCTION

This volume of *The New Encyclopedia of Southern Culture* presented distinctive planning challenges. Race is a topic that the other 23 volumes in the series treat, some more centrally than others, but it simply cannot be ignored in considerations of the American South. The topics related to race in other volumes provide an ongoing web that connects each volume to a larger southern cultural whole. Each volume has been planned, however, to stand alone in treating a major topic in southern culture, so a separate volume on race was essential. The editors made the decision to include here some articles related to race that have appeared in other volumes. We could not imagine having a volume claiming to treat race in the South without including the excellent article on "Etiquette of Race Relations in the Jim Crow South" that had appeared in the *Myth, Manners, and Memory* volume, or the article on "Criminal Justice" that had appeared in the *Law and Politics* volume. "Southern Politics and Race" similarly addressed concerns of this volume, although it originally appeared in an earlier volume.

Beyond that choice, editors commissioned new entries to reflect the *Race* volume's concern with the South as a multiracial society. The origin of this volume is the Black Life section of the original *Encyclopedia of Southern Culture* (1989), which focused on African American history and culture within a primarily biracial context. Since then, scholars have produced an exciting new literature that positions the South as a society that tried to impose rigid racial boundaries, but one that transcended those attempts, resulting in a dynamic, diverse, and fluid society, all of which is reflected in the articles herein. The authors of these entries take as a given that race is a socially constructed category, and they go on to examine ideas about racial differences within a multiracial context, providing new ways of looking at the South's racial past and future. As the overview suggests, racial diversity has nurtured the South's cultural heritage.

Much attention remains focused on African American life, given the demographic and cultural impact of blacks on the South, but the articles collectively show that the black experience looks different at different times and places in the region's history. Articles on black life range from those on black landowners to advertising stereotypes to African influences. Enduring issues of segregation and desegregation are explored through articles on education, sports, and religion. This volume's shape came out of interpretive priorities that stressed ethnic interactions, as in entries on "Asians, Mexicans, Interracialism, and Racial Ambiguities," "Jews, Race, and Southernness," and "Native Americans and African Americans." As seen, article titles are sometimes more complex than many encyclopedia descriptors, but they reflect the volume's picture of a complex, multiracial South. The volume also reflects the recent spatial turn in Southern Studies. The South's relationship to Europe and Africa, to the Atlantic, the Pacific, and the Caribbean, all provide spatial grounding to understanding race and the South's cultural development. Writers on the South have long posited a particular southern sense of place, but this volume's focus on race led to a particular appreciation not so much of place but of movement, with articles on black migration, Latino migration, and white migration.

Work has been another broad interpretive theme in this volume, as labor has long been central to efforts at racial categorization, as seen in articles on "Agriculture, Race, and Transnational Labor," "Slavery and Emancipation," "Postbellum Labor," and the "Evolution of the Southern Economy." Creative expression is a familiar theme in *The New Encyclopedia*, and authors here treat it with new articles on literature and musical recordings, through entries on the importance of race to musical genres identified with the South, and through a lean and selective list of biographies of creative southerners who addressed racial issues.

The first volume in *The New Encyclopedia of Southern Culture* was *Religion*, surely one of the most important abiding aspects of southern life, and the editors chose to close the series with this volume on *Race*, another of the most important aspects to evaluate in charting southern cultural life. In both cases, as throughout the entire encyclopedia series, the editors offer articles that reflect contemporary concerns of a South in the midst of continual change, ever trying to understand the relationship of the region's past to its future.

RACE AND CULTURE IN AN
EVER-CHANGING SOUTH

The general editors have chosen a passage from *Absalom, Absalom!* for the epigraph to introduce these volumes on southern culture, suggesting thereby that our enduring image of the American South is best captured in the fiction of William Faulkner. Faulkner portrays a place, as C. Vann Woodward once suggested, long haunted by a very *un*-American memory of defeat, a sense of social failure, a lost innocence. Enveloping his tales is the fear that the South's best days are in the past, a past that yet haunts and constrains the present, a past that's "not even past." The South's story, then, cannot be simply told; it must be unraveled, strand-by-strand. Indeed, the very rhythm of Faulkner's storytelling evokes at times an image one often finds in the popular imaginary: the South is an insular, bounded space, a world closed and relatively homogeneous.

In reality, however, Faulkner's mythic South is a far more nuanced and complex world than its conventional image, with a complicated racial landscape that a simple black and white palette cannot capture. At the center of Faulkner's *Absalom, Absalom!* saga, of course, are the relations between its black and white inhabitants, with the sins of slavery laying heavily on southern white consciences, not because of its brutality and exploitation of labor—which continued under new forms of labor control well into the 20th century—but because of the shame and confusion of the "miscegenated" bodies and cultures left in its wake. At the story's margins, however, are the descendants of Native Americans, some of them forcibly relocated along a Trail of Tears from the Southeast. Their blood flows in the veins of his black and white characters alike, and their dispossession forms a half-remembered episode in the region's guilty past. Faulkner's South also has links to the Caribbean, prefiguring in fiction the flow of people and ideas in real life that would challenge the region's ostensibly strict social separation of black and white. Upon second sight, then, Faulkner's South is not closed and insular but open, not bounded and homogeneous but overlapping and diverse. Viewed from that perspective, the region's racial past and future look very different.

More than a quarter century ago, historian Ira Berlin warned that our understanding of African American life and history was unduly limited by "a static and singular vision" of its dynamics and complexity, when in fact the black experience evolved divergently in different times and spaces. His argument for a revised perspective on black life, one attentive to its spatially and temporally "specific social circumstances and cultural traditions," applies with equal force to studies of the South as a whole and to its racial dynamics in particular. The essays in this volume underscore Berlin's charge that we must take serious account of time and space in our efforts to comprehend how ideas about racial difference have shaped the region's past and present. They make clear that the South is not simply biracial but multiracial, and has been so since the 17th and 18th centuries, when European settlers first deployed captive African labor to exploit confiscated Native American land. They show how a rich, ever-expanding racial diversity has nourished the social and material roots of the South's proud cultural heritage—of story and song, of architecture and art, of manners and cuisines. They suggest that the region's political, social, and economic history cannot be fully comprehended without taking account of this past and this present.

Susan O'Donovan elaborates how slavery—the institutional foundation of southern life and culture and of their racial scaffolding—evolved differently in the various subregions of the South and at different historical moments. The South's racial and labor relations varied over time and space, reflecting the historically specific demographic configurations of its black, white, and red inhabitants, as well as the diversity of the southern economy that evolved. The South and its race relations must be understood in this broader, more dynamic context: that from the beginning the region has been defined by and formed in relation to other slave regimes in the Americas and around the bell curve of the Atlantic slave trade that peaked in the late 18th century; by trade relations with European nations and their Caribbean colonies, both before and after slave emancipation; and by the specific geopolitical interests that all these relationships produced. The South was not and could never be, as the popular imagination would have it, an undifferentiated place, frozen in time.

Focusing on New Orleans as a simultaneously unique and exemplary case, Shannon Dawdy and Zada Johnson reveal how an ostensibly insular southern world had in fact long been open to influences from the larger Atlantic World. Indeed, as their entry and other entries in this volume will show, from the beginning the region was shaped and reshaped by crosscurrents of peoples, ideas, and institutions. Slavery and the slave trade dictated the course of those crosscurrents over the South's first two and a half centuries, during which black bondage was the core institution around which much of the region's law, labor, polity, and social life revolved. It was slavery that initially knit the South into the international economic and cultural complex formed by other slave societies in the southern hemisphere, especially in the Caribbean. Sharing similarities in climate, economy, and cultural development, New World slave societies developed similar interests, confronted similar political forces, and evolved similar ideologies of rule and social order. Thus, while "peculiar" in comparison to its northern and middle Atlantic compatriots, the South was not exceptional among its neighbors in the southern Atlantic. It is not surprising, then, that southerners looked to annex Cuba when their farther westward continental expansion seemed thwarted, or that defeated Confederates immigrated to Mexico and Brazil after the Civil War.

Fed by the Atlantic slave trade for all but 50 years of its first two and a half centuries, the South's population mix and cultural life—for blacks and whites alike—was in constant flux as new Africans poured in and their new owners remade the southern physical and social landscape in order to exploit their labor power. Given that overseas trade was essential to the plantation economy, moreover, southern ports—dotting a coastline stretching from Baltimore to Galveston, the longest in the continental United States—were openings to the world. Through these openings poured goods, people, and, occasionally, revolutionary ideas. Notwithstanding determined efforts to suppress challenges to the racial regime, therefore, the antislavery pamphlets of David Walker or the republican ideas of Haitian and Cuban refugees found their way through those openings.

For all these reasons, British colonies in the lower South manifested from the start a demographic profile and a legal and economic character more typical of the Caribbean and Latin American slave societies than the Chesapeake or northern colonies; and this produced similarities in their political cultures and social arrangements, not least of which was the relative acceptance and allocation of social space to a mixed-race population (as Faulkner shows so graphically in *Absalom, Absalom!*). The long and porous sea border on the southern Atlantic opened the South to repeated waves of diverse political and economic refugees from the Caribbean basin and, on occasion, invited southern planters to dream of expansion into the Caribbean. All in all, the region knew a dynamism and openness thoroughly at odds with its more conventional image of timelessness and homogeneity.

Moon-Ho Jung's essay alerts us to the South's historic links to the Pacific World as well as to the Atlantic, despite the absence of a port on America's western coast. Like most New World planters, white southerners looked to Asian laborers to replace their former slaves in the early years following the Civil War and slavery's destruction. The indentured laborers they brought from southern China never satisfied the planters' fantasies of docile "guest workers" who would stake no claims to economic justice or citizenship, however. Like black freedpeople, Asians came to call the South "home." They formed families and communities, and some of them mixed socially and biologically with southern blacks, whites, Creoles, and Native Americans. Southern census takers and neighbors were never quite certain how to classify these families racially, so they were all identified simply as "Chinese" until Jim Crow laws forced them onto one or the other side of the biracial spectrum.

This 19th-century Asian beachhead was relatively small and inconsequential to the broader development of the southern economy and society at the time, but it prefigured the pattern of the South's 20th-century engagement with the Pacific World and a future immigration and settlement pattern that would eventually transform the South's cultural and racial makeup. From Japan to Vietnam, 20th-century wars in the Pacific drew the United States into intense and continuing involvements with Asian nations and peoples, some of whom made their way to the southern states. Several of the places of wartime incarceration of Japanese American citizens were located in the South—namely, in Arkansas, Texas, and Louisiana—from which many of the menfolk were inducted into segregated military units. Three decades later, American military interventions in Southeast Asia resulted in thousands of displaced persons seeking refuge in southern states. New communities sprang up in Louisiana and Texas, where climate, occupational opportunities, and a welcoming Catholic Church encouraged Vietnamese refugees to settle. As a result, the Gulf Coast is now home to more than 200,000 Southeast Asians (Vietnamese, Cambodian, Laotian) alone, and there were a total of at least 2.3 million Asians scattered across the South by the beginning of the new millennium in 2000. By the early 21st century, peoples of Asian origin had become a ubiquitous presence in southern interior cities and towns—running hotels, restaurants, and other small businesses and building churches, suburban enclaves, and shopping centers—and, in a throwback to the 19th century, sometimes working for manufacturers intent on disrupting union solidarity by employing a presumably docile, non-English-speaking labor force.

The growth of the South's Asian population is impressive, but the expansion and dispersion of the Latino population is undoubtedly the driving force in the region's late 20th-century racial transformation. Between 1980 and 2000, the South's Latino population increased from 4.3 million to 11 million. By the second decade of the new century, their numbers had swelled to 16.4 million. Equally impressive was their far-greater dispersion across the region. Instead of 9 out of 10 being concentrated in Florida and Texas, as had been the case in 1980, Latinos were scattered throughout the southern states in urban and rural areas and occupations.

Although the growing presence of Latinos in many areas of the Old South is new, Spanish-speaking peoples and territories have shaped southern history from the beginning. Imperial Spain's presence in Florida, along the Gulf Coast, and in Louisiana profoundly influenced the nation's and the region's colonial and early national history. The refuge that Native Americans and escaped African and African American slaves found in Spanish territories left deep impressions on each of those peoples' cultures, including the cultural interactions and alliances between them that contact promoted. The Latino imprint would grow broader and deeper after the Mexican War of 1846 and the annexation of Texas, both of which were promoted by southern expansionists seeking to build a more impregnable slave empire. Not only did territorial expansion forever blur the regional boundary between South and West; it also provided a rehearsal of a multiracial South, as black labor and brown labor were marshaled to tame the new frontier. With the development of large-scale agriculture in south Texas after World War I, southern plantation–style relations between growers and laborers took on new forms in the context of cross-border migrations by Mexican laborers, which were alternately facilitated and shut down by an expanding border patrol. Like African Americans in states to Texas's east, people of Mexican origin in south Texas were confronted by the threat of racial violence in addition to segregation. Though lacking the legal mandate for Jim Crow generally inscribed in the constitutions of the southeastern states, the segregation of Mexican Americans in Texas was just as thorough.

The 21st-century legacy of the South's westward expansion is a far more complex racial situation than the conventional biracial paradigm can account for. The ostensibly "solid" political South now cloaks a social, cultural, and political diversity and complexity that is almost certain to find expression eventually in a new southern political regime. The recent hostility to Mexican immigrants in the southern interior is but a harbinger of that very different political future, since Latino population growth will inevitably change not only the South's political calculus but its racial discourse as well. It is possible, however, that the South's rapidly evolving racial demography will also produce more complex political alliances—ones in which black may ally with brown, or brown with white, or even black with white. The 2007 election in Louisiana of a governor and a congressman of Asian descent and conservative politics suggests something of the uncertain trajectory that a reframed political landscape in a multiracial South might take.

With the question "Where did the Asian sit on the segregated bus?" Leslie Bow frames an intriguing perspective on how demographic transformations have challenged, changed, and reinforced southern racial hierarchies. At times,

Asians were bystanders to a humiliation directed solely at blacks; at other times they were its victims; and at yet others their status was indeterminate. It was not the first nor the last time that a racial regime built to justify the subordination of black labor had trouble assimilating a nonwhite people of a different origin and history. Mexican Americans, armed with treaty rights and legally classified as white, presented similar problems early on. Similarly, southern Jews, as Allison Schottenstein shows, often had trouble finding their place within the southern racial classification system, the nature of their inclusion or exclusion from whiteness varying sharply from one era to the next.

The problem of finding a place to sit or stand in the racial order has been no less difficult for the racialized victims of that order. At various times, Mexican Americans and Asian Americans have benefited from their legal designation as "white," notwithstanding their racial denigration more generally. Yet struggles by different groups in the civil rights era to secure the Fourteenth Amendment guarantee of equal protection under the law further illuminate the racial complexity of the South. Guadalupe San Miguel informs us that Mexican Americans in Houston, influenced by the Chicano Movement, declared that they were "Brown, not White," after the school district in 1970 responded to a court desegregation order by placing whites in one school and African Americans and Mexican Americans—still classified as white—in another. Meanwhile, southern labor struggles have sometimes led African American workers to object to the competition from rapidly growing Latino and immigrant Southeast Asian, Caribbean, and Central American workforces in many southern manufacturing and food-processing plants. And, thus far, the success of politicians of Asian descent has been more likely than not to come at the expense of African American or Latino citizens. All of this suggests that racial lines may as easily be hardened as softened in a multiracial South. Far from auguring an inevitable break with the South's racist legacy, therefore, the rupture of the biracial paradigm could simply presage new lines of color and newly separate communities. It remains, then, an open question whether the racial geography of this latest New South will look more like the formerly all-black neighborhood in east New Orleans that is now an amicably mixed community of African Americans and Vietnamese or more like the separate enclaves developing in other southern cities.

The ongoing demographic transformation of the 21st-century South suggests an ironic twist on Faulkner's trenchant observation: "The past is never dead. It's not even past." Much like the region itself, southern race relations were never as static, bounded, and monochrome as typically represented. From the start, a growing mixed-race population challenged fixed black-white boundaries, in law as well as in social relations. In southern households, slave masters, unable to master their own desires, produced claimants to their property and white privilege, fostering in the process a far more complex and contested racial landscape. In southern courtrooms, white-skinned slaves sued for their freedom, making hash of the notion that "race" was indelibly marked on the bodies or in the behavior of human beings. These claimants were not the last to make manifest the fact that race was something performed as well as seen. Julia Schiavone Camacho's entry shows that the racial masquerades white-skinned slaves used to escape bondage were echoed in the hilarious send-up Chinese workers deployed to cross the U.S.-Mexican border in the early 20th century. Donning ponchos and sombreros and mumbling a few words of Spanish or singing traditional ballads, Chinese men passed themselves off as Indian or Mexican.

On the Mexican side of the border, these same Chinese created an even more complex racial identity, taking Mexican wives and fathering mixed-race children. As merchants and skilled tradesmen, they helped build their adopted nation's economy, only to be victimized once again by anti-Chinese riots and pogroms during and following the Mexican Revolution. Consequently, they found themselves once again attempting to cross the border, but this time it was U.S. border officials who misrepresented their families' racial identities—classifying them all as simply "Chinese" and sending them "back" to China.

Whether by disguise or misrecognition, therefore, race has been repeatedly revealed as ambiguous, with uncertain boundaries, constructed and reconstructed within the borderlands and contested spaces produced by the South's social-historical transformation. Perversely, perhaps, the very ambiguity of race may be a source of its enduring power— for both those who impose and those who accept any given racial identity. Similarly, the blurring of the South's geographic and demographic boundaries may mirror the blurring of its cultural origins. Its music, its cuisine, its architecture, all betray these diverse elements, all are deposits of this complex history. All this makes for a rich and complex past—and future.

THOMAS C. HOLT
University of Chicago

LAURIE B. GREEN
University of Texas at Austin

Fran Ansley and Jon Shefner, eds., *Global Connections, Local Receptions: New Latino Immigration to the Southeastern United States* (2009); Mark Bauman, ed., *Dixie Diaspora: An Anthology of Southern Jewish Life* (2006); Ira Berlin, *American Historical Review* (February 1980), *Many Thousands Gone: The First Two Centuries of Slavery in North*

America (1998); Leslie Bow, *"Partly Colored": Asian Americans and Racial Anomaly in the Segregated South* (2010); Jonathan Brennan, ed., *When Brer Rabbit Meets Coyote: African-Native American Literature* (2003); James F. Brooks, ed., *Confounding the Color Line: The Indian-Black Experience in North America* (2002); W. Fitzhugh Brundage, *The Southern Past: A Clash of Race and Memory* (2008); James C. Cobb and William Stueck, eds., *Globalization and the American South* (2005); Lucy M. Cohen, *Chinese in the Post–Civil War South: A People without a History* (1984); Stephanie Cole and Alison M. Parker, eds., *Beyond Black and White: Race, Ethnicity, and Gender in the U.S. South and Southwest* (2004); Stephanie Cole and Natalie Ring, *The Folly of Jim Crow: Rethinking the Segregated South* (2012); Pete Daniel, *Breaking the Land: The Transformation of Cotton, Tobacco, and Rice Culture since 1880, Lost Revolutions: The South in the 1950s* (2000); Allison Davis, Burleigh B. Gardner, and Mary R. Gardner, *Deep South: A Social Anthropological Study of Caste and Class* (1941); Jean Van Delinder, *Struggles before Brown: Early Civil Rights Protests and Their Significance Today* (2008); W. E. B. Du Bois, *The Souls of Black Folk* (1903); William Faulkner, *Absalom, Absalom!* (1936); Marcie Cohen Ferris and Mark Greenberg, eds., *Jewish Roots in Southern Soil: A New History* (2006); William Ferris, *Give My Poor Heart Ease* (2009); Barbara J. Fields, in *Region, Race, and Reconstruction: Essays in Honor of C. Vann Woodward*, ed. J. Morgan Kousser and James McPherson (1982); Neil Foley, *Quest for Equality: The Failed Promise of Black-Brown Solidarity* (2010), *The White Scourge: Mexicans, Blacks, and Poor Whites in Texas Cotton Culture* (1999); Jack D. Forbes, *Africans and Native Americans: The Language of Race and the Evolution of Red-Black Peoples* (1993); Laurie B. Green, *Battling the Plantation Mentality: Memphis and the Black Freedom Struggle* (2007); Michael D. Green, *Politics of Indian Removal: Creek Government and Society in Crisis* (1982); Cheryl Lynn Greenberg, *Troubling the Waters: Black-Jewish Relations in the American Century* (2006); Ariela Julie Gross, *What Blood Won't Tell: A History of Race on Trial in America* (2008); James R. Grossman, *Land of Hope: Chicago, Black Southerners, and the Black Migration* (1989); Cindy Hahamovitch, *No Man's Land: Jamaican Guestworkers in America and the Global History of Deportable Labor* (2011); Steven Hahn, *A Nation under Our Feet: Black Political Struggles in the Rural South from Slavery to the Great Migration* (2003); Grace Elizabeth Hale, *Making Whiteness: The Culture of Segregation in the South, 1890–1940* (1999); Paul Harvey, *Freedom's Coming: Religious Cultures and the Shaping of the South from the Civil War through the Civil Rights Era* (2005); Thomas C. Holt, *The Problem of Race in the Twenty-first Century* (2002); Jacqueline Jones, *Saving Savannah: The City and the Civil War* (2009); Winthrop Jordan, *White over Black: American Attitudes toward the Negro, 1550–1812* (1968); Moon-Ho Jung, *Coolies and Cane: Race, Labor, and Sugar in the Age of Emancipation* (2006); William Kandel and John Cromartie, *New Patterns of Hispanic Settlement in Rural America* (2004); Joseph Crespino and Matthew D. Lassiter, eds., *The Myth of Southern Exceptionalism* (2009); George Lewis, *Massive Resis-*

tance: The White Response to the Civil Rights Movement (2006); James W. Loewen, *The Mississippi Chinese: Between Black and White* (1972); Neil R. McMillen, *Dark Journey: Black Mississippians in the Age of Jim Crow* (1989); Tara McPherson, *Reconstructing Dixie: Race, Gender, and Nostalgia in an Imagined South* (2003); Jeffrey Melnick, *Black-Jewish Relations on Trial: Leo Frank and Jim Conley in the New South* (2000); Tiya Miles, *Ties That Bind: The Story of an Afro-Cherokee Family in Slavery and Freedom* (2005); Karl Hagstrom Miller, *Segregating Sound: Inventing Folk and Pop in the Age of Jim Crow* (2010); David Montejano, *Anglos and Mexicans in the Making of Texas, 1836–1986* (1987); Mary E. Odem and Elaine Lacy, eds., *Latino Immigrants and the Transformation of the U.S. South* (2009); Susan Eva O'Donovan, *Becoming Free in the Cotton South* (2007); Theda Perdue, *Slavery and the Evolution of Cherokee Society, 1540–1866* (1979); Theda Perdue and Michael D. Green, *The Cherokee Removal: A Brief History with Documents* (2005); Kenneth W. Porter, *The Black Seminoles: History of a Freedom-Seeking People* (1996); Hortense Powdermaker, *After Freedom: A Cultural Study of the Deep South* (1939); Albert J. Raboteau, *Canaan Land: A Religious History of African Americans* (1999); Susan Reverby, *Examining Tuskegee: The Infamous Syphilis Study and Its Legacy* (2009); James L. Roark, *Masters without Slaves: Southern Planters in the Civil War and Reconstruction* (1977); Joshua D. Rothman, *Notorious in the Neighborhood: Sex and Families across the Color Line in Virginia, 1787–1861* (2003); Tony Russell, *Blacks, Whites, and Blues* (1970); Guadalupe San Miguel, *Brown Not White: School Integration and the Chicano Movement in Houston* (2005); Claudio Saunt, *Black, White, and Indian: Race and the Unmaking of an American Family* (2005); Rebecca J. Scott, *Degrees of Freedom: Louisiana and Cuba after Slavery* (2005); Rebecca J. Scott and Jean M. Hebrard, *Freedom Papers: An Atlantic Odyssey in the Age of Emancipation* (2012); Jim Sidbury, *Becoming African in America: Race and Nation in the Early Black Atlantic* (2007); Ronald T. Takaki, *A Pro-slavery Crusade: The Agitation to Reopen the African Slave Trade* (1971); Keith Wailoo, *Dying in the City of the Blues: Sickle Cell Anemia and the Politics of Race and Health* (2000); Clive Webb, *Fight against Fear: Southern Jews and Black Civil Rights* (2003); C. Vann Woodward, *The Burden of Southern History* (1993), *The Strange Career of Jim Crow* (1974).

Advertising (Early), African American Stereotypes in

At the 1893 Columbian Exhibition, at which Ida B. Wells protested African American exclusion, Aunt Jemima drew a warm welcome. A woman named Nancy Green, an ex-slave working as a domestic for a wealthy Chicago family, played the role. Outside a gigantic flour-barrel-shaped exhibition hall constructed by the milling company that had invented the pancake mix, Green's Aunt Jemima served and sold pancakes to the fair's overwhelmingly white visitors. Making the cakes might have been easy, but Green's performance was complicated. Her character portrayed an advertising image that mimicked minstrel show performances inspired by Harriet Beecher Stowe's character Aunt Chloe, and yet it also drew from contemporary white southerners' sentimental images of black antebellum "mammies." Green was born into slavery, but Aunt Jemima was at least a copy of a copy (minstrel show "aunts") of a copy (Aunt Chloe) of a white fantasy (the black mammy)—her connection to any real black woman lost in multiple layers of commercialized popular culture. Emancipation may have freed African American bodies, but popular culture made a great deal of profit selling black images. The tremendous popularity of Aunt Jemima in the late 19th century made clear the deep racial foundations of the increasingly national consumer market.

Advertising emerged as a national enterprise in the late 19th century in the midst of a minstrel show revival—the "coon song" craze—and white southerners' sentimental Lost Cause fantasies of happy slaves. Most consumers were familiar with the standard minstrel characters: the uncles, aunties, and mammies; the "pickaninny," or comic black child; the absurd black politician; the African "savage"; and the black figure trying and failing to live in the modern world.

Minstrelsy, a form of popular theater in which white men blacked up and cross-dressed to play black characters, originated in the antebellum Northeast in white working-class fantasies of black life in the South. In the postemancipation period, minstrelsy became extremely popular across the South, with its blacked-up characters acting out white southern fears and dreams of black life. As technological advances made the production of visual imagery increasingly affordable in the 1870s and 1880s, posters and playbills for minstrel acts papered small towns and cities and advertisements for minstrel shows and the sheet music for coon songs filled newspapers. Businesses quickly put these stylized images of black "types" to work selling other commodities. These racial representations, in turn, helped generate a new understanding of consumers as buyers detached from specific localities and from regional, ethnic, religious, and even, at times, gender and class identities—as buyers linked, in effect, to a larger, more abstract category through their whiteness: the national market.

The first advertisements to make extensive use of minstrel characters were trade cards, a new genre of advertising developed in the late 1870s and 1880s, which featured images and pitches for products on small pieces of card stock. Circulated by manufacturers, country stores, and urban shopkeepers, trade or ad cards appropriated demeaning images of not only African Americans but also American Indians and Asian Americans for the promotion of branded products and stores. Many early cards made no pretense of connecting the product and pitch to the visual imagery used to catch the attention of potential consumers. Often businesses chose cheaper stock images available from lithographers and printers. "Pluto," a young black child wearing a hood and staring out of a background of flame with enlarged, whitened eyes, promoted both the Pomeroy Coal Company and McFerren, Shallcross, and Company Meats. Two black children tickling an old black man to sleep on a cotton bale appeared on cards for Trumby and Rehn furniture makers and for a photographer named Rabineau. Other images attempted to be more comic than sentimental. A Union Pacific Tea card used a minstrel show version of a black child's face, ears, and lips, exaggerated and with eyes whitened, to illustrate four different emotional expressions.

The most popular racial images used on trade cards pictured black adults trying and failing to mimic their white "superiors." Mismatched patterns and awkward clothes pairings suggested that blacks could never achieve that crucial marker of middle-class status, respectable attire. Often these outrageously dressed figures participated in elite leisure activities. On a card for Sunny South cigarettes in a scene labeled "Cape May," a young black woman wearing clashingly striped clothes tries to play croquet. Her exaggerated mouth gapes in surprise and pain as she holds up her hurt foot. She has missed the ball and hit herself with the mallet instead. The ad invites middle-class and elite white consumers from across the nation to laugh at the black figure's absurd attempt to enjoy the pastimes of a fashionable resort. A grinning, walleyed black man awkwardly rides a grinning, equally walleyed horse using a stiff saddle on a card for Vacuum harness oil. "People," the pitch announces, "cannot exist without it," effectively excluding this figure too ignorant to oil his tack from the category of humanity. In an explicit play upon whites' fears of confusing appearances, a trade card for Tansill's Punch, "America's Finest Five Cent Cigar," depicts a rear view of "Beauty on the Street." Attired in respectable clothing, well corseted, and topped with a tasteful hat, the woman lifts her skirt and holds her parasol in one hand and her purse and a dog's leash in the other. Flipping over the card reveals the joke. Beauty's "Front View" reveals the woman's face as black, coarse, and masculine. A whole category of cards made fun of wildly dressed black characters trying to use the telephone.

As advertising became more sophisticated in the late 19th and early 20th centuries, cards appeared that specifically linked stylized black images to the ad copy. On a card for the St. Louis company Purina Mills, an "African" boy stands before a background of spindly palms and naked men. He wears the Purina breakfast box like a suit, and with a western spoon and dish in hand proclaims, "I Like the Best!" Purina almost makes him civilized. Other companies chose brand names that suggested blackness and allowed for an easy use of racial images in product pitches. "Nigger head" and "Niggerhead" became common product names for tobacco, canned fruits and vegetables, stove polish, teas, and oysters from around 1900 through the 1920s. Nigger-Hair Chewing Tobacco claimed to be as thick as black people's hair. Trade cards promoted Korn Kinks cereal with pictures and stories of the adventures of the curly-headed little Kornelia Kinks. Still other companies chose brand names—Bixby's Blacking, Bluing, and Ink and Diamond Dyes' Fast Stocking Black—or wrote pitches that depended on the most visible marker of racial difference, skin color. On a card for Coates Black Thread, a white woman says to her servant, "Come in, Topsey, out of the rain. You'll get wet." "Oh!," the servant replies, "it won't hurt me, Missy. I'm like Coates Black Thread. Da Color won't come off by wetting."

In the late 19th century, black-figured items became profitable commodities themselves. Mammy and the "pickaninny" dolls, jolly-nigger banks, big-lipped and black-faced cookie jars and spoon rests, and other similar products flooded the market. An Aunt Jemima rag doll cost one trademark from the mix's packaging plus five cents. The company bragged in its advertisements that "literally every city child owned one." Not all white children could have a black servant, but all but the poorest could have their very own pancake mammies.

As magazine advertising expanded and incorporated visual imagery, it too made use of the minstrel-influenced images popular on trade cards. An 1895 Onyx Black Hosiery ad in the *Ladies Home Journal* depicted a crowd of picka-ninnies with the caption "Onyx Blacks—We never change color." Soap adver-tisements in particular used minstrel images and white racial fantasies to ex-plain how their products worked rather than to simply attract attention. In the late 19th century, Kirkman's Wonder Soap featured a mammy and two small boys to advertise its product. The mammy wears a head rag and stands over a washtub. One of her hands helps a naked black boy into the water on the right while her other hand holds a bar of white soap above a naked white boy getting out on the left. The copy describes "two little nigger boys" who hate to bathe.

A stereotypical advertisement showing an African American man playing the harmonica, ca. 1887 (Library of Congress [LC-USZ62-87637], Washington, D.C.)

Only Kirkman's soap was strong enough to perform miracles: "Sweet and clean her sons became—It's true, as I'm a workman—And both are now completely white. Washed by this soap of Kirkman."

As advertising became more sophisticated in the early 20th century, "spokes-servant" ads became increasingly popular. These ads used and extended the theme of black racialized subservience, as branded characters like Aunt Jemima worked for the company and the company's products worked for the consumer. In this way, these ads elided the service of the product with

the service of the black figures promoting it. Aunt Jemima Pancake Mix magazine advertisements used this strategy and featured the mammy figure cooking
her southern specialties, including pancakes, and serving up "Old South" hospitality everywhere she went. "I'se in town, honey," she usually said, ready to
serve white folks everywhere. The Gold Dust Twins, two pickaninny characters
who promoted Gold Dust All Purpose Washing Powder and who were almost
as famous as Aunt Jemima, appeared on a 1910 billboard. Foot-high letters announced: "Roosevelt Scoured Africa. The Gold Dust Twins Scour America."
The light within the image focused the consumer's eye first on the towering and
golden figure of Teddy Roosevelt, toward which an equally large and glowing
figure of Uncle Sam in the left foreground reaches out a hand in honor. The
smaller twins follow Roosevelt, carrying his bags, his gun, and a huge tiger car-
cass and playing the roles of housecleaning black servants and African porters.
Gold Dust, through the twins, could do the work at home that Roosevelt had
performed overseas.

In the 20th century, advertising perpetuated and extended the reach of
minstrelsy's black images, even as the traditional black-faced theatrical form
increasingly survived as a form of popular theater. Aided by popular entertainment forms—vaudeville, radio, and later television—that it supported,
advertising helped lodge minstrelsy's racist fantasies deep within American
popular culture.

GRACE ELIZABETH HALE
University of Virginia

Kenneth Goings, *Mammy and Uncle Mose: Black Collectables and American Stereotyping* (1994); Grace Elizabeth Hale, *Making Whiteness: The Culture of Segregation in
the South, 1890–1940* (1999); Tara McPherson, *Reconstructing Dixie: Race, Gender, and
Nostalgia in an Imagined South* (2003); Juliann Sivulka, *Stronger Than Dirt: A Cultural History of Advertising Personal Hygiene in America, 1875–1940* (2001); Patricia A.
Turner, *Ceramic Uncles and Celluloid Mammies: Black Images and Their Influence on
Culture* (1994).

African American Landowners

Landownership gave African Americans a measure of economic security and
greater independence from white control. Farm owners were their own bosses.
They set their hours, controlled labor within their families, selected and marketed their own crops, and exerted a great deal of control over the education
of their own children. Additionally, on their farms they were somewhat insu-
lated from the humiliations of Jim Crow culture. Accordingly, from emancipa-

tion until the Great Migration, landownership was the goal most black families sought in order to fashion for themselves a meaningful freedom. After the federal government failed to supply Reconstruction-era blacks with the promised "40 acres and a mule," they made significant progress on their own, despite widespread white hostility and prolonged agricultural depressions. By 1870, only 5 percent of all black families had achieved this goal; by 1910, a quarter of black southern families had done so.

Some African Americans became free and began purchasing land soon after they first arrived in North America as slaves in the early 1600s. But as the transatlantic slave trade brought increasing numbers of Africans into bondage, whites passed restrictive new laws to maintain them in a dependent position. As a result, the numbers of black farm owners grew very slowly. By the 19th century, two subregional patterns had evolved. Before the Civil War, few African Americans had obtained their freedom in the Deep South, but those who did frequently amassed property. While few in number, they constituted three-fourths of the South's affluent free people of color (those who had more than $2,000 worth of property). They tended to be the descendants of whites, often receiving land and education through these family ties. They saw themselves as a separate "mulatto elite" and tended to identify with whites more than with blacks. This pattern was especially marked in Louisiana, where Spanish and French customs of interracial marriage and concubinage held sway.

Conversely, most free people of color lived in the Upper South, but few of these owned land before 1830. They had gained their freedom in a general wave of manumission that swept the region in the decades following the American Revolution. Most had not been related to their previous masters and did not derive long-term advantages from kinship ties with whites. Relatively few were literate or employed in skilled occupations. Those who did acquire land held only small parcels. Unlike African American landowners in the Deep South, those in the Upper South did not conceive of themselves as a separate "brown" society. Instead, they maintained social ties and intermarried with poorer blacks and slaves. Only 1 in 14 became slave owners, whereas fully a quarter of free people of color in the Deep South did so.

In the 1830s, regional patterns began to reverse. African American landowners in the Deep South lost ground, or at best merely held on as a group. At the same time, by their second generation after manumission, free people of color in the Upper South began to work their way into the skilled trades and professions and began to purchase land, matching the total property owned in the Deep South by 1860. When general emancipation came, they accelerated this trend. Although their holdings were usually modest in size, they made extraordinary progress.

African American farm ownership peaked from 1910 to 1920 at one-quarter of black farm families. This achievement was far from evenly distributed, as 44 percent of farmers in the Upper South came to own land, whereas only 19 percent did so in the Deep South. Generally, the sparser African American population was in a state, the easier a path black farmers found to landownership. In Georgia, only 13 percent of black farmers owned their own land; in Alabama and Mississippi, 15 percent; in Louisiana, 19 percent; in South Carolina, 21 percent; in Arkansas, 23 percent; in Tennessee, 28 percent; in Texas, 30 percent; in North Carolina, 32 percent; in Florida, 50 percent; in Kentucky, 51 percent; and in Virginia, 67 percent.

Many of these black farm owners were scattered and isolated among white farmers. But in many places, such as Texas and Mississippi, they settled in freedom colonies—all-black communities that provided most of the basic needs of their members. In these settlements, they frequently had their own churches, schools, lodges, and businesses. Although they did not farm on a large scale, with aid from black county extension agents they raised enough of their own food to avoid debt. Their relative economic independence gave them greater control over their lives than that enjoyed by black tenants. For example, when civil rights workers registered rural African Americans to vote during the 1960s, they frequently stayed in the homes of black farm owners.

Black farm owners have declined in number continuously from the 1920s to the present. Many lost their land owing to the general difficulties afflicting small farmers: the boll weevil and the lower prices and higher costs brought by an industrializing, globalizing economy. Other families sold their land when their young people began to identify farming with the exploitation of slavery and sharecropping and turned increasingly away from their parents' farms and toward urban occupations. Still others lost their farms because of the liabilities of racism, in particular, difficulty in gaining equitable aid from banks and government agencies. For many decades, local administrators of USDA farm loan agencies denied loans to African American farmers, while giving them to comparable white farmers. In other cases, these agencies extended loans that were too small or too late to be useful. To seek compensation for this pattern of discrimination, thousands of black farmers brought a class-action lawsuit against the USDA, in *Pigford v. Glickman*. In 1999, a Washington, D.C., district court found for the plaintiffs and called for damages to be paid, which have amounted to nearly 1 billion dollars, the largest class-action civil rights settlement in U.S. history. Suit brought by an additional 60,000 late filers may bring the full settlement to over 2 billion dollars.

MARK SCHULTZ
Lewis University

W. E. B. Du Bois, *U.S. Department of Labor Bulletin* (July 1901); Melvin Patrick Ely, *Israel on the Appomattox: A Southern Experiment in Black Freedom from the 1790s through the Civil War* (2005); Peggy G. Hargis and Mark R. Schultz, *Agricultural History* (Spring 1998); Leo McGee and Robert Boone, *The Black Rural Landowner: Endangered Species* (1979); Gary B. Mills, *The Forgotten People: Cane River's Creoles of Color* (1977); Debra Reid, *Reaping a Greater Harvest: African Americans, the Extension Service, and Rural Reform in Jim Crow Texas* (2007); Debra Reid and Evan Bennett, eds., *Beyond Forty Acres and a Mule: African American Farmers since Reconstruction* (2012); Loren Schweninger, *Black Property Owners in the South, 1790–1915* (1990); Thad Sitton and James H. Conrad, *Freedom Colonies: Independent Black Texans in the Time of Jim Crow* (2005).

African Influences

In 1935, Melville J. Herskovits asked in the pages of the *New Republic*, "What has Africa given America?" In his answer, a radical response for the time, he briefly mentioned the influence of blacks on American music, language, manners, and foodways. He found most of his examples, however, in the South. Eighty years later, the answer to this question could be longer, perhaps less radical, but still surprising to many. Much of what people of African descent brought to the United States since 1619 has become so familiar to the general population, particularly in the South, that the black origins of specific customs and forms of expression have become blurred or forgotten altogether.

Consider, for example, the banjo. Not only is the instrument itself of African origin but so is its name. Although the banjo is encountered today chiefly in bluegrass ensembles, where it is considered an instrument of the Appalachians, it was first played by slaves on Tidewater plantations in the 17th and 18th centuries. It was only taken up into the Piedmont and the mountains during the 19th century by blacks working on railroad gangs. Although the contemporary banjo is physically quite different from its Afro-American folk antecedent, it nonetheless retains the unique sounds of its ringing high drone string and its drum head. These are the acoustic reminders of the instrument's African origins.

Linguists have noted that southern speech carries a remarkable load of African vocabulary. This assertion is all the more remarkable when we recall that white southerners have often claimed to have little interaction with blacks. Some regional words have murky origins, but there is no controversy for such terms as boogie, gumbo, tote, benne, goober, cooter, okra, jazz, mumbo-jumbo, hoodoo, mojo, cush, and the affirmative and negative expressions "uh-huh" and "unh-uh." All are traceable to African languages and usages. The term "guinea" is used as an adjective for a number of plants and animals that were imported long ago from Africa. Guinea hens, guinea worms, guinea grass, and guinea corn, now found throughout the South, are rarely thought of as exceptional, even though their names directly indicate their exotic African origins.

Beyond basic words, blacks have created works of oral literature that have become favorite elements of southern folklore. Within the whole cycle of folk-tales with animal tricksters—those put into written form by Joel Chandler Harris and others—some may be indigenous to American Indians and some may have European analogies, but most appear to have entered the United States from Africa and the West Indies. The warnings they provide concerning the need for clever judgment and social solidarity are lessons taken to heart by both whites and blacks. The legacy of artful language in Afro-American culture is manifested further in other types of performance such as the sermon, the toast, and contests of ritual insult. For people who are denied social and economic power, verbal power provides important compensation. This is why men of words in the black community—the good talkers—are highly esteemed. The southern oratorical style has generally been noted as distinctive because of its pacing, imagery, and the demeanor of the speaker. Some of these traits, heard in speeches and sermons, are owed to black men of words who of necessity re-fined much of what is today accepted as standard southern "speechifying" into a very dramatic practice.

In the area of material culture, blacks were long assumed to have made few contributions to southern life, but such an assessment is certainly in error. There have, over the last four centuries, existed distinctive traditions for Afro-American basketry, pottery, quilting, blacksmithing, boatbuilding, wood-carving, carpentry, and graveyard decoration. These achievements have gone unrecognized and unacknowledged. Take, for example, the shotgun house. Several million of these structures can be found all across the South, and some are now lived in by whites, although shotgun houses are generally associated with black neighborhoods. The first of these distinctive houses with their narrow shapes and gable entrances were built in New Orleans at the beginning of the 19th century by free people of color who were escaping the political revolution in Haiti. In the Caribbean, such houses are used in both towns and the countryside; they were once used as slave quarters. Given its history, the design of the shotgun house should be understood as somewhat determined by African architectural concepts as well as Caribbean Indian and French colonial influences. Contemporary southern shotgun houses represent the last phase of an architectural evolution initiated in Africa and modified in the West Indies and now in many southern locales dominating the cultural landscape.

The cultural expressions of the southern black population are integral to the regional experience. Although the South could still exist without banjos, Brer Rabbit, goobers, and shotgun houses, it would certainly be less interesting. The black elements of southern culture make the region more distinctive.

JOHN MICHAEL VLACH
George Washington University

J. L. Dillard, *Black English* (1972); Dena J. Epstein, *Ethnomusicology* (September 1975); Melville J. Herskovits, *New Republic*, 4 September 1935; Robert Farris Thompson, *Flash of the Spirit: African and Afro-American Art and Philosophy* (1983); John Michael Vlach, *The Afro-American Tradition in Decorative Arts* (1978), *Pioneer America* (January 1976).

Agriculture, Race, and Transnational Labor

The plantation economy that dominated the American South through the colonial and early national periods sharply defined labor and race relations in the region. Millions of African and African American slaves toiled in the tobacco, cotton, sugar, and rice fields, fueling a highly profitable cash crop economy dependent on the subjugation of their labor. The powerful labor system upon which the plantation economy was built collapsed with the advent of the Civil War and the abolition of slavery under the Thirteenth Amendment in 1865. Soon after, southern planters, hoping to rebuild their political and financial power, complained about the unreliability and inefficiency of newly freed black labor. Despite planters' efforts to stabilize and immobilize black farmworkers through a system of farm tenancy, many African Americans searched for better opportunities through migration.

As the southern agricultural economy transformed in the late 19th century, the concern over a steady labor supply became more serious. America's Industrial Revolution fostered new urban markets with growing populations requiring food and factories demanding raw materials. The development of refrigerated railway cars and the application of new machinery to agricultural production further incentivized the expansion of large-scale, capitalized farms in the South. With increasing numbers of African Americans leaving in search of better economic opportunities and social conditions, planters were left to search for alternatives to meet their growing labor needs. The Great Migration resulted in an exodus of about 500,000 black southerners between 1910 and 1920 alone. To meet these needs, planters relied increasingly on seasonal migrants, who could provide flexible and inexpensive labor.

Texas had long depended on the transnational migration of Mexican farmworkers, who after 1910 (the start of the Mexican Revolution) began arriving in greater numbers. During the same decade that black southerners left the countryside at growing rates, more than 185,000 Mexicans entered the United States in search of work. The availability of Mexican laborers facilitated Texas's transformation from a plantation and ranching economy into commercial agribusiness. Between 1900 and 1920, the number of cultivated acres on Texas farms grew from 15 million to 25 million. By this time, central Texas was the nation's leading cotton-producing region and south Texas was dominant in the truck farming of vegetables and citrus fruit. The system of agribusiness based on inexpensive, migrant, and mostly noncitizen labor that existed in Texas by World War I would soon spread across the South, pushing the region to follow a new model of farm labor relations.

While the presence of a large transnational labor force distinguished Texas from the rest of the American South in the early 20th century, other regions experimented with the use of immigrant labor following the Civil War. Several states sought to use immigration to revive agribusiness and resolve enduring political tensions. A study of South Carolina during Reconstruction shows that there was much discussion on the question of transnational labor. According to historian R. H. Woody, state leaders believed that "the West had been made powerful and prosperous through immigration, and this same factor would increase the wealth and property values of South Carolina." Labor recruiters were sent to Germany and the Scandinavian countries to lure workers to the New South. Some South Carolinians warned that "a day laborer could not compete with the Negro in the service of the former slave-owner, or in the cultivation of southern staples." To a large extent, such skeptics were right. Most of the immigrants who came to the region during the late 19th century complained about the poor climate, disorderly society, and lack of real economic opportunities.

Louisiana had more success employing immigrant farmworkers at the turn of the century. At this time, most of the sugar cultivated in the continental United States grew in the southeast and south-central areas of Louisiana. After the 1880s, Italian immigrants were recruited as replacements for low-wage, mostly unskilled black labor. The seasonal influx of Italian workers ranged from 30,000 to 80,000. Most came from established enclaves in New Orleans that worked around the citrus fruit trade, while others migrated from Chicago and

New York. Like most states seeking an immigrant workforce, Louisiana established immigration and homestead associations to encourage Italian immigration. Soon after, a successful transnational system was in place, with workers arriving directly to the cane fields at grinding time and returning to Italy immediately after. This cyclical pattern allowed Louisiana's sugar parishes to thrive. It was not until economic depression hit the sugar industry in the early 1900s that Italians left the sugar fields searching for better wages. During World War I and shortly after, restrictive federal immigration policies also served to limit Italian immigration.

The Reconstruction period also saw the arrival of Chinese labor to the Mississippi Delta. In 1869, southern growers organized the Arkansas River Valley Emigration Company, whose purpose it was to attract large numbers of Chinese laborers for the cultivation of cotton. According to historian John Thornell, labor recruiters were sent to Hong Kong in search of willing migrants, and eventually two ships arrived in New Orleans in 1870 with about 400 Chinese workers. Members of this group arrived in the Delta to work specifically in agriculture. Like their Italian counterparts, they considered themselves sojourners, expecting to return to their homeland once they had secured enough money to support their families. While their expectations were hopeful, their experiences as farmworkers were mostly unsuccessful. Exploitative labor conditions on cotton farms, which included terribly low wages for extremely physically demanding work, encouraged most Chinese migrants to reconsider their arrangements. Those that did not return to China walked off the farms to find better opportunities. Many became small business owners and opened grocery stores that catered to black farmworkers. The Chinese immigrant community could have flourished had it not been for the passage of the Chinese Exclusion Act in 1882.

Mexican migrants began arriving in the Mississippi Delta shortly after growers experimented with hiring Chinese workers. As historian Julie Weise explains, Mexicans were working in the state's lumber industry as early as 1908 as replacements for black workers who left for cities in the North and West as part of the Great Migration. During the period from 1917 to 1921, a federal guest-worker program attracted some 51,000 Mexicans to help meet World War I labor demands, mainly in agriculture. Most of the migrants who arrived in Mississippi came from north-central Mexico and were recruited at the Texas border by labor agents working for southern cotton growers. By the mid-1920s, Mexican workers realized that they could earn more picking cotton in the American South than elsewhere in the country, including Texas and California.

In 1925, a peak period in the migratory flow, some 500,000 Mexicans could be found picking cotton throughout the region. Not all of the Mexican workers were transnational migrants, however. A 1930 census figure taken in the Delta's Bolivar County revealed that one in every six Mexican farmworkers had actually been born in Texas. Few Mexican farmworkers stayed in the Delta after December, when the cotton-picking season ended. Most chose to follow the migratory route back to Texas, up north, or to Mexico.

The impermanent character of the transnational labor that came to the South after the Civil War allowed southerners to avoid altering the racial division of labor that existed in the region. Southern planters simply tried to replace African American slaves (or newly empowered black workers) with an alternative source of exploited labor to sustain productivity on their farms. In the 1930s, for example, the use of Mexican labor in the Delta would serve to undermine the solidarity black workers were building through the Southern Tenant Farmers' Union. In this way, the use of transnational labor was not just a response to black out-migration but also a means to undermine domestic workers' coalitions.

Despite their diverse origins, the Italian, Chinese, Mexican, and even German immigrants that first came to the South as farmworkers were inserted (often uncomfortably) into the existing black-white racial dyad. Their labor status alongside low-wage African American workers—at times also cohabitating, intermarrying, and organizing with blacks—tainted these migrants racially in the eyes of white society. Those that actively sought acceptance as whites by attending white schools and churches, challenging segregation in court, or elevating their class status, encountered significant barriers in transgressing the color line. For Mexican migrants, according to Weise, it was the actions of the Mexican Consulate that eventually helped them gain some of the privileges of whiteness.

The influx of immigrant labor to the South slowed during much of the mid-1920s and 1930s as the nation experienced a severe economic depression that fueled nativist sentiment and policies. It was not until the 1940s, with mounting World War II labor demands, that growers again clamored for a transnational farmworker program. The Bracero program consisted of a series of bilateral agreements between the U.S. and Mexican governments that lasted from 1942 to 1964. Over the duration of the program, more than 4.5 million Mexican farmworkers were contracted (often more than once) to work in the United States. In negotiations over the stipulations of the agreement, the Mexican government addressed the problem of racial discrimination many of its nationals experienced as U.S. workers. Several states, including Texas, Arkansas, and Mississippi, were blacklisted from participating in the program until they could guarantee better labor and living conditions, including an end to the racial prejudice Mexicans encountered.

The British West Indies Labor Program was modeled after the Mexican agreement to meet farm labor demands on the East Coast. Approximately 66,000 workers, mostly from Jamaica and the Bahamas, participated in the program from 1943 to 1947. According to historian Cindy Hahamovitch, the secretary of state for the British colonies attempted, much like Mexican officials, to regulate the discriminatory conditions workers encountered by discouraging migrants from working south of the Mason-Dixon Line. Even so, Florida growers were determined to secure guest workers and ultimately received some of the largest numbers.

The cycles of migration created by such guest-worker programs had a long-lasting affect in establishing a more permanent and visible presence of migrants in the South. Since the 1960s, particularly as African Americans gained access to industrial and service-sector jobs, the regional workforce has undergone what many describe as a "steady process of Latinization." Caribbean guest workers continue to migrate under the H-2A temporary worker program, but the rate of employment among Latino farmworkers far outnumbers any other group. Unlike past migrations, Mexican (and to a lesser extent Central American) immigrants have been arriving in the South and then settling. Since 1990, eight out of the top ten "states with fastest growing nonmetro Hispanic populations," according to the U.S. Department of Agriculture, are located in the American South.

As Latino immigrants settle in the South, local communities are faced with the challenge of integrating them beyond their roles as migratory workers. This adjustment has led to anti-immigrant hostility and the escalation of racial tension. Recently, Alabama, Georgia, and South Carolina passed anti-immigrant legislation under the guise of protecting Americans' jobs. A notable concern among nativists has also been the dilution of southern culture and values, resembling the immigration debates that occurred shortly after the Civil War. Growers generally do not support such legislation, knowing that it will undermine the current system, which provides them with cheap and vulnerable workers. Immigrant farmworkers are organizing in remarkable ways to contest the structural violence and exploitative conditions that too closely resemble the postbellum era. For example, the Coalition of Immokalee Workers, an organization of mainly Latino, Mayan Indian, and Haitian immigrants, offers a source of promise that the existing system of agribusiness can be reformed for the

better. Over time, transnational workers have disrupted the traditional structure of labor and race relations, forging a new American South.

VERÓNICA MARTÍNEZ MATSUDA
Cornell University

Neil Foley, *The White Scourge: Mexicans, Blacks, and Poor Whites in Texas Cotton
Culture* (1997); Cindy Hahamovitch, *The Fruits of Their Labor: Atlantic Coast Farm-
workers and the Making of Migrant Poverty, 1870–1945* (1997); William Kandel and
John Cromartie, *New Patterns of Hispanic Settlement in Rural America* (2004);
James W. Loewen, *The Mississippi Chinese: Between Black and White* (1971); Mary E.
Odem and Elaine Lacy, eds., *Latino Immigrants and the Transformation of the U.S.
South* (2009); Vincenza Scarpaci, *Italian Immigrants in Louisiana's Sugar Parishes:
Recruitment, Labor Conditions, and Community Relations, 1880–1910* (1980); John
Thornell, *Chinese America: History and Perspectives* (2003); Julie M. Weise, *American
Quarterly* (September 2008); R. H. Woody, *Mississippi Valley Historical Review* (Sep-
tember 1931).

Asian American Narratives between Black and White

How did Jim Crow culture view Asian Americans, those who did not fit into
a system predicated on the distinction between "colored" and white? Asian
American narratives about racial segregation in the South reveal more than
one answer to the question where did the Asian sit on the segregated bus? In
doing so, they offer important insights into the ways in which racial hierarchies
were enforced in southern culture.

Interned with other Japanese Americans in Arkansas during World War II,
Mary Tsukamoto recounts that her first trip out of camp, a bus ride to Jackson,
Miss., in 1943, offered a shocking view of racial discrimination: "We could not believe the bus driver's tone of voice as he ordered black passengers to stand at the
back of the bus." In contrast, the white driver gestured her to the front. "We were
relieved but had strange feelings," she writes. "Apparently we were not 'colored.'"

Tsukamoto's dilemma—front or back?—goes largely unnoticed in depic-
tions of segregation-era history. The fact that Mary is designated "not 'colored'"
here belies the fact that she is also a victim of racial discrimination: she is a
prisoner of war on temporary furlough from the "segregation" of a concentration camp. The story reveals complex issues surrounding the indeterminate
racial status of Asian Americans between black and white. In 1930, sociologist
Max Handman noted that American society had "no social technique for handling partly colored races." As a metaphor, the "color line" does not allow for
a middle space. One Chinese American woman living in Mississippi stated,

"Delta whites think there are only two races in the world and do not know what to do with the Chinese." Similarly, the Korean protagonist of Susan Choi's novel *The Foreign Student*, set in Sewanee, Tenn., in the 1950s, reflects upon the locals' reaction to him: "They don't know what to make me." The Asian's racial status became subject to interpretation.

Asian Americans have often been positioned in American culture as vehicles for affirming racial progress; they are continually represented as the "model minority," as proof that systemic racial barriers do not exist. Yet segregation affected Asians in the South as well as African Americans; while neither white nor black, they were not immune to the racial hierarchies enforced in southern culture. Asian American novels, ethnographies, oral histories, and memoirs about the South provide intriguing accounts of the ways in which interstitial individuals became written into the region's prevailing racial codes. These narratives reveal what it means to inhabit an in-between space, what it means to be, in Handman's words, "partly colored." While this emerging body of letters contributes to a reevaluation of the transnational aspects of southern literature by highlighting global migration to the South, Asian American literature here, like African American literature, also testifies to the effects of white supremacy, offering a powerful—if at times ambiguous—critique of social injustice.

Some accounts of Asian American experiences with segregation and its legacy simultaneously document unjust racial treatment and, curiously, deny unjust treatment. Reflecting on his fieldwork in Georgia and Tennessee in the 1960s, Korean anthropologist Choong Soon Kim poses the question "Had a proverbial 'southern hospitality' been extended to Asians?" Throughout his ethnographic writing, Kim affirms that it has. In *An Asian Anthropologist in the South: Field Experiences with Blacks, Indians, and Whites*, he assures his readers that despite witnessing racial discrimination against African Americans, he himself does not experience it while living in the South. Yet he also confesses that white people have, upon occasion, refused to shake his hand. Kim writes, "These incidents should not be interpreted in terms of racial discrimination. Such curiosities in relation to foreigners are rather natural." Kim's analysis of his own treatment points to the unreliability of autobiographical narratives: He has been snubbed because of his race but dismisses the discourtesy and its implications. His contradictory testimony unveils the ways in which individuals rationalize a loss of social status, highlighting the psychic violence that is part of segregation's legacy. The Asian American's depiction of racial hierarchy requires reading in-between the lines of the narrative.

Segregation-era oral histories and memoirs reveal that individuals will resist the implication that they are inferior because of their race or skin color. For example, Ved Mehta's account of his 1950s residence at a school for the blind in Arkansas reveals very little about what it means to be South Asian in a "whites only" institution. Rather, his memoir, *Sound-Shadows of the New World* (1985), asks us to consider another form of integration—the mobility of the blind in a sighted world. In spite of the fact that Mehta has deliberately downplayed his Indian cultural difference at school, he is moved out of the boys' dormitory and into a converted broom closet. The move is represented as an administrative concession to Ved, a privilege granted to him alone. As the white director suggests, "You want a place where you can shut the door and be by yourself, keep on with your typing and reading, listen to Indian music and think of home. Am I right?" Whether he understands this separation to be anything other than voluntary goes unremarked. Why is Mehta singled out for "special" treatment? Does the separation represent a concession to time and place, one whose motive remains veiled even to the author?

An Asian in the South, Mehta is, in Handman's terms, only "partly colored": The move *within* the white school *away* from white boys may be interpreted either as a privilege or in deference to segregation. As in contradictory anecdotal evidence of Asians traveling in the South, he is not quite white. What is telling is that Mehta refuses to allow southern norms to impact his own self-conception, preferring to see himself as simply a brown-skinned human being whose worth remains intact. In his eyes, he is not a "darky," not a "Negro." Asian American literature nevertheless reveals that the entrenched customs of the South implicate these migrants, Kim and Mehta, even as they themselves are only partially aware of it. If these memoirs refuse to document the effects of racism in overt ways, they nevertheless contribute to an understanding of southern race relations by testifying to the individual's attempts to resist racism's dehumanizing effects.

As in the most popular depiction of Asians in the South, Mira Nair's 1991 film, *Mississippi Masala*, Asian American literature denormalizes racial separation in the United States through global parallels. For example, Susan Choi's novel *The Foreign Student* (1998) offers a meditation on the artificiality of divisions in its dual settings: Korea and Tennessee in the 1950s. The demilitarized zone at the 38th parallel, the imaginary line that divided the Korean peninsula into north and south as a result of civil war, finds its analog in the Mason-Dixon Line. The novel's Korean protagonist, Chang, comes to occupy a racial DMZ, finding himself "foreign" to American racial politics at the University of the South.

The novel thus highlights a dynamic reflected in anecdotal accounts of Asian experiences with segregation: the Asian American becomes an object of intense local scrutiny and interpretation, particularly as Chang begins a relationship with a white woman. Choi describes reaction to the interracial couple as "unremitting scrutiny, disguised as politeness," and as the "tension of careful indifference . . . and steady observation." There is no communally agreed-upon response to the Asian's unwitting crossing of the color line's sexual taboo—because he is not black, their outings avoid overt hostility and confrontation, but because he is not white, surveillance is uncensored and undisguised. The novel establishes a tone of impending menace reflective of author David Mura's speculation about Japanese Americans interned in Arkansas: "There was an unspoken message all about them in the camps, especially in the South: Things are bad now, but they could be worse. We aren't lynching your kind. Yet." The gray zone of Jim Crow culture that the Asian inhabits is depicted as both similar to and distinct from that experienced by African Americans; the novel intimates that suspended evaluation and punitive action are contingent upon unspoken rules.

Abraham Verghese's *My Own Country: A Doctor's Story of a Town and Its People in the Age of AIDS* also represents an Asian American's search for home in the South. Like Choi's work, it calls upon the condition of postcolonial exile to comment on segregation—here based not only on racial division but also on lines drawn between illness and health. An immigrant of South Asian ancestry, Verghese is an infectious disease specialist who was treating individuals infected with HIV in rural Tennessee in the mid-1980s. In defiance of southern stereotyping, the doctor was readily embraced by the white population as a fellow "good ole boy." Yet as his practice with AIDS patients grows and he encounters increasing ostracism in the community, Verghese experiences his pariah status as racial alienation: "Was there some place in this country where I could walk around anonymously, where I could blend in completely with a community, be undistinguished by appearance, accent or speech?" The doctor's own difference becomes "outed" via proximity to the presumed medical and sexual deviances of those he treats, linking the memoir's representation of race to sexuality.

My Own Country's significance to southern literature lies in its highlighting alternative forms of caste making in ways that complicate community division based on race. In doing so, it also refigures lines of connection away from the identity categories that have traditionally configured southern communities. The Asian American finds a contingent home in the South by forging meaningful connections with other "migrants," in this case, white gay men who have returned home to Tennessee. The literature shows that being an outsider can provoke new forms of community.

The addition of Asian American writing to the southern canon does not simply contribute uncritically to notions of a multicultural New South. It can expand the global reach of regionalism by provoking questions about citizenship, diaspora, migration, acculturation, and transnationalism. But as significant, these narratives offer a potentially reorienting perspective on the dynamics at the heart of southern literature: racial politics between black and white. In this sense, authors such as H. T. Tsiang, V. S. Naipaul, Cynthia Kadohata, Lan Cao, Elena Tajima Creef, Patsy Rekdal, Abraham Verghese, Ved Mehta, Patti Duncan, Ha Jin, Susan Choi, Choong Soon Kim, and M. Evelina Galang who set prose narratives in the region are not "foreign" to southern letters. They too offer a critique of American racial politics, forcing a reconsideration of what it means to be "at home" in the South. The impact of white supremacy on Asian Americans might lack the immediacy of James Baldwin's recognition that, as a black man, he is "among a people whose culture controls me, has even, in a sense, created me." Nevertheless, southern Asian American literature offers insight into the complexities of social power, belonging, and denial.

Asian American narratives ask us to consider the arbitrary division between blacks and whites from the perspective of those whose place across the color line was indeterminate and often fluid. These postsegregation-era texts establish the interstitial as a site of cultural discipline, but they also give it an alternative political valence. The anomaly of the Asian in the South might be reconceived as a useful site of alienation from entrenched race relations, an estrangement that provides the space for questioning norms of racial etiquette, habit, and expectation. In this sense, the racial in-between pushes us to think beyond the lines drawn by color that constitute segregation's ongoing legacy.

LESLIE BOW
University of Wisconsin at Madison

Brewton Berry, *Almost White* (1963); Edna Bonacich, *American Sociological Review* (October 1973); Leslie Bow, *"Partly Colored": Asian Americans and Racial Anomaly in the Segregated South* (2010); Lan Cao, *Monkey Bridge* (1997); Susan Choi, *The Foreign Student* (1998); Lucy M. Cohen, *Chinese in the Post–Civil War South: A People without a History* (1984); Elena Tajima Creef, *North Carolina Literary Review* (2005); Max Sylvius Handman, *American Journal of Sociology* (1930); Cynthia Kadohata, *kira-kira* (2004); Choong Soon Kim, *An Asian Anthropologist in the South: Field Experiences with Blacks, Indians, and Whites* (1977), in *Cultural Diversity in the U.S. South: Anthropological Contributions to a Region in Transition*, ed. Carole E. Hill and Patricia D. Beaver (1998); James W. Loewen, *The Mississippi Chinese: Between Black and White* (1972); Ved Mehta, *Sound-Shadows of the New World* (1985); David

Mura, in *Under Western Eyes: Personal Essays from Asian America*, ed. Garrett Hungo (1995); V. S. Naipaul, *A Turn in the South* (1989); Robert Seto Quan, *Lotus among the Magnolias: The Mississippi Chinese* (1982); Mary Tsukamoto and Elizabeth Pinkerton, *We the People: A Story of Internment in America* (1987); Abraham Verghese, *My Own Country: A Doctor's Story of a Town and Its People in the Age of AIDS* (1994).

Asians, Mexicans, Interracialism, and Racial Ambiguities

Although Chinese men first arrived in the Spanish borderlands during the 16th century, they began arriving in northern Mexico in greater numbers after formal exclusion from the United States in 1882. Owing to gender norms in China and gendered exclusionary policy in the United States, Chinese migrations to the Americas were overwhelmingly male. Some men, intent on crossing the northern border surreptitiously, simply passed through Mexico. Others found opportunities in the burgeoning border economy and settled in local communities. Becoming both laborers and businessmen, Chinese in the latter group in particular formed romantic unions with local women. Anti-Chinese campaigns that emerged during the Mexican Revolution of 1910 and peaked with the Great Depression targeted Mexican-Chinese unions as damaging to the Mexican race and nation. Ultimately, the northwestern states of Sonora and Sinaloa drove out the vast majority of Chinese. Whether by choice or by force, their Mexican-origin families often accompanied them out of Mexico. Some passed through U.S. territory as "refugees" before beginning their lives anew in Guangdong Province in southeastern China.

Chinese men often entered the United States by passing as members of diverse minority groups across the nation's borderlands regions; in the U.S. Southwest, they disguised themselves as local indigenous peoples and Mexicans. Stories abound of Chinese men who entered the United States by posing as Mexicans, since the latter could cross the border freely through the early 20th century. Invoking the dominant racial images of Mexicans in the United States, coyotes instructed Chinese men to wear ponchos and sombreros, learn some phrases in Spanish, or even sing traditional ballads as they pretended to be part of groups of Mexican men who had been out drinking. Through such tactics, among others, the cross-border smuggling of Chinese became a profitable business enterprise by the turn of the 20th century. Mexican and American men, as well as some Chinese, profited from U.S. immigration policy as they took excluded men across the border or transported, housed, and fed those who awaited opportunities to enter the United States secretly.

Other Chinese stayed in Mexico. They fit into two broad socioeconomic categories. Agricultural laborers and unskilled employees, on the one hand, exhibited lower rates of assimilation. Skilled artisans and merchants, on the other hand, had more wealth and tended toward greater integration. As elsewhere in Mexico, the Chinese were crucial in the north as they fulfilled a number of key roles in local communities. They participated in the traditional, rural economy by becoming landowners or laboring on the haciendas, ranchos, and fields of Mexican as well as Chinese landowners. But the Chinese also helped northern states modernize by becoming the first petit bourgeois class. They established businesses either individually or in conjunction with other countrymen. They opened shops where they sold inexpensive household goods and foods. In addition to selling necessary items, they established laundries and provided vital domestic services to local people. Chinese businessmen at first enjoyed the protection of municipal authorities because they brought revenue and staples to local communities. Although some were large-scale operations, most Chinese enterprises were small and locally operated; these included street peddling. Chinese had more businesses, but less overall capital, than other immigrant groups. Rather than displacing Mexicans or other foreigners, they found new commercial openings. Chinese drew on transnational economic networks in a way that local residents or other foreigners could not. Brethren in China and other parts of the Americas contributed capital and low-cost merchandise to Chinese businesses. This helped them prosper and eventually establish a monopoly on low-end consumer goods. As the growing border economy pushed northern Mexico toward the commercial and the modern, and with a native petit bourgeoisie lacking, the Chinese found an important economic and social niche.

Chinese became incorporated into northern Mexican society because the Mexican government allowed them to immigrate, naturalize, and marry local women, at least at first. The *Porfiriato* (the reign of Porfirio Díaz, 1876–1911) encouraged Chinese to migrate to help "whiten" Mexico's dark-skinned indigenous and mestizo population during the late 19th century, since attempts to recruit southern and eastern Europeans had failed. In a key difference with diasporic patterns in the United States, many Chinese became naturalized citizens, learned Spanish, adopted naming patterns and other local norms, and entered into civil unions with Mexican or indigenous women. Besides providing companionship and love, marriages to local women helped Chinese men integrate into the society. It facilitated drawing Mexican and indigenous clientele to their businesses. Unions with Chinese men, in turn, offered economic stability and prestige to local women and their families; some parents even arranged such marriages. Chinese were known for being frugal, good providers, and saving for their children's futures. Along with the romantic feelings and love they felt for their partners, these were attractive qualities for women, and families, from the poor and working classes.

Anti-Chinese sentiment had existed in northern Mexico since the Chinese first arrived, but it was neither widespread nor organized until the Mexican Revolution of 1910. Changing notions of race, citizenship, and belonging made the ground fertile for the rise of a vicious anti-Chinese movement, which first emerged in the border state of Sonora in 1916 and eventually spread to other areas of the nation. *Antichinistas* (anti-Chinese activists) viewed Chinese men as a formidable threat to the race and nation; ejecting them from Mexico was their supreme goal. Crusaders vilified Mexican-Chinese unions, as well as cross-cultural relationships more generally. They derided as *chineras* and *chineros* those Mexicans who were friendly to or had formed ties with Chinese. A deep split came to characterize Sonora, as some worked vehemently against the Chinese while others maintained—in many cases their longtime— relationships. They did so in spite of social stigma and legal punishment as the movement gained momentum during the 1920s. Early in the decade, the state of Sonora passed a law prohibiting marriages and "illicit" unions between Chinese men and Mexican women, among other anti-Chinese measures.

The movement against Chinese culminated with forced removals during the Great Depression. Although anti-Chinese activists had by now formed campaigns in a number of Mexican states, only Sonora and Sinaloa carried out massive evictions of Chinese and many of their Mexican-origin families. It was no coincidence that these northern states took such drastic measures, as anti-Chinese hatred and exclusionary ideology had for decades circulated in the border region. Some local people had even linked the U.S. treatment of Mexicans with the future expulsion of Chinese. In 1926, Francisco Martínez wrote to Mexican president Plutarco Elías Calles from Nogales, Ariz., attaching a newspaper article entitled "Mexicans Will Be Kicked Out of California." The piece reported that 75 percent of Mexicans in California had entered the United States illegally and that a campaign to return them to Mexico was to begin immediately. Although the United States would not conduct a massive "repatriation" of Mexicans until the Depression years, U.S. newspapers reported on the formation of smaller deportation operations in California during this time. "If the Americans can do this to a neighboring country, to Mexicans," Martínez wrote, "why don't we take advantage of this idea—using it against Chinese?" The Chinese "plague," he argued, had "infested and threatened" Mexico. Displacing his frustrations onto the Chinese, the border town resident urged Mexico's leaders to counter the humiliation of the U.S. deportations of Mexicans. Dwelling on the Arizona side of the boundary, Martínez may have been an official or a businessman, a Mexican immigrant or Mexican American—or an amalgamation, as lines of identity have been historically blurry, especially in the border region. His wish, in any case, would be fulfilled half a decade later. Mexican workers, as scapegoats for the Great Depression in the United States, returned to Mexico en masse beginning in 1929. Within two years, Sonora and Sinaloa, in turn, began widespread evictions of Chinese, whom they had likewise blamed for Mexico's economic and social ills.

While many left directly from Mexican seaports, several thousand Chinese men and over 100 members of Mexican Chinese families passed through U.S. territory as "refugees from Mexico." One such family was the Wong Campoy family from the southern Sonoran town of Navojoa. After narrowly escaping cruel *antichinista* tormenters who had driven him to run away and climb a roof—from which a fall caused serious heart problems—Alfonso Wong Fang knew he could no longer remain in Mexico as before. The wife and mother, Dolores Campoy Wong, decided that she and their children, Alfonso Wong Campoy, María del Carmen Irma Wong Campoy, and Héctor Manuel Wong Campoy—all under five years old—would accompany him to keep the family together. In early 1933, the Wong Campoy family headed north and crossed the border illegally into the United States. Enforcing the Chinese Exclusion Acts, U.S. immigration agents apprehended the family and held them in an immigration jail in southern Arizona before putting them on a train to San Francisco for ultimate deportation to China with other "Chinese refugees from Mexico."

Attempting to understand and control the situation, the Immigration and Naturalization Service (INS) took statements from hundreds of Chinese men, who described the brutality they had endured in Mexico. U.S. authorities at first perceived Chinese men and Mexican Chinese families from Mexico through the decades-old lens of Chinese Exclusion. But after taking testimony, they saw a new pattern: These Chinese had fled Mexico owing to anti-Chinese hostility. Thus, they were refugees whom the agency could neither send back to Mexico in good conscience nor allow into the United States because of·the policy of Chinese Exclusion. Officials usually referred to "illegal" Chinese immigrants as "contraband" or "smuggled." In the case of the Mexican Chinese, however, the INS and the State Department used the term "refugee," even though nations in the prewar era were not yet in the regular practice of understanding the concept or employing the term in this way. The use of the term pointed to the complexity of the situation and the diplomatic issues it raised. In the end, the United States spent over half a million dollars to feed, house, and deport the Mexican Chinese in a depressed economy; the Chinese government repaid a small fraction, but Mexico never offered any reimbursement.

U.S. immigration agents deployed a gendered rubric of Chinese Exclusion as they labeled not only Chinese men but also Mexican women, whether married or unmarried, and Mexican Chinese children, as "Chinese refugees from Mexico" and ultimately deported them to China. Strikingly, the INS avoided sending Mexican women and Mexican Chinese children back to Mexico, even though it would have cost the agency far less than the trip to China; moreover, the mass forcible repatriations of Mexicans were well under way, so returning these women and children would have been a simple undertaking. With few exceptions, U.S. immigration agents did not even take Mexican women's testimony, focusing instead on gathering Chinese men's statements. The ideology of men's control over women under "coverture" and "the femme covert" legitimized the deportation to China of entire Mexican Chinese families, including women in free associations rather than legal marriages with Chinese men. Gender norms and citizenship policy commonly upheld around the world during this time stripped women of their status when they married or formed unions with foreigners. While men (unless they were excluded by race) maintained citizenship regardless of marriage, these notions defined women by the status of their husbands or companions. Mexican women would fall deeper into the interstices of the nation-state once they reached China, where in some cases Chinese men's previous marriages removed the possibility that authorities would consider these women Chinese citizens.

Chinese men arrived in Mexico with greater frequency following formal exclusion from the United States. While some entered that nation illegally through its southern border, others remained in Mexico, participated in the border economy, and started families. A highly vitriolic and hateful anti-Chinese movement ultimately expelled the vast majority of Chinese and many of their Mexican-origin families from Sonora and Sinaloa. As some passed through U.S. territory as "refugees," racial exclusion and gendered notions of citizenship guaranteed that mixed-race families would begin new lives—and face another set of obstacles—in southeastern China.

JULIA MARÍA SCHIAVONE CAMACHO
University of Texas at El Paso

Francisco E. Balderrama and Raymond Rodríguez, *Decade of Betrayal: Mexican Repatriation in the 1930s*, rev. ed. (2006); Mercedes Carreras de Velasco, *Los Mexicanos que devolvió la crisis, 1929–1932* [The Mexicans the Crisis Sent Back, 1929–1932] (1974); Patrick Ettinger, *Imaginary Lines: Border Enforcement and the Origins of Undocumented Immigration, 1882–1930* (2009); Evelyn Hu-DeHart, *Amerasia* 9 (1982), *Amerasia* 15 (1989); Erika Lee, *At America's Gates: Chinese Immigration during the*

Exclusion Era, 1882–1943 (2003), *Journal of Asian American Studies* 8, no. 5 (2005); Mae M. Ngai, *Impossible Subjects: Illegal Aliens and the Making of Modern America* (2004); Robert Chao Romero, *The Chinese in Mexico* (2010); Miguel Tinker Salas, *In the Shadow of the Eagles: Sonora and the Transformation of the Border during the Porfiriato* (1997).

Atlantic World

Although traditionally the American South has been thought about as a largely rural, agricultural area, it is also the most coastal region of the contiguous 48 states, with 2,871 miles of shoreline along the Atlantic Ocean and Gulf of Mexico. The South is anchored by port cities like Baltimore, Charleston, Miami, Mobile, New Orleans, and Norfolk, all of which have served as important points for importing goods and for immigration, while smaller fishing communities dot the beaches and marshlands that define the littoral. From the beginning of the 19th century through World War II, the South's preeminent city, New Orleans, was the second-largest port in the country by volume of trade, second only to New York City. Although the city is often held up as exceptional, the Atlantic forces that shaped New Orleans simply acted on a grander scale in the region's largest port and can be taken as exemplars of influences that have shaped and continue to shape all of the maritime South.

For the last 25 years, scholars have reframed European colonization of the 16th through 19th centuries as the making of the Atlantic World. This perspective emphasizes the multidirectional circulation of people, ideas, and commodities among the regions that border the Atlantic Ocean (West Africa, Western Europe, the Americas, and the Caribbean). Exploring the Atlantic World offers a perspective that escapes the limits of both regionalism and nationalism, opening possibilities for examining multiracial, multiethnic, multinational, and multi-imperial connections.

The foundational historical event most associated with the Atlantic World is the slave trade, which involved the transport of people primarily from the coastal regions of West and Central Africa, with nearly 500,000 brought to the American South. But since slaves, when they survived the Middle Passage, did not always continue to circulate in the Atlantic system, the continuous connections across the waters that affected racial formations may be best captured by sailors, traders, and free travelers, who throughout their restless lives experienced the South as a region connected to a larger sphere.

Free and enslaved sailors of African descent traveled extensively throughout the Atlantic World and were well versed in both African and European languages and customs. These "Atlantic Creoles," as historian Ira Berlin calls them, worked as skilled sailors and shipwrights, shipboard servants, and interpreters. Many ships' crews of the Atlantic were multihued and multilingual, and the men spent more time on the sea than on land, such that by the early 18th century many sailors thought of themselves as "nationless brethren." When they arrived in or settled in southern ports, Atlantic Creoles were instrumental in refashioning the icons and ideologies of the Atlantic World into their new lives, which inevitably affected racial experience, accounting for some of the striking differences seen between the South's port cities and its interior. It is no accident that prior to the Civil War, Baltimore, New Orleans, and Charleston had the highest percentage of free people of color, not only in the South, but in the entire United States. Still, the encounters that produced a different demography in the South's port cities were not without conflict, as evidenced by the case of one Etienne LaRue. A classic "Atlantic Creole," LaRue was a Senegalese free mulatto sailor fluent in French who arrived in New Orleans in 1747, like other sailors, to enjoy shore leave in the city's taverns. He met up with some less cosmopolitan French soldiers in the street, who addressed him with a racial slur. LaRue was comfortable enough in his status to respond in kind, addressing his verbal assailant as "Milord Bugger." While authorities were not pleased that LaRue's gun had gone off in the ensuing scuffle, the court treated the parties as legal equals (over the protests of the soldiers). Indeed, the maritime Atlantic long continued to be a virtual classroom for political rights. Although scholars dispute his birthplace, Denmark Vesey is known to have traveled through the Caribbean, working briefly in Saint-Domingue (later Haiti), before landing in the port of Charleston, where he purchased his freedom and participated in planning a major slave rebellion in 1822. In the late 19th century, many of the people who organized some of the most sustained protests against racial injustice had roots in that same Atlantic milieu.

Historian Rebecca Scott traces three generations of an Atlantic Creole family whose travels spanned Senegal, Haiti, France, Belgium, and Louisiana. Her work shows how the movement of Atlantic World émigrés fueled the tradition of public rights and anticaste thinking in New Orleans, which would eventually lead to the landmark civil rights case *Plessy v. Ferguson*. The story begins with Marie Françoise dite Rosalie, a young woman who lived in 18th-century Saint-Domingue as the property of a prosperous free woman of color. A notary recorded Rosalie as a "negresse de nation Polard," identifying her with the Peul or Fulbe people, a largely Muslim ethnic group from the Senegambia region of West Africa. In the late 1700s, Rosalie's domestic partner, a Frenchman named Michel Vincent, drew up unofficial documents that declared Rosalie and her children as his slaves to whom he wished to grant freedom. In the aftermath of the Haitian Revolution, Rosalie fled with Vincent and their four children to Havana, Cuba. While there, she presented her manumission documents to representatives of the French government, who granted her French citizenship. When refugees of the Haitian Revolution were expelled from Cuba in 1809, the family fled again, this time to New Orleans.

Rosalie's family were part of a multipronged out-migration from Haiti of free whites, free people of color, and the still enslaved to the United States (estimated to be about equal thirds of the emigrant population), who landed in port cities such as Philadelphia, New York, Baltimore, and New Orleans. In New Orleans, the immigrants had a major impact by reinfusing the francophone population in the wake of the Anglo invasion of the Louisiana Purchase territory. Many now iconic New Orleans cultural traditions have been credited to the influence of Saint-Dominguans, including the Creole cottage, voodoo, and even gumbo. Immigrants strengthened the middle classes of free whites and free people of color in the "Creole" neighborhoods of Marigny, Tremé, and the Vieux Carré, offering their skills in the building trades or becoming small business owners in Caribbean luxuries such as tobacco, coffee, and even chocolate, such as Madame Berquin, who transported her knowledge of cocoa cultivation from Saint-Domingue to open a chocolate factory in the French Quarter in the 1810s.

This circulation of people and ideas did not end with the revolutionary generation, nor did the more cosmopolitan aspirations of Atlantic Creoles. Rosalie's children and grandchildren did not stay put in New Orleans. They traveled throughout the Atlantic World in search of better opportunities and freedom from the growing racial restrictions of the antebellum and Jim Crow South. Rosalie's grandson, Edouard Tinchant, was born in France after his parents left New Orleans seeking what he would later describe in a letter as a place where the "stupid prejudices" of racial marginalization did not exist. As a student in French schools, Edouard spent the majority of his formative years as an advocate of French republicanism and suffrage. By the age of 21, Edouard had lived in Antwerp, Belgium, and Veracruz, Mexico, in an attempt to expand the Tinchant family's cigar-making business. When he arrived in New Orleans in 1862 to assist his brother Joseph with the American arm of the family business, the country was entrenched in civil war and his brother had recruited a regiment of free and enslaved Union soldiers. Edouard joined his brother's regiment and wrote an editorial in the *New Orleans Tribune* declaring his entitlement to rights as a U.S. citizen.

In the 20th century, other southern ports began to compete for New

Manuel, a five-year-old shrimp picker who speaks no English, with a mountain of
child-labor oyster shells behind him. Biloxi, Miss., 1911 (Lewis Wickes Hine, photographer,
Library of Congress [LC-USZ62-55649], Washington, D.C.)

Orleans's place in the Atlantic World, but the city held its own between the
world wars, not only as a major economic entrepôt but also as a hearth for new
immigrants, both domestic and international. Another example of the ways
in which maritime labor and travel have shaped the population of the South
is the relationship of New Orleans to the "banana boat" republics of Central
America, particularly Honduras. Latin American men who worked the plantations and boats of the New Orleans–based United Fruit Company were introduced to the city via this route, gradually settling and bringing their families.
As a result, prior to Hurricane Katrina, the New Orleans area was home to the
largest Honduran population outside the capital of Tegucigalpa. After Katrina,
the racial map of New Orleans has changed, with an estimated 20 percent loss
of the local African American population and an influx of Latino (especially
Mexican) workers and their families. While these transitions have been attended by difficult family separations and political struggles, the older history
of the city's Latin American connections is now being invoked as a recovered
memory to comprehend the ongoing process of creolization.

New Orleans's Atlantic World connections have deep historical roots that
are fully evident to even a casual tourist sampling its unique cultural flavors

and architectural facades. Other southern coastal cities have had similar links to that world. Atlantic trade stimulated immigration into Florida's fast-growing port cities, for example, culminating in 20th-century Cuban and Haitian immigrations, echoing those that shaped New Orleans in the prior century. Far from being insular, therefore, the South has always been global, looking out onto the waters of the Atlantic, especially the Caribbean Basin. As in the past, its porous coastline continues to absorb new commodities, the people that transport them, and the new ideas that float on worldly currents.

ZADA JOHNSON
SHANNON LEE DAWDY
University of Chicago

Ira Berlin, *William and Mary Quarterly* (April 1996); Shannon Lee Dawdy, *Building the Devil's Empire: French Colonial New Orleans* (2008); Nathalie Dessens, *From Saint-Domingue to New Orleans: Migration and Influences* (2007); Jack P. Greene and Philip Morgan, eds., *Atlantic History: A Critical Appraisal* (2009); Peter Linebaugh and Marcus Rediker, *The Many-Headed Hydra: Sailors, Slaves, Commoners, and the Hidden History of the Revolutionary Atlantic* (2001); Raymond A. Mohl, *Journal of American Ethnic History* (Summer 2003); Walter G. Rucker, *The River Flows On: Black Resistance, Culture, and Identity Formation in Early America* (2006); Rebecca Scott, *Current Anthropology* (April 2007).

Civil Rights, African American

The modern civil rights movement succeeded in three very important ways. First, it played a decisive role in the destruction of Jim Crow; second, it transformed the ongoing and larger black freedom struggle within which the civil rights movement transpired; and third, it transformed the status of blacks and race relations in the United States. American democracy moved closer to realizing its ideals of liberty, equality, and justice for all because of the civil rights movement.

The Fourteenth Amendment (1868) established that blacks were U.S. citizens. Blacks have consistently used the Fourteenth Amendment as the constitutional bulwark for their civil rights battles. As it evolved, the civil rights movement employed three broad and interrelated strategies: (1) moral appeal, or moral suasion, or speaking to the moral conscience, especially the white, moral conscience; (2) collective protest action, ranging from boycotts, sit-ins, and marches to nonviolent civil disobedience; and (3) legal action—employing civil rights jurisprudence rooted in the Fourteenth Amendment as a way to abolish the legal/constitutional impediments to black citizenship.

The horror of escalating disfranchisement, lynching, and Jim Crow in the late 19th and early 20th centuries only intensified the urgency of black civil rights struggles. The increasing virulence of the white supremacist offensive forced an interracial coalition to create the National Association for the Advancement of Colored People (NAACP) in 1909. The NAACP soon emerged as and has remained the single most important institutional vehicle for advancing the black civil rights struggle.

The infamous decision in *Plessy v. Ferguson* (1896) legitimized the doctrine of Jim Crow: the myth of separate but equal public accommodations and institutions for blacks and whites in the South. A legal fiction as well as a powerful institutionalization and symbol of white racism, Jim Crow and the white supremacist mind-set that rationalized it rapidly proliferated across the South. The *Plessy* decision was the legal/constitutional bulwark of the inherently separate, unequal, and white supremacist world of Jim Crow.

The southern black struggle to defeat Jim Crow lay at the heart of the 20th-century civil rights movement. At the heart of the legal/constitutional war against Jim Crow were various legal campaigns. Pioneered by Charles Hamilton Houston, the ultimately successful NAACP battle against Jim Crow began in the 1930s and 1940s with a series of important legal victories that culminated in the *Brown* decision.

The 1954 Supreme Court decision in *Brown v. Board of Education* was a watershed in the modern civil rights movement. First and foremost, the landmark decision overturned *Plessy*, the constitutional justification for Jim Crow. The court unanimously ruled that the doctrine of separate and equal schools violated the Fourteenth Amendment–protected rights of the black plaintiffs precisely because such Jim Crow arrangements were inherently unequal and thus inherently unjust.

Southern white resistance to school desegregation was widespread and intense. Massive resistance—the organized regional white opposition to racial integration—undermined both. The Supreme Court's toothless enforcement decree in *Brown II* (1955)—that the schools were to be desegregated "with all deliberate speed"—further undermined progress toward school desegregation and racial integration. In 1957, black students in Little Rock, Ark., backed up by the local black community, fought to integrate the all-white Central High School. That valiant effort in the face of furious local white opposition epitomized the kind of insurgent mobilization of local black communities necessary to realize what *Brown* mandated.

After *Brown*, the civil rights movement increasingly encompassed expanding and widespread grassroots campaigns to uproot Jim Crow in public accommodations as well as in areas like housing and schools. Indeed the insurgent spirit of *Brown* inspired a burgeoning direct-action phase of the movement, exemplified by the Montgomery Bus Boycott from December 1955 through November 1956.

The Montgomery Bus Boycott saw local blacks boycott the city buses for almost a full year in order to end the bus system's degrading Jim Crow practices. The boycott grew out of one of the most famous moments in civil rights history lore: local NAACP activist Rosa Parks's defiance of the local Jim Crow statute by refusing to give up her seat to a white person. Parks was not, as enduring legend has it, simply tired. Instead, Parks was a committed long-distance black freedom fighter.

As the head of the Montgomery Improvement Association, Martin Luther King Jr. helped lead the Montgomery campaign. The Southern Christian Leadership Conference (SCLC), the organization of ministers that King subsequently created and led, not only modeled nonviolent civil disobedience; it also served as the institutional network that backed up the many grassroots campaigns King embraced. Soon King became not just the most important black spokesman of his time and beyond, but also one of the most important leaders in all of U.S. history.

In addition to the grassroots insurgency, the Montgomery struggle fought the Jim Crow city bus system in the courts. The legal battle worked hand in hand with the grassroots insurgency. The successful litigation led to *Browder v. Gayle* (1956), in which the Supreme Court upheld a federal court ruling that declared unconstitutional the Montgomery and Alabama statues requiring racially segregated buses. The legal victory indeed underwrote the successful conclusion of the Montgomery Bus Boycott.

The Montgomery insurgency catalyzed the escalating civil rights insurgency. In early February 1960, four students at A&T College for Negroes in Greensboro, N.C., sat in at the downtown Woolworth lunch counter seeking to integrate it. The resulting desegregation campaign sparked an escalating series of desegregation campaigns throughout the South. These innumerable mobilizations contributed to the successful desegregation of stores and public facilities not only throughout the South but in the West and North as well.

Out of this student-led insurgency emerged the Student Nonviolent Coordinating Committee (SNCC), the organization that would be the radical cutting edge of the movement. Along with the King-led SCLC and the Congress of Racial Equality (CORE), SNCC modeled nonviolent direct action, especially militant civil disobedience.

The 1961 Freedom Rides tested the nation's commitment to desegregated interstate travel. In *Morgan v. Commonwealth of Virginia* (1946), the Supreme Court outlawed segregated seating on interstate buses. In *Boynton v. Virginia* (1960), the Supreme Court expanded the reach of the *Morgan* decision, outlawing segregated facilities for interstate passengers. The Freedom Riders were an integrated group that traveled from the upper South through the lower South. Mass media images of a burning bus in Anniston, Ala., the bandaged face of Freedom Rider James Peck lying in a hospital bed, and race riots in Birmingham and Montgomery, Ala., rallied the nation to the side of the Freedom Riders. In September 1962, the Interstate Commerce Commission outlawed segregated seating on interstate buses, sealing the Freedom Riders' victory.

Insurgent action proved essential to the passage of the two towering achievements of the civil rights movement: the 1964 Civil Rights Act and the 1965 Voting Rights Act. The Birmingham movement played a crucial role in forcing the passage of the Civil Rights Act. The 1965 Selma to Montgomery March pushed Congress to pass the Voting Rights Act.

The 1963 Birmingham movement was a powerful black grassroots mobilization that fought to desegregate public facilities and to end discriminatory hiring practices. Boycotts, sit-ins, and marches galvanized the insurgency. When King heeded the call of the Birmingham campaign to help out, the mobilization kicked into a higher gear. King went to jail rather than abide by local orders that he not march, from which he wrote his famous "Letter from Birmingham Jail," compellingly articulating the urgent need for direct action to bring down Jim Crow immediately.

The Children's Campaign, in which black youth participated in the marches, invited a vicious response from local police, who turned attack dogs and fire hoses on the marchers, including the children. These startling images horrified the world and made it clear that Jim Crow must be destroyed not only in Birmingham but everywhere. Coming shortly after the high of the 1963 March on Washington, the cold-blooded murder of four little girls in the September bombing of the 16th Street Baptist Church only strengthened the resolve of the Birmingham Campaign, which soon succeeded.

The Selma Voting Rights Campaign fought to register blacks in an area where they constituted a majority but where, owing to racist barriers, relatively few were able to register to vote, let alone actually vote. In late 1964, at the request of the Selma Campaign, King and SCLC joined the SNCC-led protests. In early 1965, increasingly large and militant demonstrations against the racist practices of the local voting system led to growing numbers of arrests. The murder of Jimmy Lee Jackson, a black worker, by state trooper J. Bonard Fowler outraged

Police dog attacking civil rights demonstrators, Birmingham, Ala., 1963
(Charles Moore, photographer, Birmingham News)

the campaign and led to calls for a march on Montgomery from Selma to demand immediate action on black voting rights.

On Sunday, 7 March 1965, "Bloody Sunday," over 600 blacks led by SNCC's John Lewis and SCLC's Hosea Williams began a march across the Edmund Pettus Bridge on the way to Montgomery when 90 troopers and deputies beat them, forcing them to retreat back across the bridge. Of the marchers, 56 had to be hospitalized. On 9 March, King led 2,500 across the bridge to the point of the infamous "Bloody Sunday" attack, but then heeding the police officials rather than forcing the issue, he led a controversial retreat back across the bridge.

On 17 March, however, King led 8,000, including thousands from across the nation, across the bridge. In Montgomery, King insisted before a crowd of 25,000 that victory in the voting rights struggle was imminent. The Selma Campaign generated enormous support for the Voting Rights Act, which President Lyndon Johnson signed into law on 6 August 1965.

The civil rights movement began to splinter in the mid-1960s. The failure of the Democratic Party to seat the interracial Mississippi Freedom Party delegation at the 1964 convention instead of the all-white official delegation soured many not only on the racial liberalism the party represented, but also on interracialism. The 1965 Watts Riot in Los Angeles and the many urban rebellions of the late 1960s signaled a growing black rage that the southern-based movement and its successes had left poverty and economic oppression untouched. These rebellions also clearly revealed intensifying black disenchantment with nonviolent direct action.

During the 1966 Memphis-to-Jackson "March against Fear," James Meredith was shot as he sought to show that racial progress had come to Mississippi and the South. When Stokely Carmichael and Willie Ricks shouted the words "Black Power" at a rally during the march, they captured the escalating militancy of the moment. They likewise captured the deep questioning among a growing number of blacks regarding the efficacy of nonviolence. A small yet growing number of blacks began to embrace the call of leaders like Robert Williams and Malcolm X for armed self-defense. Growing numbers of blacks rejected the integrationism of the civil rights movement in favor of the racial nationalism of Black Power.

After 1965, King's leadership showcased a growing concern for economic justice and opposition to the war in Vietnam. In 1968, when he joined the struggle of the Memphis sanitation workers for better pay and working conditions, he also spearheaded the planning for a multiracial Poor People's Campaign on behalf of economic justice. King's assassination in Memphis on 4 March 1968 traumatized the nation and, for a growing number of Americans, especially radical blacks, hammered the nails in the coffin of nonviolence. The black freedom struggle would never be the same.

WALDO MARTIN
University of California at Berkeley

Taylor Branch, *At Canaan's Edge: America in the King Years, 1965–68* (2006), *Parting the Waters: America in the King Years, 1954–63* (1988), *Pillar of Fire: America in the King Years, 1963–65* (1998); Henry Hampton and Steve Fayer, eds., *Voices of Freedom: An Oral History of the Civil Rights Movement from the 1950s through the 1980s* (1990); Vincent Harding, *There Is a River: The Black Struggle for Freedom in America* (1982); Richard Kluger, *Simple Justice: The History of* Brown v. Board of Education *and Black America's Struggle for Equality* (1975); Manning Marable, *Race, Reform, and Rebellion: The Second Reconstruction and Beyond in Black America, 1945–2006* (2007); Howell Raines, *My Soul Is Rested: Movement Days in the Deep South Remembered* (1977); Harvard Sitkoff, *The Struggle for Black Equality* (2008); Patricia Sullivan, *Lift Every Voice: The NAACP and the Making of the Civil Rights Movement* (2009).

Civil Rights, Mexican American

Mexican Americans actively struggled for civil rights in the United States throughout the 20th century. In the South and in Texas—the only southern state with a large Mexican-origin population—Mexican Americans experienced a pervasive segregation order that denied persons of Mexican descent basic equality and dignity. The Mexican American Jim Crow included the segregation of public places, neighborhood segregation, separate Mexican schools, employment discrimination and low wages, disfranchisement, and a general perception among white people that Mexican Americans were racially degenerate and inferior. Mexican Americans challenged this racism using a variety of methods, beginning in the early 1900s.

Labor organizing was at the forefront of Mexican American civil rights activism in the early 20th century. As many Mexicans and Mexican Americans understood, workers' rights were civil rights. For example, Mexican-origin workers formed the Federal Labor Union (FLU) in Laredo, Tex., in 1905. The FLU represented hundreds of skilled and unskilled laborers working on farms and for railroad companies. The union called a general strike in 1906 to protest the low pay railroad workers received. After three months, the railroad companies agreed to a wage hike from 75¢ to $1 for a ten-hour day. This general strike was so successful that the following month the mineworkers represented by the FLU walked off the job. When the FLU threatened another general strike, the mine company settled. But the mine owners reneged on their agreement, another general strike failed, and the FLU folded shortly thereafter.

Union organizing represented a nascent struggle for rights that only increased throughout the 20th century, culminating in Cesar Chavez's organization of the National Farm Workers of America in 1962. Mexican Americans successfully organized to resist poor conditions, low wages, and harassment. However, labor activism proved untenable, and victories won in one year could be lost the next. For Mexican-origin workers, as for all laborers who were economically poor, protesting was difficult because striking meant not working. Union organizing helped, but workers could not remain off the job forever.

Other groups advanced different agendas. El Congreso del Pueblo de Habla Española (Congress of Spanish-Speaking Peoples), founded in 1939, for example, pushed more aggressively for civil rights. El Congreso sought to improve the social and economic conditions of Mexicans in the United States. This meant that the group supported the New Deal, sought increased wages for the underpaid, and called for the destruction of racial discrimination. Aside from these goals, El Congreso had a bold agenda of encouraging unity among all oppressed groups, including the Mexican, Mexican American, white liberal, and African American communities. But it proved to be short lived. It was damaged by red-baiting, and the organization folded in 1942.

In addition to labor and civic group activism, many Mexican Americans looked to military service as a strategy for securing rights. Individuals and leaders hoped military service would prove to the majority Anglo population that Mexican-origin people were decent, patriotic, and honorable citizens who would sacrifice for the cause of the United States. Many also viewed military service as a route to citizenship (if they did not have it). During the two world wars, these expectations were only partially fulfilled, as many of the soldiers found racism in the military, and most returned home to find things as they had left them. While their hopes were perhaps misplaced, nearly 400,000 Mexicans and Mexican Americans served in World War II.

While Mexican-origin soldiers fought bravely throughout World War II, their compatriots at home experienced many problems. The U.S. government initiated the Bracero guest-worker program in 1942, allowing Mexican workers to legally come to the United States to work in agriculture. These "braceros" experienced a good deal of abuse and harassment, and their presence also depressed the wages of Mexican American workers. More problematically, race relations increasingly intensified between Mexican Americans and whites throughout the war period, culminating in 1943 in the so-called Zoot Suit Riots. White police and military personnel beat hundreds of men, tore off their zoot suits, cut off their long hair, and left the men bleeding in the street. These conflicts, which occurred in California, Florida, Texas, New York, and several other states, demonstrated that military service would not change the opinions of white people.

These negative events contributed to increased activism. For example, Mexican Americans had long opposed segregated education. In the 1950s and 1960s, civic groups such as the League of United Latin American Citizens (LULAC) fought several important school desegregation cases. LULAC won the 1948 *Delgado v. Bastrop Independent School District* case, primarily by arguing that Mexican Americans were white and hence segregation did not apply to them. This case serves as an example of Mexican American white racial formation. Regarded as neither white nor black in the United States, Mexican Americans fell uncomfortably into a racial hinterland. White racialization proved a natural, albeit controversial strategy for securing rights. In the *Delgado* case and in the Bastrop schools, whiteness won some benefits, but in numerous other instances white racialization did nothing.

LULAC attacked another aspect of segregation with the 1954 *Pete Hernandez v. State of Texas* case. An all-white jury had convicted Hernández of murder, sentencing him to life in prison. On appeal before the U.S. Supreme Court, Hernández's attorneys asserted that the trial neglected their client's constitutional rights because Mexican Americans had not served on the jury. Instead of arguing that the jury was all white (and hence could not be considered exclusionary since Mexican Americans were classified as white), the lawyers declared that Mexican Americans were a separate class of white people who could not be excluded from jury service. The court agreed and concluded that exclusion of Mexican Americans as a group of whites, distinct from Anglos, violated their rights.

In addition to legal activism, Mexican Americans began to politically organize in the 1950s and 1960s. One of the most important political campaigns occurred in Crystal City, Tex. In 1961, local leaders organized the Citizens Committee for Better Government (CCBG) to challenge the white families who had controlled local politics for decades. With support from the newly founded statewide Political Association of Spanish-Speaking Organizations (PASO) and funding from the Teamsters Union, the CCBG began registering Mexican American voters for the 1963 city council elections. The group also ran five candidates—"Los Cinco Candidatos"—for the election (Juan Cornejo, Manuel Maldonado, Reynaldo Mendoza, Antonio Cárdenas, and Mario Hernández). The registration and voting drive ensured that "Los Cinco Candidatos" beat all five white incumbents, replacing the Anglo council with an all–Mexican American government.

The 1963 elections were a momentous victory in the Mexican American struggle for rights. But these democratically elected officeholders were treated like political usurpers, harassed by the Texas Rangers, and voted out of office in the next election cycle by a newly developed Anglo–Mexican American political machine in 1965. Mexican Americans understood they would have to more forcefully push for rights in order to win lasting victories.

That more forceful stance appeared starkly in 1966. That year, government officials began debating the establishment of a uniform minimum wage of $1.25 per hour for farmworkers as part of the War on Poverty. But Texas governor John Connally opposed the idea. Farmworkers in the Rio Grande Valley therefore walked off the job in the summer of 1966. To dramatize their plight, they also planned a march from the Rio Grande Valley to Austin. They set out on Independence Day to highlight the symbolism of the protest. This Minimum Wage March took over 65 days to complete. The marchers hoped to meet Governor Connally in Austin and convince him that he should publicly endorse a $1.25 minimum wage, but he refused.

In the end, the strikers failed to secure the desired minimum wage. In many ways, however, the protest succeeded beyond the wildest dreams of most of its participants. The march proved to many Mexican Americans that nonviolent, direct action demonstrations could unite the Mexican-origin community. Many began to embrace a new sense of what it meant to be a person of Mexican descent living in America. This more radical or militant group of Mexican Americans looked to civil disobedience and social activism to challenge racism. They also rejected whiteness as a civil rights strategy. Mexican Americans, they argued, were brown, not white, people. With this new racial focus came a change in ethnic identification. No longer content with being Latin American, Spanish American, or even Mexican American, these activists adopted a new name for themselves—Chicano.

In Texas, the main Chicano leader was José Angel Gutiérrez. He was born and raised in Crystal City and had his first taste of civil rights activism during the campaign of "Los Cinco Candidatos." Gutiérrez helped form two of the most important Chicano organizations. The first group was the Mexican American Youth Organization (MAYO), founded in San Antonio in 1967. MAYO was a student-centered, militant, direct-action organization that protested police brutality, the Vietnam War, and racism more generally. MAYO sprouted dozens of chapters that battled for civil rights across the state.

In addition to MAYO, Gutiérrez also helped found La Raza Unida Party (RUP, the United People's Party) in 1970. RUP fielded Chicano political candidates who would be accountable to the Latino community. RUP's initial focus was on local elections in Crystal City. Gutiérrez ran as a RUP candidate for a seat on the school board. The party also fielded two candidates for city council in Crystal City and ran candidates for all at-large positions in the four counties surrounding Crystal City. A total of 15 RUP candidates won election, including Gutiérrez. RUP's first political outing was a success that inspired the Chicano community across the Southwest.

RUP next joined the 1972 Texas gubernatorial contest. The party ran Ramsey Muñiz, a Waco attorney and a popular former college football star. When the votes were tallied, Muñiz garnered an impressive 6 percent of the vote (or approximately 200,000 votes). RUP ran Muñiz for governor again in 1974. But political infighting within RUP damaged his chances for victory, and he was once again defeated (he received 190,000 votes). RUP's statewide losses in Texas fractured the party. Muñiz's defeat and his subsequent arrests for drug possession seriously damaged the party's credibility. Its demise in many ways represented the end of the Chicano movement.

The Chicano movement witnessed the headiest days of Mexican American civil rights activism. The broader Mexican American freedom struggle sought political clout, an end to anti-Mexican racism, and, in the Chicano period, the basic reframing of what it meant to be Mexican in America. While Mexican Americans sought acceptance during the initial phase of the struggle, Chicanos aggressively demanded that acceptance and inclusion. No longer were Mexican Americans viewed as white, without a past, or foreigners. Rather, Chicanos argued for Mexican American cultural pride, nationalism, self-defense, the teaching of Chicano history, and the understanding that Chicanos were a distinct ethnic minority community in the United States. The basic ways in which the Mexican American community is perceived in the United States today is largely a result of Mexican American civil rights activism in previous decades.

BRIAN D. BEHNKEN
Iowa State University

Rodolfo Acuña, *Occupied America: A History of Chicanos* (2010); Brian D. Behnken, *Fighting Their Own Battles: Mexican Americans, African Americans, and the Struggle for Civil Rights in Texas* (2011); Patrick J. Carroll, *Felix Longoria's Wake: Bereavement, Racism, and the Rise of Mexican American Activism* (2003); Ignacio M. García, *White but Not Equal: Mexican Americans, Jury Discrimination, and the Supreme Court* (2008); Mario T. García, *Mexican Americans: Leadership, Ideology, and Identity, 1930–1960* (1989); George Mariscal, *Brown-Eyed Children of the Sun: Lessons from the Chicano Movement, 1965–1975* (2005); Benjamin Márquez, *LULAC: The Evolution of a Mexican-American Political Organization* (1993); David Montejano, *Anglos and Mexicans in the Making of Texas, 1836–1986* (1987); Armando Navarro, *The Cristal Experiment: A Chicano Struggle for Community Control* (1998); Cynthia Orozco, *No Mexicans, Women, or Dogs Allowed: The Rise of the Mexican American Civil Rights Movement* (2009); F. Arturo Rosales, *Chicano! The History of the Mexican American Civil Rights Movement* (1997); Guadalupe San Miguel, *"Let All of Them Take Heed": Mexican-Americans and the Campaign for Educational Equality in Texas, 1910–1981* (1987); Zaragosa Vargas, *Labor Rights Are Civil Rights: Mexican American Workers in Twentieth-Century America* (2004).

Convict Lease System and Peonage

The convict lease system was the means by which southern states dealt with their post–Civil War prisoners. Under this regimen, convicts were leased to individuals or corporations, who thus acquired a captive labor force and at the same time agreed to supervise it. As a result, the industrial landscape of the New South was dotted with prison work camps and stockades, home to inmates who were overwhelmingly (roughly 90 percent) African American. At their worst, these facilities afforded examples of human misery that shocked contemporaries and gave southern corrections a bad reputation.

Apologists pointed out that the state governments were impoverished, that penitentiaries erected before the war were destroyed, and that state and local officials had no reliable mechanism of control over recently freed black populations. In fact, models for privately run prisons were already in place. As early as 1825, Kentucky had leased its inmates to a businessman who sought to turn the penitentiary at Frankfort into a factory. In 1846, Alabama legislators leased the "Walls" at Wetumpka to the first of a series of entrepreneurs. The lure of turning a debit into a credit through off-site labor appealed to postwar officials, Republicans and former Confederates alike.

The convict lease system should be understood as a child of slavery. White southerners (and many northerners) believed that African Americans needed the tutelage of their former masters—that left to their own devices, freedmen would fall into idleness and crime. Judges imbued with these beliefs found themselves dealing with a range of behaviors (ranging from genuinely criminal acts to mere rudeness) that once would have been handled extralegally by plantation discipline. In the post-Reconstruction world, such offenses were punished by hard labor for the state or county. Judges of the period exercised considerable discretion in sentencing, taking into account the labor needs of sheriffs or lessees. Sentences tended to be long. Of 1,200 convicts leased by Georgia in 1880, over 500 were serving terms of 10 years or more. In Texas, with more than 2,300 incarcerated in 1882, only two men were sentenced for less than 10 years.

By the 1880s, several states had given their convicts over to large corporations. This had the merit of administrative simplicity and was also financially attractive. Georgia in 1876 divided 1,100 prisoners among three companies, each of which agreed to pay the state $25,000 per year. Tennessee and Alabama made their arrangements with the Tennessee Coal and Iron Company (TCI). In 1890, more than 800 Alabama convicts worked in TCI mines, for which the state was paid more than $180,000—6 percent of its yearly income. It would be an oversimplification to argue that the South was following the "Prussian Road" of authoritarian development. On the other hand—in light of many alliances between entrepreneurs and ultraconservative Bourbon politicians—it is true that racial ideology and law converged for the benefit of New South industrialists. The latter gained both cheap labor and a ready-made strikebreaking force.

Yet the concentration of convicts made them more visible to journalists, reformers, and other critics of the system. An assertion made during the period was that convict leasing was worse than slavery—that, as Women's Christian Temperance Union leader Julia Tutwiler said in 1890, it had all of slavery's evils without the personal contact and paternalism that she viewed as "ameliorating features." She was right to think that most lessees had few occasions to look upon their laborers as individuals and only the slightest of economic motives to promote their welfare. The frequency of escapes was such that camp managers tended to fire lenient guards and to employ shackles and close confinement whenever possible. The results were poor sanitation and scandalously high mortality from disease and accidents. While 1 to 2 percent of northern prisoners died each year, death rates of 15 percent were not unknown in the South.

Critics of the system were a diverse group and included the African American leaders Booker T. Washington, W. E. B. Du Bois, and Mary Church Terrell, white women activists like Tutwiler and Georgia's Rebecca Felton, agrarian politicians and labor activists who opposed corporate power, and an intriguing number of well-placed, otherwise conventional whites who can be called "Bourbon reformers." The most celebrated of the latter was the Louisiana writer George Washington Cable, whose nonfiction work eloquently denounced racial discrimination and southern penal practices. These disparate elements did accomplish certain reforms in the 1880s and 1890s.

Administratively, these years saw the creation of stronger state regulatory boards, staffed by men who were acquainted with professional organizations such as the National Prison Association. Through these boards (and with persistent lobbying by women's organizations), the states mandated improved standards of housing, diet, and health care and began to provide educational facilities for inmates. During the same period, the states began to exclude female prisoners and minors from the camps, placing them in separate facilities. By the turn of the century, reformist and anticorporate influences were strong enough to put some states on the road to ending the lease system, initially by working convicts on state-owned farms. A leader in this development was Mississippi, which took steps to abolish the lease system in its 1890 constitution (interestingly, the same constitution that effectively disfranchised black voters) and had opened Parchman Farm by 1901.

For all these improvements, the convict lease system was irredeemably flawed. This is evident in the career of R. H. Dawson, chief inspector of the Alabama Department of Corrections (1883–96). A true Bourbon reformer, Dawson saw himself as a mediator between the convicts and TCI, the state's chief lessee. Each prisoner was expected to produce 4,000 pounds of usable coal per day; Dawson worked to ensure honest time keeping and decent living conditions. To improve morale and fend off vice, he distributed writing materials and encouraged letter writing. Thus, miners could stay in touch with their families and more easily report corporate rule breaking. He gave each convict a card with two dates written on it: the date of the man's full-sentence release and the date of his "short-time" release for good behavior. For several years, Dawson's methods seemed to work, and convicts each had a fighting chance to survive prison—and to leave it with coal-mining skills, which many proceeded to put to use.

Yet, in the 1890s, TCI officials steadily undermined Dawson's achievements. Guards goaded prisoners into riots that wrecked their "short-time" status. Company bosses bribed or pressured inmates into overtime work in exchange for company scrip that fueled gambling and black market activities. Clearly, the lessees preferred to handle overburdened, dissolute men, and Dawson concluded that the kind of order he was promoting—prison run as a school of discipline—could not take hold within the convict lease system. Gov. Thomas Goode Jones (1890–94) agreed, and under his administration the state prepared to shift its corrections to Mississippi-style prison farming. However, the Panic of 1893 touched off a crisis of state finance, and Jones's successors preserved the always-profitable mining lease.

The eventual decline of convict leasing came about as a result of several factors: middle-class concerns over child labor, illiteracy, and public health; election of progressive Democrats such as Georgia's governor Hoke Smith (a major actor in that state's 1908 abolition of the lease); and the "good roads" movement in Georgia, North Carolina, and other states, which shifted convict labor to the highways under state control. State sponsorship of private unfree labor ended with Alabama's 1928 laws terminating the convict lease. But public laws had little to do with the survival of a parallel regime—peonage—still very much alive in the 1930s.

Large numbers of African American farmers were sharecroppers who paid the landowner half their crops in addition to the value of supplies received. Declining prices of staple crops almost guaranteed that such men (and their white counterparts) fell deeper into debt each year, thus creating a class of hopeless debtors. When plantation owners compelled tenants to work out their debts, the result was peonage. Across the region, contract labor laws criminalized breach of contract, opening the way for shadowy collaborations between planters and local law enforcement. Under this system, a justice of the peace would arrange for a defaulting debtor to be arrested and fined on charges that might or might not be entered on his books. The landowner would appear, pay the fine, and be granted custody. Now the peon had to work out the fine (and the rest of his indebtedness) or risk another arrest. Though such practices appear (correctly) to modern eyes as a crude restoration of master-slave relations, they also meshed perfectly with a long-lived stereotype of black folk and poor whites alike—that the working classes must be forced to work.

Peonage was widespread in the Cotton Belt, in Florida's turpentine camps, and in other settings of isolation and poverty. Nonetheless, in the early 1900s, a number of federal officials, most of whom were Republicans, joined forces with black spokesmen and a sprinkling of Bourbon reformers to challenge these practices. Acting under an 1867 statute, U.S. attorneys brought cases before district judges Charles Swayne (Florida), Thomas Goode Jones (Alabama), Emory Speer (Georgia), and Jacob Trieber (Arkansas). Their greatest success came in Alabama, where Judge Jones and Booker T. Washington quietly supported a state case, *Alonzo Bailey v. Alabama* (1911), in which the U.S. Supreme Court overturned Alabama's contract labor law. Subsequently (in *U.S. v. Reynolds*, 1914), the High Court also struck down Alabama's practice of assigning prisoners to private citizens. Still, these victories did not end peonage. So long as debt reigned supreme, so long as planters and industrialists were patrons of local lawmen, the corrupt regime could flourish.

PAUL M. PRUITT JR.
Bounds Law Library
University of Alabama

Brent Jude Aucoin, "'A Rift in the Clouds': Southern Federal Judges and African-American Civil Rights, 1885–1915" (Ph.D. dissertation, University of Arkansas, 1999); Mary Ellen Curtin, *Black Prisoners and Their World: Alabama, 1865–1900* (2000); Pete Daniel, *The Shadow of Slavery: Peonage in the South, 1901–1969* (1990); Matthew J. Mancini, *One Dies, Get Another: Convict Leasing in the American South, 1866–1928* (1996); Blake McKelvey, *American Prisons: A History of Good Intentions* (1977); David M. Oshinsky, *Worse Than Slavery: Parchman Farm and the Ordeal of Jim Crow Justice* (1996); Paul M. Pruitt Jr., *Reviews in American History* (September 2001); Hilda Jane Zimmerman, "Penal Systems and Penal Reforms in the South since the Civil War" (Ph.D. dissertation, University of North Carolina, 1947).

Criminal Justice

In April 1963, Martin Luther King Jr. was jailed for his role in a nonviolent protest against racial segregation in Birmingham, Ala. From the jaws of the southern criminal justice system, the southern jail, King put pen to paper to write "Letter from Birmingham Jail," a powerful indictment of racial injustice that skewered white moderates for undermining progress on integration and other matters. Southern moderates, King believed, were "more devoted to 'order' than to justice." King's words resonated as the black freedom struggle confronted a white-dominated criminal justice system and well described the criminal justice system in the American South throughout much of its history: often more devoted to order than to justice, conventionally defined, and committed to an order first dedicated to and then tainted by the legacy of racial subjugation.

Criminal justice in the American South developed in the political and social climate created by slavery, as white southerners shaped its founding institutions from their position atop the backs of black slaves. The system they built operated by and large to protect the interests and human property of slave owners; this required achieving a careful balance between denying black slaves basic rights, granting white slave owners extraordinary privileges, and giving whites who did not own slaves enough power to invest them in the slave system but not enough to challenge it. The laws that governed white authority over slaves, first set down in Virginia in the early 1700s and soon reproduced around the South, extended beyond the boundaries of the plantation to establish a criminal justice system that operated according to the race of defendants and victims. It was a system that diminished the culpability of white perpetrators and enhanced the value of white victims; conversely, African American victims of crime found little protection under the law, which punished harshly those African Americans accused or convicted of crimes.

As a result, both before and after the Civil War, some forms of violence against blacks were not considered crimes, either socially or legally, including the sexual violence and the beatings—and sometimes the killings—visited on slaves by their masters. Similarly, lynchings, though technically illegal, often were not considered crimes socially, and if they were, disapproval was the only consequence suffered by the perpetrators, who were rarely arrested and charged. Furthermore, many white southerners understood lynching to work in concert with, or at least nip at the heels of, the formal legal system: opponents of lynching thought courtroom trials with satisfactory outcomes discouraged lynchings, while proponents believed lynchings encouraged "satisfactory" outcomes in courtroom trials. Thus the threat of lynching that hung over black men, even those arrested and standing trial, was both real and overt. No more so than in the 1880s and 1890s, when lynchings became increasingly frequent, brutal, and race based.

African American suspects who avoided extralegal violence entered the formal criminal justice system at considerable disadvantage, with limited or entirely curtailed rights. They were rarely found not guilty and were often punished violently and publicly, with the aim that their suffering would serve as a lesson for their peers. Judges and justices wrestled over a crucial irony here: as defendants in court, slaves were treated as human beings, even more gravely accountable for their actions than whites, but outside the courtroom, they were considered property. This dual identity meant slaves were more likely to face harsh punishments both within the formal criminal justice system and under the more informal slave justice system they faced outside it. Free blacks often found themselves constrained by and punished under the same laws that regulated slave behavior.

The period between the end of the Civil War and the civil rights era found much of the criminal justice apparatus in the South bent toward controlling the social, political, and working lives of African Americans. Many whites who subscribed to the tenets of white supremacy in the segregated South, whether vicious racists or naive paternalists, believed that the point of contact between African Americans and whites should be control. White elites' desire for control became particularly urgent after the Civil War, when hundreds of thousands of freed slaves sought their place in southern society. As a result, new laws targeted African Americans by criminalizing normal behavior, such as gathering in groups, carrying a firearm, entering town with empty pockets, or not holding a job, sending many to prison.

Prisons were notably absent from the southern landscape before Reconstruction. Historians have suggested a number of reasons for southerners neglecting their prisons (and for being slow to build a functioning court apparatus): the South's low population density in the 19th century, southerners' distrust of centralized power, and their reliance on settling disputes personally. However, it was primarily race that stunted the growth of the antebellum prison system before the Civil War and race that nourished it afterward. Under slavery, white southerners were repulsed by the idea that whites might be confined—and forced to work—like black slaves. Afterward, the need for black labor propelled the prison industry, laying the foundation for the thriving correctional industry of today.

The stewards of the rigidly segregated southern prisons reserved their worst treatment for African American convicts, who suffered privation and torture not only in jails and prisons but also in the far-flung work camps, where convicts labored for state government or for private companies that leased their labor. Widely publicized horror stories did little to stem southern states' reliance on convict leasing and chain gangs to keep their prison population and punishment budgets manageable. Convict leasing and chain gangs lasted well into the 20th century, long after they were condemned as cruel and unusual.

They were often miserable places, but southern prisons were no more horrible than their northern counterparts, whose early experiments with penology, including forced silence and isolation, today are considered forms of torture. In fact, the chain gang may be the southern criminal justice system's only truly unique feature. Often, all-black chain gangs became a potent symbol of the region's slave legacy, especially when exported north, as in the 1932 film *I Am a Fugitive from a Chain Gang.*

As the penitentiary put down roots in the South, so, too, did the death penalty. Like imprisonment, the death penalty was once a punishment reserved almost exclusively for slaves, who were executed brutally and publicly to frighten the slave population into submission. In the early 20th century, southern governments centralized executions, taking control from sheriffs and executing criminals in a central location. The death penalty in the South claimed the lives of a disproportionate number of African Americans. Southern states alone maintained rape as a capital crime, executing virtually only African American men convicted of raping white females. As late as the 1960s, when African American civil rights activists were loudly objecting to the influence of white supremacy on law enforcement, black men were being executed for raping white women after convictions by all-white juries. Such convictions and executions represented the criminalization of social contact between African American men and white women and held fast the line drawn by lynching decades earlier and the antimiscegenation laws that followed.

Well into the 20th century, court officials in the South maintained virtually all-white juries, finding legal justifications—such as "low moral character" or "insufficient intelligence"—to exclude African Americans without admitting to doing so on account of their race. These maneuvers helped skew trial outcomes against African American defendants and victims, even as the civil rights movement scored blows against racial discrimination. African Americans and other minorities facing trial before all-white juries faced predictable outcomes, given a criminal justice system that diminished the culpability of whites and inflated it for African Americans.

Historians have noted that African Americans and other minorities, such as American Indians, were not subject to uniform discrimination in the criminal justice system, pointing to the frequent paroles and clemencies granted to minority criminals. For instance, during many periods and in many southern states, African Americans on death row received commutations at a higher rate than whites. However, they often did so because trials of minority defendants were more likely to be marred by errors; because guilty verdicts often followed intense community desire for a death sentence, regardless of guilt; or because southern governors extended mercy to an African American criminal on behalf of the white community. Such acts of clemency often resulted from petitions by white citizens who vouched for the prisoners' good behavior. Thus, the extension of mercy further demonstrated the power of the white community over the lives of African Americans.

The profound influence of race on criminal justice did not preclude interregional variation. In states like Virginia and North Carolina, reformers agonized about the inefficiencies of the criminal justice system and introduced frequent changes intended to increase efficiency and fairness, often before their northern neighbors did so. Such changes—including the centralization of the death penalty process—not only altered procedures but also moved southern states away from the personal, community-driven justice that embedded racial codes in the legal culture. Yet new processes often changed the criminal justice system more in form than in function, as dramatically revealed in Tim Tyson's *Blood Done Sign My Name*, an account of the 1970 murder of a black man in Oxford, N.C. The man's white killer was never convicted.

Edward Ayers, whose *Vengeance and Justice* remains the authoritative historical work on criminal justice in the American South, argues that crime and punishment demonstrate the region's continuity with its past, writing that "among every new generation walk the ghosts of the old." Yet unlike the specters left behind by duelists and brawlers, the pernicious influence of race on the administration of criminal justice remains real in the modern-day South. African Americans and other minorities are imprisoned at disproportionately high rates, are executed in numbers too high to be explained by any factor other than race, and remain underrepresented in courtrooms, except as defendants. Around the South, lawmakers have rewritten laws to define crimes and administer punishments in less discriminatory fashion, but nowhere is the power of history more evident than in the profound and enduring influence of race on criminal justice in the American South.

SETH KOTCH
University of North Carolina at Chapel Hill

Edward L. Ayers, *The Promise of the New South: Life after Reconstruction* (1992), *Vengeance and Justice: Crime and Punishment in the Nineteenth-Century American South* (1985); W. Fitzhugh Brundage, *Lynching in the New South: Georgia and Virginia, 1880–1930* (1993); Michael Steven Hindus, *Prison and Plantation: Crime, Justice, and Authority in Massachusetts and South Carolina, 1767–1878* (1980); Heather Ann Thompson, in *The Myth of Southern Exceptionalism*, ed. Joseph Crespino and Matthew D. Lassiter (2009).

Etiquette of Race Relations in the Jim Crow South

In "The Ethics of Living Jim Crow," black novelist and autobiographer Richard Wright described the "ingenuity" required of black southerners who wanted "to keep out of trouble" with whites. "It is a southern custom that all men must take off their hats when they enter an elevator," Wright explained. "And especially did this apply to us blacks with rigid force." Unable to remove his hat in an elevator one day because his arms were full of packages, Wright faced two white men who stared at him "coldly." Finally, one of the men took off Wright's hat and placed it on top of his packages. "Now the most accepted response for a Negro to make under such circumstances is to look at the white man out of the corner of his eye and grin," Wright wrote. "To have said: 'Thank you!' would have made the white man *think* that you *thought* you were receiving from him a personal service. For such an act I have seen Negroes take a blow in the mouth. Finding the first alternative distasteful, and the second dangerous, I hit upon an acceptable course of action which fell safely between these two poles. I immediately—no sooner than my hat was lifted—pretended that my packages were about to spill, and appeared deeply distressed with keeping them in my arms. In this fashion I evaded having to acknowledge his service, and, in spite of adverse circumstances, salvaged a slender shred of personal pride."

Many autobiographers, historians, and other observers have commented on the customs that guided day-to-day encounters between blacks and whites in the Jim Crow South. Like Wright, they have noted that the definition of good manners depended on one's race, that there were "accepted responses" for blacks to use with whites and vice versa, and that rules of appropriate behavior applied to blacks with especially rigid force. Increasingly, this "etiquette of race relations" has attracted the attention of scholars interested in its purpose and effects, as well as its significance to historical interpretations of the Jim Crow era.

Among the first and most influential of these scholars was sociologist Bertram Wilbur Doyle, author of an often-cited 1937 book titled *The Etiquette of Race Relations in the South: A Study in Social Control*. Doyle outlined customary forms of deference and paternalism between slaves and masters in the Old South and then offered myriad examples of how these practices continued, with some alteration, up to his own day. He also emphasized, and indeed encouraged, blacks' "adjustment" to unjust social relations to a degree that seems difficult to comprehend, given that he was himself a black southerner. However, Doyle was also a student of pioneering sociologist Robert E. Park at the University of Chicago and, according to Gary D. Jaworski, believed in a "race relations cycle" delineated by Park and his colleague Ernest W. Burgess, in which accommodation was a step toward inevitable, if gradual, assimilation, during which time any evidence of conflict between the races signified a lack of progress. Doyle recognized that blacks' performance of humility could be insincere, a matter of survival rather than belief. But his model provided very little room for theorizing black resistance.

Although more recent scholars have not adequately addressed the question of continuity versus change in racial etiquette and have almost universally disagreed with Doyle's portrayal of black southerners as fully accommodated to racism, they have frequently adopted the word "etiquette" and drawn on Doyle's work (as well as that of John Dollard, Hortense Powdermaker, Allison Davis, Charles S. Johnson, and other Depression-era social scientists) to detail the codes that governed interpersonal relations between blacks and whites under Jim Crow. In brief, these codes required blacks to demonstrate their subordination and supposedly natural inferiority, while whites demonstrated white supremacy. For example, whites denied blacks common courtesies, above all the titles "Mr.," "Mrs.," and "Miss," while insisting that blacks be polite, respectful, and even cheerful toward whites at all times. In addition to using racial epithets and calling blacks of all ages by their first names, white southerners often substituted generic names such as "George" or "Suzy," "boy" or "girl," or the somewhat more respectful (from the white point of view) "uncle" or "aunt." White men did not tip their hats to blacks, including black women, and to shake hands with a black person was a self-conscious gesture denoting unusual intimacy or noblesse oblige. Blacks, on the other hand, were expected to tip or remove their hats in the presence of whites, step out of whites' way on sidewalks, and enter white homes only by the back door. In some communities, whites' demands for precedence even extended to the roadways, making it perilous for a black driver to pass a white one. Blacks could also expect to be kept waiting in stores rather than being helped on a first-come, first-served basis, and many stores that relied on black customers refused to allow them to try on hats, gloves, and other articles of clothing because to do so would make the items unfit to sell to whites.

As this prohibition illustrates, racial etiquette distinguished between not only dominant and subordinate but also pure and impure, embodying the principle that, as Mary Douglas explained in her classic *Purity and Danger*, dirt is "essentially disorder" or "matter out of place" and thus can be threatening to the social order itself. "The most important of all rules of purity involved sexual contact," historian J. William Harris adds, noting that "sexual contact between black men and white women was an extraordinary symbolic threat precisely because it occurred at the point where systems of race and gender intersected in the southern cultural matrix." Within this matrix, whites sometimes perceived little distance between the breaking of one taboo and the breaking of another; thus, prohibitions against blacks and whites eating and drinking together on a basis of equality were upheld with almost as much force as prohibitions against interracial sex. (And both prohibitions were nonetheless also breached, as much recent scholarship on interracial sex in the South indicates.)

"All told, this was a social code of forbidding complexity," historian Neil McMillen summarizes. Not only local customs but also individual whites' expectations could vary, yet blacks had to try to anticipate what was expected of them. Failure to do so could result in a verbal rebuke, a beating, or even arrest and imprisonment or lynching. For all of its capriciousness, however, racial etiquette was "anything but irrational." As McMillen explains, "If violence was the 'instrument in reserve'—the ultimate deterrent normally used only against the most recalcitrant—social ritual regulated day-to-day race relations." Racial etiquette "assured white control without the need for more extreme forms of coercion."

Like McMillen, historians Jacquelyn Dowd Hall, David R. Goldfield, Leon F. Litwack, and others have wisely emphasized the role of violence in maintaining racial etiquette as an everyday form of social control. Important essays by J. William Harris and Jane Dailey have reiterated this connection but also theorized racial etiquette at a deeper level. Arguing that "race" is "a matter of culture; it is part of a system of meanings," Harris understands racial etiquette as not merely reflective of racial power relations but as constitutive of "race" itself. Dailey is most interested in blacks' everyday forms of resistance and the extent to which blacks' and whites' shared recognition of what civil behavior was and what it meant allowed "the discourse of civility itself" to become "a primary mode of confrontation" for blacks and whites in street-level encounters. Dailey also notes parallels between post–Civil War practices of racial etiquette and older notions of "honor" that, as Bertram Wyatt-Brown and other historians have argued, had long been dear to white southerners, especially white men.

Focusing on racial etiquette can result in valuable insights about the "public transcript" of white dominance. Recognizing that racial etiquette and other "vertical" and largely face-to-face forms of domination continued to operate in white households, on farms, and in urban spaces such as stores and sidewalks that were difficult to regulate, Jennifer Ritterhouse argues that the "horizontal" system of segregation has occupied too prominent a place in historical scholarship. Although both legal and customary forms of white supremacy were important, it was largely the continued salience of racial etiquette that allowed the majority of white southerners to convince themselves that white supremacy was "natural" rather than violently and governmentally enforced. Considering the significant role that racial etiquette played in white children's racial socialization (and, in an oppositional mode, in black children's as well), Ritterhouse also sheds light on the social reproduction of the South's racial culture and on women's, especially mothers', very important contributions to patterns of domination and resistance.

Used with care, the notion of an "etiquette of race relations" can reveal a great deal about southern culture. Nevertheless, as Richard Wright's explanation of how he managed to "salvage a slender shred of personal pride" indicates, blacks were able to keep their emotional distance from the demands of racial etiquette and, despite the ever-present threat of violence, often refused to provide the "accepted responses" that Jim Crow customs required.

JENNIFER RITTERHOUSE
Utah State University

Jane Dailey, *Journal of Southern History* (August 1997); Allison Davis, Burleigh B. Gardner, and Mary R. Gardner, *Deep South: A Social Anthropological Study of Caste and Class* (1941); John Dollard, *Caste and Class in a Southern Town* (1937); Mary Douglas, *Purity and Danger: An Analysis of Concepts of Pollution and Taboo* (1966); Bertram Wilbur Doyle, *The Etiquette of Race Relations in the South: A Study in Social Control* (1937); David R. Goldfield, *Black, White, and Southern: Race Relations and Southern Culture, 1940 to the Present* (1990); Jacquelyn Dowd Hall, *Revolt against Chivalry: Jessie Daniel Ames and the Women's Campaign against Lynching* (1979; rev. ed., 1993); J. William Harris, *American Historical Review* (April 1995); Gary D. Jaworski, *Sociological Inquiry* (May 1996); Charles S. Johnson, *Patterns of Negro Segregation* (1941); Leon F. Litwack, *Trouble in Mind: Black Southerners in the Age of Jim Crow* (1998); Neil R. McMillen, *Dark Journey: Black Mississippians in the Age of Jim Crow* (1989); Hortense Powdermaker, *After Freedom: A Cultural Study of the Deep South* (1939); Jennifer Ritterhouse, *Growing Up Jim Crow: The Racial Socialization of Black and White Southern Children, 1890–1940*; James C. Scott, *Domination and the Arts of Resistance: Hidden Transcripts* (1990); Richard Wright, in *Uncle Tom's Children* (1936); Bertram Wyatt-Brown, *The Shaping of Southern Culture: Honor, Grace, and War, 1760s–1880s* (2001), *Southern Honor: Ethics and Behavior in the Old South* (1982).

Evolution of the Southern Economy

The temptation is strong to read our own ideas about race backward in time. What we know and experience today becomes the historical pattern. When considered this way, racial ideas and experiences assume an unchanging and fixed character. They become phenomena that are outside of human control, something natural or inevitable. But that is not the way racial understandings and experiences actually operate. When viewed from the perspective of the past and over a long period of time, ideas about human difference show themselves to be as much a creature of the specific conditions of a specific time and place as any other set of ideas or social practice.

In the context of the American South, a region long associated with some of the most labor-intensive of staple economies, ideas about race were tightly linked to productive and political life. Thus, as those economies came and went, expanded and contracted, and in some cases, disappeared altogether, what it meant to be black and white evolved and changed, too. Never static, never the same from one age or place to another, race and its meanings are a constantly moving target. Race has taken on the exclusionary characteristics of segregation and Jim Crow; it has been understood in the more inclusionary if equally as oppressive language of "my family, black and white." Race has often been deployed by the propertied and the powerful to advance their own interests: as landowners, employers, bosses, women, and men. In some places and times, race has not mattered at all, and even when race mattered a lot, those notions of difference and the ideals they expressed sometimes mapped imperfectly, if they mapped at all, onto the day-to-day realities of southern life. Indeed, expressions of race and racial difference can be sometimes considered prescriptive as much as descriptive. Stuart Hall once famously wrote that race is the idiom through which class is lived. Class is messy, contingent, and contentious. It stands to reason that race is, too.

But racial difference did not initially matter, at least not very much. Other attributes and behaviors tended to matter more. Early colonial Americans categorized and divided along religious lines, seeing themselves and others as Puritans, Catholics, Anglicans, and pagans (to name just a few). They also organized themselves around lineage and community and split people between the savage and the civilized, a line of demarcation that was often deployed to distinguish Europeans from Native Americans. Products of a turbulent early Atlantic world, these ideas about difference grew out of and reflected a world in which English, French, Spanish, Portuguese, and Dutch adventurers jostled with each other and with native peoples for a foothold in the New World. This is not to say that notions of race did not matter. Both Europeans and Native Americans recognized racial distinctions. But during the early years of settlement, no particular economy grew up around black people's labor. As a result and as Ira Berlin explains in *Many Thousands Gone*, the kind of racial divisions that would become appallingly common in later periods were all but absent for most of the 17th century. Neither law nor custom, for example, made any significant distinction between black workers and white ones. Instead, they routinely worked side by side—sawing logs on the Carolina frontier and hoeing tobacco on Chesapeake plantations. When not at work, white servants, and the small number of black slaves who had gradually joined them, lived together, played together, prayed together, absconded together, and, not infrequently, married and raised families together. In a society in which it mattered more if a person was Christian than if a person was colored, even slavery itself was not firmly established. Burdened by none of the later assumptions that to be black was to be forever a slave, opportunities existed for early colonial slaves to change their status, and many did. Francis Payne, who had once been known as "Francisco a Negro," brokered a deal with his Chesapeake owner that resulted in the freedom of Payne and his entire family. Others found their loopholes in early colonial laws that allowed men like John Graweer, who lived in a society that generally agreed that Christians ought not to be slaves, to win his child's freedom by proclaiming a wish to raise the youngster in the Anglican faith. By the middle of the 17th century, as many as 30 percent of the Chesapeake's black people were free, and a good many of them had accumulated substantial property in livestock, houses, and land.

But the world was changing around the Paynes, the Graweers, and all the others who had taken advantage of an early colonial society that was concerned about much more than race. By the last quarter of the 17th century, American planters had begun to reconfigure their labor forces. It was a process that began on Chesapeake tobacco plantations when, as access to and control over indentured servants began to slip, landowners shifted their attention toward African slaves. Once deemed too expensive and for cultural reasons too inefficient for plantation labor (everyone was bound to die in less than a decade, and it was easier to boss workers who spoke the boss's language than it was to direct the labor of linguistic strangers), the percentage of slaves shot skyward. By 1700, slaves represented 20 percent of the Chesapeake population, up from 7 percent only 20 years earlier. In the Carolinas and what would become Georgia, the transition took a little longer. But Lowcountry colonists eventually abandoned their initial trade in deer hides for the more lucrative—and labor-intensive— trade in indigo and rice. Following the example of their northern neighbors, Carolinians and Georgians looked to Africa to meet those labor needs. By 1720, slaves in those colonies accounted for an astonishing 60 percent of the entire population, and a nervous white minority began to conflate blackness and slavery into a singular state.

Simply conflating color and caste was not enough for America's colonial planters. They strove to institutionalize control over the people on whom their own fortunes depended by redefining race and its role in American society. In short order, the southern colonies developed new bodies of law that instead of treating workers alike, which had been 17th-century practice, departed from English common law to draw explicit legal lines between those who were slaves and those who were not. In Virginia, Maryland, the Carolinas, and Georgia, legislators began to reserve the harshest punishments for the enslaved, decreed that children born to enslaved mothers would themselves be enslaved, and demolished any lingering possibility that Christianity might provide an escape route from slavery. To further distinguish free from slave, black from white, and to further secure the dominance of planter capital over plantation labor, colonial slaveholders assigned black workers demeaning, mocking, and dehumanizing names. They loudly condemned the growing population of the African-born for their "gross bestiality" and alien customs and reduced the quality and quantity of clothing customarily provided to colonial servants, denying to their bound workers the most visible trappings of "civilization." This was a new idea of race and one that took deep hold among American colonialists, who, slaveholders or not, had come to appreciate the wealth slaves and their labor could generate. Thus, even in the wake of a revolutionary war fought for principles of democracy and manhood rights, the nation could rally behind leaders who, like Thomas Jefferson, claimed forthrightly that Africans and their descendants were a people apart, and a substandard people at that. Ignoring the children he had already fathered with the slave Sally Hemmings, it was Jefferson who, in a tortured logic that itself had been shaped by colonial racism, argued in his *Notes on the State of Virginia* that any improvement Africans enjoyed "in body and mind" from admixture with Europeans proved without a doubt that black "inferiority [was] not the effect merely of their condition of life."

Jefferson's words were more prescriptive than descriptive—wishful thinking of an intellectually and certainly self-interested sort—for even as he penned those sentences, exceptions abounded. Race in the abstract should not be confused with race in reality. Shaped as they were by specific historical circumstances, racial ideas and practices differed radically not only across time but across space too. Thus while the tobacco grandees of the colonial Chesapeake and Lowcountry rice planters were pulling out all stops to draw rigid lines between white people and black, other colonial Americans challenged those lines. In Charlestown (Charleston), S.C., for example, a city surrounded by densely populated plantations but also a city that depended on enslaved hucksters for food for their tables, white residents chose to excuse the aggressively entrepreneurial market women from racial proscription. In a very literal attempt to have their cake and eat it too, hungry townspeople redefined the women in ways that separated color from caste by recoding the hucksters as unruly women rather than punishing them as unruly slaves. Similarly, the Spanish and French, who had established toeholds along the Florida and Gulf coasts, subordinated racial difference to imperial political concerns, and, even as racial lines hardened in Virginia, Maryland, and the coastal Carolinas, the European colonists to their south welcomed Africans into their Catholic communities, stood as grandparents to black babies, and, with hostile forces always on the horizon, recruited black men (including former slaves) into their colonial militias.

But it was not just other Europeans who envisioned and enacted early America's many and competing racial orders. Black people did too, and everywhere both slaves and free people doggedly articulated a sense of self that belied American slaveholders' efforts to push Africans and their descendants to the outermost margins of social and political life. The female hucksters who staked out places at the center of colonial Charlestown's public markets and the black men who drilled with Spanish commanders were not alone in promoting alternative racial orders. Throughout the Chesapeake, where planters' practice of assigning small groups of workers to noncontiguous units of land gave rise to a culturally, geographically, and politically literate labor force, slaves quickly learned their owners' language, adopted their owners' dress, and, as front-row witnesses to souring relations between colony and crown, demanded that the principles of liberty and universal right be extended to all people, not just free and white. By the eve of the Revolutionary War, slaves in Maryland and Virginia were pressing up against—and threatening to march across—the racial divide on which their owners depended. Hundreds did once war broke out, abandoning slavery and slaveholders when the last royal governor of Virginia offered to free "all indented Servants, Negroes, or others" in exchange for military service.

Slaves further south were equally as creative, but in the swampy and sickly environment of the coastal Carolinas and Georgia the circumstances of colonial slavery gave rise to one of the most distinctive racial orders in mainland North America. There, a combination of superior numbers, isolation, knowledge of rice cultivation, and the presence of diseases particularly deadly to Europeans allowed enslaved women and men to win unusual control over their lives and their labor. But instead of appropriating European practices, as did their counterparts in the urban and Upper South, Lowcountry slaves created an African-influenced hybrid. Known as Gullah north of the Savannah River and Ogeechee south of it, theirs was a culture set apart by language, diet, dress, art, religion, music, and tools. Even the everyday practices of planting, irrigating, and processing the chief staple crop—rice—bore more than a passing resemblance to West African tradition. To be sure, the social and cultural order that emerged on Lowcountry estates continued to emphasize racial distinction, but what slaves created in the hinterlands of Charlestown and Savannah resisted the hierarchical system their owners aspired to. Different, yes—subordinate or savage, no.

The struggle for independence thrived on and ushered in a host of new ways of thinking about black women and men and the roles they should play in a young nation. The change registered most visibly in the Chesapeake region, where the combined effects of war, a declining tobacco economy, and a widespread commitment to Enlightenment ideas opened up fissures in a racial order inherited from colonial slaveholders. Determined to reconfigure labor forces and practices to meet new economic and moral imperatives, farmers and planters manumitted hundreds of slaves in the last decades of the 18th century and then hired them back as free workers. Between 1790 and 1800, the free black population in the Chesapeake region more than tripled. It was not change enough to restore the early colonial world of Francis Payne and John Graweer, where race had been just one of many markers. Nor were white citizens universally inclined to embrace the abolitionism that had begun to spread across the Atlantic and into New England communities. Nevertheless, the once-tight association between blackness and status weakened throughout Virginia, Maryland, Delaware, and portions of North Carolina in the decades immediately following the American Revolution. In some locations, most notably North Carolina and the new state of Tennessee, free people of color even won the right to vote. But the effects of racial rethinking were limited to the Upper South. In South Carolina and Georgia, where the colonial staples of rice and Sea Island cotton retained their market value despite the disruptions of war, planters swiftly and violently reasserted control over their slave forces. Their assault paid off. By the last decade of the century, rice production had surpassed colonial levels, reinvigorating Lowcountry planters' commitment to both slavery and its justifying ideas of race.

Despite the promises of the postrevolutionary era, slavery and its racialist substructure soon revived in the Chesapeake region. With the introduction of short-staple cotton as a viable commercial crop, the opening of the trans-Appalachian frontier, and, in 1808, the closing of the transatlantic slave trade, Upper South slaveholders quickly rediscovered a value in and market for excess laborers. Rather than freeing the black people they no longer needed, Virginian and Maryland owners elected to sell them. By the early 19th century, the Chesapeake had become a major slave-exporting area. Thus, even as antislavery advocates picked up momentum from Pennsylvania northward (regions that not incidentally had never developed a comparable dependence on slave labor), slavery's champions were joining forces with a sympathetic national government to open a kingdom for cotton on the western frontier. Like tobacco and rice before it, cotton was a labor-intensive crop and one that growers thought best served by slave labor. And like the slavery that sprang up in the late 17th century, the exploitative system that arose in Alabama, Mississippi, Louisiana, and east Texas took shelter behind a welter of racialist ideas and the laws that enforced them. But the ideas of difference that slaveholders articulated as cotton drew them west reflected the social and political realities of a world in which slavery was coming under sharp attack by an increasingly radical antislavery coalition. Gone were the open references to black savages and the imposition of names that recalled barnyard livestock that had been all too common during the colonial era. Gone too were more visible manifestations of the brute force on which New World slavery always rested: amputations, mutilations, and the decapitated heads of dead rebels that colonialists would line up along busy roads in a grisly display of class power. Instead, more and more antebellum slaveholders chose to represent themselves as fatherly figures, stern yet benign paternalists who opened their homes to the perpetual children who were also their slaves.

Antebellum paternalism was a far more inclusionary vision of race than any previous American configuration, and one that brought black people into human society, albeit on a severely constrained basis. Permanent children, after all, require permanent parenting. It was a more explicitly defensive racism too, and its proponents hedged their bets by planting supportive struts in science, theology, and political economy. Eager, for instance, to deflect abolitionists' complaints that slavery did violence to black people's families as well as to Christian beliefs, slaveholders distanced themselves from slave traders, cautiously established religious missions to slaves, and argued loudly, as Virginian George Fitzhugh did in his 1857 *Cannibals All! Or Slaves without Masters*, that not only did the Christian Bible sanction man's ownership of man, but that the nation's slaves enjoyed a much higher quality of life than did northern and foreign wageworkers. These were powerful arguments, which resonated far beyond the boundaries of the slaveholding states, but science too found a national audience. Especially compelling was the work of Swiss paleontologist Louis Agassiz, whose belief in a hierarchically ranked animal kingdom informed American scientists, including Alabama physician Josiah Nott, who in 1854 helped to popularize a new human order, one that located Africans at or near the bottom of a taxonomy of man.

Historians call this multifaceted articulation of race the antebellum "proslavery defense." It was a defense meant less to describe than to hide the horrors that continued to define black people's lives. To be sure, the practices of slavery had evolved since the Revolution. The 19th century's greatest staple — cotton — had its own rhythms and routines, characteristics that set it apart from tobacco, sugar, and rice. In contrast to the Lowcountry, where planters continued to organize agricultural enterprise around the task system, and the Chesapeake, where mixed farming and the intensification of industrial work gave rise to a much more elastic, diverse, and in many respects self-directing labor force, the slaves who made cotton labored in large gangs under the close supervision of an owner or his agent. They worked longer days and more of them, as planters seized back the Sundays and holidays that slaves in the Upper and seaboard South continued to enjoy. The slaves who made cotton often labored as strangers too, thrown together in new constituencies by an interstate trade that was notorious for fracturing families. Indeed, in the Chesapeake region alone, as many as half of all slave sales separated parents from children and one-quarter tore husbands from wives. Social and affective ties were not all that slaves lost to a changing commercial and political context. In this period, state governments banned the education of slaves, ordered ships' captains to quarantine or confine black sailors on arrival in southern ports, sharply restricted the ability of slaves to gather together without white supervision, and debated evicting free people of color from slaveholding states, all part of an effort by slaveholders to strengthen their grip on black workers by isolating them from other influences.

As much as these changes disrupted black people's lives, slaveholders once again failed to make reality conform to their rhetoric of race. Instead, the enslaved fought back, rejecting the world their owners thrust toward them. But what slaves managed to make of and for themselves continued to be shaped in small and large ways by the specific circumstances of their day-to-day lives. In the Upper South, where tobacco continued its long decline, new opportunities had opened for slaves in skilled work, mobile work, and industrial work, arrangements that destabilized slaveholders' authority by giving slaves expanding authority over their lives. Agricultural routine likewise changed in ways that worked in black people's favor. One of the most noticeable developments was the replacement of white overseers with black, men who were often slaves and often related to those whose labor they supervised. Edmund Ruffin, for instance, employed a black man named Jem Sykes at his Virginia plantation, and in relaying to Sykes, "& through him to his fellows, correct information" about John Brown's attempt on Harpers Ferry, Ruffin implicitly recognized a shifting racial dynamic. Relations between black people and white people were not all that changed in the Chesapeake as cotton revolutionized the southern economy. Domestic order changed, too, and as a booming trade in labor continued to sweep enslaved teens and young adults away to Deep South plantations, those left behind reconfigured family and family obligations in order to accommodate a population that skewed toward the very young and the very old.

It was the vast stream of forced migrants, however, that faced perhaps the biggest challenge. Unlike the loved ones they had left behind, the slaves who followed cotton south and west had no choice but to restore order to their lives on new ground, among new faces, and against the heavy demands of planters whose primary interests revolved around profit. It was a slow and fitful process, for few antebellum slaves went to their graves without being sold several times, and changes of ownership invariably meant starting all over again. Nevertheless, cotton's forced migrants eventually made friends, friends became families, and families gave birth to new generations. Some of cotton's migrants were able to convert skills or a personal relationship with an owner into the right to keep a small garden or raise a few chickens. Rural churches appeared, too. But what slaves made for themselves on cotton's terrain was at best a dim and distorted reflection of what they had known in their old homes. The difference registered most vividly in the case of gender relations and the ways in which cotton's migrants understood their roles as women and men. Torn out of a world of increasing urbanization and economic diversification, one that invited women as well as men into public spaces, migrants to the Deep South discovered that by virtue of agricultural technology and tools, men and women occupied distinct geographic and, by extension, social and political places. The chores women performed for their owners kept them, by and large, confined to their home plantations: sowing, hoeing, and harvesting. Men did all that, too, but it was men far more frequently than women who delivered that finished cotton to market, who built and maintained public roads, and who, during slack periods in the agricultural year, were dispatched by their owners to join slave men from elsewhere in the South to work Appalachian and western mines, to turn timber into turpentine, and to lay the hundreds of miles of railroad track that proliferated in the slaveholding states by the late 1850s. These were experiences that introduced male slaves into a multicultural world described by one North Carolinian slaveholding '49er as a "heterogeneous comminglement" of all the people of the civilized world. It was a world that most Deep South black women knew only indirectly and by secondhand means. Thus, while slaves in the Upper and seaboard South were reordering families and family roles to take into account the loss of what amounted to a whole generation, those who were made to migrate rebuilt their lives on a very differently gendered terrain.

Slavery died along with the Confederacy in April 1865. Its demise stripped southern landowners, planters, and employers of the chief mechanism by which they had for generations forcibly appropriated black people's labor. The end of slavery did not, however, sever the relationship between the southern economy and race. Nor did war and emancipation mark the decline of cotton. Thus, while changing economic imperatives in the postrevolutionary era had prompted Upper South planters to reconsider (at least for a time) a racial order developed during the colonial period, the importance former Confederates continued to attach to cotton helped to keep intact a long-standing association between race and staple production. It was an expectation made manifest almost immediately following the Confederate surrender as former slaveholders scurried to recast labor relations on a free-labor basis. Determined to halt the revolution before it completely subverted a cherished—and exceedingly profitable—old order, planters generally acknowledged that henceforth they must pay for labor services once stolen, but few ceded much else. In most planters' minds, managers, not workers, would be the sole arbiters of productive relations and brusquely denied to their ex-slaves any role in the bargaining process. Former slaveholders likewise anticipated "wield[ing] the bone and muscle of the negro" in freedom, as had been their custom in slavery, and insisted on the same obsequious deference from free people that they had demanded of slaves. It was a vision one Georgia planter captured in contractual terms when he described in 1865 ex-slaves turned wageworkers as the "Negroes once owned by him and now controlled by him." The same vision informed the notorious and fortunately short-lived Black Codes, the body of law developed in late 1865 and early 1866 by southern state governments that represented an explicit attempt by ex-slaveholding constituents to restore capital's sovereignty over black labor.

Former slaves were not impressed. Spurning both planters' efforts to remand them back to a subordinate class and the racial structures that would keep them there, the newly emancipated envisioned—at least for a time—the possibility of a color-blind world. Believing that in leaving behind slavery they had also left behind the racisms that had been used to justify their oppression, a number of black Floridians spoke for the many when in the summer of 1865 they confidently announced to a senior Freedmen's Bureau official that "we have no massa now—we is come to the law now." But while it is important to understand that former slaves rejected ex-slaveholders' efforts to use racialist ideas to secure working-class order, it is just as important to understand that freedpeople's aspirations for their futures had been deeply shaped by their lives as slaves. Even as legal slavery expired, past experiences helped to give rise to what historians now acknowledge were a welter of black "freedoms": those sets of ideas and expectations that guided black southerners as they sought to define who they were and the positions they should occupy in a free nation. Thus it was that the black men of the South Carolina Lowcountry articulated desires that emerged out of a past distinctly their own. Products of a labor regime characterized by a relative demographic and social stability, as well as by tasking, and convinced that they had earned a right to occupy, in freedom, land they had made productive in slavery, these men (and it was wholly men in this instance) pushed the national government to make good on its wartime promises to redistribute land to ex-slaves. "General," pleaded one such community, "we want Homesteads," positioning themselves in opposition not only to those who, like Louisiana's sugar workers, accepted a future as wageworkers but to black southerners who had accumulated enough of their own property to look askance on any program that might jeopardize those holdings. In urban areas, it was often black women who articulated the freshest vision of freedom, drawing on personal experiences as hucksters and market women to lay claim to what most Americans—southern and northern—understood to be masculine civil, political, and public spaces. Indeed, in Portsmouth, Va., a group of longtime female entrepreneurs upended those mainstream assumptions by speaking not only for themselves but for their husbands too. It was an articulation of gender and race that their rural counterparts could not embrace. There, in the so-called Black Belt, where cotton continued to reign and where planters now looked upon black women and their babies as an economic liability (the "incubus among them," some declared), black women elected to slip in the opposite direction. Rather than subverting conventional gender order, the women of the plantation South used what their husbands, brothers, and fathers knew and could do as workers to secure access to subsistence and shelter.

Southern African Americans reasserted themselves as classes, too, in the postemancipation nation. And while such expressions opened up yet more fissures among the region's black population, it was also perhaps the one aspect of their efforts to define new roles for themselves in freedom that most unnerved white southerners. After all, it had been the very real threat of a working-class revolt that had prompted 17th-century colonial planters to abandon a mixed labor force for one composed almost wholly of slaves. But without the customs and laws of slavery to divide workers along racial lines, white planters and their allies had to devise new mechanisms by which to control and contain the black labor, upon which they continued to depend. Their answer was a lethal combination of terror, debt peonage, vagrancy codes, disfranchisement, and segregation known as Jim Crow. So long as federal forces remained on the ground in the former Confederacy and so long as northern attention remained fixed on southern affairs, white capitalists had to bide their time. They also had to systematically destroy any alliances black workers had forged with white workers and to convince the latter that their interests would be best served in a world defined not by class but by color. White supremacy, as Stephen Kantrowitz explains in a biography of South Carolina's Ben Tillman, was hard work. But by the last decades of the 19th century, white supremacy was reaching its apogee. An endless cycle of sharecropping defined the lives of most rural black people, segregation trapped the black residents of southern cities into new urban slums, and reworked state constitutions had all but silenced what had once been powerful black political voices. Where black people refused to accept a new and exclusionary racial order, and where biracial alliances stubbornly stood their ground—as happened in Wilmington, N.C., in 1898—white supremacists pulled out their guns, confident that a North that was by then distracted by its own social, political, and economic problems would no longer rally to black southerners' defense.

It is tempting to call this the end of the story, and too often we do. But stopping our analysis with Jim Crow requires that we accept as definitive a late 19th-century racial order that historical scholarship suggests was anything but. It also requires severing a long-standing connection between race and class. Neither of these is possible. The southern economy continued to evolve in the 20th century, pushed in new directions by the development of coal mines deep underground in Birmingham, Ala., by the final demise of rice as a profitable commercial crop, and by the growth of a timber industry that in the early decades of the 20th century would give rise to the corporate plantations that made the Mississippi Delta an American Congo. World war sent another shock wave through the once-slaveholding South, opening up new opportunities for rural black workers in northern industry, a tectonic shift that, among other things, prompted southern employers to begin replacing men with machines. And as had happened in the past, as the region's economy continued to change, so too did ideas about race. Liberated from the vicious constraints of Jim Crow (though, importantly, not from discrimination), southern transplants in northern cities reconfigured themselves the most quickly and helped to animate a cultural renaissance, but as migration strengthened channels of communication leading in and out of the South, those who remained behind on rural plantations likewise explored and then advanced new sensibilities. Some embraced the internationalism of Marcus Garvey's Universal Negro Improvement Association, Pan-Africanism, or the Communist Party. Others— like the railroad men whom Scott Reynolds Nelson encountered in his search for the historic John Henry and the laundresses who amused themselves by dancing the nights away in Atlanta's juke joints—put to music a black working-class aesthetic and, in the process, unwittingly laid the groundwork for what has become a global industry. What no one did as Jim Crow peaked and the world went to war was to stop moving, and neither have we in the 21st century. Though the southern labor force has grown progressively more complex with the introduction of Asian and Latino populations and the southern economy has dissolved into a global marketplace, race remains as it was in the 17th century: the preeminent idiom by which we organize—and reorganize—our lives.

SUSAN EVA O'DONOVAN
University of Memphis

Ira Berlin, *Many Thousands Gone: The First Two Centuries of Slavery in North America* (1998); Tera Hunter, *To 'Joy My Freedom: Southern Black Women's Lives and Labors after the Civil War* (1997); Philip C. Morgan, *Slave Counterpoint: Black Culture in the Eighteenth-Century Chesapeake and Lowcountry* (1998); Susan Eva O'Donovan, *Becoming Free in the Cotton South* (2007); Calvin Schermerhorn, *Money over Mastery, Family over Freedom: Slavery in the Antebellum Upper South* (2011); Nan Woodruff, *American Congo: The African American Freedom Struggle in the Delta* (2003).

Jews, Race, and Southernness

From the colonial period to the civil rights era, southern Jews have striven to acculturate into southern society, fighting to be defined as white in order to gain acceptance. Considering the racial hierarchies of the South, whiteness guaranteed Jews a safer position, even in a region considered less anti-Semitic than others. A chronological view of southern Jewish history reveals how, from colonial times to the Civil War, Jews have been excluded from white southern culture because of their religious practices, how, in the antebellum period through the Civil War, Jews who adopted a white southern mentality tended to be accepted as white, how, before and after the Civil War, Jews who crossed white southern racial lines faced ostracism from their families and society, how economic changes in the 1890s caused Jews to be scapegoated by white southern society, and how 20th-century fears of anti-Semitism forced Jews to embrace whiteness. In these ways, from colonial times to today, Jews have struggled to fit into white southern society.

From the colonial period to the Civil War, the practice of Judaism prohibited Jews from fully integrating into southern white society. Because they were few in number, Jews were perpetually aware that they were different. Christian fundamentalists—Protestants, specifically—considered both German and Sephardic Jews to be "Christ Killers." In an effort to blend in, Jews emulated their southern Christian peers by modeling their synagogues after churches and moving Sabbath services from Friday to Sunday. Revered as the people of the Old Testament, Jews nonetheless enjoyed few political rights. The Virginia Law of 1705 prohibited them from marrying Christians or acquiring Christian servants. Both South Carolina and North Carolina prohibited Jews from political office. North Carolina law stipulated that in order to obtain office, one had to believe in the sanctity of the New Testament. Therefore, Jews could not hold office until 1858.

In the Civil War era, southern Jews were permitted to play a part in southern politics, but senators Judah Benjamin and David Yulee gained political access only by declining to openly practice Judaism. Indeed, both Yulee and Benjamin were discriminated against and even described as having African features. Despite the fact that he married a non-Jew, Benjamin was blamed for numerous problems the Confederacy encountered during the Civil War. Even when Jews disassociated themselves from their religion, they faced persecution from white southern society.

Judaism continued to complicate acculturation, but as long as antebellum Jews were able to embrace the ideals of what it meant to be southern and white, they could potentially fit in. Because they were perceived to be of an unstable racial identity, they had to prove their whiteness. To do so, some owned slaves— a way of asserting class privilege and confirming their place in the black and white binary of southern life. Jews who opposed slavery did so privately for fear of anti-Semitism, wanting to emphasize that Judaism was only a religion, not a complex identity. Another way Jews reinforced their identification as southern was by enlisting in the Confederate army during the Civil War. Ironically, Jews had escaped Europe to avoid military service, but in the South Jews enlisted to affirm their white southern status.

From the antebellum period to the 1890s, some Jews transgressed southern whiteness at the risk of ostracism, both inside and outside of the Jewish community. David Isaac, a German Jewish immigrant, and Nancy West, a free woman of color, raised children in a common-law marriage in Virginia before being brought to Albemarle County court. Effectively, their relationship had been ignored for 20 years because the South viewed Jews as being ambiguously white. Escaping the punishments usually meted out to interracial relationships, the couple saw charges dropped against them, paid no penalty, and were not imprisoned. Although not all relations between Jews and African Americans were prosecuted, Charles Moritz and Dorcus Walker of Pine Bluff, Ark., as well as Adolph Altschul and Maggie Carson of Natchez, Miss., established similar relationships. When German immigrant and peddler Altschul married Carson—a former slave—his family disowned him. In Natchez, Miss., the Jewish population had integrated well with southern society, so Moritz and Walker chose not to marry in order to conform to southern white racial hierarchies.

Other interactions with African Americans demonstrated how Jews transgressed southern whiteness. During the Reconstruction and after, Jews engaged in economic relations with African Americans. Furthermore, new Jewish immigrants to the South—largely Eastern European—held a different perspective on African Americans because they did not have a problem in identifying themselves as Jews. Lacking the history German and Sephardic Jews had experienced in the South, Eastern European Jews recognized a similarity in experience between themselves and African Americans. Jews had fled from the pogroms, while African Americans had faced the plight of slavery. The influx of Eastern European immigrants to the South was admittedly limited, but the few who arrived were markedly different from the Jews who had preceded them— to the extent that some were even accused of being black. With the exception of Eastern European Jews and a few others, in the post–Civil War period southern Jews mostly desired to maintain their whiteness and disassociate themselves from African Americans.

During the depression of the 1890s and after, surging anti-Semitism caused the whiteness of southern Jews to again be questioned. In a no-longer agrarian-based economy, Jews represented industrialization and conspiracy. The Populist Movement of the 1890s waged war against Jews, blaming them for the economic hardships of the South and causing the vandalizing of Jewish-owned businesses in Louisiana and Mississippi. Early 20th-century literature also reflected this mind-set. Albert Abernathy's *Jew a Negro* (1910), the folk ballad "The Jew's Daughter," and Lucian Lamar Knight's "Twentieth Century of the Jews" depicted the close intersection of Judaism and race, while the unstable position of Jews as whites came under even greater scrutiny during the Leo Frank case.

In 1913, Frank, a prominent Jewish pencil factory owner, was falsely accused of raping and murdering Mary Phagan, a white southern girl. An easy scapegoat, Frank was both Jewish and an industrialist. Even though the other suspect was an African American janitor named Jim Conley—whom a witness had reportedly spotted in a blood-stained shirt—Frank became the prime suspect. Newspapers sensationalized the case, paralleling Frank's sexual behavior with that of African Americans and attributing his deviant sexual behavior to his innate Jewishness. Tragically, Frank was taken from his prison cell and lynched. His murder at the hands of an anti-Semitic mob signaled to southern Jews that they continued to be dangerously marginalized by white southern society.

The Frank case made southern Jews fearful of anti-Semitism, which inevitably caused them to be leery of joining the civil rights movement. Indeed, Jews embraced their whiteness during the civil rights era for fear that if they showed sympathy for African Americans it would only make them more vulnerable to anti-Semitism. Throughout the 20th century, the Ku Klux Klan had reminded southern Jews that they were different and vulnerable even if they were not always its target. Nonetheless, many southern Jews could not remain silent during the civil rights era. Not only had northern Jews and Jewish agencies (for example, the American Jewish Congress) championed African American rights, but the passage of *Brown v. Board of Education* associated Jews with the African American cause, inciting anti-Semitism throughout the South in the 1950s through the 1960s. Because Jews were blamed for the civil rights movement, white Christian groups like the Stoner Anti-Jewish Party opposed not only desegregation but the entire American Jewish presence as well. Out of fear, a significant portion of southern Jews opposed desegregation, and a few even considered joining anti-Semitic prosegregation groups like the Citizens' Council. In addition, southern Jews even battled with northern Jews and Jewish agencies for publicly showing visible support for civil rights and heightening their precarious position within white non-Jewish southern society.

Southern rabbis at the center of the civil rights movement hailed predominantly from the North because there were no seminaries in the South. Temple bombings that occurred throughout the South in 1957 and 1958 and again in 1967 only reinforced southern Jewish fears of anti-Semitism. As spokespersons for the Jewish community, rabbis defended southern Jews for acquiescing to the white southern majority and fought Jewish agencies for pressuring them to join the civil rights movement. Southern Jews may have been more liberal than their white non-Jewish counterparts, but they remained reluctant to fight for African American rights during the civil rights era. This fear of being perceived as nonwhite persisted until the demographics of the southern Jewish community began to change. After the 1980s, southern identity shifted as more northern Jews moved to the South. With this came an ethnic revival (for example, openly wearing Stars of David) and a greater desire to appear more openly Jewish. The long-standing desire of southern Jews to conform to standards of southern whiteness was beginning, at last, to change.

ALLISON SCHOTTENSTEIN
University of Texas at Austin

Katya Gibel Azoulay, *Black, Jewish, and Interracial: It's Not the Color of Your Skin, but the Race of Your Kin, and Other Myths of Identity* (1997); Mark Bauman, ed., *Dixie*

Diaspora: An Anthology of Southern Jewish Life (2006); Mark Bauman and Berkley Kalin, eds., *The Quiet Voices: Southern Rabbis and Black Civil Rights, 1880s to 1990s* (1997); Jack E. Davis, *Race against Time: Culture and Separation in Natchez since 1930* (2001); Leonard Dinnerstein, *Anti-Semitism in America* (1994); Leonard Dinnerstein and Mary Dale Palsson, *Jews in the South* (1973); Eli Evans, *The Provincials: A Personal History of Jews in the South* (1997); Marcie Cohen Ferris and Mark Greenberg, eds., *Jewish Roots in Southern Soil: A New History* (2006); Seth Forman, *Black in the Jewish Mind: A Crisis of Liberalism* (1998); V. P. Franklin et al., eds., *African-Americans and Jews in the Twentieth Century: Studies in Convergence and Conflict* (1998); Eric Goldstein, *The Price of Whiteness: Jews, Race, and American Identity* (2006); Cheryl Lynn Greenberg, *Troubling the Waters: Black-Jewish Relations in the American Century* (2006); Bertram Korn, *Jews and Negro Slavery in the Old South, 1789–1865* (1961); Julius Lester, *Lovesong: Becoming a Jew* (1988); Jeffrey Melnick, *Black-Jewish Relations on Trial: Leo Frank and Jim Conley in the New South* (2000); Robert N. Rosen, *The Jewish Confederates* (2000); Joshua D. Rothman, *Notorious in the Neighborhood: Sex and Families across the Color Line in Virginia, 1787–1861* (2003); Clive Webb, *Fight against Fear: Southern Jews and Black Civil Rights* (2003).

Labor, Postbellum

Since emancipation, the question of race has been at the heart of organized labor's efforts in the South. As early as the 1860s, the nascent American labor movement confronted the dilemma that faced it well into the 20th century, namely whether to *exclude* black workers from unions as a means of limiting the labor supply, or to *recruit* African Americans in behalf of common interests. The leaders of the American Federation of Labor (AFL) (established 1886) often proclaimed the latter position, but in fact many of its affiliated unions, as well as the independent railroad brotherhoods, followed the former option. Most barred blacks from membership or relegated them to second-class status. Meanwhile, more inclusive organizations such as the Knights of Labor (KOL) (founded 1869) and the Industrial Workers of the World (IWW) (founded 1905), along with a handful of AFL unions, welcomed blacks, albeit with varying degrees of enthusiasm.

A more egalitarian strand of biracial organization emerged in the 1930s and 1940s, as the Congress of Industrial Organizations (CIO) (established 1935–38) focused attention on the increasingly important role of black workers in the southern economy. Also important was the determination of black workers to form their own unions, sometimes apart from the mainstream labor movement. The most notable example of this development was the Brotherhood of

Sleeping Car Porters, founded in 1925, which, under the leadership of Florida-born A. Philip Randolph, provided a base for labor and civil rights activism in southern communities. For most of the 1865–1980 period, racial factors were expressed as a black-white binary, but by the turn of the 21st century, the presence of large numbers of Latino immigrant workers was complicating southern labor's historic narrative.

In the first decades of its existence, the AFL's ambivalence toward inclusion of African Americans became clear. In 1891, the AFL convention castigated unions that "exclude from membership persons on account of race or color." Many of its affiliated unions, however, barred blacks, either outright or indirectly, sometimes through their control of municipal licensing ordinances. One important example was the International Association of Machinists (IAM), founded in Atlanta in 1888. The IAM initially barred blacks from membership but eventually accepted a technical modification of its constitution that left the policy of racial exclusion intact. Meanwhile, the pages of the *American Federationist*, the AFL's national organ, were peppered with dismissive commentary about black workers' suitability as unionists. White-controlled railroad unions in the South were aggressive in their attacks on African Americans, often using violence and intimidation to drive black firemen out of locomotive cabs and marginalize them in the roundhouses and repair shops.

Despite long odds, biracial union activism sometimes emerged. The KOL, which flourished briefly in the mid-1880s, recruited thousands of black miners and agricultural workers. In the 1900s and 1910s, the IWW's militant industrial unionism attracted activists of both races who built short-lived biracial organizations in southwestern mines and timberlands. In the coal mines of Alabama and in the Gulf ports, black and white workers practiced forms of biracial organization. The story in the Birmingham area, a rapidly expanding iron- and steel-producing center, however, was different and more characteristic. There, white metalworkers and smelter workers excluded blacks from their unions and insisted that they remain in subordinate job categories.

During World War I, opportunities for more equal treatment seemed at first possible. Federal agencies sometimes followed the logic of wartime mobilization to intervene on behalf of black workers in urban transport, in laundries, and on the railroads, but the sudden end of the war aborted this tendency. With the government's backing, the brotherhoods quickly resumed efforts to drive blacks out of the operating trades.

The rise of the CIO in the 1930s and the labor demands of World War II, however, brought a more egalitarian brand of unionism to the South. Even before the birth of this federation of industrial unions in 1935, the United Mine

Workers had reorganized in Alabama along biracial lines, and the Southern Tenant Farmers' Union recruited impoverished agricultural workers of both races. CIO activists appreciated the key role played by black workers in southern industries and sought to challenge the conservative political orientation of the Solid South. Communists and other radicals organized woodworkers, metalworkers, smelter workers, tobacco and food-processing workers, and others in integrated unions.

By the end of the war, the CIO could count about a quarter-million black members, perhaps half of them in the South. Even so, CIO activists found that they had to perform a balancing act in southern workplaces. Union-supported upgrading of black workers sometimes triggered violent resistance among the white majority. The textile industry, the South's largest by far, remained lily-white, and white workers' resistance to Communist-oriented CIO affiliates in cigarette manufacture, food processing, and metalworking remained strong.

Challenged by the rival CIO, the AFL began cautiously to address the problems faced by black workers. To be sure, during the war, affiliated unions that practiced blatant discrimination, notably in the booming shipyards and aircraft plants, flourished. Even so, AFL leaders aligned themselves verbally with the cause of racial equality. And some black workers in the South did find opportunities within segregated unions to attain leadership roles and to link their union activities to civil rights struggles in southern states and communities. By the end of the war, the AFL counted about 700,000 black members, over 400,000 of them in southern states.

After the war, both labor federations sought to increase their southern membership. In the politically conservative postwar environment, however, neither was very successful. Moreover, as the issue of Communism, both domestic and foreign, came to dominate public discourse, the leaders of the CIO distanced the industrial union body from its pro-Soviet affiliates, several of which had been in the forefront of biracial unionism.

Throughout the postwar period, the most significant developments affecting the relationship between organized labor and African American workers in the South involved the changing legal environment. Especially after passage of the Civil Rights Act of 1964, whose Title VII outlawed racial discrimination in employment, African American membership in unions representing southern pulp and paper workers, textile workers, and other industrial, transport, and service workers expanded, owing in part to litigation brought by private parties and supported by the federal Equal Employment Opportunities Commission. In general, the national unions in these fields supported black workers' employment rights and welcomed African American workers into the unions. In many cases, however, on the local union level, African Americans found white fellow workers, along with managerial and supervisory personnel, hostile and resentful. In some cases, black workers, deeming their unions little more than agents of white privilege, petitioned the National Labor Relations Board to terminate union representation altogether.

Just as black workers made inroads into previously all-white industries and trades, employment patterns in the South began shifting away from these very sectors. Thus, for example, in the 1960s and 1970s, African Americans made major employment gains in the textile and pulp and paper industries and began to gain entry into skilled positions on the railroads and steel mills, even as these industries began to shrink or to relocate. At the end of the century, the deindustrialization of the South accelerated, devastating southern unions in metalworking, transport, pulp and paper, and textiles and reversing employment gains African American workers had made.

African Americans in the South enjoyed somewhat more enduring success in the realm of public employment. In Memphis, in spring 1968, Dr. Martin Luther King Jr. eloquently connected the efforts of the city's poorly paid and ill-treated sanitation workers—to gain improved conditions, recognition of their union, and respect—to the ongoing struggle for civil rights. Victory in the strike was, of course, tempered by the tragic murder of Dr. King in Memphis on 4 April. Sanitation workers in other southern cities, along with hospital and other institutional workers, boosted minority membership in such unions as the American Federation of State, County, and Municipal Employees, Hospital Workers District 1199, and the Service Employees International Union (SEIU), organizations that stressed the connection between the civil rights movement and the efforts of low-skilled, poorly paid minority workers to gain both tangible improvements and greater respect on the job. The civil rights–labor connection, however, was fragile. Thus, for example, in 1977, Atlanta's African American mayor Maynard Jackson fired striking sanitation workers wholesale, lest their rights-based activism jeopardize relations with the city's white-owned banks and corporate investors.

By the turn of the new century, the demographic profile of the southern working class was shifting dramatically. Whole new industries such as poultry raising and processing emerged, employing thousands, many of them recent Central American migrants. In 1980, 2.5 percent of the South's population was Hispanic; by the mid-2000s, the figure had climbed to over 8 percent. Examples of multiethnic and black-Hispanic union activism did emerge, notably in the entertainment, senior care, and institutional medical sectors. In Florida, for example, SEIU pulled together multiethnic coalitions of church and civic organizations to support organizing campaigns among low-wage native and immigrant nursing home and health care workers. At the same time, concerns about competition from immigrant workers and emotional public discourse over immigration reform highlighted perceived conflicts of interest between native black workers and their immigrant counterparts.

The history of the relationship between African Americans in the South and the American labor movement reveals a drift on the part of the latter toward ever-increasing degrees of acceptance and even cultivation. As organized labor's presence in the South (and nationally) has continued to shrink, a labor movement once characterized by racial exclusivism has become increasingly dependent on minority workers (and female workers), especially in the expanding service sector. There is thus an irony at the heart of the story of black workers and the labor movement in the South: Even as organized labor has become more accommodating and progressive in its racial attitudes and policies, it has continued to diminish as a factor in southern life.

ROBERT H. ZIEGER
University of Florida

Michael K. Honey, *Going Down Jericho Road: The Memphis Strike, Martin Luther King's Last Campaign* (2007); Timothy J. Minchin, *Hiring the Black Worker: The Racial Integration of the Southern Textile Industry, 1960–1980* (1999); Robert H. Zieger, *For Jobs and Freedom: Race and Labor in America since 1865* (2007).

Literature

Race has been a prominent theme in southern literature since the colonial era. It has been central to such southern literary genres as pastoral, plantation fiction, local color, and modern realism. In the 19th century, white writers generally supported white supremacy, and they used their works to create a normative assumption about the inevitability of white control and black submission. Slave narratives challenged such views, as did postbellum black writers. In the 20th century, a new critical realism came to dominate the literature of the region, exposing the ugliness of Jim Crow society. Southern writing has always been rooted in specific southern places, with racial issues tied in with local economic and social particularities varying from the Appalachian Mountains to the Tennessee hill country to the Mississippi Delta.

John Smith's writings on Native Americans in early Virginia may lay claim to the earliest glimmers of a southern pastoral, working a dynamic between the Noble Savage in American nature and the violent heathen in the wilderness. Images of the southeastern parts of North America as a Garden of Eden early took root in promotional materials. The garden suggested biblical authority but also a pastoral tradition going back to the classical age, which projected images of innocent people in an idyllic version of nature. But the garden pastoral contained ominous premonitions of impending loss, the inevitability of displacement. Early writers offered a particularly Virginian version of this that came to characterize the developing regional pastoral—the slave was in the garden. Southern writers would have to labor to invent images of an idyllic, innocent community that was built on an exploitative slave system resting ultimately on violence. William Byrd's *Westover's Secret Diary, 1709–1712* and Thomas Jefferson's *Notes on the State of Virginia* were early efforts to use the plantation as a setting for an emerging literature with regional focus. Jefferson created the white yeoman as an American type, a representation of Virgil's shepherd. Jefferson's status as a slave owner and his ambivalent views on blacks compromised his ability to define a convincing southern pastoral, a problem that would thereafter haunt southern white writers.

Plantation fiction became the defining literary genre of southern literature in the three decades before the Civil War, and its romanticized appeal would last a generation after the Civil War. It was a response to abolitionist fiction and nonfiction, which became widespread in the North in the antebellum era, attacking slavery on plantations as immoral and brutal. Slave narratives became a major African American literary form, the beginning of a long-standing literature of protest that has characterized black writing. Slave narratives portrayed cruel slave masters and mistresses and slave traders destroying black families, debunking romantic images of contented slaves. White masters would not acknowledge their mixed-race children in William Wells Brown's *Clotel; Or the President's Daughter* (1853), depicting specifically the child of Thomas Jefferson and his slave mistress. Frederick Douglass's narrative, originally published in 1845, portrayed Douglass as longing understandably for freedom but restrained by slave owners who were barbaric. Harriet Jacobs's *Incidents in the Life of a Slave Girl* (1861) presented a virtuous young slave woman trying to negotiate a system that encouraged sexual exploitation. In the 1850s, *Uncle Tom's Cabin* (1852) drew on many of the tropes of plantation fiction, and in the immediate years after its publication, white southern writers wrote more than a dozen proslavery novels defending slavery's racial arrangements. In response to slave narratives and other abolitionist literature, white writers used the family metaphor, picturing the plantation as an idyllic scene for kind masters and contented slaves bound together in a patriarchal household. Scholars see John Pendleton Kennedy's *Swallow Barn* (1832) as the first full-blown plantation novel. Its setting is a run-down but genteel James River plantation, where a northerner visits and recounts stories of singing slaves and courtly masters and belles. William Gilmore Simms was one of the best-known antebellum southern writers. He wrote a series of Revolutionary War historical novels, but he later became an aggressive defender of slavery, with *Woodcraft* (1852) portraying an isolated plantation with childlike slaves and a paternalistic planter family.

Race also appears as a theme in the history of Native Americans in the early 19th century in the Southeast. White land hunger led to a desire for Indian removal, at the same time that whites were increasingly imagining a South that would be defined by white racial dominance over Indians as well as black slaves. The physical removal of most southeastern Indian tribes to the West effectively removed, until recently, consideration of southern Indians as a part of southern culture, including southern literature, and left a view of the South as simply a biracial, black and white, place. Such Cherokee writers as Elias Boudinot and John Rollin Ridge wrote fiction and nonfiction that preserved the trauma of their southern experience.

Writings about the plantation and its racial patterns continued after the Civil War, its pastoral images now overlapping with a stress on picturesque elements, which appealed to the growing audience for local-color writing in the late 19th century. Such writers as Thomas Nelson Page, Sherwood Bonner, and Joel Chandler Harris were popular local-color writers in national magazines, with stories that looked back nostalgically on the time of the antebellum plantation as a golden age. The former slave became a key figure in this writing, offering fond reminiscences of the moonlight-and-magnolia plantation life and lamenting its loss. Many such stories were in dialect, including Harris's popular Uncle Remus tales. Harris drew from African American folktales, most notably the trickster Brer Rabbit, whose subtext was always subversive of the slave regime.

Place was important to local-color writings, and one sees that significance in such Louisiana writers as George Washington Cable, Grace King, and Kate Chopin, all of whom were more critical of slavery than other southern white writers and who pictured south Louisiana's complex racial identities. Two other southern writers, Mark Twain and Charles Chesnutt, offered the most direct response to the white racism inherent in plantation fiction. Huck Finn became a naive but insightful poor white observer of southern racial injustice, becoming a rebel against it, even if he did believe he would be condemned to hell for violating his society's racial strictures. His slave friend, Jim, was an ironic black voice that punctured the plantation legend of a happy interracial family. The image of Huck and Jim on the raft presented the possibilities of an interracial friendship. Twain's *Pudd'nhead Wilson* (1894) denounced slavery and the unwillingness of whites to acknowledge mixed-race children. Chesnutt's *The Conjure Woman* (1899) was a collection of stories that featured a black character, Uncle Julius McAdoo, whose folksy stories taught visiting northerners that the antebellum South was far from an idyllic place and time, challenging the predominant tone of the southern pastoral with examples of slavery's injustices. Chesnutt's novels *The House behind the Cedars* (1990) and *The Marrow of Tradition* (1901) dealt with light-skinned blacks who passed for white and with the conditions relating to the Wilmington race riot in 1898.

Other black writers of the late 19th and early 20th centuries constituted an important force in refuting demeaning stereotypes of blacks and protesting conditions in the Jim Crow South. Anna Julia Cooper's *A Voice from the South* (1892) emphasized the need for black women's education in achieving black middle-class respectability. Ida Wells-Barnett had to flee the South because of her forthright criticism of lynching, but her book *Southern Horrors: Lynch Law in All Its Phases* (1892) continued her documentation of racial violence. James Weldon Johnson, from Florida, offered psychological insight into the life of a light-skinned African American passing for white in *The Autobiography of an Ex-Colored Man*. Jean Toomer's *Cane* (1923) was one of the most critically praised works on southern black life. Part one of the book paints a lyrical portrait of the southern landscape and black folk culture. The second part of the book portrays black life in the urban North, with none of the passion and beauty of southern black life but nonetheless home to increasing numbers of black migrants out of the segregated South.

The writers of the Southern Literary Renaissance, white and black, made race a major theme. Some, such as the Vanderbilt Agrarians, defended agrarian society as the defining feature of the South, virtually masking the role of race in regional life. But most writers embraced literary modernism, with its critical realism. William Faulkner was at the forefront of white writers who confronted the region's racial realities and sketched memorable characters beyond stereotypes. Joe Christmas in *Light in August* (1936), Lucas Beauchamp in *Intruder in the Dust* (1948), and Dilsey in *The Sound and the Fury* represent a range of black characters centrally positioned in Faulkner's work. The burdens of southern history preoccupied Faulkner, and he saw race relations as at the center of the region's history. Dispossession of Indian land became the region's original sin, and white injustice toward blacks was the recurring theme. *Absalom, Absalom!* presented Thomas Sutpen, a self-made planter who had come from the Appalachian Mountains, went to Haiti to make his success as a planter, and then came to the Mississippi wilderness to build his empire. Faulkner uses Sutpen to connect the South's colonial story to that of the Caribbean Islands' slave plantation society, and Sutpen's refusal to acknowledge his mixed-race son critically addresses the white South's obsession with miscegenation. *Light in August* (1936) presented the confused racial identity of Joe Christmas in a society determined to draw racial boundaries. *Go Down, Moses* (1942) explores the human interactions that laid the basis for acknowledging a biracial South.

Faulkner's fellow Mississippian, Richard Wright, was at the forefront of a 20th-century tradition of protest against racial injustice by African American writers. Like Wright, many of these black writers were exiles from the South. Wright examined the psychological trauma of living in the Jim Crow South. His memoir *Black Boy* (1945) was about the aspiring artist growing up in an authoritarian society, recounting repeated experiences of daily humiliation and physical and psychological danger. Zora Neale Hurston represented a differing approach, celebrating black life in the South, seeing the rural black folk culture offering grounds for survival of racist conditions and a strong African American community. She insisted on the possibility of creativity and achievement, beyond the victimization that Jim Crow suggested. Hurston's work looked at the private context of racially defined life, with less concern for political protest at segregation's injustices. An anthropologist, she documented that black folk culture that her writing celebrated.

Race continues to be a central concern of southern literature in the contemporary period. Black writers like Toni Morrison in *Beloved* (1987) and Alice Walker in *The Color Purple* (1982) go back into southern history to explore the traumas and strengths of black culture. Larry Brown in *Dirty Work* (1990) and Madison Smarrt Bell in *Soldier's Joy* (1989) write of the opportunities and limitations of interracial friendships among men wounded in the Vietnam War. Ellen Douglass's *Can't Quit You Baby* (1988) offers a rich study of two women, a black servant and a white employer, who have been linked by a lifetime of fraught interaction. Ernest Gaines's novels, such as *A Gathering of Old Men* (1983), unravel the south Louisiana ethnic and racial landscapes, with interactions among African American and Cajun men. The civil rights movement has been the subject of literary production, including Alice Walker's *Meridian* (1976), Mark Childress's *Crazy in Alabama* (1993), and Nanci Kinkaid's *Crossing Blood* (1992).

Two of the most important recent writers offering fresh perspectives on racial interaction are Natasha Trethewey and Randall Kenan. Trethewey, who won the Pulitzer Prize for poetry in 2007 and was named the nation's poet laureate in 2012, offers through her poetry a reimagined southern history, with women and blacks as central figures. She revises a long-standing southern literary theme in her 2002 sonnet "Southern Pastoral," which pictures her in the

Richard Wright, Mississippi-born writer
who was at the forefront of a 20th-century
tradition of protest of racial injustice by African
American writers, ca. 1940 (Archives and Special
Collections, University of Mississippi Library,
Oxford)

nonpastoral black metropolis of Atlanta, having a drink with the all-white, all-male Agrarian writers of the past. She also unravels the South's mixed-race heritage through poems about her own family's experience. Kenan used his childhood memories, growing up in a small North Carolina town that became the basis for his fictional Tim's Creek, where characters recur throughout many stories. In his short story collection, *Let the Dead Bury the Dead*, he draws from rural black folk culture, and his magical realism stories include African lore, ghosts, and haunted memories. He writes of gay characters who often cross racial lines.

Increasingly, writers from a variety of social and ethnic perspectives are producing works that show the changing context of race in the South. Robert Olen Butler writes of Vietnamese in Louisiana in *A Good Scent from a Strange Mountain* (1992), and Susan Choi's *The Foreign Student* (1998) explores a protagonist haunted by his childhood during the Korean War, as well as his embrace of southern small town life. Cynthia Shearer's *The Celestial Jukebox* (2005) presents a vibrant Mississippi Delta, with Asian, Latino, African, African American, Lebanese, and other ethnic characters suggesting a diverse cultural context. Native American writers such as LeAnne Howe (Choctaw), James Harris Guy (Chickasaw), and Diane Glancy (Cherokee) continue to write of tribal history and contemporary Native life with southern settings. Writers and scholars now see race as a socially constructed concept, and contemporary southern literature deals with race through blurred boundaries between ethnic groups beyond racial categorization.

CHARLES REAGAN WILSON
University of Mississippi

Thadious Davis, *Southscapes: Geographies of Race, Region, and Literature* (2012); Minrose Gwin, *Black and White Women of the Old South: The Peculiar Sisterhood in American Literature* (1985); Barbara Ladd, *Nationalism and the Color Line in George W. Cable, Mark Twain, and William Faulkner* (1996); Robert Stepto, *From Behind the Veil: Study of Afro-American Narrative* (1970); Eric Sundquist, *To Wake the Nations: Race in the Making of American Literature* (1993); Floyd C. Watkins, *The Death of Art: Black and White in the Recent Southern Novel* (1970); Joel Williamson, *The Crucible of Race: Black-White Relationships in the American South since Emancipation* (1980).

Lynching and Racial Violence

Lynching was arguably the most conspicuous form of a long-standing American tradition of vigilantism. In popular usage, it referred to a killing perpetrated by a group of persons working outside the law to avenge an alleged crime or to impose social order. By the 20th century, however, lynching also came to stand for racial oppression at its most horrifying, a result of the vast numbers of lynchings committed against African Americans during the Jim Crow era as a means to instill racial terror and enforce white supremacy. Even today, the term denotes an act of violence perpetrated out of racial animosity, fueled by a mob mentality that is quick to ascribe guilt outside the bounds of due process. Lynching, however, has had a long and complex history in the United States. The meaning of the term has changed considerably over time, and acts of lynching are not easily categorized.

The origin of the term has most commonly been attributed to Col. Charles Lynch of Virginia, whose extralegal "court" sentenced Tories to floggings during the American Revolution. "Lynch law" at first referred to any form of extralegal corporal punishment. By the mid-19th century, however, it came to refer primarily to lethal punishments. Hanging was the most common form of lynching, although mobs also shot their victims, dragged, beat, and tortured them, or burned them at the stake. Despite the gruesomeness of the practice, it was considered, through most of the 19th century, to be a legitimate, community-sanctioned form of violence. It was rooted in traditions of popular justice and local sovereignty, according to which a community punished crimes and established social order outside official legal institutions. In the antebellum period, lynching was not a predominantly southern practice; it was most commonly practiced in frontier regions, particularly in western states and territories. At this time, whites, Mexicans, and Native Americans were more likely to be the victims of lynchings than African Americans, although historians are uncovering more and more the extent to which slaves were subject to lynching. Lynching began to increase in the South just before the Civil War, when southern vigilantes, particularly in Louisiana and Texas, routinely inflicted death upon outlaws and on individuals suspected of plotting slave insurrections.

The Civil War and Reconstruction intensified lynching activity in southern states. Vigilantism in Texas alone during the war probably accounted for over 150 deaths. Lynching became even more widespread during Reconstruction and was directed mostly at ex-slaves as a form of political terror. The Ku Klux Klan and other vigilante groups killed hundreds of African Americans, as well as white Republicans, in what were often ritualized ceremonies that presaged the ritual and public nature of many Jim Crow lynchings. Significantly, however, these killings were not at the time called "lynchings," since that term still connoted community sanction, and the violence of Reconstruction did not garner widespread and undisputed white support.

After a brief decline in violence just after Reconstruction, lynching rose in both intensity and frequency in the mid-1880s, peaking in 1892 and 1893, and, though on the decline after the 1890s, the practice persisted well into the 20th century. Although lynchings still took place throughout most of the United States in this period, the vast majority occurred in the southern states and involved white mobs targeting African Americans. Indeed, by the turn of the 20th century, the term came to be primarily associated with racial control and oppression, even as defenders of the practice still sought to justify it as a legitimate form of criminal vengeance. In fact, many African Americans supported the practice of lynching as a form of community vigilantism in the late 19th century, even engaging in acts of lynching themselves. Once lynching came to be seen as a tool of white supremacists to exert racial control, however, their support for the practice withered.

Lynching increased at the start of the Jim Crow era for a number of reasons. Economic stress and uncertainty provoked struggling white farmers and petty merchants to lash out at African Americans seeking political and economic advancement and impelled white planters to exert control over their black labor force. Moreover, increased urbanization and industrialization threatened traditional racial hierarchies and created a sense of social instability. In southern towns and cities, fears of black advancement and diminished white power be-

Lynching of Gus Goodman, Bainbridge, Ga., 1905
(Georgia Department of Archives and History, Atlanta)

came coupled with intense fears of black criminality—in particular the fear that black men would rape white women and thus violate white purity. In this context, lynching coincided with the institutionalization of white supremacy, in the form of segregation and disfranchisement, and served as a means to enforce new racial codes and to protect white male authority.

Efforts made to gather data on lynching across the United States did not begin until 1882. For this reason, the numbers of lynching before 1882 may be underestimated. And even this post-1882 data is not comprehensive, since many lynchings went unreported or uncounted. Nevertheless, scholars have ascertained that from 1882 through the early 1950s, by which time lynching had virtually ended, at least 4,739 persons reportedly died at the hands of lynch mobs in the United States. The likely total is probably nearer to 6,000. Over 80 percent of lynchings occurred in southern states, and almost 90 percent of those were committed by white mobs against African American men. These statistics do not include those who died in race riots; nor do they include inter-racial homicides. Among the southern states, Mississippi, Georgia, and Texas saw the most lynchings, although, in proportion to the African American population in each state, lynching rates were actually higher in Florida, Arkansas, and Kentucky.

Other ethnic minorities, especially Mexicans, as well as immigrant and native-born whites, were also the targets of lynch mobs in this period. The largest mass lynching in the country, which took place in 1891 in New Orleans, was committed against 11 Italian immigrants who had been indicted for the assassination of the local police chief. A mob of thousands stormed the jail where the men were detained and dragged them to the street, shooting to death 10 of them and hanging the other.

Lynchings drew more attention in the Jim Crow period, not only because of the sheer numbers but also because a good number were committed as public rituals, before crowds of hundreds, and sometimes thousands, of spectators. The spread of newswires in the late 19th century ensured that Americans across the country were more likely to learn of the most horrific lynchings. On the whole, the news media became more sensationalistic in this period, and reports of lynchings lingered over the ghastly details of mob executions. Not infrequently, local photographers, and sometimes members of the mob, snapped pictures of the violence, often making them into postcards to send to family and friends.

The 1899 lynching of Sam Hose in Newnan, Ga., was one such sensationalized and gruesome event, which garnered national attention after news of the lynching spread across the wires. Hose was a black farm laborer, accused of murdering his white employer and raping his wife. A mob tortured and mutilated Hose before burning him to death. Crowds swarmed the town to witness the lynching, and excursion trains brought spectators in from Atlanta. Hose's body parts were distributed and sold afterward, and a photographer advertised the sale of photographs of the lynching in the local newspaper. That lynching set off a series of lynchings throughout the countryside around Newnan, as local whites feared a black conspiracy to attack and kill white citizens.

The lynching of Sam Hose was atypical in its excess, but most lynchings received the same kind of widespread community sanction. Lynch mobs are not easily categorized since they were made up of men from all strata of society. Lynching is most associated with the poorest members of white society, those who might have been in direct economic competition with African Americans. But that stereotype is only true of a segment of lynchings. Many mobs were made up of yeoman farmers as well as solid working-class and lower-middle-class townspeople. Mobs also operated with the tacit, and at times vocal, approval of wealthy planters, civic and business leaders, ministers, judges, lawyers, and newspaper editors. Very few participants in lynch mobs were prosecuted in any state, and prior to World War II almost none ever served time in prison.

Lynching especially garnered public support when the target of the mob was accused of sexually violating a white woman. Those lynchings that resulted from accusations of rape were also more likely to be public and sadistic. Ridding society of "black brutes" who violated white women was indeed the most common justification for lynching. South Carolina governor Cole Blease echoed the sentiments of many white southerners when he declared in one infamous speech: "Whenever the Constitution comes between me and the virtue of the white women of South Carolina, then I say 'to hell with the Constitution.'" In fact, however, only about one-third of all lynching victims were suspected of rape or attempted rape. Murder or attempted murder was more often the alleged crime. Others who died at the hands of lynch mobs were accused of transgressions of descending importance, such as arson, burglary, slapping a white person, stealing chickens, chronic impudence, or simply being "vagrant and lewd." Whatever the supposed crime, most southern whites considered lynching to be a significant deterrent to black criminality. In cases in which they felt white authority or white purity to be threatened, many southern whites believed that the law was too slow and that it bestowed too many rights upon criminals; some crimes, they believed, simply stood beyond the purview of man's law — they required a form of justice that was swifter and more severe.

Although white southerners largely defended the practice until the 1930s, lynching rates decreased with each decade in the 20th century, except for brief flare-ups just after World War I and at the start of the Great Depression. This decline was due to a number of factors. As southern blacks increasingly migrated to the North and West in the 1910s and 1920s, white elites were less likely to condone the violence. Local police departments, meanwhile, were professionalizing and thus took greater pains to protect potential lynching victims. Moreover, antilynching activists, both inside and outside the South, were increasingly successful at publicizing the atrocity of lynching. And in light of the NAACP's campaign for federal antilynching legislation, local and state officials grew more willing to arrest and indict alleged mob members, if only to keep federal involvement at bay. Over time then, public attitudes toward lynching shifted, and by the start of World War II white southerners for the most part had come to disdain the practice. Lynchings still occurred in the 1940s and into the civil rights era, but they were, significantly, not committed publicly.

The public presentation of lynching photographs and postcards in the past decade has focused renewed attention on lynching, and a spate of academic studies reflects the growing interest in lynching and its role in southern culture. This recent attention to lynching led to a U.S. Senate resolution in 2005 that officially apologized for the Senate's repeated failure to pass antilynching legislation in the 1920s and 1930s.

WILLIAM I. HAIR
Georgia College

AMY LOUISE WOOD
Illinois State University

Edwin T. Arnold, *What Virtue There Is in Fire: Cultural Memory and the Lynching of Sam Hose* (2009); Edward L. Ayers, *Vengeance and Justice: Crime and Punishment in the 19th-Century American South* (1984); Bruce E. Baker, *This Mob Will Surely Take My Life: Lynchings in the Carolinas, 1871–1947* (2008); Ray Stannard Baker, *Following the Color Line* (1908; reprint 1969); Richard Maxwell Brown, *Strain of Violence: Historical Studies of American Violence and Vigilantism* (1975); W. Fitzhugh Brundage, *Lynching in the New South: Georgia and Virginia, 1880–1930* (1992); William Carrigan, *The Making of Lynching Culture: Violence and Vigilantism in Central Texas, 1836–1916* (2004); James H. Chadbourn, *Lynching and the Law* (1933); James E. Cutler, *Lynch-Law: An Investigation into the History of Lynching in the United States* (1905); Phillip Dray, *At the Hands of the Unknown: Lynching of Black America* (2002); Michael J. Pfeifer, *Rough Justice: Lynching and American Society, 1874–1947* (2004); Arthur F. Raper, *The Tragedy of Lynching* (1933); Stewart E. Tolnay and E. M. Beck, *Festival of Violence: An Analysis of Southern Lynchings, 1882–1930* (1995); Christopher Waldrep, *The Many Faces of Judge Lynch: Extralegal Violence and Punishment in America* (2002); Walter White, *Rope and Faggot* (1929); Amy Louise Wood, *Lynching and Spectacle: Witnessing Racial Violence in America, 1890–1940* (2009); George C. Wright, *Racial Violence in Kentucky, 1865–1940: Lynchings, Mob Rule, and "Legal Lynchings"* (1990).

Medical Care and Public Health

In the antebellum South, Americans were vulnerable to many diseases and conditions that scientific and medical knowledge have rendered rare in the present-day United States. Without antibiotics, advanced surgical techniques, understandings of infection, or vaccines or effective sewage systems, antebellum Americans suffered from postpartum infection, tuberculosis, and a host of other problems. But African Americans, particularly southern slaves, had health issues that sprang directly from their enslavement. Among these were malnutrition, parasites, tuberculosis, and childbirth complications. Whippings, which were carried out across the South from the colonial era through the Civil War, injured skin, muscle, and occasionally internal organs. Slaves' labor was also frequently physically dangerous. Domestic work such as cooking and laundry carried risks of burns and other injuries. Agricultural labor exposed slaves to injuries from machinery and livestock.

Most African American slaves moved between two parallel medical systems. Over the years, slave communities developed their own system of medical treatments and understandings of health and illness. Slave practitioners who were largely illiterate received medical training from other slaves. Their treatments tended to rely heavily on local flora. For these healers, curing the body often intersected with the patient's spiritual and emotional health as well as the patient's relationship to family and community. Largely divorced from concerns of the market and labor production that informed white doctors' treatment, African American medicine was a key component of slave community and spiritual life.

Slave owners, on the other hand, wanted healthy slaves who would be able to labor productively or bring a high price on the market. Often masters relied on a mixture of patent medicines, homeopathy, and their own medical skill or an overseer's to treat a wide variety of chronic and acute conditions. Many masters, particularly when dealing with slaves "in their prime," spent considerable resources treating illness. Many called in white doctors, paid for medicines and surgeries, and asked one another and professionals for advice on keeping slaves healthy.

White doctors' interest in slaves extended beyond desires to cure them for humanitarian or financial interest. White physicians in the South often used slave patients as research subjects and the remains of deceased slaves for autopsies and educational purposes. While some of these experiments and procedures attempted to locate the physical essences and implications of racial difference, most focused on treatments that they hoped would apply to white patients. Unsurprisingly, white doctors almost never asked slaves or their next of kin for permission to use dead bodies or to perform research on the living. White doctors could hire slaves with specific conditions to serve as research subjects.

The most well-known of these projects is the work of Dr. J. Marion Sims of Alabama. Sims performed 30 vaginal surgeries on three slave women suffering from vesicovaginal fistula, a debilitating and humiliating condition, between 1845 and 1849. Sims used no anesthetic during these operations and eventually perfected a surgical technique and invented instruments that became standard for vaginal exams and surgeries. Sims's work, and indeed most medical practice under slavery, was predicated on slavery's central tenet—that a person could own another person's body, as opposed to just their labor. When the Civil War and emancipation put an end to bodily ownership, the systems of medical care that had developed under slavery changed as well. In 1862, President Abraham Lincoln signed the Militia Act, which allowed black men, regardless of their status, to enlist in the Union army. Black men who served in the military received an initial physical exam from an army physician. These records reveal a great deal about the general health of African American men (northern and southern) in the mid-19th century. African American soldiers, both those who had been slaves and those who enlisted as free men, suffered higher mortality rates and received less care than their white counterparts, as the army assigned few trained physicians to African American regiments. Since proportionally fewer of them served in combat roles, their rate of battle wounds was lower than that of white soldiers. The reasons for their high mortality rates converge around a number of factors. For example, many rural African Americans had not been exposed to childhood contagious diseases and were vulnerable to these in the close military quarters. In addition, African American troops performed much of the army's dangerous and physically taxing labor, such as digging fortifications and clearing land. The poor quality of many of the African American troops' uniforms and rations also weakened their defenses against illness.

In addition to African American men on active duty in the military, thousands of African Americans—men, women, and children—escaped plantations and fled to refugee camps administered by the Union army. These people often arrived in poor health and found that the crowded conditions, poor sanitation, and scarcity of food and shelter rendered them vulnerable. They sought out medical treatment from Union army doctors and the volunteers and employees of freedmen's aid organizations who staffed the camps.

After emancipation, the federal government created the Bureau of Refugees, Freedmen, and Abandoned Lands. The bureau did provide various forms of relief for freedpeople, as did a number of private agencies, but from its inception it resisted providing free and complete medical care to African Americans. Despite this practice, the bureau established a number of hospitals and dispensaries across the South. A number of Freedmen's hospitals provided leadership roles for African Americans. For example, Alexander Augusta, a black physician who had trained in Canada and served as a Union army surgeon, worked at the Freedmen's Hospital in Georgia and later at the Freedmen's Hospital in Washington, D.C. This hospital, which was largely funded by African Americans, grew into part of Howard University's medical school.

Many African Americans were unable or unwilling to rely on Freedmen's

Public health doctor giving tenant family medicine for malaria, near Columbia, S.C., ca. 1939 (Marion Post Wolcott, photographer, Library of Congress [LC-USF33-030425-M5], Washington, D.C.)

Bureau hospitals and instead tried to negotiate medical care into their labor contracts with employers. Still others formed mutual aid societies that negotiated with physicians as a group to provide benefits for their members. Many of these groups engaged in philanthropy as well, providing medical care for indigent black people in their communities.

During Reconstruction and through the turn of the century, black and white philanthropists invested in black schools throughout the South. As part of this movement, religious groups, preexisting colleges, philanthropists, and even entrepreneurs founded a number of medical and nursing schools. Medical education was largely unregulated during this time, and like institutions that catered to white students, African American medical schools were wildly uneven in terms of curriculum and quality. In 1909, in a major step toward regulating medical education and creating national standards, Abraham Flexner was commissioned by the Carnegie Foundation to make a tour of medical colleges in the United States and Canada to evaluate their quality. Flexner assigned a grade to each school and occasionally explicitly recommended that a school close. Even before state and medical board authorities put in formal regulation measures, a low mark from Flexner effectively crippled a school's attempt to raise funds and recruit students. Flexner gave low marks to all but three African

American medical schools: Howard University Medical School in Washington, D.C., Meharry Medical College in Nashville, and Leonard Medical School in Raleigh. While the Flexner Report did shut down substandard medical schools, these schools had provided a basic medical education to African Americans who then went on to serve black patients. White medical schools that survived the Flexner Report did not admit black students, and the American Medical Association remained segregated. In response to these conditions, a group of African American medical professionals formed the National Medical Association, which is ongoing.

In the midst of these developments in African American medical education and institution building, experimentation on African Americans' bodies continued. The Public Health Service organized and funded the most notorious of these experiments. The Tuskegee Syphilis Study took place in Macon County, Ala., home of the Tuskegee Institute. In this study, which ran from 1932 until 1972, African American men who had tested positive for syphilis were followed and studied for years. The aims of the study were to learn the effects of untreated latent stage syphilis, more specifically on black men. Over the years, under the direction of both black and white doctors and one black nurse, the men received what they thought was treatment but in fact was aspirin and iron tonics. Men in the study were discouraged from seeking out legitimate syphilis treatment and remained ineligible for the draft during World War II since the military demanded testing and treatment for syphilis for all inductees. After providing data for 12 academic papers in medical journals, the study ended in 1972 amid a flurry of bad publicity. President Clinton issued a formal apology for the study in 1997.

In 1946, 14 years into the Tuskegee study, the U.S. Congress passed the Hill-Burton Act, originally named the Hospital Survey and Construction Act, which provided grants and loans for underserved areas to build medical infrastructure, mainly hospitals and nursing homes. Institutions that accepted the funds were obligated to provide a "reasonable volume" of services to people unable to pay. The Hill-Burton Act funded the construction of hospitals all over the South, and although the original language in the bill stipulated that projects that the initiative funded could not discriminate on the basis of race, the funding of separate-but-equal facilities continued until 1963.

The years since 1963 have seen increasing desegregation of medical schools, nursing schools, and hospitals. However, demographic patterns and access still translate into racial imbalances in many institutions and medical specialties. African Americans in the 21st century still suffer disproportionately high rates of asthma, obesity, type-2 diabetes, infant mortality, and HIV infection. These statistics emerge from a constellation of causes. Poverty, lack of health insurance, lack of access to primary care, poor nutrition, and environmental factors all play a role in the illnesses that African Americans get, how those illnesses are treated, and the outcomes of that treatment. A marked disparity between the health of African Americans and white people has persisted since before the nation's founding and continues today.

GRETCHEN LONG
Williams College

Sharla Fett, *Working Cures: Healing Health and Power on Southern Slave Plantations* (2002); Margaret Humphreys, *Intensely Human: The Health of the Black Soldier in the American Civil War* (2008); Susan Reverby, *Examining Tuskegee: The Infamous Syphilis Study and Its Legacy* (2009); Todd L. Savitt, *Medicine and Slavery: The Diseases and Health Care of Blacks in Antebellum Virginia* (1978), *Race and Medicine in Nineteenth- and Early Twentieth-Century America* (2007); Maria Schwarz, *Birthing a Slave: Motherhood and Medicine in the Antebellum South* (2006); Karen Kruse Thomas, *Journal of Southern History* (November 2006).

Medical Science, Racial Ideology, and Practice, to Reconstruction

Slavery in the American South presented a unique catalyst for growing questions and concerns about race within the practice of medicine. The arrival of the first Africans in Jamestown, Va., in 1619 laid the foundation for future medical preoccupations with physical differences between blacks and whites. Ideas governing disease causation remained closely tied to the relationship between region, climate, and physical constitution and the South's distinctive ecology. Hot and humid summers and frequent spells of yellow fever led to pervasive beliefs that the southern climate was too harsh for the constitutions of white laborers but perfectly suited for Africans. Southern physicians made broad assessments about morbidity and mortality along racial lines. Most notable was the enduring belief that African Americans were immune to yellow and malarial fevers.

Whites saw black skin as both a biological advantage and a mark of degeneracy because although it offered protection from the ill effects of the climate it was also viewed as a sign of primitiveness. In *Notes on the State of Virginia*, Thomas Jefferson lamented that "Negroes" were too different from whites for equal coexistence because their physical differences were "fixed in nature." In the 1850s, Josiah C. Nott, a respected and outspoken southern physician, cited black features as evidence of separate origins of the races of mankind—a controversial theory known as polygenesis. Polygenesis remained the hallmark of Nott's race theories and the cornerstone of his beliefs in black biological inferiority.

Even as white physicians claimed that African Americans were biologically different from whites, they relied on African American bodies for dissections, experiments, and anatomical demonstrations. In Charleston, S.C., the medical college made no secret of its use of "anatomical material" taken from the "colored population." Southern physician J. Marion Sims, a pioneer in surgical techniques and "father of gynecology," used three female slaves, Lucy, Betsy, and Anarcha, to find a treatment for vesicovaginal fistulas. Despite his success, and the relief his new treatment offered to women of all races, his rise to fame rested upon experimental surgeries performed on enslaved African American women.

Bold claims about black inferiority gained momentum in the decades leading up to the Civil War. Proslavery medical thought worked in tandem with "Herrenvolk democracy" to justify attitudes of white supremacy. Southern physicians fashioned themselves as experts on slave health, and antebellum medical articles on "distinctive Negro" physiology proliferated in medical journals. Samuel A. Cartwright, onetime chairman of the Medical Association of Louisiana, authored "A Report on the Diseases and Peculiarities of the Negro Race," published in 1851 in the *New Orleans Medical and Surgical Journal* and later reprinted in *De Bow's Review*. Cartwright's report was more of a political invective interspersed with spurious medical claims than a medical overview of Negro diseases, and in it he infamously coined the term "drapetomania"—the disease causing slaves to run away.

The Reconstruction era brought new trends in medical ideas about race as well as views of slavery, which were more nostalgic than accurate. Whites argued that, prior to the Civil War, slaves' health was guaranteed by their benevolent masters and that the troubles that freed African Americans faced after emancipation were consequences of their inability to look after their own welfare. Physicians pathologized freedom and published articles on increases in the rates of tuberculosis and insanity among African Americans in the South. At the Alabama Insane Hospital, freedom was cited as a cause of insanity among African American patients. The traits of African Americans, before seen as advantages for laboring in the South, became the loci of their postbellum health complaints. Social Darwinists claimed that African Americans would become extinct because they could not compete in society at the same level as whites. In the aftermath of slavery, African Americans continued to face challenges in gaining control over their health care as a result of deliberate and institutional-ized neglect caused by Jim Crow policies at the turn of the century.

RANA ASALI HOGARTH
Yale University

George M. Fredrickson, *The Black Image in the White Mind: The Debate on Afro-American Character and Destiny, 1817–1914* (1987); John S. Haller Jr., *Medical History* (July 1972); Reginald Horsman, *Josiah Nott of Mobile: Southerner, Physician, and Racial Theorist* (1987); John S. Hughes, *Journal of Southern History* (August 1992); Kenneth Merrill Lynch, *Medical Schooling in South Carolina, 1823–1969* (1970); Gary Puckrein, *Journal of American Studies* (August 1979); Todd L. Savitt, *Journal of Southern History* (August 1982), *Medicine and Slavery: The Disease and Health Care of Blacks in Antebellum Virginia* (1978); Alden T. Vaughan, *William and Mary Quarterly* (July 1972); John Harley Warner, in *Science and Medicine in the Old South*, ed. Ronald L. Numbers and Todd L. Savitt (1989); Christian Warren, *Journal of Southern History* (February 1997).

Migration, Black

To black southerners, migration has symbolized both the limitations and the opportunities of American life. As slaves, many suffered forced migrations with the attendant heartbreaks of separation from family and community. As freedmen and freedwomen, they seized upon spatial mobility as one of the most meaningful manifestations of their newly won emancipation. Subsequently, black southerners sought to better their conditions by moving within the rural South, to southern cities, and finally to northern cities, in a frustrating quest for equality and opportunity. Simultaneously, white southerners acted to restrict such movement because, until the mechanization of cotton culture, black geographic mobility—like black social and economic mobility—threatened the racial assumptions and labor relations upon which the southern economy and society rested.

The first significant migration of black southerners followed the American Revolution and the subsequent opening of the trans-Appalachian West to settlement by slaveholders. The enormous expansion of cotton cultivation in the early 19th century, combined with the closing of the foreign slave trade (1808), soon transformed a forced migration dominated by planters carrying their own slaves westward to one increasingly characterized by the professional slave trader. Although the Chesapeake remained the major source for the inter-state slave trade, after 1830 North and South Carolina, Kentucky, Tennessee, Missouri, and eventually Georgia also became "exporters" of slaves. The plantations of Alabama, Mississippi, Louisiana, Florida, Arkansas, and Texas were worked largely by these early black "migrants" and their children. Although it is difficult to determine the volume of the domestic slave trade, one historian has recently estimated that over 1 million black southerners were forcibly relocated between 1790 and 1860.

The forced migrations of the antebellum South were complemented by barriers against voluntary movement. Although each year hundreds of slaves escaped, they represented but a fraction of the southern black population. Even free black southerners were hemmed in, and by the 1830s their movement across state lines was either restricted or prohibited.

During the Civil War, white fears and black hopes generated opposing migration streams. Many slave owners responded to the approach of Union troops by taking their slaves west, either to the western, Upcountry areas of the eastern states, or from the Deep South to Texas and Arkansas. Thousands of slaves, on the other hand, fled toward the advancing army.

Ex-slaves continued to move away from plantations after the war ended. For many, like Ernest J. Gaines's fictional Miss Jane Pittman, the act of moving constituted a test of the meaning of emancipation. Others sought to reunite with family separated by antebellum forced migration. Much of the movement grew out of a search for favorable social, political, and economic conditions, especially the chance for "independence," which was closely associated with landownership. The flurry of migration generally involved short distances, often merely to the next plantation or a nearby town or city.

Southern cities offered ex-slaves the protection of the Freedmen's Bureau and the Union army, higher wages, black institutions, political activity, and freedmen's schools. But under pressure from whites—and often faced with the prospect of starvation—many of the thousands who moved cityward soon returned to the plantations. Urban whites considered the black city dweller a threat to social order, and planters sought to stabilize and reassert dominance over their labor forces. Vagrancy laws provided a temporary mechanism, and even after the legislative reforms during Reconstruction, the economic structure of the cities limited the urbanization of the black population. Few jobs outside the service sector were available to blacks, and black men especially found that survival was easier in the countryside. Black southerners continued to migrate to cities in modest numbers; by 1910, less than one-fourth lived in communities larger than 2,500. Some people moved back and forth, mainly between farm and small town, following seasonal labor patterns. This kind of mobility also characterized rural nonfarm labor and established what one historian has called a "migration dynamic," which later facilitated movement to northern cities.

Most black southerners who migrated longer distances in the 19th century headed for rural destinations, generally toward the south and west. During the 1870s and 1880s, rumors and labor agents drew blacks living in the Carolinas and Georgia to the Mississippi Delta and other areas in the Gulf states with promises of higher wages and better living conditions. Usually, migrants found social and economic relations similar to what they had left behind. The search for "independence" continued, with black southerners trying Kansas in the 1870s and then Arkansas and Oklahoma between 1890 and 1910. Movement became as central to southern black life as it has been to the American experience in general. Because blacks for so long had been unable to move freely, however, it acquired a special mystique manifested as a major theme in black music and symbolized by the recurrent image of the railroad as a symbol of the freedom to move and start life anew. By the 1890s, one black southerner in twelve would cross state lines during the decade in search of the still-unfulfilled promise of emancipation. Local moves remained even more frequent.

The direction and historical impact of black migration shifted dramatically during World War I. Northern industrialists, previously reluctant to hire blacks when they could draw upon the continuing influx of white immigrants, turned their attention southward as immigration ceased and production orders began pouring in. Some sent labor agents into the South, but news about opportunities and conditions in the North traveled more often via an emerging black communications network comprising letters from earlier migrants, northern newspapers (especially the *Chicago Defender*), and railroad workers. Observers and subsequent scholars offered various catalogs of "economic" and "social" factors that "pushed" migrants from the South and "pulled" them toward the North. Floods, boll weevil infestations, and credit contractions contributed to the urge to move to northern cities offering higher wages than those available to black southerners. Jim Crow, lynching, disfranchisement, and discrimination in the legal and educational systems contrasted with seemingly more equitable and flexible race relations in the North. Most migrants left because of a combination of motivations, which they often summarized as "bettering my condition." For the first time, however, thousands of black southerners looked to industrial work, rather than landownership, in their hopes to enjoy the prerogatives of American citizenship.

Nearly half a million black southerners headed north between 1916 and 1920, setting off a long-term demographic shift, which would leave only 53 percent of black Americans in the South by 1970, compared with 89 percent in 1910. Nearly all of these migrants went to cities, first in the Northeast and Midwest and later in the West. Most followed the longitudinal routes of the major railroads, although by World War II California was drawing thousands of migrants from Texas, Oklahoma, Arkansas, and Louisiana. At the same time, black southerners moved to southern cities, which by 1970 contained two-thirds of the region's black population. Even the massive urban unemployment of the Great Depression only moderately slowed the continuing flow northward, and movement accelerated to unprecedented levels during World War II and the following decades.

Many white southerners initially responded to this "Great Migration" by continuing the tradition of constructing barriers in the paths of black migrants. As always, landlords and employers feared the diminution of the labor supply, a threat that in the 19th century had stimulated the enacting of legislation designed to limit labor mobility. As a social movement and a series of individual decisions, however, the Great Migration also constituted a direct— although unacknowledged—threat to the fiber of social and economic relations in the South. The system rested upon the assumption that blacks were by nature docile, dependent, and unambitious. The decision to migrate and the evolution of a "movement" suggested dissatisfaction, ambition, and aggressive action. As they had in the past, white southerners tended to blame the movement on "outside forces" (in this case, labor agents), and localities ineffectively sought to stem the tide by tightening "enticement" laws and forcibly preventing blacks from leaving.

The Great Migration transformed American urban society and African American society, as migrants adapted to urban life while retaining much of their southern and rural culture. It was not unusual for southern communities to reconstitute themselves and their institutions in northern cities. Frequent visiting back and forth between relatives from the South and the North has contributed to this interchange between regional cultures, and the South is still "down home" to some northern black urbanites.

The 1970s saw a return of blacks to the South, a reverse migration that escalated in the 1990s. According to Census 2000 figures, the non-Hispanic black population of the South surged in the 1990s by 3,575,211 persons, more than in the Northeast, Midwest, and West combined, doubling the black population that the South had attracted in the 1980s (1.7 million). Southern cities, especially Atlanta, attracted most of these African American migrants in the late 1990s, at the same time that such major urban areas as New York, Chicago, Los Angeles, and San Francisco experienced the largest out-migration of blacks.

Demographers have attributed the dramatic reversal of the Great Migration north during the early 20th century to the South's economic development, its improved race relations, the growth of a black middle class in southern cities, and historic, cultural, and family ties to the South.

As a historical process, black migration within and from the South suggests some important continuities suffusing much of southern history: the coercive implications of white dependence on black labor; the refusal of blacks to accept their "place" as defined by whites; and the search for identity and opportunity, articulated by black writer Richard Wright, whose personal migration experience began with the hope that "I might learn who I was, what I might be."

JAMES R. GROSSMAN
University of Chicago

William H. Frey, in *Immigration and Opportunity*, ed. Frank D. Bean and Stephanie Bell-Rose (1999), *Population Today* (May/June 2001); James R. Grossman, *Land of Hope: Chicago, Black Southerners, and the Black Migration* (1989); Florette Henri, *Black Migration: Movement North, 1900–1920* (1975); Allan Kulikoff, in *Slavery and Freedom in the Age of the American Revolution*, ed. Ira Berlin and Ronald Hoffman (1983); Nicholas Lemann, *The Promised Land: The Great Migration and How It Changed America* (1991); Larry Long, *Migration and Residential Mobility in the United States* (1987); Nell Irvin Painter, *Exodusters: Black Migration to Kansas after Reconstruction* (1976); Arvarh Strickland, *Missouri Historical Review* (July 1975); Carter G. Woodson, *A Century of Negro Migration* (1918).

Migration, Latino

During the last two decades of the 20th century, Latino immigration represented a key demographic transformation across most of the South. Previously, the New South was a frontier to Latinos, with two exceptions, Texas and Florida. In 1980, the U.S. Census Bureau reported that the South was home to approximately 4.3 million Hispanics, with nearly 90 percent concentrated in parts of Florida and more broadly settled in Texas. By 2000, over 11 million Hispanics were counted by the Census Bureau, with the 2009 population estimates for the South revealing a 47.9 percent increase, to nearly 16.4 million Hispanics.

While the absolute increase in *nuevo* southerners is dramatic, the greater impact is related to the spreading of Latino newcomers outside of the former settlement zones. Consider that between 2000 and 2009 the number of Hispanics living outside of Texas and Florida nearly doubled, growing from 1.7 to 3.3 million residents. At the community level, this means that urban and rural places across the region, long bypassed by ethnic immigrants, are receiving streams of Latino newcomers from other parts of the United States and international locations.

In turn, the arrival of these newcomers has complicated social relations and class structures attached to the black-white binary. In a region where skin color situates a person's class position, brown means "in-between" and quickly labels one as an outsider. As a result, Latinos risk discrimination from blacks and whites alike.

Although Latinos share roots of Iberian colonization and are overwhelmingly Spanish speaking, they come from disparate nations and cultural groups. Moreover, their settlement experiences in the South vary widely. When Latinos settle in places like south Florida or the Texas Metroplex, they connect into existing social frameworks that ease stresses and enable newcomers to settle in more quickly. In contrast, Latinos arriving in large parts of the Deep South, Appalachia, or Coastal Plains are often viewed as outsiders. And social infrastructure—family, church, and community—are absent.

Historically, temporary immigrant labor has been a key production tool in southern agriculture and forestry industries. Seasonally, waves of international laborers with temporary work permits augmented domestic farmworkers across the South's agricultural landscapes—planting, pruning, or picking crops as needed. Since the middle of the last century, Latino workers have been a growing segment of this invisible agricultural workforce. These sojourners filled critical labor needs during labor-intensive phases in the production process and then moved on to the next work site.

More recently, Sunbelt cities in metropolitan areas like northern Virginia, Atlanta, Charlotte, Nashville, Raleigh, Greenville-Spartanburg, Orlando, and Greensboro have attracted large streams of Latino laborers, drawn by the rapid growth in low-wage service-sector jobs. During the earliest stages of the immigration process, the urban migrants often fit a "pioneer profile," that is, young male workers, absent families, expecting to live in the United States temporarily and then return home. With maturing immigration streams, the single male prototype has been replaced by families establishing homes, building communities, and connecting to local place.

As Latino immigrants have moved from temporarily occupying places toward establishing lives in urban neighborhoods and rural landscapes, nativists and xenophobes have resisted the newcomers. For them, ethnic immigration challenges the vestiges of racial and class privilege. Often, the hostility directed toward Latinos by right-wing groups is expressed through the invocation of place, represented by defense of community and culture. Public discourse around Latino immigrants uses metaphors like "invaders" or even "animals" to demonize Latino immigrants. The late Sen. Jesse Helms referred to Latinos as burglars breaking into a home (the country) to steal law-abiding citizens' property. Increasingly, the Ku Klux Klan and other white supremacist groups have shifted their hate speech toward brown-skinned Latino immigrants.

Where local and state governments are drawn into efforts to defend their communities against Latino settlers, the processes and ordinances are more sophisticated but carry similar themes. Across the South, some municipalities and counties have actively sought to discourage Latino settlement or control immigrant place-making activities. The range of government actions includes bans on Spanish-language signage, requiring the speaking of English on job sites, restricting the location of *loncheras* (food vending trucks) along city streets, rewriting zoning rules to forbid multiple-family housing (presumably favored by Latinos), and outlawing day-labor hiring sites. In similar fashion, state governments have put in place legislation to restrict the issuance of drivers' licenses, deny access to public services and/or higher education, and punish employers hiring undocumented labor. The recent publicity surrounding the Arizona anti-immigrant legislation has attracted legislative supporters.

Although Latinos face strong hostility from conservatives in the public arena, southern business interests have been strong supporters of northward labor migration under the H-2A guest-worker program and the North American Free Trade Agreement. During the economic boom of the last decades of the 20th century, Latino labor built the southern cities and sustained the rural industrial and agricultural economies. Throughout the region, employers view Latinos as hardworking bodies who are easily disciplined and controlled. In many instances, they are preferred over local African American workers. Limited or prejudiced views of brown-skinned newcomers lead to "work ethic" myths. Not unexpectedly, the overwhelming majority of international Latino migrants moving to the South come from working-class backgrounds and fill jobs in the blue-collar labor market. In urban North Carolina, for example, Latinos dominate the trade and landscaping sectors.

The competition for construction, manufacturing, and service jobs between African Americans, who have traditionally dominated these job categories, and Latinos has created tensions between the communities. Some black leaders and scholars contend that Latino immigrants have displaced African American workers and kept wage levels low for all workers. As early as 1979, *Ebony* magazine warned that undocumented Mexican immigrants in Florida and North Carolina posed "a big threat to black workers." Many labor market researchers offer an alternative explanation. They report that Latinos are not displacing African Americans in low-wage jobs. Rather, immigrants are filling "replacement" jobs. In other words, immigrants are taking jobs that African Americans have bypassed because they pay the lowest wages and are the most dangerous or dirty.

The color line inextricably undergirds class status in the South and frames belonging and place. Among Latino immigrants, the importance of skin color is not entirely new. Ethnographic research finds that racializing or skin-color stereotypes affect attitudes even within the Latino community. For example, South American migrants look down upon Mexican and Central American migrants as being less intelligent, submissive, and better suited to physical labor. Ethnic origin, reflected in skin tone and physical appearance, is broadly stigmatized. Darker skin color and physical features are associated with Indo-Latino (Latinos with indigenous ancestry) or Afro-Latino (Latinos with African heritage) groups and are viewed by light-skinned Latinos as having a lower class status.

Recent Latino immigrants, especially those with darker skin color, perceive greater discrimination from whites. Research comparing first-generation immigrant parents and U.S.-born children shows that the two groups view race and race relations differently. The first-generation perspective finds greater discrimination from white southerners and more favorable attitudes toward African Americans. In contrast, their children report less-positive relations with African Americans. Other research has found that white-Latino relations are comparatively more positive than white-black relationships. These data suggest that Latinos are making faster gains toward achieving the privileges of whiteness. In turn, the economic and social advantages of whiteness provide even stronger incentives for Latinos to create social distance from African Americans.

Social justice issues for Latinos are very different from the traditional agenda of the South's civil rights movement. Among Latino activists, skin color or racial identification is far less significant for explaining discrimination or unequal treatment in the South than national origin or legal-immigration status. Consequently, Latino immigration-rights advocates appeal for solidarity based upon the underlying principle that we are "a nation of immigrants." But for many in the African American community, the implication that citizenship bestows privilege is unacceptable. They remind Latinos that the black experience in the South is indelibly linked to racism and oppression.

Efforts to bridge the divides between Latino and native southerners are often built along three lines. The first, collaborations of color, is structured around bringing together black southerners and Latinos based upon discrimination and their common experiences as people of color. Racial profiling by law enforcement, housing or employment discrimination based upon skin color, hate speech, or violent targeting by racist groups are examples of the issues that foster activist coalitions between black and brown southerners.

A second form of collaboration arises from seemingly race-neutral issues. However, there are often racial undertones related to de facto discrimination and white privilege when access or equity of public resources is examined. Among the issues that bring together these coalitions are concerns arising from public school quality, inadequate health care, or environmental racism. A final bridging framework is traditional class-based community organizing. Commonly associated with workplace conditions or labor organizing, working-class southerners will put aside racial or ethnic prejudices to address shop-floor working conditions or the benefits of workers. Recent union efforts to organize meat- and food-processing workers in parts of the region reflect this pan-ethnic activity.

OWEN J. FURUSETH
University of North Carolina at Charlotte

Fran Ansley and Jon Shefner, eds., *Global Connections, Local Receptions: New Latino Immigration to the Southeastern United States* (2009); Karen D. Johnson-Webb, *Recruiting Hispanic Labor: Immigrants in Nontraditional Areas* (2003); William Kandel and John Cromartie, *New Patterns of Hispanic Settlement in Rural America* (2004); Raymond A. Mohl, in *Globalization and the American South*, ed. James C. Cobb and William Stueck (2005); Mary E. Odem and Elaine Lacy, eds., *Latino Immigrants and the Transformation of the U.S. South* (2009); Debra J. Schleef and H. B. Cavalcanti, *Latinos in Dixie: Class and Assimilation in Richmond, Virginia* (2009); Barbara Ellen Smith and Jamie Winders, *Transactions of the Institute of British Geographers* (January 2008); Heather A. Smith and Owen J. Furuseth, eds., *Latinos in the New South: Transformations of Place* (2006); Roberto Suro and Audrey Singer, *Latino Growth in Metropolitan America: Changing Patterns, New Locations* (2002).

Migration, White

In the first several hundred years of settlement of the U.S. South, white southerners migrated west from the Atlantic Coast and helped form the characteristic features of an Upland South and a Lowland South. In the 19th century, they took their cultures farther west, forming yeoman and plantation cultures that mixed in varying degrees with African American and Native American cultures. In the 20th century, the South's economic problems and the appeal of other American places promoted a massive out-migration that took forms of white southern culture north and west.

In the 1700s, between 130,000 and 250,000 Scots-Irish and 200,000 German settlers migrated to the American colonies, many coming through Philadelphia and down the Shenandoah Valley and then westward across the Appalachian Mountains. These settlers sought out similar landscapes they had known in Europe, mostly as small farmers and herdsmen. Their mountain and hill country settlements combined European folk culture with Native American culture in the areas they spread across. In the early 19th century, white settlers from the Atlantic Coast and Piedmont areas moved into what became the Deep South, after the removal of Native American tribes in the 1830s, establishing the Cotton Kingdom. White migrants came with their slaves and established plantation cultures in places like the Alabama Black Belt and the Mississippi Delta.

Throughout the 19th century, white southerners went west. Virginians, for example, settled farmlands north of the Ohio River, in Indiana and Illinois, flowing into Missouri and Kansas and later into Colorado and New Mexico, seeking quick wealth in western gold rushes. They entered into the borderlands guerrilla warfare in the 1850s for control of the West against northerners. White southerners originally from South Carolina and North Carolina spread westward, pushing the frontier settlement into the Southwest. The end of the Civil War brought a new kind of migration, as white southerners who feared northern rule in Reconstruction or who sought greater economic opportunities than the impoverished postwar South could offer left the region. Between 4,000 and 6,000 former Confederates moved to Central America, with most settling in small colonies in Mexico. Matthew Fontaine Maury, Confederate general and a distinguished oceanographer, served as commissioner of immigration for Mexico after the war, as the Mexican government promoted the settlement. Other former Confederates went to Honduras and the Caribbean Islands. Thousands of white southerners went to Brazil in the five years after the war, attracted by a government that offered them cheap land and immigration assistance in the hope that former southern planters would help develop that nation's plantation districts. Most of these postwar migrants returned to the South after 1870, but many became permanent residents in Brazil.

The American West attracted, however, more white southerners after the war than did Central America. "Gone to Texas" was a common sentiment in the 1870s South, as white southerners joined freedpeople in moving west for a fresh start in that state's postwar cattle industry. Such northern cities as Philadelphia, Boston, and especially New York City attracted the most white southerners after the war, as mostly young, well-educated whites went north to seek economic opportunities. Southern landowners who had fallen on hard times, professionals, and businesspeople all made the trip. By the end of the 19th century, almost 40,000 white southerners lived in New York City, establishing a network of southern heritage associations and Confederate veterans groups. They preserved relics from the antebellum South and promoted intersectional commercial relations.

Historian James N. Gregory, the closest student of white southern migration, estimates that during the 20th century, 20 million white southerners left the region, migrating in two distinct phases. The first began in the first decade of the 20th century and peaked in the 1920s. White migrants had left the South during the 19th century for farming opportunities, but World War I saw many white southerners leave to work in northern industries in need of labor with the end of European immigration to the United States. Most who left had been raised on farms, so the adjustment to migration included accommodation to city life and factory work demands. This first wave also included southern well-educated whites and those with particular skills, such as salespeople and professionals who saw greater opportunity in northern commercial centers than in the South. Better-off southern farmers became investors and developers of agricultural fields in Texas and California in the 1910s and 1920s. Writers and artists left to tap the greater institutional framework in the North for certain kinds of creativity.

As with black migration, white migration generally dropped off during the Great Depression, and an unknown number of former southerners returned home, plugging back into home places and kin who had not left. In one dramatic example, a special census in 1934 showed that the southern-born population of Flint, Mich., had decreased by 35 percent since 1930. The Depression did see one particular example of increased white migration, though, as southern farmers fled the environmental and economic devastation of the Dust Bowl in the Southwest. By 1940, California had added more than 300,000 white southerners to its population.

A second wave of migration began with World War II and lasted until the 1970s. Increased military and defense industry production created millions of new jobs, sometimes drawing rural and small-town southern whites (as well as blacks) to new coastal industrial centers and sometimes attracting them to booming economic locations outside the South. Migration rates of white Appalachians, in particular, increased, as they were drawn to automobile production sites in the industrial Midwest. They were among the most visible white southern migrants, as the image of "hillbilly bars" in Detroit, Chicago, and Cleveland became a new symbol of white southern migration. The 1970s saw an end to white migration; with improving economic opportunities through economic diversification and economic development, more formerly exiled southern whites returned.

The story of white southern migration mirrored that of the Great Migration of African Americans out of the South in the 20th century, but there were differences as well. In contrast to African American migration, one characteristic of white southern migration was the high rate of return to the South by migrants. In most five-year periods, the return rate was 10 percent or higher. In the 1950s, for every 100 white southerners leaving the South, 54 came home. Less than half of the 20 million whites who migrated out of the South thus left permanently. The largest numbers of white migrants went to the Great Lakes states, as was true for African American migrants, but the Middle Atlantic states were much less a destination for whites than for blacks. The exception to this generalization was New York City—that economic and cultural capital lured southerners of both races. California was also a popular area of white southern settlement, with more than 1.6 million white southerners there in 1970. Popular culture stereotyped the white migration to California through the 1960s television series *The Beverly Hillbillies*. White migrants did not achieve the levels of unity and political organization that black southerners who left the region did. Despite the stereotype of the hillbilly bar, they typically did not cluster together in white southern enclaves. Middle-class white migrants often did not feel common cause or social connectedness with working-class white southern migrants, thus limiting the opportunities for institution building and political organization. On the other hand, white migrants from the South did spread conservative evangelical Protestantism into the Midwest and West, and the nationalization of country music can be traced to white southern migrants who wanted the comforts of regional music even in places far away from the southern places that had given birth to the music.

CHARLES REAGAN WILSON
University of Mississippi

Chad Berry, *Southern Migrants, Northern Exiles* (2000); David Hackett Fischer and James C. Kelley, *Bound Away: Virginia and the Westward Movement* (2000); Neil Fligstein, *Going North: Migration of Blacks and Whites from the South, 1900–1950* (1981); James N. Gregory, *American Exodus: The Dust Bowl Migration and Okie Culture in California* (1989), *The Southern Diaspora: How the Great Migrations of Black and White Southerners Transformed America* (2005); Eugene C. Harter, *The Lost Colony of the Confederacy* (1985); Jack Temple Kirby, *Journal of Southern History* (November 1983); Phillip J. Obermiller, Thomas E. Wagner, and Bruce Tucker, eds., *Appalachian*

Odyssey: Historical Perspectives on the Great Migration (2000); Daniel E. Sutherland, *The Confederate Carpetbaggers* (1988).

Music, Recordings

Blues and country, jazz and pop, hip-hop and indie rock: it is difficult to talk about the history, the sound, and the meaning of southern music without invoking racial categories. It can appear as if the region is home to separate black and white musical traditions, reaching back across the Atlantic to Europe and Africa and continuing through the contemporary country and R&B charts. Forays across the musical color line—from Elvis's boogie and Stevie Ray Vaughan's blues to the country music of black artists such as Ray Charles and Charlie Pride—can appear transgressive, the exceptions that prove the rule of historical relationship between music and race in the South. Far from indelible, however, the racial music categories of the 20th century can largely be traced back to the twin emergence of southern segregation and the phonograph industry.

Thomas Edison invented the phonograph in the year of the Compromise of 1877. The commercial market for musical recordings matured alongside white southerners' development of a legal system of racial segregation. The commercial recording industry maintained a complex relationship with Jim Crow segregation, which echoed throughout the 20th century and beyond.

Some music had developed racial connotations before the advent of sound recording, of course. People of African descent in slavery and freedom had used music—from the spirituals and the ring shout to field hollers and the additive rhythms of Congo Square in New Orleans—to forge a collective identity, to signify a common history, or to express a shared condition. White southerners likewise used music—including European-derived art music and, beginning in the 1830s, blackface minstrelsy—to express an ever-changing white identity. Yet black and white southerners never limited themselves to making or enjoying music that expressed their own racial identities, no matter how important and vibrant those traditions were. Southerners partook of the vast array of music available to them, and they did so for a variety of reasons, including to express themselves, to imagine themselves part of a larger, perhaps better world, or simply to feel pleasure. Southerners' musical lives were never constrained by the racial categories that have come to represent them.

The advent and spread of phonograph recordings changed the ways in which many understood the relationship between music and race. Records enabled the separation of music from musicians. Disembodied sounds floated free from their source. Ultimately, this separation led many commentators and consumers to ascribe racial and regional identities to sounds themselves rather than to the people who made them. In the early years of the phonograph business, a time when black performers largely were barred from recording, this division facilitated a thriving market for white performers' renditions of what they claimed to be "Negro" music. The industry promoted minstrel ditties, spirituals, and blues recorded by white singers as genuine black music. Black artists successfully challenged industry segregation and minstrelsy in the 1920s by insisting on the correspondence between racial sounds and racial bodies. Black music was made best by black people.

The resulting "race records" market was a boon to African American artists and consumers. For the first time, music by black Americans was widely commercially available on record. At the same time, however, the new configuration reversed previous conceptions of the relationship between race and music. Phonograph companies insisted that African American performers only record what the industry considered to be black music. This resulted in wonderful and important blues and jazz recordings, but black artists often were barred from recording other parts of their repertoires, such as pop songs, Broadway hits, classical selections, or folk songs. A similar process occurred with the marketing of white southern recording artists. Long engaged with the wide variety of music echoing through the nation, they were marketed as "hillbilly" or "old-time" singers.

The segregated marketing of "race" and "hillbilly" music did little to represent the vibrant, complex, interregional everyday world of southern music. It did, however, correspond to the new concepts of racial distance and separation that white citizens were promoting in the Jim Crow South. It also provided the template for categorizing and marketing southern music according to race for the rest of the 20th century.

KARL HAGSTROM MILLER
University of Texas at Austin

Karl Hagstrom Miller, *Segregating Sound: Inventing Folk and Pop in the Age of Jim Crow* (2010); Tony Russell, *Blacks, Whites, and Blues* (1970); Elijah Wald, *Escaping the Delta: Robert Johnson and the Invention of the Blues* (2004).

Native American Removal, 1800–1840

When the invention of the cotton gin made upland cotton a viable cash crop for thousands of Upcountry settlers, Georgia and the territory that became the states of Mississippi and Alabama were home to 32,800 first people, 53,400 free people, and 30,000 enslaved people. By 1840, when the first postremoval censuses were taken, the same region was home to 922,000 free people and 737,000 enslaved people. Census takers failed to note any remaining Cherokees, Creeks, Choctaws, and Chickasaws because nearly all of them had been expelled from the region during the previous decade.

Why would state and federal governments forcibly expel people whose ancestors had inhabited the land for millennia? President Andrew Jackson had advocated removal since his days as the commander of the Tennessee militia in the Creek Civil War and cited the threat that so-called Indians posed to settler society as well as the incompatibility of the two cultures. Rather than await what everyone expected to be their inevitable extinction, Jackson believed that the federal government had to remove the indigenous people to the West where they could perpetuate their "race." Despite considerable opposition to the proposal in both houses, Jackson garnered enough congressional support to see the measure pass, and he signed the Indian Removal Act on 29 May 1830.

Choctaws were the first to experience removal under the auspices of the Indian Removal Act, and subsequent treaties with the Creeks in 1832, the Chickasaws in 1834, and the Cherokees in 1835 secured the removal of those nations and the cession of their land. All told, the federal and state governments expelled just more than 50,000 people from their homelands, some in chains, others at gunpoint, and acquired almost 30 million acres of land for settlement, taxation, and development. In the ongoing construction of a society whose citizens saw the world in terms of white freedom and black slavery, there was simply no place for "Indians."

The federal government kept no systematic records of the removals, so it is difficult to ascertain how many people died. Perhaps a third of removed Choctaws perished, while the tally of 4,000 Cherokee deaths on the Trail of Tears, one quarter of the total number of Cherokees removed, is a likely estimate. Perhaps 10,000 Cherokees who would have lived or been born had removal not occurred were wiped from the face of the earth. Such death tolls must also be understood in the context of the loss of land. Indeed, for Choctaws, separation from their homeland meant for them death, and Choctaw conceptions of the West as a place where spirits were lost only compounded their misery, sense of loss, and despair for the future. One of their leaders, a man named George Washington Harkins, understood all of this. As he departed his homeland, his mother earth, on a steamer bound for Fort Smith, Ark., he mourned the total destruction of his people's world. "We found ourselves," he wrote from the ship's railing, "like a benighted stranger, following false guides until surrounded by fire and water—the fire is certain destruction, and a feeble hope was left of escaping by water."

For the Mississippi House Indian committee, however, the removals, the deaths, and the despair augured a new beginning, "the dawn of an era . . . when . . . this state would emerge from obscurity, and justifiably assume an equal character with her sister states of the Union." Indeed, to the United States, the removals were a triumph. Land had been opened for settlement, the "Indians" had been saved, and the unrelenting expansion into the West could continue unabated. But what did the South lose with the removals? Were the removals acts of ethnic cleansing akin to what happened in the Balkans in the late 20th century? And why are not "Indians" remembered in the same way that the slaves and planters of the early 19th century South are? Is it because they were removed from our memories as well? Such questions suggest that even today we have failed to come to grips with what removal meant to the South then and what it means to the South today.

JAMES TAYLOR CARSON
Queens University

Donna Akers, *American Indian Culture and Research Journal* (1999); James Taylor Carson, *Searching for the Bright Path: The Mississippi Choctaws from Prehistory to Removal* (1999); Michael D. Green, *Politics of Indian Removal: Creek Government and Society in Crisis* (1982); Lucy Maddox, *Removals: Nineteenth-Century American Literature and the Politics of Indian Affairs* (1991); Ronald Satz, *American Indian Policy in the Jacksonian Era* (1975); Russell Thornton, in *Cherokee Removal: Before and After*, ed. William L. Anderson (1991).

Native Americans and African Americans

Native peoples in the South and African newcomers to North America first encountered one another at least by the early 16th century when Africans traveled through the indigenous Southeast with Spanish explorer Hernando de Soto. De Soto's ruthless 1539–40 expedition in which he pillaged for gold and Indian slaves included more than 600 soldiers, some of whom were enslaved blacks. In the wealthy Mississippian chiefdom of Cofitachequi (present-day South Carolina), the de Soto party met a woman chief known thereafter as "the Lady of Cofitachequi." Draped in a fine white fabric, the Lady was carried on a litter and transported in a decorative canoe by slaves from another indigenous group. De Soto and his men plundered pearls, desecrated the temple, and took the Lady captive. She escaped into the woods with a cache of recovered pearls and later encountered a group of enslaved, Spanish-speaking soldiers who had also stolen away from de Soto's party. The Lady of Cofitachequi partnered with a black man from this group in perhaps the first recorded example of Native American and African (American) marriage. The layered context of their coupling—European invasion, greed, violence, multinational slavery, and the quest for freedom and belonging—would also influence Native American and black relations to come.

A century after this encounter, hundreds of "charter generation" Africans arrived on slave ships to labor in European colonies. When Africans first appeared at the side of Europeans on Atlantic shorelines or in newly established frontier settlements in Virginia or Carolina, speaking European languages and wearing European clothing, they would have been grouped with Europeans by Native American observers who drew lines of distinction around cultural practice rather than race. Not until the early 1700s for tribes that traded most heavily with Europeans, and the late 1700s for geographically isolated tribes, did Native people witness and absorb the organizing principle of racialized chattel slavery. As the English held a growing number of dark-skinned Africans in permanent and inheritable chattel bondage, Native people could not help but recognize race as a marker of difference that mattered.

Concurrent with the importation of black slaves was the rise of an Indian slave trade in the middle and late 1600s. Southern Indians had long taken captive members of enemy Native groups and kept those who were not adopted or ritually murdered as slaves. However, the scale and purpose of Indian slavery shifted as European colonists sought capital to finance plantations through the sale of human beings, as well as an inexpensive labor force with which to derive value from usurped Native lands. European planters incentivized and coerced Indians to sell captives taken in intertribal conflicts. In order to ensure their supply of highly valued trade goods and to protect their own communities from attack, groups like the Westos and the Chickasaws engaged in slaving raids to provide captives to the English. As the European quest for slaves mushroomed, the Indian slave trade enveloped most southern nations, catapulting them into excessive intergroup conflict, population loss, forced migration, and retrenchment as confederacies. At the same time that an African diaspora was being forged through the dispersal of enslaved blacks, an "American diaspora" was being shaped through the dispersal of enslaved Native Americans.

Many of these Indian slaves were sold to the Caribbean, Europe, and New England; some were sold to the Upper South, and the minority was retained in the Lower South. Charles Town was the main location for the sale of both black and Indian slaves, who stood on the same auction blocks and traversed the Atlantic on the same ships. As blacks and Indians were both ensnared in the changing dynamics of human slavery, the merger of lives, communities, and cultures followed. Intermarriage between blacks and American Indians took place on southern plantations, as evidenced by descriptions of mixed-race runaway slaves in colonial newspaper advertisements. In addition to intermarriage, shared circumstances of enslavement led to the exchange and re-creation of cultural forms. African concepts of place, holistic spirituality, respect for ancestors, and the oral tradition corresponded with Native American notions, thereby facilitating this process. Cultural practices that reflect black and Native comingling in the South include a corn-based Indian diet that influenced black "soul food," the augmentation of black women's basket-weaving skills with Native patterns and plant preferences, black men's dugout canoe building learned from Indian companions, cross-cultural influences in Colonoware pottery recovered by archaeologists in Indian towns and on Virginia and South Carolina plantations, plant use as herbal medicines and gourd use as containers, and trickster rabbit story traditions that share character, theme, and plot connections.

Small but noteworthy numbers of free and runaway blacks moved through Native communities in the 1700s. They did so at first as cultural and familial outsiders. Because blacks lacked kinship ties, they were treated as foreigners and held at a distance until or unless they established connections. Such ties were most successfully based in kinship relationships through intermarriage or adoption into Native clans. However, Africans without demonstrable links to Native communities could face suspicion, exclusion, and harsh treatment, as did any uninvited outsider. While one "Negro Fellow" who sought to trade with the Catawbas was met with anger in the 1750s, another "free Negro . . . live[d] among the Catawbas, and [was] received by them as a Catawba, that [spoke] both their language and English, very well." In these early years of black and Native interaction, race was not a distinguishable factor. Native people instead determined how they would relate to Africans on a case-by-case basis, depending on circumstance, cultural dictates, and mutual need. Blacks seeking free spaces and better lives would also have assessed the Native people they encountered with discernment.

Native slavery decreased after 1720 and was gradually outlawed in the southern colonies by the mid- to late 1700s. But even as the Indian slave trade faded and the importation of Africans skyrocketed, Native people remained aware of the threat of the Euro-Americans' expanding race-based plantation regime. Witnesses to and previous victims of the brutality of chattel slavery reserved for dark-skinned peoples, Native Americans feared the continuing seizure of their lands and also being grouped with "a great 'colored' underclass." The major southern tribes that survived the "shatter zone" of the Indian slave trade and consolidated their peoples—the Cherokees, Creeks, Choctaws, and Chickasaws—began to draw their own color lines and practice race slavery by the turn of the 19th century.

The outcome of the American Revolutionary War, in which the major southern tribes had aided the British, placed increased pressure on these nations to adopt white American ways of life, including race slavery. As U.S. representatives pushed "civilization" and urged Indian men to give up hunting and turn to agriculture, they also modeled and encouraged black slave ownership. The first treaties negotiated with the Cherokees, Choctaws, and Chickasaws after the war took place on the Hopewell plantation of Brig. Gen. Andrew Pickens in 1785–86. With black slaves in the background presenting a cautionary contrast, Indians were assured that the Continental Congress would promote their welfare "regardless of any distinction of colour." After the Hopewell treaties had secured large land cessions, Benjamin Hawkins, U.S. agent for southern Indian affairs, developed a model plantation complete with black slaves.

By the early 1800s, minorities within the Cherokee, Choctaw, Chickasaw, and Creek nations held black slaves on small farms and large plantations. Native slaveholders sometimes inherited blacks from white fathers, held blacks taken in the Revolutionary War, and traded for blacks in Indian towns and southern cities. Native governments sanctioned slavery and black political exclusion, and prohibitions against intermarriage developed in the Cherokee and Creek nations in the 1820s. Nevertheless, intimate relations across the color line persisted in slaveholding Indian nations. Some of these couplings were engaged in by choice; others were coerced or forced. The experience of blacks owned by Indians differed depending on circumstance but in many ways echoed that of slaves in the white South. Blacks enslaved by Native people resisted in various ways, including escape. Those who remained in Indian bondage learned Native languages, prepared Indian foods, and wore Indian dress. Native slaveholders' dependence on black slaves' linguistic and interpretive skills in missionary, trading, and treaty negotiation contexts is widely documented and distinguishes black slavery in Indian locales.

Among the large slaveholding tribes, the Seminoles were exceptional. They were themselves a nation made up of survivors—runaways and refugees of various Indian groups, particularly Creek minorities. Rather than adopting chattel slavery, Seminoles created a system that borrowed from older Native chiefdom models of central and dependent towns. Aware of the uniqueness of Seminole views, black slaves fled to Florida and established towns of their own within Seminole territory. With an estimated population of 800 in 1822, Seminole maroon communities thrived, paying a required tribute in crops to powerful Seminole towns. While black Seminoles were not formally free, they lived lives characterized by relative autonomy and mobility. Interracial marriage between blacks and Seminoles occurred but was not the norm, as social life focused within rather than across the settlements. Black headmen emerged not only as leaders of black Seminole towns but also as go-betweens, and black male interpreters served in diplomatic talks between the Seminoles and the United States. In the First and Second Seminole Wars (1817–18, 1835–42), waged with the United States over Florida lands, black Seminoles fought alongside Seminoles, who in turn protected them from being returned to slavery in the states. Maj. Gen. Thomas Jesup's warning to the secretary of war—"The two races, the negro and the Indian, are rapidly approximating; they are identified in interests and feeling"—captured the strength of the alliance as well as the anxiety it caused. The alliance faltered, however, when Jesup offered freedom to black Seminoles if they abandoned the resistance movement and immigrated to Indian Territory. After Seminole removal, bands of Seminoles and black Seminoles led by former warriors Wildcat and John Cavallo (Horse) continued the alliance and departed Indian Territory for Mexico together. However, relations as a whole deteriorated in the West, and the interdependent chiefdom system was not restored.

Following the Indian removal period of the 1830s and 1840s, Native Americans and African Americans in the South came into significant contact at Hampton Institute in Virginia. A black industrial school by design, Hampton became a biracial institution and an early site of government-funded education for Indians at the start of the boarding-school era. Indians first entered Hampton in 1878, 10 years after the school's founding, when Capt. Richard Henry Pratt transported Plains tribes prisoners of war to study under the directorship of Hampton founder Samuel Chapman Armstrong. The goal of educating Native students at Hampton was civilizational and industrial training, as Indians were expected to learn habits of white society that would enable their cultural transformation and eventual assimilation. In 1879, when Hampton launched its Indian Program, Native students studied alongside blacks in a regimented, semisegregated setting that encouraged racial comparison and competition. School administrators imagined black students as willing workers because of the legacy of slavery, while they pictured Indians as wild, proud, and hostile to whites. Placed higher on a projected scale of civilization, black students were expected to set an example of good cheer and hard work for Indians. Notions about black and Indian students at Hampton fluctuated, however, with each group being shifted on an ideological hierarchy of races. The Hampton Indian program ended in 1922, in large part owing to the loss of congressional funding in 1912 and a growing inability to recruit Indian students to attend a predominantly black institution at a low point in African American history.

Native American and African American interrelated cultural lives have been rich, complex, and varied. Brought together in the 1500s by European exploration, colonization, and slavery, thousands of Native Americans and African Americans came into intimate contact by circumscribed choice as well as duress. They forged familial, cultural, and political connections and engaged in intergroup conflicts that continue to reverberate. Together with whites, blacks and Indians were important, if often unwilling, partners in the forging of a new southern world.

TIYA MILES
University of Michigan

Ira Berlin, *Many Thousands Gone: The First Two Centuries of Slavery in North America* (1998); Kathryn E. Holland Braund, *Deerskins and Duffels: Creek Indian Trade with Anglo-America, 1685–1815* (1993); Jonathan Brennan, ed., *When Brer Rabbit Meets Coyote: African–Native American Literature* (2003); Chester B. Depratter, in *The Forgotten Centuries: Indians and Europeans in the American South, 1521–1704*, ed. Charles Hudson and Carmen Chaves Tesser (1994); Robbie Ethridge and Sheri M. Shuck-Hall, eds., *Mapping the Mississippian Shatter Zone: The Colonial Indian Slave Trade and Regional Instability in the American South* (2009); Jack D. Forbes, *Africans and Native Americans: The Language of Race and the Evolution of Red-Black Peoples* (1993); Thomas Foster, ed., *The Collected Works of Benjamin Hawkins, 1796–1810* (2003); Alan Gallay, *The Indian Slave Trade: The Rise of the English Empire in the American South, 1670–1717* (2002), ed., *Indian Slavery in Colonial America* (2009); Charles Hudson, *Knights of Spain, Warriors of the Sun: Hernando de Soto and the South's Ancient Chiefdoms* (1997), *The Southeastern Indians* (1976); Barbara Krauthamer, in *New Studies in the History of American Slavery*, ed. Edward E. Baptist and Stephanie M. H. Camp (2006); Almon Wheeler Lauber, *Indian Slavery in Colonial Times within the Present Limits of the United States* (1970); Donal F. Lindsey, *Indians at Hampton Institute, 1877–1923* (1995); James H. Merrell, *Journal of Southern History* (August 1984); Tiya Miles, *The House on Diamond Hill: A Cherokee Plantation Story* (2010), *Ties That Bind: The Story of an Afro-Cherokee Family in Slavery and Freedom* (2005); Patrick Minges, *Black Indian Slave Narratives* (2004); Kevin Mulroy, *Freedom on the Border: The Seminole Maroons in Florida, the Indian Territory, Coahuila, and Texas* (1993); Celia Naylor, *African Cherokees in Indian Territory: From Chattel to Citizens* (2007); Greg O'Brien, ed., *Pre-removal Choctaw History: Exploring New Paths* (2008); Theda Perdue, *Ethnohistory* (Fall 2004), *Slavery and the Evolution of Cherokee*

Society, 1540–1866 (1979); Theda Perdue and Michael D. Green, eds., *The Columbia Guide to American Indians of the Southeast* (2001); Kenneth W. Porter, *The Black Seminoles: History of a Freedom-Seeking People* (1996); Claudio Saunt, *Black, White, and Indian: Race and the Unmaking of an American Family* (2005), in *Confounding the Color Line: The Indian-Black Experience in North America*, ed. James F. Brooks (2002); Claudio Saunt et al., *Ethnohistory* (Spring 2006); Theresa A. Singleton, ed., *I, Too, Am America: Archaeological Studies of African-American Life* (1999); Christina Snyder, *Slavery in Indian Country: The Changing Face of Captivity in Early America* (2010); Gabrielle Tayac, in *Documents of United States Indian Policy*, ed. Francis Paul Prucha (1975; 1990), ed., *IndiVisible: African–Native American Lives* (2009); Peter H. Wood, *Black Majority: Negroes in Colonial South Carolina from 1670 through the Stono Rebellion* (1974); J. Leitch Wright, *The Only Land They Knew: The Tragic Story of the American Indians in the Old South* (1981); Gary Zellar, *African Creeks: Estelvste and the Creek Nation* (2007).

Pacific Worlds and the South

Often depicted as isolated and xenophobic, at least in relation to other parts of the United States, the American South at first glance appears to have little relevance to lands and peoples across the Pacific. But the South's transpacific connections run deep. And it is through those connections forged by empire and capital that Asians have arrived in the South (and the Americas in general). Indeed, within the field of Asian American Studies, the South is where that history first took root. When the Spanish claimed the Americas and the Philippines in the 16th century, they envisioned and pursued an imperial world of mercantile capitalism, including the galleon trade plying between Manila and Acapulco. It was not uncommon for Filipino sailors, who had been impressed to work on the galleons, to jump ship in Mexico. Possibly as early as the 1760s, when the Spanish Crown ruled over Louisiana, some of these sailors sought refuge in St. Bernard Parish, establishing perhaps the oldest Asian American community in the present United States.

As the example of Louisiana's Manilamen, as they would be called, suggests, the South was not always what it has become (or, more precisely, what it has come to represent)—a region within the United States, usually defined by its distinctly biracial (black-white) history. The Spanish, French, British, and American empires have laid claims to different parts of southeastern North America, making it, at varying points, the northern, eastern, western, or southern node in wider imperial formations. (Our geohistorical groundings would become more unsettled if we were to include the perspectives of American Indians.) Exploring how and why Asians have come to call the South home, if only temporarily at times, compels us to contend with these larger histories, to see the South's imbrication in national and global developments that were never simply black and white, North and South, or West and East.

New Orleans, the Old South's leading port city, and the surrounding sugar parishes constituted the southern hub of ideas and movements concerning Asia and Asians in the 19th century. For proslavery ideologues like J. D. B. De Bow, Asia and Asians were very much at the heart of struggles over American slavery. Observing the transport of thousands of indentured Asian workers to British, Spanish, and French colonies of the Caribbean in the 1840s and 1850s, the influential journalist of New Orleans denounced what he saw as the hypocrisy of abolitionism. "The civilized and powerful races of the earth have discovered that the degraded, barbarous, and weak races may be induced *voluntarily* to reduce themselves to a slavery more cruel than any that has yet disgraced the earth," De Bow concluded, "and that humanity may compound with its conscience, by pleading that the act is one of *free will*." If condemning their Caribbean neighbors' resort to Asian workers helped to justify American slavery, the Civil War and its aftermath drew southern planters' eyes increasingly to Asia and the Caribbean. "Those pent-up millions of Asia want room, want food, want the opportunity to work," a southern champion of Chinese labor argued in 1868; "we, in the Valley of the Mississippi, want labor; we must have it; we have farms for millions, work for tens of millions."

With the onset of Radical Reconstruction, southern planters' fascination with Asian workers as a potential alternative to black labor reached a feverish pitch, enough to generate a mass regional convention in Memphis, Tenn., in July 1869. In both the South and the Caribbean, a leading organizer of the meeting stated, "experience taught that the great staples could not be produced by voluntary labor, but under coerced labor systematized and overlooked by intelligence . . . labor that the owner of the soil can control." He and many of the delegates clamored openly for a new form of slavery, labor "which you can control and manage to some extent as of old." With discussions on labor conditions in the Caribbean, Hawaii, California, and elsewhere, the Memphis convention also conveyed the New South's worldly (and imperial) ambitions. Its delegates resolved to form the Mississippi Valley Immigration Labor Company to bring "into the country the largest number of Chinese agricultural laborers in the shortest possible time," with an invitation to "capitalists and planters" everywhere to purchase stocks. It was a resolution and a movement simultaneously to revive slavery and to modernize the South.

Such brash talk of recruiting "coerced" workers from Asia generated vehement opposition from two seemingly dissimilar sources, reflective of intensifying battles over Reconstruction and Chinese migration. Fearful of southern white designs to thwart recent political advances, prominent abolitionists and Republicans objected to what Frederick Douglass called "the selfish inventions and dreams of men!" Immediately after the Memphis convention, Secretary of the Treasury George S. Boutwell instructed the New Orleans collector of customs "to use all vigilance in the suppression of this new modification of the Slave Trade." The growing ranks of dispossessed whites in the South likewise rejected the prospect of Asian workers flooding the region, not for humanity's sake but for their own salvation. "We will have again a fat and pampered aristocracy, worse than it ever was, and far more haughty and overbearing," an anti-planter editorial declared. "It will then be 'how many Coolies does he work?' instead of 'how many negroes does he own?' so commonly used *ante bellum*." Echoing anti-Chinese rancor on the Pacific Coast, many southern whites articulated and translated their critique of monopoly capital in racial terms.

These local, national, and global forces firmly linked Asian workers with slavery in American culture and, in turn, steered thousands of Chinese migrants to the South, especially Louisiana, in the 1860s and 1870s. Largely restricted to the richest planters, who could afford the high costs of recruitment and shipment, a coterie of southerners, targets of fanfare and optimism as much as of chagrin and scorn, pursued Chinese workers on imperial routes crisscrossing the globe—from Cuba, China, Martinique, and, increasingly after the completion of the transcontinental railroad in 1869, California. "Physically they are fine specimens, bright and intelligent," the *New Orleans Times* rejoiced, "and coming, as they do, from the low districts of China, within the tropics, there is nothing to be apprehended on the score of climate." But Chinese migrants failed to solve planters' labor "problems," for they behaved no differently than black workers. Planter after planter drew the same conclusion—the Chinese were "fond of changing about, run away worse than negroes, and . . . leave as soon as anybody offers them higher wages," as a newspaper put it—even as they ironically and continually lured Chinese workers away from their neighbors' estates, with the hope of stabilizing their labor force.

As Chinese workers ran away to various plantations, to small towns and larger cities, and to California and elsewhere, they seemed to vanish from the South as fast as they had appeared. Outside the public eye, however, many Chinese migrants formed families and communities, with one another and with local peoples. They made the South their home. In Natchitoches Parish, La., for example, Chinese men established families with black, white, Creole, and American Indian women, whose progeny have continued to recognize (and at times vehemently deny) their Chinese ancestry for generations. U.S. census records failed to capture their diverse histories though. In 1880, the multiracial children of Chinese migrants were categorized as "Chinese," but within two decades, amid the onslaught of Jim Crow laws, those same individuals were reclassified as either "black" or "white." Later on, some embraced their "Mexican" identity, a classification that enabled them to straddle the hardening color line. In contrast to their forebears, who were in demand as plantation workers precisely because they were neither black nor white, most descendants of Chinese migrants were compelled to identify as either black or white in the 20th century.

As in other regions of the United States, Asian Americans in general had no choice in racial matters. The state decided for them. Born and raised in the segregated world of Mississippi, Martha Lum and her parents attempted to enroll her in the all-white Rosedale Consolidated High School in 1924. Readily admitting that their client was not white, Lum's lawyers simultaneously insisted that she was not "colored," which, they argued, had been defined historically as persons with "negro blood." Placing the "Mongolian" apart from the "colored" and next to the "Caucasian," Lum's appeal to the U.S. Supreme Court rested on doubling (and troubling) claims of racial discrimination. "The white race may not legally expose the yellow race to a danger that the dominant race recognizes and, by the same laws, guards itself against," Lum's lawyers pleaded. "This is discrimination." The highest courts of Mississippi and then the United States disagreed. Upholding *Plessy v. Ferguson* (1896) and other legal precedents on racial exclusion and segregation, they ruled that Lum "may attend the colored public schools of her district, or, if she does not so desire, she may go to a private school." She was indeed "colored."

U.S. military campaigns across the Pacific, which began in the 19th century and proliferated in the 20th century, have driven new waves of Asians to the South. In the wake of U.S. entry into World War II, the federal government rounded up Japanese Americans living along the Pacific Coast and ordered them at gunpoint to embark on a trail of dispossession and misery eastward. Tens of thousands of them ended up in the South, incarcerated in concentration camps (in Rohwer and Jerome) in Arkansas and internment camps in Texas and Louisiana and inducted into a segregated military unit in Mississippi. "Being at Rohwer was just a lonely feeling that I can't explain," recalled Miyo Senzaki. "You couldn't run anywhere. It was scary because there was no end to it. You could run and run and run but where are you to go? . . . We felt like prisoners." Though victims of segregation before World War II, for many

Japanese Americans, including the legendary activist Yuri Kochiyama, it was in Arkansas and Mississippi that they awakened to a new political consciousness, a new awareness of white supremacy's reach and depth. Jim Crow in the concentrations camps, in the military, and in the surrounding southern landscape ruled their lives.

Three decades later, U.S. military intervention in Southeast Asia drove thousands of refugees to the South, a flow of Asian migrations created by the colossal U.S. military industrial complex and the living legacies of Spanish, Portuguese, and French colonialisms. Among the first to arrive in 1975 were Vietnamese Catholics, whose religious lineage dates back to Spanish and Portuguese colonizers of the 16th century and French colonial rule beginning in the 19th century. Deemed collaborators of French rule and then of the U.S. military by the Communist leaders of Vietnam, Vietnamese Catholics sought refuge for decades, first in southern Vietnam (after the decisive defeat of French troops in 1954) and then in the United States and elsewhere (upon the "fall" of Saigon in 1975). These refugees were first flown to Guam and the Philippines and then to four military bases on the U.S. mainland, including Camp Chafee in Arkansas and Elgin Air Force Base in Florida, from which volunteer organizations sponsored them for resettlement across the United States. Thousands of Vietnamese refugees accepted an open invitation from the head of the New Orleans archdiocese, finding a refuge, a new home, in a Catholic city, not far from where the Manilamen had landed two centuries earlier.

Vietnamese refugees and their families were among those devastated by Hurricane Katrina in 2005, a storm that pushed race to the fore of U.S. politics, albeit framed almost universally in black and white. Largely below the media radar, racial dynamics in the Village de L'Est neighborhood of New Orleans were radically different. With mass white flight since the 1960s, it was a neighborhood made up almost completely of blacks and Vietnamese. In Katrina's aftermath, both Vietnamese and black residents returned much earlier and in larger numbers than anticipated or desired by city, state, and federal officials. Almost immediately upon their return, they encountered a new threat nearby, in the form of a makeshift landfill ordered into existence by Mayor C. Ray Nagin. With support from the Southern Christian Leadership Conference, Martin Luther King Jr.'s organization, the Southern Poverty Law Center, and other civil rights groups, local residents mobilized successfully to shut it down. "The landfill struggle, everything we're fighting for out here—this is about the Vietnamese and the blacks together," a Vietnamese American organizer stated. Village de L'Est is a neighborhood not devoid of racial tensions and conflicts, but, like many rural and urban pockets across the South today, it is a place of complex memories and histories, a place that growing numbers of Asian Americans are calling home.

MOON-HO JUNG
University of Washington

Leslie Bow, *Partly Colored: Asian Americans and Racial Anomaly in the Segre-gated South* (2010); Sucheng Chan, *Asian Americans: An Interpretive History* (1991); Lucy M. Cohen, *Chinese in the Post–Civil War South: A People without a History* (1984); Marina E. Espina, *Filipinos in Louisiana* (1988); Diane C. Fujino, *Heartbeat of Struggle: The Revolutionary Life of Yuri Kochiyama* (2005); *Gong Lum et al. v. Rice et al.*, 275 U.S. 78 (1927); Moon-Ho Jung, *Coolies and Cane: Race, Labor, and Sugar in the Age of Emancipation* (2006); Karen J. Leong et al., *Journal of American History* (December 2007); Gary Y. Okihiro, *Margins and Mainstreams: Asians in American History and Culture* (1994); *Rice et al. v. Gong Lum et al.*, 139 Mississippi 760 (1925); Eric Tang, *American Quarterly* (March 2011); John Tateishi, ed., *And Justice for All: An Oral History of Japanese American Detention Camps* (1999).

Racial Terror and Citizenship

"There is a perfect reign of terror existing in the several counties, so much so that I cannot do justice to the subject," wrote an official with the U.S. Bu-reau of Refugees, Freedmen, and Abandoned Lands in 1866. The phrase this superintendent chose to characterize the late-night home invasions, plunder, murder, and rape being carried out by a vigilante gang of white men against former slaves in his region of Tennessee — "a perfect reign of terror" — appeared repeatedly in official descriptions of similar white-on-black violence that oc-curred across the South after the Civil War. This violence was generally well planned and carried a clear political message: regardless of their new status as free people, African Americans would not be permitted to exercise the rights of citizenship. It also initiated patterns of racial and political violence that en-dured across the South well into the 20th century.

During Reconstruction, former slaves seized opportunities for political par-ticipation, while the federal government — through legislation and the Four-teenth and Fifteenth Amendments — recognized them as citizens and guaran-teed the right to vote without regard to race. Active black citizenship, though, upended a southern antebellum political culture wherein a voice in public af-fairs had been the exclusive privilege of white men. Black male suffrage threat-ened not only white men's control over politics but also the significance of their whiteness, which had previously depended on a clear distinction between white "freemen" and black slaves. Violent white reactions to the challenges posed by emancipation began immediately after the war, when bands of white men roamed rural areas of the South, disarming black Union soldiers, stealing freedpeople's property, and threatening and often killing black community leaders. The "reign of terror" also included "riots"—in fact, premeditated massacres of freedpeople—in cities such as Memphis and New Orleans. It was repeated scenes of such violence in the former Confederacy that convinced many northern white Republicans to support federal protection of black rights in the South, and specifically suffrage. Yet as the resultant federal law took effect in the late 1860s, white-on-black violence only spread into widening realms.

At this time, vigilante gangs began wearing disguises and calling themselves the Ku Klux Klan. The Reconstruction-era Klan, though, was far less a centralized organization than a label used by disparate white gangs across the South who sought the anonymity offered by Klan-style practices. Attacks by these disguised bands followed a common pattern. Late at night, masked men surrounded freedpeople's homes, dragged their victims outside, plundered their belongings, and stripped, beat, whipped, raped, or murdered them. White vigilantes also subjected many to scenes of racial and sexual submission. Through their words and deeds, assailants compelled their victims to enact a return to a pre-emancipation racial order, that is, one in which black men were rendered incapable of protecting their families and black women were obliged to provide white men with sex on demand. In effect, assailants attempted to impose upon black men and women their putative unsuitability for citizenship by forcing them to perform dishonorable masculine and feminine roles.

Many African Americans responded to Klanlike attacks by participating in local militias to protect their communities from violence. Especially in rural areas where African Americans were in the minority, though, the power of terrorist gangs frequently overwhelmed local law enforcement. Indeed, some gangs included police officials as members. Some Reconstruction-era governors imposed martial law to put down the Klan, but in most states only federal action was effective in stopping the violence. In 1870–71, the Enforcement Acts made violence or intimidation with the intent of impeding voting a federal offense, allowing the federal government to oversee elections and to arrest Klan members. Under these acts, hundreds were prosecuted. Although few served significant jail time, Klanlike vigilante terrorist groups were effectively ended for the time being. Suppressing the violence led to an impressive expansion of black political participation between 1872 and 1874.

This high point in black political power, though, also marked the beginning of the next round of terrorist violence in the South, as armed auxiliaries of the Democratic Party mounted new campaigns to push African Americans out of the political process. African Americans organized in self-defense but were usually out-armed and out-numbered, and hundreds were killed in clashes during the mid-1870s. In summer 1876, a federal official again used the familiar phrase "a perfect reign of terror" to describe the violence in one region of South Carolina. But this time attackers operated in the open, emboldened by an apparent federal retreat from backing African Americans' rights in the South. This retreat was evident when, in *United States v. Cruikshank et al.* (1876), the Supreme Court overturned convictions under the Enforcement Acts, arguing that the federal government had authority only over actions taken by states, not individuals. Thereafter, the power to police vigilante violence returned to state governments, which were now all under Democratic control and often complicit in terror.

With the alliance between African Americans and northern white political leaders that had made possible the Reconstruction era's dramatic revolution in citizenship now ended, the threat of violence rather than the force of law would regulate the exercise of political power in the South for decades to come. Not until the 1960s did renewed federal attention drive white terror underground, from where assailants nonetheless carried out plans to bomb black churches and to kidnap and murder civil rights activists. White violence thus effectively barred African Americans from the citizenship they had sought, and had momentarily enjoyed, after emancipation until the civil rights movement's successes a century later.

HANNAH ROSEN
University of Michigan

Jane Dailey, *Before Jim Crow: The Politics of Race in Postemancipation Virginia* (2000); Eric Foner, *Reconstruction: America's Unfinished Revolution* (1988); Glenda Elizabeth Gilmore, *Gender and Jim Crow: Women and the Politics of White Supremacy in North Carolina, 1896–1920* (1996); Steven Hahn, *A Nation under Our Feet: Black Political Struggles in the Rural South from Slavery to the Great Migration* (2003); Stephen Kantrowitz, *Ben Tillman and the Reconstruction of White Supremacy* (2000); Hannah Rosen, *Terror in the Heart of Freedom: Citizenship, Sexual Violence, and the Meaning of Race in the Postemancipation South* (2009); Allen W. Trelease, *White Terror: The Ku Klux Klan Conspiracy and Southern Reconstruction* (1971).

Racial Uplift

Racial uplift is an African American ideology that had its greatest impact in response to the increasing oppression blacks faced between 1880 and World War I. Earlier versions of its concern for achieving social respectability in the eyes of whites appeared in the North before the Civil War, among free blacks trying to claim their rights. The end of slavery and the gaining of freedom for southern slaves led to an optimistic period for African Americans during Reconstruction. But the frustration that came afterward with Jim Crow segregation laws, disfranchisement, economic marginalization, bigoted and crude representations in American culture, and racial violence led to a variety of efforts to counter white racism, with leaders advocating for public protest, migration, industrial education, or higher education. In this context, the black middle class embraced the idea of uplift, a belief that advocates who called themselves the "better classes" should nurture black respectability as a way toward social advancement. This outlook called for black elites to assume responsibility for working with the black masses to encourage them to follow middle-class values of temperance, hard work, thrift, perseverance, and Victorian-era sexual self-restraint. The expectation was that as most blacks came to practice middle-class virtues, they would earn the esteem of white America.

The ideology countered antiblack stereotypes by stressing class differences among African Americans, with black elites the symbols of racial progress. Its advocates demanded recognition by white elites of the role of black elites as torchbearers for "civilization" and "progress." This approach encouraged intraracial class tensions and overlooked the deeply racialized categories of civilization and progress in the age of empire and the "white man's burden." By endorsing the idea of backward black masses, racial uplift ironically seemed to endorse the white racist representations of blacks. In the realm of culture, racial uplift endorsed Western European forms of music. The Fisk Jubilee Singers, for example, converted the folk spirituals of slavery into a choral style that would appeal to white audiences as they toured the nation and Europe itself. Black middle classes disliked, in turn, the raw emotions of blues music and black gospel music, seeing them as survivals from a primitive age of black culture. Black elites did not appreciate ways that black folk culture offered individual psychological resources and communal social class cohesion to counter the trauma of white racism.

The ideology was firmly patriarchal in its assumption that male-headed families should be the norm, with male authority sometimes taken for granted, although black women leaders often challenged this latter assumption. African American women, in fact, were among the chief advocates for racial uplift and were responsible for some of its greatest achievements. The black Baptist Women's Convention Movement drew from an emergent middle class in the late 19th century of school administrators, journalists, businesswomen, and social reformers that served an all-black community in the age of Jim Crow.

Black religious women promoted bourgeois ideals as missionaries, teachers, and sometimes just as influential wives of ministers, all of which made them conveyers of culture to the larger black community. They also vocally attacked the nation's failure to live up to its ideals. One of the most prominent Black Baptist women leaders was Nannie Burroughs, who was the first president of the National Baptist Convention's National Training School for Women and Girls. She had introduced the idea for the school to the Women's Convention and stoked enthusiasm for it. "This is going to be the 'national dream' realized," she wrote, insisting that "a million women in our churches will make us have it." The convention's interest in the welfare of the working poor and its interest in employment possibilities after graduation led to founding the institution as an industrial school rather than a liberal arts college. Its motto was "Work. Support thyself. To thine own powers appeal." The school's founders saw productive labor as contributing to individual self-help and responsibility, but it also encouraged "race work," pride in racial identity and responsibility for the collective black community.

The Woman's Christian Temperance Union (WCTU) became a prime organizational context for African American women to promote the middle-class ideals of uplift. The image of the drunken husband and father had no innate racial component, but black women reformers saw how whites often represented that figure as a black man. They argued that alcohol had a pernicious effect not only on families but on the black community in general. They used the WCTU to show that black leaders were witnessing for temperance with dignity and industriousness, and that not all blacks failed to achieve this particular middle-class ideal. Working for temperance brought black women uplifters into collaborative work with white women, in a conspicuous example of interracial cooperation for the time period. White women saw black women, though, as junior partners in the collaboration, working in a segregated institution and reporting to white women. At a time when some African Americans were still able to vote, white women recognized the potential for recruiting black voters in temperance elections, encouraging this cross–racial line cooperation. Black women reformers had long worked through churches for temperance reform and resented the often-patronizing attitudes of white women. Still, black women saw in the WCTU the opportunity to build a Christian community that might serve as a model for interracial cooperation on other fronts, which could aid very tangibly the social needs of the black masses.

Black ministers were also among the most important and successful advocates for racial uplift. The ideology had roots in the communal religious activities of the slave community before the Civil War, and the New Testament ideal of community offered a specifically religious theology supporting the concept. The Christian image of the shepherd inspired black ministers as they rose in denominational hierarchies, and they affirmed the need to care for less-fortunate blacks and to inculcate the Protestant work ethic as an illustration of racial uplift ideals. The National Baptist Convention (NBC) supported both industrial education and higher education as vehicles for middle-class black aspirations, and both Booker T. Washington and W. E. B. Du Bois were often in attendance at the convention's activities. Black religious leadership of the era often reflected a Gilded Age success formula. Thomas Fuller, for example, the minister of a large Nashville congregation at the turn of the 20th century, preached a popular sermon, "Work Is the Law of Life," which projected an optimistic, self-help philosophy encouraging his hearers to success through hard work. Another black minister, Elias Camp Morris, was the first president of the NBC, beginning in 1895, and remained its leader for a quarter of a century. He urged blacks to support "the business side of the race" by patronizing black-owned businesses. He urged that there be no let-up "of our efforts to become taxpayers, owners of homes, and constructive builders of our own fortunes."

Although the racial uplift ideology had its limitations, it counted many solid achievements in terms of social improvements for African Americans at a time regarded as the nadir for black life in the South and the nation. Advocates worked through schools and colleges, civic and fraternal organizations, Social Gospel churches, settlement houses, newspapers, and trade unions to improve the life of black communities. The ideology failed, though, in its assumption that embracing middle-class values would overcome the disadvantages from American society's racist structures that stacked the deck against those very middle-class aspirations of African Americans.

CHARLES REAGAN WILSON
University of Mississippi

Kevin Gaines, *Uplifting the Race: Black Middle-Class Ideology and Leadership in the United States since 1890* (1996); Evelyn Brooks Higginbotham, *Righteous Discontent: The Women's Movement in the Black Baptist Church, 1880–1920* (1994); Angela Hornsby-Gutting, *Black Manhood and Community Building in North Carolina, 1900–1930* (2009); Karen Ann Johnson, *Uplifting the Women and the Race: The Educational Philosophies and Social Activism of Anna Julia Cooper and Nannie Helen Burroughs* (2000); Edward Wheeler, *Uplifting the Race: The Black Minister in the New South, 1865–1920* (1986).

Religion, Black

The religious life of the majority of black southerners originated in both traditional African religions and Anglo-Protestant evangelicalism. The influence of Africa was more muted in the United States than in Latin America, where African-derived theology and ritual were institutionalized in the communities of Brazilian Candomblé, Haitian Voodoo, and Cuban Santeria. Nevertheless, in the United States, as in Latin America, slaves did transmit to their descendants styles of worship, funeral customs, magical ritual, and medicinal practice based upon the religious systems of West and Central African societies.

Although some slaves in Maryland and Louisiana were baptized as Catholics, most had no contact with Catholicism and were first converted to Christianity in large numbers under the preaching of Baptist and Methodist revivalists in the late 18th century. The attractiveness of the evangelical revivals for slaves was due to several factors: the emotional behavior of revivalists encouraged the type of religious ecstasy similar to the danced religions of Africa; the antislavery stance taken by some Baptists and Methodists encouraged slaves to identify evangelicalism with emancipation; blacks actively participated in evangelical meetings and cofounded churches with white evangelicals; and evangelical churches licensed black men to preach.

By the 1780s, pioneer black preachers had already begun to minister to their own people in the South, and as time went on, black congregations, mainly Baptist in denomination, increased in size and in number, despite occasional harassment and proscription by the authorities. However, the majority of slaves in the antebellum South attended church, if at all, with whites.

Institutional church life was not the whole of religion for slaves. An "invisible institution" of secret and often forbidden religious meetings thrived in the slave quarters. Here slaves countered the slaveholding gospel of the master class with their own version of Christianity in which slavery and slaveholding stood condemned by God. Slaves took the biblical story of Exodus and applied it to their own history, asserting that they, like the children of Israel, would be liberated from bondage. In the experience of conversion, individual slaves affirmed their personal dignity and self-worth. In the ministry, black men exercised authority and achieved status nowhere else available to them. Melding African and Western European traditions, the slaves created a religion of great vitality.

Complementing Christianity in the quarters was conjure, a sophisticated combination of African herbal medicine and magic. Based on the belief that illness and misfortune have personal as well as impersonal causes, conjure offered frequently successful therapy for the mental and physical ills of genera-tions of African Americans and simultaneously served as a system for venting social tension and resolving conflict.

The Civil War, emancipation, and Reconstruction wrought an institutional transformation of black churches in the South. Northern denominations—black as well as white—sent aid to the freedmen and missionaries to educate and bring them to church. Freedmen, eager to learn to read and write, flocked to schools set up by the American Missionary Association and other freedmen's aid societies. These freedmen's schools laid the foundation for major black col-leges and universities such as Fisk, Morehouse, Dillard, and others. Eager to exercise autonomy, freedmen swarmed out of white churches and organized their own. Some affiliated with black denominations of northern origin; others formed their own southern associations.

Black ministers actively campaigned in Reconstruction politics and in some cases were elected to positions of influence and power. Richard H. Cain, for example, was elected to the U.S. House of Representatives from North Caro-lina and Hiram R. Revels was elected to the Senate from Mississippi. With the failure of Reconstruction and the disfranchisement of black southerners, the church once again became the sole forum for black politics, as well as the eco-nomic, social, and educational center of black communities across the South.

By the end of the century, black church membership stood at an astounding 2.7 million out of a population of 8.3 million. Most numerous were the Bap-tists, who succeeded in 1895 in creating a National Baptist Convention, fol-lowed numerically by the black Methodists, as institutionalized in the African Methodist Episcopal (AME) Church and the African Methodist Episcopal Zion Church, both founded in the North early in the century, and the Colored Meth-odist Episcopal Church, formed by an amicable withdrawal from the Methodist Episcopal Church, South, in 1870.

Though too poor to mount a full-fledged missionary campaign, the black churches turned to evangelization of Africa as a challenge to Afro-American Christian identity. The first black missionaries, David George and George Liele, had sailed during the Revolution, George to Nova Scotia and then to Sierra Leone, Liele to Jamaica. Daniel Coker followed in 1820 and Lott Carey and Colin Teague in 1821. But in the 1870s and 1880s, the mission to Africa seemed all the more urgent. As race relations worsened, as lynching mounted in fre-quency, as racism was legislated in Jim Crow statutes, emigration appeared to black clergy like Henry McNeal Turner to be the only solution. Others saw the redemption of Africa as the divinely appointed destiny of black Americans, God's plan for drawing good out of the evil of slavery and oppression.

Connections between southern black churches and northern ones developed as blacks from the South migrated or escaped north and as northern missionaries came to the South after the Civil War. Several southern blacks assumed positions of leadership in northern churches. Josiah Bishop, a Baptist preacher from Virginia, became pastor of the Abyssinian Baptist Church in New York, and Daniel Alexander Payne and Morris Brown, both of Charleston, became bishops of the AME Church. Beginning in the 1890s and increasing after the turn of the century, rural southern blacks migrated in larger and larger numbers to the cities of the North. Frequently, their ministers traveled with them and transplanted, often in storefront or house churches, congregations from the South.

In the cities, southern as well as northern, black migrants encountered new religious options that attracted some adherents from the traditional churches. Catholicism, through the influence of parochial schools, began attracting significant numbers of blacks in the 20th century. Black Muslims and Jews developed new religioracial identities for African Americans disillusioned with Christianity. The Holiness and Pentecostal churches stressed the experiential and ecstatic dimensions of worship while preaching the necessity of sanctification and the blessings of the Spirit. They also facilitated the development of gospel music by allowing the use of instruments and secular tunes in church services.

Though urbanization and secularization led to criticism of black religion as accommodationist and compensatory, the church remained the most important and effective public institution in southern black life. The religious culture of the black folk was celebrated by intellectuals like W. E. B. Du Bois and James Weldon Johnson, who acclaimed the artistry of the slave spirituals and black preaching.

In the late 1950s and 1960s, the civil rights movement drew heavily upon the institutional and ethical resources of the black churches across the South. Martin Luther King Jr. brought to the attention of the nation and the world the moral tradition of black religion. Today, black religion is more pluralistic than ever. Most African Americans continue to worship in predominantly black denominations, although they also form identifiable caucuses with biracial denominations. Black liberation theology associated with southern-born writers like James Cone and Pauli Murray has been an influence on some of the faithful for decades. Roman Catholics and Muslims include significant communities of African Americans in the South. Black religious leaders and laypeople continue to work for racial justice and to cooperate in racial reconciliation efforts in the South. Churches remain important political organizing sites and encourage political participation among their members. Although the church is no longer the only institution that blacks control, it still exerts considerable power in black communities.

ALBERT J. RABOTEAU
Princeton University

Hans A. Baer, *The Black Spiritual Movement: A Religious Response to Racism* (1984); Yvonne Chireau, *Black Magic: Dimensions of the Supernatural in African American Religion* (2000); James Cone, *For My People: Black Theology and the Black Church* (1984); W. E. B. Du Bois, *The Souls of Black Folk* (1903); Sylvia R. Frey and Betty Wood, *Come Shouting to Zion: African American Protestantism in the American South and British Caribbean to 1830* (1998); Samuel S. Hill, ed., *Religion in the Southern States: A Historical Study* (1983); C. Eric Lincoln, ed., *The Black Experience in Religion* (1974); Donald G. Mathews, *Religion in the Old South* (1977); William E. Montgomery, *Under Their Own Vine and Fig Tree: The African American Church in the South, 1865–1900* (1993); Albert J. Raboteau, *Canaan Land: A Religious History of African Americans* (1999), *Slave Religion: The "Invisible Institution" in the Antebellum South* (1978); Clarence Walker, *A Rock in a Weary Land: The African Methodist Episcopal Church during the Civil War and Reconstruction* (1982); James M. Washington, *Frustrated Fellowship: The Black Baptist Quest for Social Power* (1986); Joseph R. Washington, *Black Religion: The Negro and Christianity in the United States* (1964).

Religion, Latino

Specific forms of Latino Catholicism have a long historical trajectory in the geographic extremes of the South, but in the past decade Latino religion has become increasingly pervasive and varied throughout the region. Tejano (Mexican Texan) religion dates back to Mexico's ceding of Texas to the United States, which was completed with the Compromise of 1850. In the late 19th century, mestizos in the region, whose indigenous ancestors had been evangelized by Franciscans during Spanish military expeditions, identified as Catholic but had tenuous ties to the institutional church. As the U.S. Catholic Church assumed ecclesiastical control of the region, many factors hindered Tejano participation in the church: only a handful of functioning parishes already existed in the region; Tejanos had a long history of anticlericalism, which resulted from the Catholic Church's alignment with Spain against Mexican independence; and as Anglo-American clergy arrived in Texas, most brought with them a strong bias against Mexican Texans, with a few notable exceptions (such as the Oblates of Mary Immaculate, who worked extensively with Tejanos in the south Texas borderlands). Nevertheless, many Tejanos practiced a vibrant home-centered religion that revolved around devotions to Mary and the saints, as well as a range of syncretic practices such as *curanderismo*, a blend of Catholicism with ancient Mesoamerican healing rites that continues to thrive among Mexicans in the South.

Between 1910 and 1940, Tejanos were joined by hundreds of thousands of Mexican immigrants, who had been pushed from the interior of Mexico by the Mexican Revolution (1910–19) and the Cristero Rebellion (1926–29). The new Mexican government's persecution of the Catholic Church and popular revolts in support of the clergy resulted in the exile of Catholic faithful, nuns, and priests. Once in Texas, these exiles worked together to build their own churches, parochial schools, and service centers. Nevertheless, many remained underserved by Catholic diocesan structures, which remained focused on "Anglo" (non-Mexican) Catholics. In some regions of Texas, religious (order) priests were given the responsibility of ministering to Mexicans in separate churches. In 1954, the Oblates of Mary Immaculate constructed a large shrine in the Lower Rio Grande Valley to honor the Virgin of San Juan, to whom many Mexican immigrants in the area had a powerful devotion. Currently, almost 1 million visitors pass through the doors of the Shrine of Our Lady of San Juan del Valle annually, making it the most visited Catholic pilgrimage destination in the United States.

As Texas was beginning its secession from Mexico, another form of Latino popular religiosity was establishing a presence in the South: that of Cuban immigrants to Florida. The first Florida Cuban communities formed in Key West in 1831 and Ybor City, Tampa, in 1886. Both of these communities were made up of cigar makers and their families, who were supporters of Cuban independence from Spain and of José Martí's Partido Revolucionario Cubano. As in Mexico, support of the revolution was generally accompanied by a strong dose of anticlericalism, since the Cuban Catholic Church aligned with Spanish colonial powers. Nevertheless, Ybor City's first Catholic church was established by a Jesuit priest in 1890, and a second Cuban parish opened in 1922. Although the Catholic Church was widely regarded as a weak and relatively insignificant institution in Ybor City, some evidence exists that home-based popular religiosity and African-based syncretic religious practices thrived there.

In 1961, as a result of the Cuban Revolution, two-thirds of the Catholic clergy of Cuba were evicted, and they were accompanied by almost 80,000 anti-Communist exiles. These exiles, and hundreds of thousands more in the years to come, took refuge in the primarily Protestant, typically southern city of Miami. With the help of exiled clergy, they quickly set about re-creating some of their religious institutions, including numerous Catholic schools and student associations, in Miami. Unlike their Mexican counterparts in Texas earlier in the century, they also encountered a Catholic diocese that was eager to assist them, provided a wide range of material resources, and expected them to rapidly and fully assimilate into already existing "American" parishes. In 1966, perhaps to temper well-documented Cuban Catholic resistance to this plan for assimilation, the bishop of Miami established a shrine for Our Lady of Charity, Cuba's patroness. This sacred site annually attracts hundreds of thousands of pilgrims, making it the sixth-largest Catholic pilgrimage site in the United States.

Currently, the south Florida Shrine of Our Lady of Charity and the south Texas Shrine of Our Lady of San Juan del Valle anchor Latino religion in the South. Both popular pilgrimage destinations juxtapose Cuban or Mexican nationalism with tensions between heterodox and orthodox Catholicism, since they are inevitably sites for practices associated with Santeria and *curanderismo*, respectively. Santeria has steadily grown in popularity in Miami as a result of both the Mariel boatlift in the early 1980s, which brought proportionally more practitioners of Afro-Cuban religions than earlier migrations, and U.S. Supreme Court proceedings of 1993, which increased the status and publicity of Santeria in the United States. Such practices receive strong disapproval and are often dismissed as "superstition" or worse by the Catholic hierarchy, which uses the popular shrines to evangelize Latinos, encouraging them to practice a more orthodox and church-centered Catholicism.

In the past decade, the exponential growth of the Latino population in the traditional Bible Belt has meant that Latino religion is no longer confined to the South's geographic extremes. According to the 2000 U.S. Census, six of the seven states that have experienced a more than 200 percent increase in Hispanic population since 1990 are located in the historically "Baptist South" (North Carolina, South Carolina, Georgia, Alabama, Tennessee, Arkansas). Two of the states in which this increase has been most profound are Georgia and North Carolina, where the foreign-born population has exploded as a result of changing migration patterns of Mexicans and the increasing presence of immigrants from throughout Central and South America, particularly Guatemala, Honduras, El Salvador, Colombia, and Peru. What constitutes contemporary "Latino religion" in these states is, in fact, the religion of very recent Latin American immigrants, most of whom are young, mobile, and undocumented residents of the United States. Many can also be characterized as transmigrants, because they maintain close ties to their places of origin. Such ties are often religiously mediated through Catholic activities like feast-day celebrations for local, regional, and national saints or through the connections that evangelical and Pentecostal churches have to parent organizations in their members' places of origin.

As they reshape the religious contours of these southern states, new immigrants radically impact the presence and role of the Catholic Church, change the traditional mission fields for established Protestant churches, and introduce a range of new religious practices and organizations. Georgia and North Carolina are home to four of the six Catholic dioceses in the United States with the fastest-growing Hispanic membership (Charlotte, Atlanta, Raleigh, and Savannah). Currently, 46 percent of the churches in the Archdiocese of Atlanta offer Spanish masses, and the Diocese of Raleigh offers such masses in 61 percent of its churches. Beyond offering mass, the Catholic Church is struggling to respond appropriately to these newcomers and defend against what it perceives to be the dangerous lure of Pentecostal and evangelical churches. The most popular strategies used by the Catholic Church to be more inviting to Latinos and counteract the appeal of Protestant churches are to offer a broad range of social services and to establish charismatic worship groups.

There are two primary sources of Latino Protestant congregations in the South. The first, and less prevalent, type results from a perceptible shift in the home mission field of well-established denominations. An association of Hispanic Baptists in Georgia, for instance, now includes more than 70 congregations, many of which are associated with the Southern Baptist Convention. In Georgia and North Carolina, Lutherans, Episcopalians, Methodists, and Presbyterians have all worked to establish Latino congregations, often recruiting Latino clergy from other parts of the United States, but they have been less successful than their Baptist counterparts. Baptist churches offer less arduous routes to both ordination and the formation of new congregations, and non-Catholic Latino churches in the South appear more likely to thrive when they are independent and pastored by Latino newcomers. The second, and more prevalent, type of Latino Protestant congregation in the region is an extremely heterogeneous collection of small evangelical and Pentecostal groups that are unaffiliated with an established denomination in the region and pastored by Latin American immigrants. Interestingly, some such churches, such as Iglesia de Cristo Ministerios Elim, or La Luz del Mundo, have been brought with migrants from Guatemala and Mexico, respectively, to the South.

Home-based popular Catholicism continues to be the most pervasive (and varied) form of Latino religiosity in the South. Most recent Latin American immigrants to the region, like their predecessors, practice a religion that does not necessitate regular participation in particular churches. However, for many immigrants, religious organizations have assumed another kind of responsibility. In many parts of the South, Latino immigrants have sometimes arrived in unwelcoming, predominantly white destinations. Even when not resistant to their presence, southern cities and towns offer few, if any, services, advocacy groups, or even public gathering places for Latinos. In some such places, churches fill all of these roles, becoming sites for the defense and protection of undocumented immigrants, in particular. As they strive to provide much more than spiritual assistance to a minority group experiencing persecution and discrimination, these Latino religious organizations follow a route paved by African Americans in the South, along which churches become, for marginalized groups, centers of economic, social, educational, and political life.

MARIE FRIEDMANN MARQUARDT
Emory University

Gilberto M. Hinojosa, in *Mexican Americans and the Catholic Church, 1900–1965*, ed. Jay P. Dolan and Gilberto M. Hinojosa (1994); James Talmadge Moore, *Through Fire and Flood: The Catholic Church in Frontier Texas, 1836–1900* (1992); Lisandro Pérez, in *Puerto Rican and Cuban Catholics in the U.S., 1900–1965*, ed. Jay P. Dolan and Jaime R. Vidal (1994); Thomas A. Tweed, *Our Lady of the Exile: Diasporic Religion at a Cuban Catholic Shrine in Miami* (1997), *Southern Cultures* (Summer 2002); Manuel A. Vasquez and Marie Friedmann Marquardt, *Globalizing the Sacred: Religion across the Americas* (2003); Martha Woodson Rees and T. Danyael Miller, *Quienes Somos? Que Necesitamos? Needs Assessment of Hispanics in the Archdiocese of Atlanta* (25 March 2002).

Religion, Native American

For millennia, religious practices enabled Native Americans in the Southeast to maintain or restore vital balances disrupted by human action or the actions of other living beings. Across the Southeast, Native Americans perceived spiritual values and meanings in a wide range of activities, events, and phenomena. They found holiness in a comet's sweep across the sky, the earth's rumbling in a quake, turbulence in a river, and the flight of a bird. Their dreams foretold the future, warning of impending sickness and death, or, more auspiciously, a successful hunt. Their systems of belief and morality shaped how they understood weather, birth, courtship, healing, death, horticulture, warfare, and diplomacy. Their pottery, baskets, clothing, jewelry, stories, place-names, art, and architecture invoked creation stories, mythic beings, and cosmic symbols. Their sacred sites, holy times, and festivals embodied their distinctive spiritual orientations toward the world.

Embedded so deeply in daily life and diffused so widely across so many activities, Native American religions were very influential, but ironically, they were to some extent invisible as religion. Many Native peoples did not think of religion as a separate thing or coin a word to name it. On the other hand, if there was not a well-bounded or tightly circumscribed phenomenon called "religion" in ancestral Native America, there were among many peoples special ceremonies, sacred buildings, and ritual specialists that stood out, possessed special names, and evoked extraordinary treatment. This was especially the case in nonegalitarian social formations, such as the Mississippian society that flourished 1,000 years ago along that river and to the east.

Mississippian society (900–1550 C.E.) consisted of chiefdoms, alliances of a village and outlying farmsteads dominated by particular chiefly lineages that exacted tribute from or waged war with other chiefdoms. Although remarkably unstable, these polities produced some monumental architecture, most notably, large, flat-topped earthen mounds that served as political and spiritual foci. Some of the most spectacular of these were located at Moundville, Ala. These ceremonial mounds, although constructed over many years by communal labor, were not open to the general public. On these square-topped platforms, priests and chiefs performed vital ceremonies to pay homage to the chiefly lineage, to gather power for warfare against other chiefdoms, and to orchestrate the community's agricultural activities. Centuries later, these mounds, in spite of a lack of care and in the face of serious threats posed by modern development, still represent the largest religious structures ever built in the Southeast. Their silent monumentality belies the dynamism of the societies that constructed them.

Long before contact with Europeans and well before the Mississippian period, Native men and women changed their traditions in many ways, some local and almost invisible, others far more dramatic, systemic, and public. Because Native traditions were holistically connected to the rest of life, any significant change in one aspect of life could produce profound religious repercussions. When corn moved from Mexico to the American Southwest and then later to the Southeast, it arrived not simply as a plant, but as an embedded part of a distinctive and highly spiritualized cultural tradition. Symbols and rituals, gods and ceremonies accompanied the plant, as a cultus came with the corn. Corn gave rise to the Mississippian religiopolitical system and other maize-centered religious practices, stories, and sacrifices. Corn changed in fundamental ways how people lived, related, and believed. All of this occurred long before Columbus.

After contact with non–Native Americans, mound building declined significantly. Disease epidemics brought by Europeans and the violence of conquistador armies caused the greatest loss of life ever experienced in the Southeast and severely disrupted Mississippian society and its religious system. Nevertheless, although mound building declined, many Mississippian beliefs, values, and practices survived and helped shape the traditions of post-Mississippian groups such as the Muskogee (Creek), Choctaw, and Cherokee Indians. Hunters did not forget to offer pieces of meat to the fire, and women took care to sequester themselves during their menses. And everyone kept tending corn and, in annual communal ceremonies, celebrated its significance as a gift from self-sacrificing sacred beings.

With the spread of Spanish missions in La Florida during the 16th and 17th centuries, many southeastern Indians learned the rites and tenets of Catholicism. But missionized Indians continued to hold onto some precontact traditions. They also occasionally revolted against priestly authority. Over time, a complex, hybridized world—part Spanish, part Indian—emerged in these missions. It did not last. At the beginning of the 18th century, English-led armies from South Carolina destroyed all of the missions and enslaved and/or deported the Christianized Indians. For the next century, few missionaries of any sort sought to convert southeastern Indians, but Christianity, especially Protestant Christianity, continued to percolate into Indian country, brought by traders, settlers, agents, and runaway slaves. They shared stories from the Bible.

Different Native American groups in the Southeast responded differently to Protestant Christianity. The Creek Muskogees, for example, expressed a very low tolerance for Christian preaching and harassed Protestant missionaries when they arrived in the early 19th century. Indeed, among the Creeks, anticolonial American Indian prophets found a receptive audience. These prophets rejected the economic dependency associated with the deerskin trade and decried class divisions emerging among southeastern Indians. In 1811, a significant faction of Creeks, known as the Redsticks, launched a dramatic movement to restore the symbolic boundaries between Indians and whites. Political revolt became a sacred cause involving 9,000 Muskogee men, women, and children, but American armies and their Choctaw, Cherokee, and Creek allies crushed this revolt decisively, destroying dozens of villages in the process and changing the future of the region and all of its peoples.

In the wake of the Creeks' defeat, all southeastern Indians faced intensified threats to their political and cultural sovereignty. Having witnessed the Creeks' defeat and recalling other earlier defeats experienced by Cherokees and others, southeastern Indians knew that overt revolt against the invasion of their lands was hopeless. Rising white racism in the era had further marginalized the Native tribes. Some left, moving west. Others, especially among the Choctaws and Cherokees, began welcoming Protestant missionaries into their midst, attending their schools, translating hymns, and converting to Christianity in small numbers. Missionaries condemned, initially to no avail, popular practices, including the ball playing, traditional medicine practices, conjure, and all-night dances. Methodist and Baptist itinerants soon outnumbered the missionaries from the American Board of Commissioners for Foreign Missions and from the Moravian Church, and in the long run, most southeastern Indians joined these evangelical branches of Christianity, modifying them in the process in ways that have yet to be fully studied or appreciated. Enduring Indian Removal in the late 1830s and the Civil War, southeastern Indians somehow survived in the region and also in Oklahoma. By the end of the 19th century, most of them had become Protestants. Baptists predominated among the Native peoples of Virginia as they did elsewhere. Methodists also abounded among many southeastern Indian groups, but Mormons won the hearts of Catawbas. Regardless of the denomination, in the era of Jim Crow individual churches served as important symbolic centers for rural Indian communities and helped them negotiate the challenges of living in a rigidly biracial society that had little room for peoples who were not black or white.

Protestantism continues to prevail among southeastern Indians today. Most are conservative Christians, not unlike their non-Native neighbors, with whom they have often intermarried. Some Native men and women consider their Christian confession to be at odds with ancestral traditions, or, at the very least, think religions exist on parallel paths and should not be mixed. Among Creeks in Oklahoma, one is expected to affiliate either with a church or with a ceremonial square ground, but not both at the same time. In contrast, eastern Cherokees connect being truly Cherokee with being truly Christian. To win the highest respect among the eastern Cherokees, one needs to be able to read the Cherokee New Testament or sing Cherokee hymns. In the past, the syllabary was also used by individual conjurers to scribble down formulas related to matters of witchcraft and sorcery. While this esoteric knowledge might also be considered part of Cherokee religion, it is occult, secretive, and not shared in public. The knowledge recorded in those writings is feared, not revered like the Cherokee translation of John or the Cherokee version of "Amazing Grace."

After centuries of struggle just to survive as distinct peoples, some southeastern tribes today are thriving economically, thanks to their own entrepreneurial talents. Now possessing the economic and political means to exercise much fuller self-determination, several tribes have created formalized educational programs and institutions to revitalize ancestral language, arts, and culture. Poarch Creeks hired an Oklahoma medicine man to teach their young in Alabama the Muskogee language. Eastern Cherokees have sought to buy back lost lands, to protect sacred sites, and to establish positive ties with the Cherokee Nation in Oklahoma, symbolically healing the long-standing breach between east and west.

Old challenges still exist, and new ones will no doubt emerge that will directly or indirectly affect Native American religions. Mass communications, electronic media, improved transportation systems, and increased exposure to tourists make it more difficult to revitalize distinctive cultures and indigenous languages. The good news, however, is that in spite of terrible travails — epidemic diseases, invasion and loss of most of their lands, forced removal from their sacred ancestral landscapes and geographical separation from their kin, racial subjugation, transgenerational poverty, and social marginalization — some southeastern Indian peoples have finally regained some security in the Southeast. It is as if the world of southeastern Indians, long imbalanced, has finally begun to be righted.

JOEL MARTIN
University of California at Riverside

Margaret Bender, *Signs of Cherokee Culture: Sequoyah's Syllabary in Eastern Cherokee Life* (2002); Vernon Knight Jr., *American Antiquity* 514 (1986); Joel W. Martin, in *Native Religions and Cultures of North America*, ed. Lawrence E. Sullivan (2000), *Sacred Revolt: The Muskogees' Struggle for a New World* (1991); Bonnie G. McEwan, ed., *The Spanish Missions of La Florida* (1993); William G. McLoughlin, *Cherokees and Missionaries, 1789–1839* (1984); J. Anthony Paredes, ed., *Indians of the Southeastern United States in the Late Twentieth Century* (1992).

Religion, White Supremacist

White supremacist racial thought emerged early in the modern world. It fatally shaped interactions between Europeans and Africans from the 15th century forward. Religious divisions drawn by Europeans between those of Christ and those in the heathen world became part of defining what race meant. "European" or "English" meant "Christian," and in future centuries that also came to mean "white." "African" meant "heathen." Thus, from early in southern history, religion created race, and race thereafter shaped religion.

Early colonizers in the Americas faced first the question of whether Christianity would apply to Indians and black slaves at all. The answer required, in part, deciding on whether Native peoples in North America, Africans, and African Americans were fully human — a debate that raged for several centuries and indeed continued on into the post–Civil War era of scientific racism.

Once slavery took root in the Americas, it virtually was inevitable that religious authorities would decree that if slavery existed, God must have a reason for it—and that reason must be in the Bible. But slavery in the Americas was specifically a *racial* form of bondage. This was in contrast to traditional forms of slavery found worldwide, which were not "racial" in the modern sense. This religious justification of slavery would have to clarify God's providence in having one race of people enslave another. In this way, Euro-Americans developed some of the meanings of "race" in the modern sense. They began to define what constituted whiteness and blackness, categories that would long outlive slavery itself. And those categories were, at least initially, fundamentally religious ones.

When some Africans converted to Christianity and claimed their freedom as a result, colonial assemblies in Maryland (1664) and Virginia (1667) responded by dissociating baptism from freedom. From that point forward, Christianity and slavery were not antithetical. Children born of slave women, even Christian slave women, would be bondpeople for life. A few decades later, the plantation complex in the Chesapeake took off, resulting in the importation of large numbers of Africans. By the 1730s, in Virginia as in South Carolina, very few planters evinced any interest in imparting Christianity to the slaves. Those missionaries who made it their task to do so generally met resistance by the slave owners and indifference among the slaves.

Yet the inescapable fact remained that white southerners somehow had to fit black people into God's providence. Passages from the Old Testament, especially Genesis 9:18–27, outlined the curse on Canaan, son of Ham, who had originally espied Noah's naked drunkenness and thereafter was consigned to slavery. "A servant of servants shall he be," the verse proclaimed. Once properly exposed to exegesis, it provided at least a start at a religiomythical grounding for modern racial meanings, and a long-lived one. The passage was still being cited in segregationist literature of the 1950s and remains an ideological part of certain fringe groups, such as the so-called Christian Identity Movement, down to the present day. Respectable theologians often skirted the son of Ham story, as it smacked more of folklore than "high" theology. Moreover, as the historian Colin Kidd has argued, the major thrust of Christian theology weighed in against the varieties of racism that cast particular groups out of the category of humanity. That being said, the fable of Ham deeply penetrated the religious consciousness of white southerners, who were for the most part biblical literalists.

The son of Ham saga served well in the sense that it seemed to explain how black people could be free Christians and unfree slaves at the same time. But

the curse on Ham was at best a shaky foundation for religioracial mytholo-
gizing, for the passage invoked was simply too short, mysterious, and fablelike
to bear up under the full weight of the interpretations imposed upon it. More
respectable proslavery theologians worked feverishly through the antebellum
era (1800–1860) to enunciate a Christian proslavery apologetic, one that would
preserve boundaries of whiteness/blackness while also supporting their efforts
to Christianize the slaves. Contrary to views in the 17th and 18th centuries,
which often set in dichotomous relief whiteness and Christian freedom versus
blackness and unchristian unfreedom, by the 19th century the missions to the
slaves had been successful enough that many whites came to see "black" religion as peculiarly fervent and reassuringly orthodox. Later in these years, the
development and full-fledged exposition of a proslavery argument explained
away the obvious contradictions of slaveholding in a free republic and justified
the daily repression required to enforce enslavement even in the midst of the
rapid Christian evangelization of the South.

White supremacy was an ideology of power that enveloped white southerners in an imagined community. Southern whites inherited a theological
regime grounded in conservative notions of hierarchy; and 19th-century white
southern theologies of class and blood (sometimes expressed formally, more
often disseminated in everyday speech, Sunday sermons, and self-published
tracts and pamphlets) buttressed white southern practice. Southern theological
figures preached that God ordained inequality.

The Civil War fundamentally challenged and shook up the supposedly
secure southern racial hierarchy. The postwar years saw a growing bitterness
and desire for separation among white believers who previously had declared
slaves part of their "family." The term "Redemption," used by historians to
describe the end of Reconstruction in the mid-1870s, assumed an especially
powerful meaning for white southern believers. Redemption signified individual salvation as well as the deliverance of society from "cursed rulers."

As would be the case a century later during the civil rights movement, white
Democratic politicians during Reconstruction employed an evangelical language of sin and redemption combined with measures of political organization
and extralegal violence. When some African American men exercised rights of
political citizenship, it appeared to white conservatives as an overturning of a
divinely ordered hierarchy. Southern Redemptionists battled to restore a white
supremacist order and claimed, without any consciousness of hypocrisy, that
their churches were undefiled by the politics that disgraced northern and black
religious organizations. White southern Christians viewed their Redemptionist

activity as essentially religious, an extension of the cosmic struggle between order and disorder, civilization and barbarism, white and black.

To do its work in a devout society, the ideology of racism required Christian underpinnings for the brutal exercise of power. The proslavery argument filled this void. Post–Civil War southern theologians responded to defeat in the Civil War by emphasizing human weakness, fallibility, and dependence on God. For many white southern theologians, defeat in the Civil War also shored up orthodoxies of race and place. The Negro—as a beast, a burden, or a brother—was there to be dealt with by whites, who were the actors in the racial dramas. By using the term "Redemption," white southerners expressed a deeply religious understanding. The divinely ordained social/racial hierarchy had been restored by southern martyrs, and the South atoned, renewed.

Once again, the southern white consensus on race and hierarchy was challenged during the civil rights years. A certain stratum of religious moderates and a few liberals moved toward some support for civil rights. The major southern denominations, for example, came out in favor of following the dictates of the *Brown v. Board of Education* decision of 1954. However, the bulk of white southern believers distrusted the official pronouncements put out by denominational authorities and clung to arguments based on connecting whiteness with purity and godliness. During the civil rights era, white believers throughout the South connected the preservation of race purity with the fear of miscegenation and defense of southern social customs. Most arguments employed some form of received wisdom and familiar folklore—the immutable "nature" of the Negro, the "impurity" that would inevitably accompany integration, or time-honored scriptural staples such as the Old Testament story of Noah and his progeny. Denominational ethicists and theologians consistently showed how the ancient and cryptic Old Testament stories in no way buttressed the specific 20th-century social system of segregation. But this biblical jousting was beside the point, for the theoreticians of Jim Crow were by definition suspicious of officially sanctioned modes of scriptural interpretation.

After World War II, the American creed of democracy and equality effectively put white southern religious conservatives on the defensive. To justify inequality, they resorted to constitutional arguments ("interposition"), appeals to tradition, outright demagoguery, and obscurantist renderings of Old Testament passages. At that point, however, the raw exercise of power that white supremacy entailed appeared naked, without any compelling theological justification. God-ordained racial inequality crumbled in the hypocrisy of endorsing equality while practicing racism.

By the 1970s, many white southern believers accommodated themselves to the demise of legal segregation. Thus, in the recent controversies within southern church organizations, race has been one of the very few items usually *not* in dispute. Since the 1960s, southern religious conservatives, for the most part, have repudiated the white supremacist views of their predecessors, as seen in the 1995 Southern Baptist Church resolution officially apologizing for the evangelical and denominational role in slavery and segregation.

Yet the standard biblical arguments against racial equality, now looked upon as an embarrassment from a bygone age, have found their way rather easily into the contemporary religious right's stance on gender. A theology that sanctifies gendered hierarchy has become for the post–civil rights generation what whiteness was to earlier generations of believers. For religious conservatives generally, patriarchy has supplanted race as the defining first principle of God-ordained inequality.

PAUL HARVEY
University of Colorado

David Chappell, *Stone of Hope: Prophetic Religion and the Death of Jim Crow* (2004); Erskine Clarke, *Dwelling Place: A Plantation Epic* (2005); Paul Harvey, *Freedom's Coming: Religious Cultures and the Shaping of the South from the Civil War through the Civil Rights Era* (2005); Paul Harvey and Edward Blum, *Jesus in Red, White, and Black* (2012); Winthrop Jordan, *White over Black: American Attitudes toward the Negro, 1550–1812* (1968); Colin Kidd, *The Forging of Races: Race and Scripture in the Protestant Atlantic World, 1600–2000* (2006); Michael Pasquier, *Fathers on the Frontier: French Missionaries and the Roman Catholic Priesthood in the United States, 1789–1860* (2010); Charles Reagan Wilson, *Baptized in Blood: The Religion of the Lost Cause* (1980).

Segregation, Desegregation, and Resegregation

Segregation is the practice of physically separating categories of individuals on the basis of socially determined ethnic, gender, racial, or religious attributes. Segregation can be voluntary or involuntary, sanctioned by law (de jure) and by custom (de facto). Desegregation is the process of undoing the different legal, social, economic, and political practices supporting segregation; resegregation refers to reverting to segregation practices, though sometimes in different ways. In the South, the segregation of blacks was woven into the entire scope and scale of the community. Desegregation attempted to end segregation by challenging it through particular institutions deemed egregious—schools, lunch counters, public transportation. Through the flight of better-educated and wealthier people—white and black—from communities in recent decades, the remaining poor (and usually black) residents have been subject to a re-segregation perhaps more pernicious than the previous forms of segregation.

Social practices arising around segregation are usually justified by an ideology of one group's superiority over another. In the South, the justification for segregation was the belief in white supremacy, that whites were inherently better—morally, physically, and intellectually—than blacks (the principles of white supremacy continue to permeate the American consciousness today, particularly in white opposition to immigration). Though voluntary segregation was more likely in the North, involuntary physical separation of blacks from whites was the predominant structure of segregation in the South.

Slaves had no choice but to live in close proximity to their masters in rural areas. The few free blacks in the South had a tenuous status and lived in designated sections of towns, barred from most public accommodations. Yet during this period, free blacks created their own separate community by forming their own religious, fraternal, and benevolence institutions. These segregated institutions helped to sustain a distinct black identity in the face of white hostility and widespread discrimination.

During the antebellum period and continuing just after the Civil War, the status of blacks was defined by Black Codes or laws enacted by all states in the Deep South. These statutes defined the near-absolute power slave owners had over their slaves, including over their sexual relationships and offspring. Though these codes prohibited slaves from marrying anyone, particularly whites, they also contributed to an ideology of white racial purity, which was given form through appeal to white women. The belief in an inviolate white womanhood or rape myth provided a ready excuse for lynching blacks who were too "uppity," serving to maintain strict racial boundaries separating whites and blacks.

After the Civil War, the Thirteenth Amendment (1865) abolished slavery; blacks were granted citizenship with equal rights, and black males were then granted voting rights (Fourteenth Amendment, 1868). The Fifteenth Amendment (1870) prohibited racial discrimination in voting. These and other federal laws initially protected blacks' civil liberties and civil rights during Reconstruction. But after the withdrawal of federal troops in 1877, the less-frequent interventions in the South by Congress and the tightening of local control by white elites allowed the reinstating of exclusionary social practices toward blacks.

Between 1890 and 1965, southern states sponsored a system of racial segregation, colloquially termed "Jim Crow." Jim Crow laws covered the segregation of public schools, public places and public transportation, and restrooms and restaurants for whites and blacks. Segregated institutions were established to circumscribe racial mixing in every conceivable facet of social life, covering churches, libraries, schools, theaters, and restaurants. This then followed the pattern of segregation, desegregation, and resegregation: segregation by Black Codes, desegregation by the federal government during Reconstruction, and resegregation by Jim Crow laws.

Toward the end of the 19th century, industrialization and urbanization fueled growth and demand for more housing and public transportation. In response to the demands, and under pressure from whites uncomfortable with the changes occurring, southern states responded by sanctioning further segregation of the races in political parties, housing, unions, and other private businesses—even to the extent of prohibiting shopping or working in certain stores and working at certain trades. For example, "restricted covenants" barred the sale of homes to blacks (or Jews or Asians), thus ensuring that neighborhoods remained racially segregated. These policies had particular impact in urban areas.

As the 19th century came to a close, several state and local laws were enacted sanctioning discriminatory practices and extending segregation to dictating where someone sat in a railroad car. One challenge to Louisiana's segregated railroad cars eventually made its way to the Supreme Court as *Plessy v. Ferguson* (1896). This case deemed segregation constitutional in public accommodations as long as both races received equal treatment in public. In response, after 1896, all public facilities, including public schools, were subject to segregation, putting an end to informal, sporadic patterns of integration for other nonwhite racial and ethnic groups. (The introduction of public conveniences such as drinking fountains, restrooms, and phone booths resulted in additional Jim Crow laws.)

In *Rice v. Gong Lum* (1927), the Mississippi Supreme Court maintained that white children must be segregated from all other races, including Asians. Originally brought in to displace black laborers after the Civil War, Chinese immigrants thought they were well liked by the local townspeople until they tried to send their children to white schools. Racial segregation in the South did not allow for any ambiguity in terms of defining who was white.

Over the next 50 years, between 1896 and 1956, black leaders responded to the systematic exclusion of blacks in the South in two ways: accommodation or protest. One prominent black leader, Booker T. Washington, argued on the side of accommodation in a speech he delivered in 1895. In the "Atlanta Compromise" speech, he argued that blacks and whites should be like the separate fingers of the same hand. This image reinforced the basic premise of segregation but also allowed for a notion of racial equality within separate institutions.

African American man going in "colored" entrance of movie house on a Saturday afternoon, Belzoni, Mississippi Delta, Miss., ca. 1939 (Marion Post Wolcott, photographer, Library of Congress [LC-USF331-030577-M2], Washington, D.C.)

The rising new middle class of black professionals (ministers, teachers, business owners) began to have a vested interest in segregated businesses and was inclined to be conservative by subscribing to the accommodation viewpoint, largely due to this economic self-interest.

Those blacks who did want to protest against segregation did so, in sporadic challenges—against a railroad company, grocery store, or restaurant—usually in response to a personal instance of exclusion. Unlike the mass mobilizations of the 1950s and 1960s, these types of protest sought to create small, individual openings within the existing system of race relations. Early civil rights protests objected to racial segregation as perpetuating racial prejudice and validating the treatment of blacks and other nonwhites as inferior. These initial, almost tentative, dissents did not stem the incremental growth in segregation but did help to question the morality of such a system in a supposedly democratic society.

By the early 20th century, creating and maintaining "separate-but-equal" facilities became increasingly costly for southern states and cities, particularly as the increasingly urbanized South tried to keep up with the demand for more public schools and other services. Funding for black schools fell ever further behind that of white schools, and many southern states were no longer able to sustain even a pretense of separate-but-equal. Recognizing the economy of scale lost in maintaining separate school systems, along with a range of other public facilities, black attorneys formulated challenges to segregation demanding that states actually provide and maintain equal separate institutions as required by *Plessy*.

There had been some advances on that front: the Supreme Court began to overturn Jim Crow laws on constitutional grounds, starting with a ruling overturning a Kentucky law requiring residential segregation (*Buchanan v. Warley*, 1917), and more generally in *Shelley v. Kraemer* (1948), in which it held that "restrictive covenants" were unconstitutional. The Supreme Court also no longer permitted segregation in interstate transportation (*Irene Morgan v. Virginia*, 1946).

A series of cases aimed at equalizing higher education and black teachers' salaries were initiated in the 1930s by the NAACP and later by NAACP Legal Defense and Educational Fund, Inc. In *Missouri ex rel Gaines v. Canada* (1936), the black plaintiff was denied access to the University of Missouri Law School, even though the state of Missouri did not provide a separate-but-equal accommodation. Small victories against segregation were claimed whenever state or lower federal courts ruled in favor of black plaintiffs who sought equalization of resources.

After World War II, there was a shift in strategy from trying to achieve equalization of facilities to directly challenging the constitutionality of segregation. The 1954 *Brown v. Board of Education* case argued that even when black institutions and white institutions were allotted equal resources, as they were in Topeka, Kans., separate-but-equal institutions forever imprinted a "badge of inferiority" on black children. The court held that *all* separate facilities were *inherently* unequal in the area of public schools, effectively overturning *Plessy v. Ferguson* and outlawing Jim Crow in other areas of society as well. This landmark case included complaints filed in two southern states, South Carolina (*Briggs v. Elliott*) and Virginia (*Davis v. County School Board of Prince Edward County*), along with Delaware (*Gebhart v. Belton*) and Washington, D.C. (*Spottswode Bolling v. C. Melvin Sharpe*).

In the South, the *Brown* decision was met with massive resistance at both the state and the local level. Many southern white congressional members signed the "Southern Manifesto," providing justification for a doctrine of states' rights, declaring the federal court illegitimate and its decisions null. *Brown* caused southerners to re-revisit the role of the national government in regulating local issues. Century-old arguments, reminiscent of the debates over slavery, were revived to defend the primacy of states' rights over federal jurisdiction.

Words like "interposition" and "nullification"—the same language used to defend slavery—were heard again in defense of segregation. *Brown* also revived fears of miscegenation as a threat to white supremacy. These fears were realized when *Loving v. Virginia* (1967) ended all race-based legal restrictions on marriage.

In conjunction with the massive resistance to *Brown*, public protests against segregation intensified in the South. Partially in response to this increased activism and to circumvent further school desegregation, the White Citizens' Council (wcc) was formed in Mississippi and quickly expanded to other southern states. Some communities simply closed their public schools, while others reopened their public schools as private "council schools" for white children only and sponsored by the wcc. In Prince Edward County, Va., all public schools were closed for a decade after the *Brown* decision in an attempt to avoid desegregation. These tactics to prevent desegregation were largely successful— by 1964, 10 years after *Brown*, only 2.3 percent of southern black children attended desegregated schools.

The southern mass mobilizations of the civil rights movement in the 1950s and 1960s were successful in raising awareness of racial segregation as undemocratic at home and abroad. This appeal to American core values of fairness and equality increased the likelihood of federal intervention when desegregation was blocked. Additional pressure from the federal government was placed on southern political leaders, as images of southern police brutality in Birmingham, Ala., in 1963, for example, were beamed around the world and used to fuel anti-American propaganda by the Soviet Union and other undemocratic regimes. In a largely symbolic protest against desegregation, Alabama governor George Wallace became famous for his "Stand at the Schoolhouse Door" in June 1963, in which he attempted to bar the enrollment of black students Vivian Malone and James Hood at the University of Alabama.

Resistance to desegregation led to numerous state and federal lawsuits. In 1968, the *Greene v. County School Board* case of Virginia reaffirmed school desegregation as a means to build a color-blind society: no longer would dual school systems be tolerated. In order to achieve racial parity, desegregation would now be force-remedied through a variety of means, including extensive busing of students. A few years later, in North Carolina, the Supreme Court upheld busing as a means to desegregate the South (*Swann v. Charlotte-Mecklenburg Board of Education* [1971]).

Though *Greene* and *Swann* sought to circumvent attempts to avoid school desegregation, they could not address the economic, political, and social factors working against the implementation of integrated schools. In the South, long-established residential housing patterns of racially isolated neighborhoods contributed to the continuance of dual school systems for many years after *Brown*. Using busing to integrate schools contributed to the virtual abandonment of public education by white and black elites to lower-class whites and blacks in many southern communities. Desegregation had thereby stripped public schools of the upper economic strata of society, creating institutions that were resegregated, on the basis of economic resources rather than race.

In *Parents Involved in Community Schools v. Seattle School District No. 1 et al.* (2007), the Supreme Court ordered that race could no longer be a factor in assigning students to schools. In a 5–4 decision striking down public school choice plans in Seattle, Wash., and Louisville, Ky., Chief Justice John Roberts argued that in keeping with the goal of a color-blind society, using race to assign students to schools was unconstitutional. But, as Justice Breyer remarked in his dissent, this redefinition of a color-blind society gave all races equal weight and ignored any past injustices created by racial segregation. The *Parents* opinion obliquely referenced resegregation in the South by distinguishing between de jure segregation as being created by school systems and de facto segregation as a result of individual choice in terms of buying homes in more affluent, segregated areas.

Resegregation is evident in residential housing patterns and school board policies, and today southern neighborhoods are as much segregated by social class as they are by race. In the absence of racially explicit laws, de jure discrimination is ever present, underpinning the legality of resegregation in the present context.

JEAN VAN DELINDER
Oklahoma State University

Michael J. Klarman, *From Jim Crow to Civil Rights: The Supreme Court and the Struggle for Racial Equality* (2004); Jean Van Delinder, *Struggles before Brown: Early Civil Rights Protests and Their Significance Today* (2008); C. Vann Woodward, *The Strange Career of Jim Crow* (1974).

Segregationists' Use of Media

Many of the most enduring media images generated during the civil rights struggles of the 1950s and 1960s feature segregationists. Crucially, however, the vast majority of those images were not made on segregationists' terms; rather, they were products of the increasingly sophisticated media strategies developed by their civil rights opponents, most notably the Southern Christian Leadership Conference. Decades of historical research have led to a nuanced understanding of the use of media by civil rights proponents, but, despite Hodding Carter III's contemporaneous reference to a segregationist "offensive by duplicating machine" and Numan Bartley's 1969 formulation of a "southern informational offensive," no similar appreciation yet exists for the strategies of segregationists. This continuing gap in historians' collective knowledge is the product of a number of interrelated issues: a paucity of relevant archival sources, with incomplete print runs of segregationist magazines and newspapers, and piecemeal recordings of broadcasts; a mixture of changing societal views on race; the politics of historical commemoration and patterns of popular memory that ensure greater investigation of proponents of civil rights than their opponents; and, ultimately, desegregationists' sharper and more complete understanding of the power of the media than their segregationist adversaries.

Segregationists attempted to use various forms of media to promote and defend their way of life, particularly when their racial mores were under sustained attack from both civil rights activists and the federal government in the decades after World War II. The multifaceted ways in which they attempted to do so reflect their own heterogeneity, their lack of a clearly defined overarching strategy, and the unevenness of the arguments that they sought to disseminate. In quantitative terms, the ease with which written newspapers, pamphlets, broadsides, and cartoons could be produced ensured that print was segregationists' most commonly used medium, although imaginative use was also made of local radio broadcasts. Forays into television were rare by comparison but on occasion offered access to a national audience that was otherwise all too often unobtainable. All such outputs were intended either to shore up the resolve of white southerners to resist desegregation or (in far fewer cases) to win sympathy from a national audience for the segregationist cause.

The most prolific disseminators of printed matter devoted to the segregationist cause were the Citizens' Councils and affiliated white supremacist groups around which active segregationists organized themselves from the mid-1950s onward. Many councils produced their own newspapers, such as the White Citizens' Council of Arkansas's *Arkansas Faith*, the Montgomery Citizens' Council's *States' Rights Advocate*, and the Defenders of State Sovereignty and Individual Liberty's *Defenders' News and Views*. Although their production values varied considerably, their shared aims were reflected in an inevitability of content as each publication attempted to bolster the morale of local segregationists with a mixture of editorials, opinion pieces, reprinted speeches, and crude cartoons. Collectively, the groups' printings were never widely read beyond their own membership bases, with the exception of the *Citizens' Council*, a tabloid newspaper produced by two groups from the Magnolia State, the Mississippi Association of Citizens' Councils and the Citizens' Councils of America. Printed in Jackson under the editorship of William J. Simmons, it made inflated boasts of a circulation of 40,000 to 60,000. Redesigned in 1961, it reemerged in magazine format as *Citizen*, with a circulation estimated to be closer to 3,000. Both publications sought to add a sheen of respectability to the base racism of grassroots white supremacist rhetoric by highlighting the intellectual credentials of their contributors and concentrating on such ideas as the primacy of states' rights, biblical justifications for segregation, the historical separation of the races, and a subversive presence lurking behind the civil rights movement. Citizens' Councils and their affiliated groups were also prodigious disseminators of reprinted speeches, government reports, treatises, broadsides, and pamphlets, two of the most significant being Mississippi judge Tom P. Brady's *Black Monday* and *The Congressional Committee Report on What Happened When Schools Were Integrated in Washington D.C.*

The vast majority of southern newspapers and editors supported the segregationist line; indeed, it is easier to identify those few who opposed the segregationist position, such as the *Atlanta Constitution*'s Ralph McGill or the *Arkansas Gazette*'s Harry Ashmore, than those who offered routine support. At times, southern newspapers provided crucial forums for the development of segregationist ideology, most notably when the *Richmond News Leader*'s James Jackson "Jack" Kilpatrick used a series of editorials in November 1955 to resurrect arguments for legal "interposition." Similarly, segregationists were capable of using local newspapers to help wage political campaigns. In Louisiana, for example, state senator William M. "Willie" Rainach's Joint Legislative Committee to Maintain Segregation (JLC) paid for an advertisement in the *New Orleans Times-Picayune* in November 1954 as part of a final bid to ensure a strong turnout—and to send a virulent antidesegregation message—in a referendum to legalize the use of police powers to maintain separate schools in the Pelican State.

In one sense, segregationists were forced into producing their own material, for they were routinely denied a forum for their views in newspapers and magazines that boasted national circulations. Access to these venues, in fact, was extremely limited: Clifford Dowdey of Richmond, Va., penned his thoughts in the *Saturday Review* in 1954; Thomas R. Waring managed to put "The Southern Case against Desegregation" to readers of *Harper's Magazine* in 1956; in the same year, James F. "Jimmy" Byrnes argued that "The Supreme Court Must Be Curbed" in *U.S. News and World Report*; Herbert Ravenel Sass wrote on "Mixed Schools and Mixed Blood" in the *Atlantic Monthly*; and Perry Morgan made "The Case for the White Southerner" in *Esquire* in January 1962.

Publishing houses gave segregationist tracts similarly short shrift, although there were again notable exceptions, including William D. Workman Jr.'s *The Case for the South*, published by Devin-Adair of New York in 1960, and Kilpatrick's own *The Southern Case for School Segregation*, published in Richmond by Crowell-Collier in 1962.

As a result, devoted segregationist agencies changed tactics. In 1956, Rainach and the JLC secured northern coverage by paying for a full-page advertisement in the *New York Herald Tribune*. Written in the form of an open letter "To the People of New York City," it represented an attempt to portray Jim Crow as a friend of the whole nation, given that racial strife was, in the JLC's words, heading northward as southern black migration continued. Most imaginatively, the state-sponsored Mississippi State Sovereignty Commission (MSSC), which was established on 29 March 1956 to "give the South's side" to a national audience, invited 21 New England newspaper editors to experience Mississippi life firsthand, in the belief that direct experience would overturn their anti-segregationist prejudices. The MSSC's public relations director, Hal C. DeCell, crafted a carefully organized itinerary for the junket, but it failed to have the desired effect on the visitors.

The Mississippi legislature's decision to bankroll the MSSC's activities removed many of the financial constraints that continued to hamstring the majority of privately organized segregationist groups and allowed the organization to extend its propaganda activities across all media. It was, for example, involved in various capacities in the production of three documentary films. DeCell was a surprising collaborator with the Fund for the Republic's Newsfilm Project in the making of director George M. Martin Jr.'s *Segregation and the South*. Originally entitled *Crisis in the South* before DeCell's intervention, it was broadcast by ABC in June 1957. In 1960, the MSSC released its own 35-mm propaganda film, *The Message from Mississippi*, which cobbled together interviews and newsreel footage to extol states' rights and segregation. Made by the Dobbs-Maynard Advertising Company in Jackson, the 27-minute film cost triple its original estimate, at nearly $30,000. Finally, MSSC supporters Gov. Ross R. Barnett and Lt. Gov. Paul B. Johnson filmed interviews for a 43-minute film, *Oxford USA*, made by Dallas's Patrick M. Sims, which sought to highlight the brutality of federal marshals during the 1962 rioting that accompanied James Meredith's attempted enrollment at the University of Mississippi.

Unknown to the vast majority of both contemporary segregationists and Mississippi taxpayers, the MSSC became central to the funding of the *Citizens' Council Forum*, the only regularly televised segregationist propaganda show in the nation. Anchored by the Association of Citizens' Councils of America's public relations director, Richard "Dick" Morphew, *Forum* began airing in 1955 on WLBT as a series of 15-minute studio-based interviews with segregation's apologists. Production values improved markedly in the spring of 1958, when, at the invitation of John Bell Williams and James O. Eastland, filming of the show moved to U.S. government studios in Washington, D.C. Morphew announced in 1961 that the program was going "coast to coast" for the first time, but commentators have long questioned the breadth of its appeal and the scope of its transmission. Having recently retired from the MSSC, in 1961, De-Cell openly ridiculed *Forum* producer William J. Simmons's claims to a "vast audience" across all states, and local investigative reporter Robert Pittman concluded that, in fact, only eight stations—all southern—regularly carried the show. Only when the MSSC's sealed archives were opened in 1998 did it emerge that the MSSC had spent nearly $200,000 in state funds to underwrite *Forum*'s production. Although payments were ended in December 1964, production limped on until 1966.

On the local level, support for segregation was staunch. The largest television station in Jackson, Miss., the Fred Beard–owned NBC affiliate WLBT, for example, had its broadcasting license revoked in 1969 for what was diplomatically termed "perceived discrimination"—in reality the replacement of the station's daily broadcast of the national anthem with "Dixie" and repeated announcements urging viewers to join the Citizens' Council. Exposure on nationally syndicated telecasts, however, remained extremely limited: the producers of NBC's long-running current affairs show *Comment* deemed Jack Kilpatrick sufficiently erudite and eloquent to be invited onto the program to debate segregation in summer 1958; two years later, it was again the Richmond-based newspaperman who was invited on the air by the network, this time to debate Martin Luther King Jr. face-to-face on *The Nation's Future*.

If the MSSC held a near monopoly on segregationist interest in filmmaking and television production, its work in promoting radio transmissions was matched by others. By the end of 1964, the producers of the *Citizens' Council Forum* claimed to have sent out 6,668 radio tapes to local radio stations, although most scholars believe this number to be vastly inflated. By contrast, archival sources verify that North Carolina's Jesse Helms was responsible for writing and delivering 2,732 radio editorials for Raleigh station WRAL, many of which reflected his deep conservatism, support for segregationist political candidates, and defense of Jim Crow. Indeed, local radio stations offered a relatively cheap transmission means for segregationists, and they were regularly used to broadcast propaganda, such as Virginia's Defenders of State Sovereignty and

Individual Liberty's bulletins on "The Southern Manifesto" and "Mixed Blood and Mixed Schools," and, more dramatically, to urge white southerners to defy federally mandated desegregation, most notably when Gen. Edwin A. Walker attempted to rouse segregationists into joining the angry crowds at Ole Miss in 1962 with a demagogic speech on KWKH in Shreveport.

GEORGE LEWIS
University of Leicester

Numan V. Bartley, *The Rise of Massive Resistance: Race and Politics in the South during the 1950s* (1969); Erle Johnston, *Mississippi's Defiant Years, 1953–1973* (1990); Yasuhiro Katagiri, *The Mississippi State Sovereignty Commission: Civil Rights and States' Rights* (2001); George Lewis, *Massive Resistance: The White Response to the Civil Rights Movement* (2006); Neil R. McMillen, *The Citizens' Councils: Organized Resistance to the Second Reconstruction, 1954–1964* (1994).

Slavery and Emancipation

The topics of slavery and emancipation trouble southern culture, raising issues that make many, regardless of race, uncomfortable. Slavery and emancipation combine as stories of liberation and loss, of identities gained and identities shattered, a history that places conflict and domination at the center of the region's past. Representing the promise of freedom and equality on one hand and the broken dream of plantation slavery on the other, the transition from slavery to freedom is above all else a shared history of conflict. Yet where does a revolution—one that pitted southerner against southerner—fit in the construction of a common southern identity or a shared southern culture? This dilemma so challenges the South that this history has been quieted and domesticated in the myths of the region.

The dominant white southern parable of emancipation transforms the moment of freedom from a political act to a personal one. Freedom, according to this story, left African Americans bereft, compelled to return home to their white folks. In *The Unvanquished*, William Faulkner recounted the tales of his youth, writing that those "who had followed the Yankees away . . . [had scattered] into the hills [to] live in caves and hollow trees like animals I suppose, not only with no one to depend on but with no one depending on them, caring whether they returned or not or lived or died or not." Noble white southerners, such as the Sartorises, took African Americans back in, both the faithful Ringo, who had never left, and the unfaithful Loosh, who had walked off declaring, "I going. I done been freed . . . ; I dont belong to John Sartoris now; I belongs to me and God." According to Faulkner and his peers, whether African Americans claimed freedom or not, the end result was the same: former slaves returned to the plantation household.

Our national narrative recognizes the political significance of emancipation by emphasizing that Abraham Lincoln waged a four-year bloody civil war to free the slaves. Yet this story elides the fact that it was not Lincoln, the U.S. military, or the federal government that freed the slaves. The push for emancipation began in the South.

Enslaved black southerners freed themselves during the Civil War, altering the course of the war and the nation. In what historian Steven Hahn writes was "the most sweeping revolution of the 19th century, [slaves] shifted the social and political course of the Atlantic world." Because of their actions, the U.S. Congress adopted the Thirteenth Amendment in 1865, abolishing slavery across the nation. Emancipation, therefore, is largely a southern story defining a region and a people.

At the outset of the Civil War, slaves identified Pres. Abraham Lincoln and the Union army as their allies in the struggle for freedom. Yet the Lincoln administration was a reluctant partner. As Lincoln stated in 1862, "My paramount objective in this struggle is to save the Union and is *not* to either save or destroy slavery. If I could save the Union without freeing any slave I would do it, and if I could save it by freeing all the slaves I would do it; and if I could save it by freeing some and leaving others alone I would also do that. What I do about slavery, and the colored race, I do because I believe it helps to save the Union." Southern institutions, including slavery, would be respected in order to bring the South back into the nation.

As early as May 1861, African Americans declared themselves free by running away and entering Union army camps. As the Union army invaded Virginia, South Carolina, and the Mississippi Valley, slaves stood ready to run for freedom. The land of liberty suddenly lay within reach as the Civil War brought the North into the South.

Making policy as they waged war, Union generals responded to the freedpeople's exodus in a number of ways. Gen. John C. Frémont simply freed every slave who came within his lines. Outraged, Lincoln removed him from his command. Gen. Benjamin Butler decided to keep former slaves within his lines not as free people but as "the contraband of war." Slaves, he reasoned, were valuable property—instruments of war—that could be used to assist either the Confederacy or the Union. From Butler's perspective, it was better to have slaves serve the Union than the enemy. As word spread that Butler permitted the black southerners to stay and work within his lines, hundreds of slaves began to make their way to Union lines across the South. They liberated themselves. Eventually, over 400,000 slaves freed themselves by walking across Union lines. Subsequently, Lincoln legitimized these actions through the Emancipation Proclamation on 1 January 1863, which abolished slavery in the Confederacy.

While the national narrative embraces the political significance of emancipation, it is slower to recognize that slavery is a national story as well. Slavery disturbs core American ideals: the belief in freedom, equality, and democracy. Therefore, we locate slavery in the South to set it apart from mainstream American history. This evasion ignores the fact that slavery existed north and south, east and west, in our early republic. More important, slavery is deeply (and paradoxically) intertwined with the nation's early history and founding institutions. As historian Edmund Morgan reminds us, American slavery created American concepts of freedom. To unravel this, we turn to the South to help explain our origins.

Slavery was a foreign institution to English settlers. From 1607 (when the first successful English colony was established in Jamestown) to 1691 (when legal codes hardened race-based slavery), colonial governments struggled with the concept of modern slavery. It took four generations for European Americans to accept and institutionalize "the peculiar institution" that (1) turned people into property, (2) made that status inheritable, and (3) justified dehumanization based upon an emerging concept—race.

American slavery rested on the distinction that people could be separated into "black" and "white." As such, these categories had to be made and maintained. Indeed, the construction of the new category of "white men"—not Englishmen, Scottish, Dutch—proved essential to the institution. To keep slavery intact required the combined self-interest of the new group of people— free white men. Before slavery, any concept that all white men might share a common interest was absurd. Class divided masters from servants, ladies from wenches, gentlemen from farmers. These tensions continued, but the legal code began to blur differences by granting white people a set of common civil rights. One of the first legal expressions of whiteness appeared in the 1691 Virginia legal codes, which stated that all white men (regardless of whether that white man owned enslaved people or not) shared the right to regulate, detain, and punish any black person. Race-based slavery, therefore, provided a foundation for nascent American democracy by declaring a certain kind of equality between all white men regardless of class, religion, nationality, or station in life.

The special rights accorded to those who could prove their whiteness established the founding template for race in the United States. Americans can forget the place of slavery and race in the founding of the nation because the words "slavery" and "slave" do not appear in the U.S. Constitution. Instead, slavery is obliquely referred to by its opposite: "free persons." Who is fully free, however, still rests on "race," as more and more Americans discover (Latinos, Asians, and American Indians, among others). A "nonwhite" status undermines access to full civil rights and equal opportunity.

Emancipation established by the passage of the Thirteenth Amendment (abolishing slavery), the Fourteenth Amendment (establishing federal citizenship rights for black and white Americans), and the Fifteenth Amendment (granting African American men the right to vote) disrupted the correlation between whiteness and citizenship. Moving into politics, the marketplace, and the public square, African Americans challenged white people's concept of themselves and their nation.

In the South, African Americans claimed freedom as southerners. Liberty, for most, rested on family, land, and the crop because each of these promised a kind of self-sufficiency and independence from outsiders. Black southerners and white southerners shared these values, and this fact brought them into direct conflict.

Many, but not all, white southerners refused to share public space or political power with black southerners. Viewing emancipation as a zero-sum game, planters felt that their freedom would be sacrificed if African Americans became fully free. Many whites would not acknowledge African American claims because land, family, and the crop (not to mention the political and civil rights that accompanied them) were integral to white identity and power. To grant African Americans rights threatened an erasure of white manhood.

Emancipation exposed the fiction of white men's independence. Planter men found themselves "dependent" on free labor, "dependent" on their women for financial support, and, in the case of the wounded, literally "dependent" on others for mobility. More profound, as black southerners took up arms and asserted their claims, they challenged what the white man saw as *his* household—*his* land, *his* crops, and *his* workers. As plantation slavery dissolved, mastery, whiteness, and manhood all lost their moorings.

White southerners fought back, limiting black southerners' access to voting rights, civil rights, and the public sphere and freedom from fear. Each limitation took a toll on the public remembrance of emancipation. Immediately following the war and up to the turn of the century, black southerners celebrated Emancipation Day with parades and speeches, retelling the story of how they won their freedom. As each southern state imposed segregation (and turned a blind eye to lynching), violence disrupted and finally stopped these celebrations across much of the South. States filled the silence created in the absence of Emancipation Day ceremonies with newly minted histories that defamed Reconstruction, credited the Yankees with emancipation, and depicted black southerners as either bestial or childlike. Black southerners—Carter Woodson, Pauli Murray, Susie King Taylor, and Anna Julia Cooper, to name just a few— responded with histories of their own. The history of emancipation became a segregated history—and, in many ways, it still is. The history of emancipation tends to be written either as an African American freedom struggle (the study of "Emancipation" and "Reconstruction") or as the study of whites' loss, mourning, and nostalgia for an invented past (the study of "the Lost Cause").

Yet slavery and emancipation are a shared history, one that reminds us how brutal, contested, and revolutionary sharing has been. If southern culture emphasizes stasis, tradition, and a common identity, then the transition from slavery to freedom represents its opposite—the struggle between white and black, slave and free, rights and privilege. This truth disturbs southern myth by exposing the fact that each of these histories is dependent on the others. Far from being opposed, southern culture and emancipation are contingent upon one another. Southern culture, in large part, is the act of forgetting emancipation and its implications. Manners, congeniality, and honor work to paper over conflict and to refuse to speak of southerners' unpleasantness to southerners. Slavery and emancipation, therefore, are an unspoken referent, a hidden heart, of southern culture.

NANCY BERCAW
Smithsonian Institution

David W. Blight, *Race and Reunion: The Civil War in American Memory* (2001); Elsa Barkley Brown, *The Black Public Sphere: A Public Culture Book* (1995); Kathleen M. Brown, *Good Wives, Nasty Wenches, and Anxious Patriarchs: Gender, Race, and Power in Colonial Virginia* (1996); W. E. B. Du Bois, *Black Reconstruction in America: An Essay toward a History of the Part Which Black Folk Played in the Attempt to Reconstruct Democracy in America, 1860–1880* (1935); Barbara J. Fields, in *Region, Race, and Reconstruction: Essays in Honor of C. Vann Woodward*, ed. J. Morgan Kousser and James McPherson (1982); Thavolia Glymph, *Out of the House of Bondage: The Transformation of the Plantation Household* (2008); Larry J. Griffin and Don H. Doyle, eds., *The South as an American Problem* (1995); Ariela Julie Gross, *What Blood Won't Tell: A History of Race on Trial in America* (2008); Steven Hahn, *A Nation under Our Feet: Black Political Struggles in the Rural South from Slavery to the Great Migration* (2003); Thomas C. Holt, *The Problem of Race in the Twenty-first Century* (2000); Winthrop Jordan, *White over Black: American Attitudes toward the Negro, 1550–1812* (1968); Stephanie McCurry, *Confederate Reckoning: Power and Politics in the Civil*

War South (2010); Tiya Miles, *Ties That Bind: The Story of an Afro-Cherokee Family in Slavery and Freedom* (2005); Edmund S. Morgan, *American Slavery, American Freedom: The Ordeal of Colonial Virginia* (1975); Jennifer L. Morgan, *Laboring Women: Reproduction and Gender in New World Slavery* (2004).

Southern Indians and the Problem of Race

Native southerners only gradually and incompletely adopted the concept of race as inherent, immutable, and transgenerational differences grounded in phenotype. When Europeans first arrived in the South in the 16th century, indigenous people were members of extended kin groups and subjects of powerful chiefs who exercised secular and religious authority. Chiefdoms warred with each other, enslaved captives, reduced lesser polities to tributary status, and periodically reconfigured the population into new polities. As chiefdoms collapsed after the European invasion, kinship alone came to define political relationships, and individuals were either kin or enemies. By the 18th century, southern Indian tribes began to adopt as well as enslave Europeans and Africans as well as enemy Indians. Slaves had no rights, but Indians did not distinguish between members born into tribes and adoptees, regardless of their physical appearance.

As Indians acquired the racial attitudes of southern whites, they increasingly held only people of African descent in bondage. By the late 18th century, they regarded blacks and whites as distinct from each other and from the large, diverse group called "Indian." But "Indian" contributed far less to their identity than did their nations. In an 1826 address, for example, Cherokee Elias Boudinot sought to counter "repelling and degrading" stereotypes of his "race" by chronicling the accomplishments of his own people. Being "Indian" meant being a citizen of an Indian nation.

Contemporaries tended to use "tribe" and "nation" interchangeably, as do modern scholars and southern Indians. By the 1820s, the Cherokees, Chickasaws, Choctaws, and Creeks had the defined territories, laws, and delegated political power that made "nation" more accurate. At the same time, citizenship and kinship intertwined, as they do in "tribal" societies. Southern Indians continued to consider a range of people whose ancestry included Africans and Europeans to be tribal citizens and, therefore, "Indian." In addition to adoptees and their descendants, the offspring of intermarried whites and blacks were considered Indian, especially if their mothers belonged to the clans that formed the basis of a matrilineal kin network. These people were not "mixed blood" from a Native perspective: either they were Indian by virtue of tribal membership or they were not. Having kin conveyed both a tribal and a racial identity.

Some colonial officials had promoted the intermarriage of whites and Indians as the solution to the Indian problem because they assumed that the offspring would become a part of Euro-American society. In fact, the opposite occurred, and by the 1820s intermarriage had produced many of the leaders in the large southern nations that held land in common. As Native resistance to forced removal from the South mounted in the late 1820s, politicians increasingly disparaged tribal leaders who had white ancestry as charlatans who pretended to be Indians. As far as the Indian nations were concerned, these men were Indians.

In the late 18th and early 19th centuries, the federal government developed a policy to "civilize" Indians, whom they thought of collectively even while they dealt with them tribally through the negotiation of treaties. Grounded in Enlightenment ideas, the "civilization" policy sought to make Indians culturally indistinguishable from Euro-Americans in order to assimilate them into white society. The Cherokees, Chickasaws, Choctaws, Creeks, and Seminoles selectively adopted aspects of the policy, and their success at cultural transformation earned them the designation "Five Civilized Tribes," a term that scholars no longer use. The accomplishments of these tribes did not protect them from the consequences of a shift in racial attitudes in the early 19th century. Increasingly, policy makers rejected ideas behind the "civilization" program and came to believe that Indians were an inherently inferior race that must be expelled from the South. Federal commissioners negotiated fraudulent treaties with the five tribes and forced them into what is today eastern Oklahoma. By 1842, most of their citizens were west of the Mississippi.

No tribal governments recognized by treaty remained in the South. The absence of polities readily identifiable as Indian tribes or nations rendered racial categorization more difficult and haphazard. The Choctaw removal treaty made those Choctaws who chose to remain in Mississippi legally white, and the Georgia and Alabama legislatures declared a handful of Creeks and Cherokees white. But the vast majority of southern Indians—both remnants of removed tribes and members of tribes never slated for removal—remained in legal limbo. Over the next century, the Cherokees, Choctaws, and Seminoles managed to secure federal recognition as tribes, but other southern Indian communities struggled to create nations that outsiders would recognize. Following the Civil War, it became even more difficult for Indians to carve out a place in a legal system that normally provided for only two races.

Having federally recognized tribal governments did not necessarily mean that the three tribes escaped the discrimination inherent in Jim Crow. White schools in western North Carolina, for example, denied admission to Cherokee students in the 1890s. The white school in Indiantown, Fla., expelled the four or five Seminoles who had enrolled in 1916 because local whites objected, and as late as the 1950s Mississippi Choctaws were "generally treated as colored," despite the treaty provision that made them white. When the federal government tried to intervene on their behalf, state and local authorities insisted that "colored" facilities were available to these Indians. The other southern tribes that received federal services in the age of Jim Crow—the Chitimachas and Coushattas in Louisiana and the Catawbas in South Carolina—often found themselves on the other side of the color line from whites and suffered discrimination in education, social services, employment, and public accommodations.

Whites considered "Indian" to be a race, but both they and Native peoples recognized enormous diversity that undermined tendencies to essentialize Indians. Some state legislation applied to "Indians" generally, but other acts named specific tribes. Not all tribes were the same. The University of North Carolina, for example, officially admitted Cherokees, but by the 1930s it had closed the door to Lumbees. The reason was the perception that Lumbees had African American ancestry and Cherokees did not. Indeed, tainted blood became a familiar explanation for discrimination against Indians. An attorney involved in an attempt to dispossess Chitimachas explained: "We call them Indians out of respect for the aboriginal red skin from whom they are only remote descendants. They have intermarried with negroes and with rare exceptions with white persons, so that there is not now a full-blooded Indian upon the property." Therefore, Indians began to assert the purity of their "blood." A Coushatta wrote the Office of Indian Affairs: "We are not Choctaw and not Chittimache. We all belong full blood of Coushatta Indians." Some tribes, especially those with federal recognition, instituted "blood quantum," or ancestry, requirements for membership in the 20th century.

The omnipresence of white racism prompted tribes to police their racial borders. In 1921, for example, the North Carolina legislature created a "blood" committee, composed of Lumbees, that determined whom to admit to Lumbee schools, and in 1954 the Poarch Creeks in Alabama insisted that an Indian woman whose children had an African American father withdraw the youngsters from their state-funded Indian school. Tribes also evaluated the racial purity of each other. In 1946, the Cherokee chief and the agency superintendent visited the Pamunkeys in Virginia to determine whether or not the boarding school at Cherokee would admit them. The concern was the "good deal of negro blood apparent among some of these eastern remnants of tribes," and the decision was that Pamunkeys as well as "children of similar appearance" could enroll. Southern Indians could not divorce themselves from racism.

Dennis Wolfe, a full-blooded Cherokee, in Cherokee, N.C., ca. 1980–90 (Carol M. Highsmith, photographer, Library of Congress [LC-HS503-3028], Washington, D.C.)

The federal government had a constitutionally sanctioned relationship with tribes, not individuals, and the Office of Indian Affairs (OIA) tried with little success to mitigate the impact of Jim Crow on recognized tribes. In 1934, the Indian Reorganization Act extended OIA responsibility to individuals of "one-half or more Indian blood." As a result, bureaucrats obsessed over the ancestry of Indians who were not federally recognized. They combed official records, interviewed local whites, consulted anthropologists, and made fact-finding tours. Since the colonial period, there had been so much intermarriage among many peoples in the South that quantifiable evidence of ancestry eluded them, so the OIA turned to anthropometry. In 1936, in an effort to determine if the Lumbees of North Carolina were Indian, a physical anthropologist measured, plucked, scratched, and photographed 209 of them. The conclusion that 22 were at least one-half Indian and that others had predominantly African and European ancestry led to questions about the racial authenticity of Lumbees. Though not based on "scientific" study, similar questions arose about other southern Indians.

In one sense, a tribal identity separated Indians from race, and nationhood provided Indians a platform for political engagement. Consequently, most southern Indian peoples have sought recognition of their tribal sovereignty rather than individual civil rights. A primary attribute of sovereignty is the right to determine membership, and criteria for membership vary from tribe to tribe. Although some southern tribes require a specific fraction of tribal ancestry, others have decided that demonstrable descent is sufficient for enrollment. Southern Indians, therefore, have found it difficult to be a "race" when their conception of themselves is as tribal nations.

THEDA PERDUE
University of North Carolina at Chapel Hill

Malinda Maynor Lowery, *Lumbee Indians in the Jim Crow South: Race, Identity, and the Making of a Nation* (2010); Theda Perdue, in *The Culture of Jim Crow: Rethinking the Segregated South*, ed. Stephanie Cole and Natalie Ring (2011); Christina Snyder, *Slavery in Indian Country: The Changing Face of Captivity in Early America* (2010).

Southern Politics and Race

Race is the single biggest divider in southern politics, education, and culture. Today the South is still home to the nation's largest African American population. According to the 2000 U.S. Census, roughly 54 percent of all American blacks live in the South, about 15.8 million of the 30 million in total. Political schisms based on race are not a new phenomenon for the South. Largely because of slavery and race, southern political history includes war, Reconstruction, and a long era of second-class citizenship.

Black southern political history fits into six distinct epochs: slavery, the Civil War, Reconstruction, the post–Reconstruction Jim Crow era, the civil rights movement, and the post–civil rights era. Slavery was the most apolitical time for southern blacks, as bondage prevented them from even the most rudimentary political participation. While by and large blacks were not actually political participants, their presence was the great political issue. The slavery question framed the concepts of states' rights and federalism and debates about admission of states into the Union.

The Civil War was fought largely over slavery, and race was also central to Reconstruction, a period from 1866 to 1877. Because of Abraham Lincoln's Emancipation Proclamation and the Radical Republican–led ratification in the U.S. Congress of the Thirteenth, Fourteenth, and Fifteenth Amendments, blacks mostly voted Republican. The Thirteenth Amendment declared an end to slavery throughout the United States. The Fourteenth Amendment provided for equal protection and due process and clarified citizenship, overturning the notorious *Dred Scott v. Sandford* (1857) decision, which said that the framers of the Constitution had not intended for blacks to be citizens. The Fifteenth Amendment declared that the right to vote shall not be abridged on account of race.

Reconstruction witnessed unprecedented black political growth in the South. Largely because of armed Union troops protecting voters and candidates from violence and intimidation, African Americans voted with unprecedented strength and fielded candidates for all levels of political office. At this time, blacks, the majority population in Mississippi and South Carolina, were able to use this numerical advantage to elect their own to the U.S. Congress, including Sen. Hiram Revels of Mississippi in 1870.

Yet this political surge ended almost as quickly as it began. Following the Compromise of 1877, white southern elites, known as Bourbon Democrats, used the conclusion of Reconstruction to their advantage. These plantation elites instituted a series of laws and regulations that served the purpose of removing blacks from political power and placing a whole host of day-to-day humiliations on the black population. The Supreme Court's decision in *Plessy v. Ferguson* (1896) provided national sanction to the doctrine of separate-but-equal in public transportation.

Jim Crow quickly dissolved the political progress made by blacks during Reconstruction. There were several Jim Crow political restrictions—most harmful and pernicious were those that limited the vote. American states generally could impose restrictions on the vote because judicial interpretation of the U.S. Constitution at the time regarded voting as a "reserved" power belonging to the states, not a fundamental right belonging to all American citizens.

Many states instituted literacy tests, which the Supreme Court found legal in *Williams v. Mississippi* (1898). Written in a race-neutral manner but mostly applied to blacks and very poor whites, these tests required voters to interpret

"TIME WORKS WONDERS."

IAGO. (JEFF DAVIS.) "FOR THAT I DO SUSPECT THE LUSTY MOOR
HATH LEAP'D INTO MY SEAT: THE THOUGHT WHEREOF
DOTH LIKE A POISONOUS MINERAL GNAW MY INWARDS." ___ OTHELLO.

A cartoon published on 9 April 1870 showing Jefferson Davis looking over his shoulder at Hiram Revels seated in the U.S. Senate. (Thomas Nast, Library of Congress [LC-USZ62-108004], Washington, D.C.)

a legal statute or clause of the state constitution. Whites were often exempted from the rigors of these tests through an "understanding clause," which gave the voting registrar wide discretion to decide who was fit to vote on an individual basis. Particularly good at nullifying the vote was the poll tax. This tax charged a fee to vote and, since most blacks during the Jim Crow era were in the economic underclass, thus served the purpose of encouraging blacks not to vote. The grandfather clause dictated that unless your grandfather was eligible to vote, you were not eligible to vote, although *Guinn v. United States* (1915) declared this particular practice unconstitutional. State legislators often wrote these laws in a race-neutral manner, but rarely were they applied as such.

An additional form of voting discrimination was the white primary. The period 1876–1944 saw one-party voting, in which the Democratic Party dominated in local, state, and national elections. As a result of the ineffectiveness of the Republican Party in the era, general elections were largely irrelevant because the Democratic primary was the real election. To exclude black voters, the Democratic Party declared itself a private organization that could limit participation in its internal affairs, resulting in the white primary. This lasted until *Smith v. Allwright* (1944), when the Supreme Court declared that the Democratic Party was not actually private.

Nonetheless, Jim Crow persisted throughout the first half of the 20th century. Characteristic of the legal struggle for equality during this time was the failure of the Dyer Antilynching Bill, which died in the U.S. Senate in 1918. Southern senators were able to kill legislation making lynching—mob punishment—a federal crime. Southern congressmen were generally successful at keeping the federal government out of civil rights and out of the South until the civil rights movement prompted federal intervention.

Eradication of Jim Crow segregation and political restrictions was the larger goal of black protest. To that end, the civil rights movement, a large-scale effort led by southern blacks emphasizing nonviolent resistance, affected all Americans. Southern blacks who played a particular role include Ralph Abernathy, Medgar Evers, James Farmer, Martin Luther King Jr., John C. Lewis, James Meredith, and Rosa Parks. The NAACP, the Congress for Racial Equality (CORE), the Student Nonviolent Coordinating Committee (SNCC), the Little Rock Nine, the Greensboro Four, and countless other individuals and groups combined to end Jim Crow in the South.

The first successful moments of the civil rights movement came from the Legal Defense Fund of the NAACP. Based in New York City and led by Charles Hamilton Houston and later Thurgood Marshall, these legal eagles sued to end Jim Crow racial discrimination in public accommodations, public transportation, and voting. Arguably the most important case was *Brown v. Board of Education* (1954), which declared separate-but-equal in public education unconstitutional.

Of the many notable events of the civil rights movement, five are particularly significant, along with the numerous individuals who sacrificed time, energy, money, and, in some instances, their lives. On 1 December 1955, in Montgomery, Ala., police arrested Rosa Parks for refusing to give up her seat on a bus to a white man and violating the city's law requiring segregation on its buses. Casting him into a role of national prominence, Rev. Martin Luther King Jr. helped lead a 381-day boycott of the Montgomery bus system. Eventually, the courts held segregation on intrastate public transportation unconstitutional and ended the boycott.

In 1957, the Little Rock, Ark., school board voted to integrate the school system, but segregationist governor Orval Faubus thwarted the plan. The integration plan was relatively tame, as the school board permitted just nine students to integrate Little Rock's Central High School. This form of token integration was common in the South following the Supreme Court's 1955 order to desegregate with "all deliberate speed." Governor Faubus's actions, including withdrawing protection for the nine students, prompted a constitutional crisis, and President Dwight Eisenhower sent the 101st Airborne Division to protect the students from mob violence.

Countless incidents similar to Little Rock played out throughout the South in the ensuing years as blacks tried to integrate local schools. Many whites were laissez-faire, yet many more, perhaps emboldened by the Strom Thurmond–penned Southern Manifesto, fiercely resisted. The White Citizens' Council best epitomizes this massive resistance. Formed in Indianola, Miss., in 1954, members resisted efforts to integrate public life in the South.

Nonetheless, blacks and white liberals persistently attacked southern Jim Crow. The Freedom Riders, in 1961, an integrated collection of northern college students, attempted to ride public buses from Washington, D.C., to New Orleans. Beaten, bloodied, and arrested in Alabama and Mississippi, the riders did not reach Louisiana. In 1963, during Freedom Summer, northerners attempted to register black Mississippians to vote. The murder of three of these civil rights workers cast a pall over the effort. However, these events stigmatized the South while also encouraging moderate whites in Congress eventually to take decisive action.

Prompted by Police Commissioner Eugene "Bull" Connor's 1963 unleashing of police dogs on civil rights demonstrators in Birmingham, Ala., the 1964 Civil Rights Act protected individuals against arbitrary discrimination. Passage of this legislation was not easy. Enacted after the longest filibuster (83 days) in Senate history, the 1964 Civil Rights Act outlawed discrimination in hotels, motels, restaurants, theaters, and all other public accommodations engaged in interstate commerce; guaranteed equal protection for blacks in federally funded programs by prohibiting discrimination on the basis of race; banned discrimination in employment in any business on the basis of race; and established the Equal Employment Opportunity Commission.

Following passage of the 1964 Civil Rights Act, advocates still sought legislation protecting the franchise for blacks. Despite the Fifteenth Amendment outlawing the abridgement of voting based on race, southern states in particular used numerous tactics to discourage blacks from voting, including literacy tests, poll taxes, and intimidation. The weakness of the Civil Rights Act of 1957 was evident by the paucity of black voters in the South. The 1965 Voting Rights Act became the single most important piece of legislation for increasing political participation of southern blacks. Between March 1965 and November 1988, the black-white gap in registration closed almost to nothing.

As written, the Voting Rights Act allowed federal registrars in areas where less than 50 percent of eligible voters were actually registered. These so-called covered jurisdictions must obtain preclearance from the Justice Department before they change, or implement any changes in, their voting practices, in order to prevent any return to discriminatory practices. The fear is that jurisdictions might approve a policy that suffers from retrogression.

The increase in black voter registration and office holding during the 1960s altered the South's political scene. In 1960, 1,414,052, or 28 percent, of eligible black adults voted. By the end of the decade, 64.3 percent participated in the electoral process. Tennessee (92.1 percent), Arkansas (77.9 percent), and Texas (73.1 percent) were the southern states with the highest numbers of registered black voters.

In 1975, the number of black elected public officials in the South stood at 1,600. Within five years, the number had jumped to nearly 2,500, and by January 1985 there were 3,233 black elected officials in the South. By 1993, there were 4,924 African Americans holding office in the South, representing 60 percent of such officials in the nation. In 2001, there were 6,179 black elected officials in the South, representing 68 percent of the nation's total.

In the post–civil rights era, southern black partisanship has been reliably Democratic. Since President Lyndon B. Johnson signed the 1964 Civil Rights Act into law, southern blacks have voted Democratic, with 1964 serving as a realigning election. Republican nominee Barry Goldwater, famous for his opposition of the 1964 Civil Rights Act, won only five states, his home state of Arizona and the four Deep South states of Louisiana, Mississippi, Alabama, and South Carolina.

Even so, for most white southerners the move from Democratic to Republican partisanship was gradual. An important distinction is the ideological difference between southern and national Democrats. Until the 1994 congressional elections, southern Democrats were considerably more conservative than their national counterparts in Washington, D.C., which enabled white southerners to vote in a bipartisan manner yet consistently vote for the conservative candidate. Not until the 1980 election of Ronald Reagan did Republicans attract conservative southern candidates at the state and local levels. Nonetheless, while the Republican Party is the dominant party in the South today, Republican hegemony in the South is not nearly as complete as Democratic hegemony was during the Solid South era. For instance, Democrats still controlled the Mississippi House until 2012, although it remained a reliably conservative legislative body.

In the post–civil rights era, two issues are particularly relevant to southern black politics—affirmative action in education and criminal justice. Affirmative action policies are designed to correct past discrimination against racial minorities. Two Supreme Court cases provide guidelines on affirmative action as it relates to higher education. First, in *Regents of the University of California v. Bakke* (1978), the Court declared a special admissions program for minorities unconstitutional and specified that quotas violate the equal protection clause of the Fourteenth Amendment. To justify affirmative action as a remedy, a plaintiff had to show that an institution had engaged in past discrimination. However, universities can use race as a plus factor along with other factors. More recently, in *Gratz v. Bollinger* (2003), the Supreme Court affirmed a university's right to use race as a plus factor in admissions to obtain a "critical mass" of minority students, because diversity in higher education is a compelling governmental interest as long as the program is "narrowly tailored" to achieve that end. In a companion case, *Grutter v. Bollinger* (2003), the Court stated that the Constitution "does not prohibit the law schools' narrowly tailored use of race in admissions decisions to further a compelling interest in obtaining the educational benefits that flow from a diverse student body." Justice Sandra Day O'Connor wrote, however, that universities should not allow affirmative action a permanent status, working instead to implement a "color-blind" policy.

The penal system, the death penalty in particular, has hit African American males particularly hard. Roughly 10.4 percent of all black males between the ages of 25 and 29 are either incarcerated, paroled, or on probation. Out of the 1,066 executions in America since 1976, 363, or 34.1 percent, have been black defendants; blacks now make up 41.8 percent of death row inmates. The death penalty is most prevalent in the South. Out of the 1,066 total executions since 1976, 749, or 70.3 percent, took place in the South, and out of the 363 black executions, 275, or 75.8 percent, took place in the South. This is particularly significant given the large number of exonerations, although southern states are slow to embrace the moratorium movement currently sweeping the nation.

Today, the issue of race and politics in the South is more than just black and white. The South is a dynamic and changing environment, as recently exemplified by the sizable number of recent immigrants to the region from Mexico and beyond. This influx will likely be the next great challenge to the South.

MARVIN P. KING JR.
University of Mississippi

Numan V. Bartley, *The Rise of Massive Resistance: Race and Politics in the South during the 1950s* (1969); Merle Black and Earl Black, *The Rise of Southern Republicans* (2002); David A. Bositis, *Black Elected Officials: A Statistical Survey* (2001); Dan T. Carter, *From George Wallace to Newt Gingrich: Race in the Conservative Counterrevolution* (1996); Joseph Crespino, *In Search of Another Country: Mississippi and the Conservative Counterrevolution* (2007); Robert A. Goldwin, *A Nation of States: Essays on the American Federal System* (1961); Ira Katznelson, *When Affirmative Action Was White: An Untold History of Racial Inequality in Twentieth-Century America* (2005); V. O. Key, *Southern Politics in State and Nation* (1949).

Sports and Segregation/Integration

Many sports historians have argued that sports have been a reflection of American culture, particularly when it comes to race. That institutional racism prevented the participation of minorities in specific sports just as it prevented their participation politically, economically, and socially in American society. However, an argument can be made that sport is more than a mere reflection of society; it also has the ability to shape individuals, opinions about race, and opportunity. Without question, the laboratory that has conducted the most racial experiments has been the American South. Individual states that were vehemently committed to slavery, lynching, and segregation are now just as committed to having successful football teams, on which the majority of the players are African American. The integration of many schools in the South took Supreme Court decisions, and today these same institutions spend millions of dollars recruiting the best African American athletes to enroll and play various sports.

In 1962, it took U.S. marshals and the U.S. Army to enroll James Meredith at the University of Mississippi; in 1997, this same institution gave Deuce McAllister a football scholarship and welcomed him with open arms. Meredith needed U.S. marshals to attend class, eat in the cafeteria, and sleep in the dormitory. McAllister was embraced by University of Mississippi fans as he walked through the Grove before games, was a part of a marketing campaign aimed at helping him to win the Heisman trophy, and would finish his career as arguably the greatest running back in the history of football at the University of Mississippi.

During the 20th century, several individuals and events shaped sports long before black players like McAllister were allowed to play college football. The first black heavyweight boxing champion, Jack Johnson, challenged notions of black inferiority, particularly in the rigidly segregated South. Johnson challenged white ideas of black inferiority when he became champion in 1908 by easily defeating Tommy Burns, and he openly dated white women at a time when black men were routinely lynched for being accused of looking at white women. Although he did not view himself as a role model for African Americans, they clearly viewed him as such and with great pride and admiration embraced his achievements in the ring. Blacks and whites alike recognized that during this era his habit of whipping white men in the ring was a political act of far-reaching dimensions—none more so than his defeat of Jim Jefferies, the "Great White Hope," on 4 July 1910. As a result of Johnson's victory in the ring, whites attacked blacks in riots all across America, with the vast majority taking place in the South. Johnson was finally defeated by Jess Willard in 1915 as a result of a controversial knockout; quite possibly he threw the fight in the hope of appeasing the federal government, which had brought charges against him of violating the Mann Act. With his defeat, white America let out a grateful sigh of relief, expecting that things would return to normal in the sports world. For African Americans, the reality of Johnson's defeat caused them to look inward and create new heroes in another sport, baseball.

The Negro Leagues were a relatively successful black business during their existence from 1920 until 1960. More important, they served as the premier form of entertainment for many African Americans in the South and in urban northern cities. Outstanding players such as Andrew "Rube" Foster, Satchel Paige, Josh Gibson, Cool Papa Bell, Oscar Charleston, Judy Johnson, Buck Leonard, and Ray Dandridge were not allowed to play major league baseball prior to 1947. They played on teams in the South, such as the Atlanta Black Crackers, the Birmingham Black Barons, the Chattanooga Black Lookouts, the Memphis Red Sox, and the Nashville Elite Giants. There were also several successful northern teams, such as the Cleveland Buckeyes, the Homestead Grays,

Jack Johnson challenged white ideas of black inferiority when he became heavyweight boxing champion in 1908 (photographer unknown, Library of Congress [LC-USZ62-93412], Washington, D.C.)

the Indianapolis ABCs, the Kansas City Monarchs, the Newark Eagles, the Philadelphia Stars, and the Pittsburgh Crawfords. These players and teams did not see themselves as being inferior. Just the opposite, black players felt that the talent in the Negro Leagues was better than that in major league baseball. This was proven in numerous exhibition games played between Negro League players and their major league counterparts. Sports historian John Holway estimated that teams made up of Negro League players won 57 percent of those games over teams made up of white major leaguers. World War II interrupted major league baseball, but after the war, in 1945, the signing of Jackie Robinson to a major league contract by the Brooklyn Dodgers sent shock waves throughout America. Robinson's journey through the minor leagues in 1946 caused many people to overlook professional football, as four black players were added to the rosters of the Los Angeles Rams of the National Football League (NFL) and the Cleveland Browns of the All-American Football Conference.

Pro football had allowed black players to participate since Charles Follis was paid as the game's first black professional in 1904, but a color barrier was established in the NFL after the 1933 season. Thus the signing of Kenny Washington and Woody Strode by the Rams and Bill Willis and Marion Motley by the Browns began the reintegration of pro football. Jackie Robinson's successful debut with the Dodgers in 1947 opened the doors of baseball, and black talent from the Negro Leagues poured in. Larry Doby, Roy Campanella, Satchel Paige, Monte Irvin, Willie Mays, Minnie Minoso, Ernie Banks, Elston Howard, and Hank Aaron established records and took baseball to heights it had never before seen. But the accomplishments of these great players on the field did not matter when they trained and traveled in the South. They were housed with black families or required to stay in black hotels, and they could not frequent the same restaurants as their white teammates. But by the late 1950s and early 1960s, an organized movement was taking place that directly challenged legal segregation in the South.

The *Brown* decision, the Montgomery Bus Boycott, and the murder of Emmitt Till provided the fuel for the civil rights movement, which forever changed the South. The three major college football conferences in the South — the Atlantic Coast Conference (ACC), the Southwest Conference (SWC), and the Southeastern Conference (SEC) — also underwent change as black players slowly integrated onto their respective teams. Arguably the University of Mississippi, which was forcibly integrated in 1962 by James Meredith, represented the last obstacle to African Americans in their pursuit of higher education. During the 1960s, black students trickled into southern colleges and universities, as well as onto their football teams.

Darryl Hill has been called the Jackie Robinson of southern college football. He was the first African American player at the U.S. Naval Academy, and when assistant coach Lee Corso at the University of Maryland convinced Hill to transfer to the Terps, he became their first black player. After sitting out one season, Hill became the first black player in the ACC when he made his debut against North Carolina State at wide receiver. "One of the toughest places I played was Clemson University. You know, 50,000 drunk southern gentlemen are waiting to see this brother come out on the field. Not a black person in the stands anywhere. The black people had to sit outside the stadium on a red dirt hill . . . and that's where they watched the game." Clemson used pass coverages that included double and triple teaming Hill, but he still set the ACC single-game pass-catching record with 10 catches. "I can remember they came down from the hill, when the game was over to the bus—and they were congratulating me. And that was a good feeling."

In 1966, Jerry Levias became the first African American scholarship player at Southern Methodist University, thus breaking the color barrier in the SWC. The 5-foot, 9-inch, 177-pound wide receiver set career records for the Mustangs and was one of the most exciting players in college football. One year later, in 1967, Nat Northington broke the color barrier in the SEC when he took the field for the University of Kentucky and played wide receiver in a 26–13 loss against the University of Mississippi. Northington would play in only three more games before leaving the team after being distraught over the death of Greg Page, who had been recruited with Northington in 1966 with the expectation that both black players would integrate the SEC. Page was injured during practice in August, and he died in September 1967.

The SEC has long been one of college football's strongest conferences. From 2006 to 2010, it produced five national champions. Without question, black players on these teams have been largely responsible for this success on the field, which has made the SEC the second-most-profitable conference in college football when it comes to television revenue. Although the Big 10 generated slightly more revenue than the SEC from television in 2010, that will likely change when future deals with national networks begin to produce funds. So schools like Mississippi and Alabama that fought hard against integration now fight each other in the recruitment of black athletes. Race is now viewed as an asset on the field, but not off the field. In college football, it is obvious that African Americans can play the game, but they cannot be head coaches who garner the same opportunities as their white counterparts. Jim Caldwell was the first black head football coach in the ACC when he coached Wake Forest from 1993 to 2000. In the old Southwestern Conference, which became the Big 12, Bob Simmons became its first black head coach when he took over Oklahoma State in 1995 and coached the Cowboys through the 2000 season. The SEC was the last of the major conferences in the South to integrate its head-coaching ranks, choosing to wait until the 21st century, when Mississippi State University hired Sylvester Croom in 2004.

The story of sports in the American South prior to World War II, like other aspects of this region, has been largely shaped by barriers based on race. The postwar period was largely shaped by the willingness, determination, and ability of African Americans to break down those same barriers. The process of adding athletes of color to football teams, basketball teams, baseball teams, track teams, golf teams, tennis teams, women's basketball teams, softball teams, volleyball teams, and other teams has taken place in secondary schools, high schools, colleges and universities, and professional teams throughout this region. Arguably on-the-field integration has been embraced and can be seen clearly in a sport like football, which brings southern towns and communities together, beginning on Friday nights for high school games and on Saturday for college games. During these brief two-to-three-hour contests, many blacks and whites cheer together, complain about calls made by officials, and second-guess plays by coaches, united in their love of the game. Without question, sport allows human beings to briefly experience a connection that few other aspects of society can provide.

CHARLES K. ROSS
University of Mississippi

HBO, *Breaking the Huddle: The Integration of College Football* (16 December 2008); Charles Martin, *Benching Jim Crow: The Rise and Fall of the Color Line in Southern College Sports, 1890–1980* (2010); Charles K. Ross, *Outside the Lines, African Americans and the Integration of the National Football League* (1999).

African Americans, Appalachian

African Americans have a long history in Appalachia. Arriving first in the 18th and 19th centuries as slaves, their numbers remained relatively small until the opening of the coalfields in the late 19th century. The need for miners encouraged a dramatic in-migration of free African Americans from the Deep South.

In West Virginia, the heart of central Appalachian coal country, the number of African American miners increased from just under 5,000 in 1900 to over 11,000 a decade later. By 1930, West Virginia had 22,000 African American miners. In Kentucky, African American miners numbered 2,200 in 1900 and 7,300 in 1930. These miners either followed family members to the central Appalachian region or were directly recruited by coal companies. While dispersed throughout the region, significant numbers of African Americans found their way to Kanawha and McDowell counties in West Virginia and Harlan County in Kentucky. In the region's coal towns, African Americans generally stood on more equal footing with European Americans as coal companies strove to maximize profits by keeping racial antagonism low and placing the most skilled workers in the appropriate jobs, regardless of race. As Appalachians, African Americans presently experience the myriad effects of poverty, including dilapidated housing, low educational attainment, and limited access to health and social services that typify this marginalized subregion. As a minority among mountain people,

African Americans additionally suffer the historical consequences of racism.

Any discussion of African Americans in Appalachia relates to a demographic understanding of Appalachia itself. The region, as delineated by the Appalachian Regional Commission in the 1960s, includes counties in 12 states stretching from Mississippi to New York. African Americans make up just under 8 percent of the Appalachian population across three subregions. In the southern, central, and northern subregions, African Americans make up 13, 2.2, and 3.6 percent of each subregion's population, respectively. Of the almost 8 percent (1.7 million) Appalachian African Americans, approximately 76 percent reside in the southern subregion, 22 percent live in the northern subregion, and 2.8 percent live in the central subregion. The 10 Appalachian counties with the highest percentages of African Americans are in Mississippi and Alabama. Additionally, those counties with the highest numbers are urban or adjacent to urban areas.

Implicit in any discussion of blacks in Appalachia is their distinctiveness from other African Americans in the South based on their mountain experience. Practicing the religious and musical traditions of their Deep South kinfolk, rural Appalachian African Americans also had ties to industrializing America, with the skills to match. These African Americans, however, have largely been ignored in the media and in scholarship. In their "discovery" of Appalachian culture in the late 19th and early 20th centuries, outsiders

Black coal miners in Appalachia, date unknown (Victor Howard Collection, Archives and Special Collections, University of Mississippi Library, Oxford)

stereotyped Appalachian residents as isolated, backward, violent, and, not least of all, Anglo-Saxon. Over the past 20 years, the people of Appalachia, including African Americans, have become increasingly critical of their pejorative representation in mainstream America.

Accompanying the rise of "place-based" studies and identity politics in the 1990s, African Americans began actively claiming an Appalachian identity. William H. Turner and Edward J. Cabbell's *Blacks in Appalachia* considered specific African American communities in the mountains and black coal miners. In the early 1990s, a Kentucky-based performance group, the Affrilachian Poets, began to give voice to the frustra-

tions of African Americans in Appalachia who feel excluded from historical and contemporary understandings of what it means to be from Kentucky and/or Appalachia. In Pennington Gap, Va., the county's first colored school, Lee County Colored Elementary School, has become the Appalachian African American Cultural Center. The center collects oral histories, photographs, copies of slave documents, and material culture pertaining to the African American historical experience in the region.

MICHAEL CRUTCHER
University of Kentucky

Dwight B. Billings, Gurney Norman, and Katherine Ledford, eds., *Back Talk from*

Appalachia: Confronting Stereotypes (1999); William H. Turner and Edward J. Cabbell, eds., *Blacks in Appalachia* (1985); F. X. Walker, *Affrilachia* (2000).

Afro-Cubans

"Afro-Cuban" (*afrocubano*) is a term that was invented by Cuban anthropologist Fernando Ortiz in the early 20th century. Those whom the term designates often suggest it fails to capture the nuances of Cuban history and seems to qualify citizenship in the nation that Cubans of African descent were instrumental in creating. Historically, the African population was proportionately much larger in Cuba than in the United States. Expanded sugar production in 19th-century Cuba rested on the labor of African slaves. Yet there were many more free people of color in Cuba than in the South under slavery. Afro-Cuban mutual aid societies (*los cabildos de naciones*) enabled retention of African languages and fostered syncretic Afro-Catholic religions (for example, Santeria). African-derived music and folklore have strongly influenced Cuban popular culture. Afro-Cuban music has enjoyed sustained popularity in the United States. Dizzy Gillespie's mid-20th-century collaboration with Cuban musicians Tito Puente, Mario Bauza, and Celia Cruz helped to establish a strong audience for salsa. Drums and metaphors from African religious traditions flavor this musical genre, which continues to draw broad interest, exemplified in the successful revival of the Buena Vista Social Club.

More than half of the soldiers in the Cuban revolt against Spain in 1895 were black or mulatto. It was during this revolution (and the earlier revolt of 1868) that Afro-Cubans first migrated to Florida and Louisiana. Cigar production in Key West and Tampa attracted Cuban settlers. Afro-Cubans accounted for about 15 percent of these 19th-century Cuban migrants. Smaller settlements of cigar workers located in Jacksonville and New Orleans. In addition to cigar workers, these early communities included a large number of Cuban intellectuals and political figures prominent in exile political organizations.

The end of the war against Spain in 1898 coincided with the rise of Jim Crow laws. Afro-Cubans were adversely affected by these laws. Segregated social clubs formed. The Sociedad La Unión Martí-Maceo, founded in Tampa in 1900, still remains in existence, as does El Círculo Cubano, the white Cuban club founded in 1899. The leading center of Cuban settlement in the United States during the early 20th century, Ybor City and West Tampa, were enclaves with elaborate social, recreational, and political organizations. Afro-Cubans were integrated into these enclaves, but with growing distance from white compatriots.

Cigar manufacture migration to Florida slowed during the Depression of the 1930s and ended completely with the 1961 embargo against Cuban tobacco imports. The very large influx of anti-Castro Cuban exiles, beginning in 1959, targeted Miami far more than Tampa; the Cuban histories of Key West and Jacksonville were by then nearly forgotten. Fewer than 10 percent of the immediate post-1959 immigrants were Afro-Cuban. Second- and third-generation Afro-Cubans in Tampa became more isolated, cut off from contact with Cuba and increasingly involved with African Americans.

The "Mariel" influx of Cubans in 1981 included a much larger proportion of Afro-Cubans, many of whom remained in Miami. More recent waves of immigrants and refugees on rafts have continued to include Afro-Cubans. Despite an increase in numbers, black Cubans of Miami have remained spatially and socially separate from white Cubans. Jim Crow and southern patterns of residential segregation explain only part of this phenomenon. The issue of racial diversity among Cubans has a long history of ambivalence. José Martí, who sought national unity, urged Cubans to ignore racial differences and forget past injustices. However, this discourages discourse about racial problems and has made Afro-Cubans relatively invisible.

Average incomes of Cuban immigrants exceed those of all other Latino ethnic groups in the United States. Black Cubans, however, have been shown to earn significantly less than their white counterparts. In Miami, especially, segregation between black Cubans and white Cubans is greater than for the population as a whole. Nevertheless, among recent immigrants and their children, there remains a strong identification with Cuba, and cultural practices such as food and music continue to favor the homeland. In Tampa, descendants of past immigrants are more varied in identification and cultural preferences. Fewer speak Spanish or regularly eat Cuban food. Many still

attend the St. Peter Claver Catholic Church, and a smaller number continue to belong to the Sociedad La Unión Martí-Maceo. The majority of descendants, however, more strongly identify as African American.

SUSAN D. GREENBAUM
University of South Florida

Alejandro de la Fuente, *A Nation for All: Race, Inequality, and Politics in Twentieth-Century Cuba* (2001); Susan Greenbaum, *More Than Black: Afro-Cubans in Tampa* (2002); Guillermo Grenier and Alex Stepick, eds., *Miami Now! Immigration, Ethnicity, and Social Change* (1992); Pedro Perez Sarduy and Jean Stubbs, eds., *Afro-Cuba* (1993); Madeline Zavodny, Working Paper 2003–10, Federal Reserve Bank of Atlanta (July 2003).

Afro-Seminole Creole

Afro-Seminole Creole is an offshoot of 17th- and 18th-century Gullah, traceable to the Africans who escaped from the British plantations in the southeastern Crown colonies of Georgia and South Carolina. These slaves, along with Creeks and other indigenous tribes, were allowed refuge in Spanish Florida, where they were called *cimarrones* 'fugitives,' possibly from a Native word referring to a kind of wild grass. *Seminole* comes from the Creek pronunciation (*siminoli, similoni*) of this Spanish word. When Florida joined the United States, slavery was still legal, and the African Seminoles petitioned to move west to Indian Territory (now Oklahoma), which they did in 1837. Others went to the Bahamas or Cuba. Still subject to slave raids in the United States, in 1849 they again petitioned to move, this time into northern Mexico, where they were granted 25 square miles of land at Nacimiento, in the state of Coahuila. In 1870, they were invited by the Texas Rangers to become scouts to help clear south Texas of Lipan Apaches and other tribes for European settlement. This they did, basing themselves in Fort Clark in Brackettville and in Fort Nicholas at Eagle Pass. In 1914, with the dissolution of the garrisons, some returned to Nacimiento and some remained in Brackettville. Today, the three main areas inhabited by Afro-Seminoles are Brackettville, Nacimiento (where they are known as Maskogos), and Wewoka, Okla. (where they are known as Freedmen). Their genetic and cultural makeup is traceable to various African and Native American peoples. They refer to themselves as "Negro Indians."

The food and the culture of Afro-Seminoles also include African and Amerindian elements. At a revival meeting, African gospel rhythms eventually move into the "Seminole stomp," which is clearly Native American, as is the preparation of frybread, *suffki*, and a flour from the royal palm (called a *coonteh*). Use of a large pestle and mortar to grind rice and corn probably has dual origins.

Historically, Gullah has developed into two independent branches: Sea Island Creole (SIC) and Afro-Seminole Creole (ASC). Their separation took place before the large-scale influence from Upper Guinean languages into the Georgia/Carolina region in the mid-18th century modified Gullah to become the variety described by Lorenzo Dow Turner and others in the 20th century. By contrast, ASC has been influenced by Spanish and indigenous languages. SIC resembled ASC more in the late 19th century than it does today. ASC negates solely with *no* (*hunnuh no bin yeddy um* 'you didn't hear her') and pluralizes with postnominal *dem* (*duh wisseh de knife dem dey?* 'where are the knives?'), both of which are now rare in contemporary SIC. It retains forms such as *warra* 'what' and *darra* 'that,' recorded only as archaic in other Creoles, such as Jamaican. Its future marker is *en*, from *gwen* 'going' (*e n'en talk turrum* 'she won't talk to her'), not found in SIC, where the similar-sounding *ain'* is today the common verbal negator. Some indigenous American words in ASC include *suffki*, *stamal*, and *polejo*, all foodstuffs prepared from corn. Spanish words include *calpintero* 'woodpecker,' *banya* 'wash,' *metati* 'mortar,' and many others. Quite a few African-derived words are shared with SIC (*pinda* 'peanut,' *coota* 'turtle,' *tabby* 'mud'), but that language has many more African-derived words not found in ASC. SIC also admits African phonological features, such as the doubly articulated stops /kp/ and /gb/, not found in ASC. ASC does not share with SIC such words as *buntas* 'buttocks,' *skiffi* 'pudenda,' and so on (though variants of both of these occur in some Caribbean Creoles).

ASC is a very private language, and when asked, its speakers typically deny any knowledge of it. At a gravestone dedication attended by the Seminole and non-Seminole Brackettville community, a woman greeted her friend in English from a distance as she approached her, then repeated the whole greeting in ASC quietly in her ear as she bent to hug her. ASC is not being passed on to younger generations. While ASC speakers know what they are speaking—Creole or English—at any given time, the English of the oldest generation is clearly influenced grammatically and phonologically by ASC. Speakers are also aware that ASC was "deeper" in earlier times; a younger speaker who said *trow-way* for 'spill' was corrected by an older speaker, who told her that the proper pronunciation was *chuwway*. Likewise, the "proper" pronunciation of the name of the language is said to be *Shiminóleh*, not *Siminóle*, as it is commonly pronounced. Young people today can mimic the distinctive English pronunciation of their elders but cannot produce the language.

None of the pidgin or creole languages spoken in the South are in good shape today. Mobilian Jargon (or Mobilian Yamá), once spoken in the Lower Mississippi Valley, is extinct. Louisiana Creole French has fewer than 30,000 speakers and is not being learned by children. Sea Island Gullah of South Carolina and Georgia shows an ongoing drift toward English. Fewer than 400 people today can speak Afro-Seminole Creole fluently, none of whom is younger than about 60.

IAN HANCOCK
University of Texas at Austin

Thomas A. Britten, *A Brief History of the Seminole-Negro Indian Scouts* (1999); Cloyde I. Brown, *Black Warrior Chiefs: A History of the Seminole Negro Indian Scouts* (1999); Joshua R. Giddings, *The Exiles of Florida* (1858); Ian Hancock, *Hablar, Nombrar, Pertenecer* (1998), in *Language Variety in the South: Perspectives in Black and White*, ed. Michael Montgomery and Guy Bailey (1986).

Alabama Blacks to Mexico

The Tlahualilo labor recruitment project in Alabama was the largest single private Mexican migration effort in Mexican history in the 19th century. The project sought to move up to 20,000 African American tenant farmers to plant and establish cotton fields in the Mapimi basin in northern Mexico. The first stage of the Tlahualilo cotton project involved building a 60-mile-long private irrigation canal to the privately owned dry Tlahualilo lakebed. The second phase involved recruiting approximately 100 families from towns along the Tuscaloosa River Valley in Alabama. The Tlahualilo Agricultural Company hoped that this large investment in black labor might yield enough cotton to begin to cover the capital expenses associated with building a private canal and trunk line to the Tlahualilo lakebed.

In Alabama, news that a large agricultural syndicate wanted skilled African American agricultural labor roared through black farming communities across the state. The actual handbill that followed the rumors promised a larger share of the cotton crop (on the halves), transportation costs, bountiful forests and plains, and a political climate that offered equal rights and that valued black immigrants over Chinese and Italian labor.

The Tlahualilo Agricultural Syndicate's recruitment of black families turned into something of a black exodus. William Ellis, a Texas-based businessman and black emigration activist, was the main contractor and chief contact between Mexico's president, Porfirio Díaz, the Tlahualilo Agricultural Company, and Ralph Williams, the agent for the labor recruitment project. Ellis pushed this labor arrangement as the best solution to the dire economic and political straits facing black voters across the American South. The Tlahualilo venture promised profits and freedom, and Ellis stood to enjoy his freedoms and profit in Mexico.

The Tlahualilo project was not without its critics. In Mexico, according to *El Tiempo*, "this way of stopping the lynchings and helping get rid of a race which the Yankees detest is very harmful and disquieting to Mexico." The *Economista Mexicano* believed that it would be "better we continue seeing our fields deserted and living with a small population than to admit North Americans of the Negro race." In Alabama, Republicans decried the loss of votes in Alabama's swing counties after the nationally controversial election in 1894. Others celebrated the departure of the more difficult element among sharecroppers in Tuscaloosa County. Most observers seemed to agree that the collective departure of black southern workers for Mexico was a symbol of things to come in the New American South.

The families, once they arrived at the Tlahualilo hacienda in February, did not take to their assigned roles as symbols of political defeat in Alabama. They rejected their difficult working and living conditions: roofless housing, snow, un-

built churches, a dry desert lakebed, no individual farm plots, and immediate ongoing oversight. Some took the next train back to Alabama. The majority started demanding familiar food, a slower work pace, and a day's wage for a day's work. Ellis acceded to these demands, but when people refused to work more than four days a week planting cotton, Ellis detained the people he considered ringleaders and had his foremen drag them in front of their friends and neighbors. The colonists rebelled. Some fled the plantation and sought American consular intervention.

News of the outrages in the Tlahualilo plantation circulated widely. The State Department, under pressure from congressional representatives from Alabama, ordered an investigation. Workers and their families responded to the investigation by leaving the plantation and walking, as a group, to the Torreon, Coahuila, train station. They demanded a return to Alabama, and, after news of smallpox and a tense military standoff in the middle of Torreon made its way to Grover Cleveland, the U.S. government agreed to reimburse the Southern Pacific for the journey. Their odyssey did not end there.

The Texas State Health Office detained all the migrants, regardless of smallpox status, at the Texas border. Once it became clear that Texas was refusing to try to provide adequate care, the U.S. Marine Hospital Service (USMHS) took over the quarantine and the migrants, providing the best care possible and even testing a barely experimental serum vaccination therapy at Camp Jenner. Once it became clear the serum failed, the USMHS placed the migrants in the hands of the local American consul and the African American church community in Texas. The USMHS cleared them for travel once the governor of Alabama gave the Southern Pacific permission to bring the colonists into Alabama, only 45 days after the last actual smallpox case in Eagle Pass. The numbers are dismal—78 people died in Tlahualilo and 58 people died in Camp Jenner. All in all, 107 people stayed in Tlahualilo, and 353 people officially returned to Tuscaloosa County. Their status as wards of the state prompted white southern pundits to claim that this Mexican experience proved that African Americans needed white southern oversight. The *Memphis Commercial Appeal* bluntly stated, "This is another instance of the inability of the Negro to live without the white man." Ellis himself mourned, "The impression is now before the world that the Negro as a colonist is a failure and must remain in the southern United States and there work out his destiny." The dismal news of their detention and return reverberated across Alabama's communities. Concerns with Mexico and Liberia were in the air when Booker T. Washington called on white employers and black workers to "cast their bucket where they are" and invest their time and energy in the southern economy.

The Mexican odyssey of 866 residents of central Alabama should also be an impressive example of transnational political organizing put into place by working-class Alabama-based black southerners. That they received military and medical assistance in Mexico and at the Texas border under conditions far from their choosing simply underlines the challenges the Tlahualilo colonists faced when they sought to make their American civil rights relevant to their workplace in Mexico. The actions taken by black working-class residents of Alabama in Mexico and the political responses by business and political elites in Mexico, Alabama, and Washington, D.C., remind us that the boundaries of the New South are both porous and changing and that southern history is made inside and outside the South, even outside the United States.

JOHN MCKIERNAN GONZALES
University of Texas at Austin

Karl Jacoby, *Alabama Heritage* (Winter 1995), in *Continental Crossroads: Remapping U.S.-Mexico Borderlands History*, ed. Samuel Truett and Elliott Young (2004); J. J. Kinyoun, *Annual Report of the Supervising Surgeon General of the United States Marine Hospital Service of the United States Treasury for the Fiscal Year 1897* (1899); Jerrold M. Michael and Thomas R. Bender, *Public Health Reports* (November/December 1984); Nell Irvin Painter, *Exodusters: Black Migration to Kansas after Reconstruction* (1976); Edwin Redkey, *Black Exodus: Black Nationalist and Back-to-Africa Movements, 1890–1910* (1969); Alfred Reynolds, *Alabama Review* (October 1952); Fred Rippy, *Journal of Negro History* (January 1921); Milton Rosenau, in *Annual Report of the Surgeon General of the United States Marine Hospital Service for the Fiscal Year 1896*, ed. Walter Wyman (1896).

Armstrong, Louis

(1900–1971) JAZZ MUSICIAN AND
ENTERTAINER.

Born 4 July 1900 in New Orleans,
Daniel Louis "Satchmo" Armstrong
achieved acclaim as a jazz emissary to
the world. Duke Ellington once called
him "the epitome of jazz." As a child,
Armstrong played music on the streets
of New Orleans and received musical
training in the public schools and at the
Coloured Waif's Home (1913–14). He
heard and was influenced by such early
jazz performers as Charles "Buddy"
Bolden, William "Bunk" Johnson, and
Joseph "King" Oliver, who became his
mentor. Armstrong performed briefly
in a New Orleans nightclub at age 15
but did not become a full-time professional until he was 17. He joined Edward
"Kid" Ory's band in 1918 and thereafter
played with other jazz greats and led
his own groups, especially the Hot Five
and the Hot Seven, in the 1920s. His
recording debut was with Oliver in 1923.
Recordings made him a celebrity, and
he toured widely in the 1930s, including
a trip to Europe in 1932. He acquired his
nickname "Satchmo" in England from
the editor of a music magazine. Armstrong made a historic recording with
Jimmie Rodgers, the "father of country
music," on 16 July 1930. Rodgers sang
his "Blue Yodel No. 9" with accompaniment by Armstrong on the trumpet and
his wife, Lillian Hardin Armstrong, on
piano.

Armstrong was a popular international figure by the 1940s and thereafter
performed around the world; he played
at major jazz festivals; he recorded frequently; he performed in Broadway mu-
sicals, on radio, and later on television;
and he appeared in 60 films, including
Cabin in the Sky (1943), *New Orleans*
(1947), *High Society* (1956), *Satchmo
the Great* (1956), *Jazz, the Intimate Art*
(1968), and *Hello, Dolly* (1969). He died
in New York City on 6 July 1971.

Armstrong's powerful trumpet and
soulful, gravelly singing voice, as well as
his infectious smile and effusive good
humor, helped to establish the image
of the archetypal jazzman. "Satchmo"
communicated to everyone the irre-
pressible message that jazz was "good-
time" music. His nickname, as well as
his use of street vernacular for expressions of endearment and cordiality,
reflected the communal New Orleans
roots of the music.

The jazz personality that Armstrong
helped create grew out of the southern
urban underclass found most clearly in
New Orleans. Armstrong's demeanor
was as a loose-mannered, self-assertive
(that is, "bad"), somewhat "hip" good-
time person whose music was a refuge
from the external world. The jazz personality that emerged with Armstrong
from the southern urban world included a bold and flirtatious manner,
a zany sense of humor, a familiarity
bordering on impertinence in interpersonal contact, a flashy, fancy code
of dress, and an open and adventurous
attitude toward life. Certainly, all jazz
people have not fit this personality
mold, but Armstrong—the most influential role model available to early jazz
performers—did much to implant that
abiding notion in the public mind.

Armstrong's jazz personality reflected certain aspects of the black culture in the South. He found his niche through music entertainment, a common pattern among blacks in southern urban areas. He drew on the vernacular tradition of black street and saloon life. His loose manner reflected an easygoing tolerance essential to the southern black underclass and fit squarely into the laid-back folk tradition. The hip mentality infusing the jazz personality is also a form of pride, validating the jazzman's self-assertiveness ("badness") in musical activities.

CURTIS D. JERDE

W. R. Hogan Jazz Archive
Tulane University

Louis Armstrong, *Louis Armstrong, in His Own Words: Selected Writings*, ed. Thomas Brothers (2001), *Satchmo* (1954), *Swing That Music* (1936); Laurence Bergreen, *Louis Armstrong: An Extravagant Life* (1997); Gary Giddins, *Satchmo: The Genius of Louis Armstrong* (2001); Robert Goffin, *Horn of Plenty: The Story of Louis Armstrong* (1947); Max Jones and John Chilton, *Louis: The Louis Armstrong Story, 1900–1971* (1971).

Baker, Ella Jo

(1903–1986) CIVIL RIGHTS ACTIVIST. Ella Jo Baker, the daughter of Georgianna and Blake Baker, was born in 1903 in Norfolk, Va. When she was seven, Baker's family moved to Littleton, N.C., to live with her maternal grandparents, who owned a plantation where they had previously worked as slaves. The absence of adequate public schools for blacks in rural North Carolina and her mother's concern that she be properly educated resulted in Baker's

attending Shaw University in Raleigh, where she received her high school and college education. Following her graduation in 1927, she moved to New York City to live with a cousin, where she worked as a waitress and, later, in a factory.

The product of a southern environment in which caring and sharing were facts of life and of a family in which her grandfather regularly mortgaged his property in order to help neighbors, Baker soon became involved in various community groups. In 1932, she became the national director of the Young Negroes Cooperative League and the office manager of the *Negro National News*. Six years later, she began her active career with the NAACP, working initially as a field secretary in the South. In 1943, she was appointed national director of the branches for the NAACP. In both capacities, Baker spent long periods in southern black communities, where her southern roots served her well. Her success in recruiting southern blacks to join what was considered a radical organization in the 1930s and 1940s may be attributed, in part, to her being a native of the region and, therefore, best able to approach southern people. Baker, who neither married nor had children of her own, left active service in the NAACP in 1946 in order to raise a niece. A short while later, she reactivated her involvement with the NAACP, becoming president of the New York City chapter in 1954.

In 1957, Baker went south again, this time to work with the Southern Christian Leadership Conference (SCLC), a newly formed civil rights organization. The student sit-in movement of the 1960s protested the refusal of public restaurants in the South to serve blacks and resulted in Baker's involvement in still another civil rights group. As the coordinator of the 1960 Nonviolent Resistance to Segregation Leadership Conference, which brought together over 300 student sit-in leaders and resulted in the formation of the Student Nonviolent Coordinating Committee (SNCC), Baker is credited with playing a major role in SNCC's founding. Severing a formal relationship with SCLC, she worked with the Southern Conference Educational Fund. In recognition of her contribution to improving the quality of life of southern blacks and to the founding of the Mississippi Freedom Democratic Party, Ella Baker was asked to deliver the keynote address at its 1964 convention in Jackson, Miss.

Ella Baker spent the remainder of her life in New York City, where she served as an adviser to a number of community groups. Prior to the release of Joanne Grant's film *Fundi: The Story of Ella Baker*, few people outside of the civil rights movement in the South knew about Baker's long career as a civil rights activist, but since then a number of leadership programs and grassroots organizations, such as the Children's Defense Fund's Ella Baker Child Policy Training Institute and the Bay Area's Ella Baker Center for Human Rights, have been named in her honor. Nevertheless, she is probably less well known than many other civil rights workers, because she was a woman surrounded by southern men, primarily ministers, who generally perceived women as sup-

porters rather than as leaders in the movement, and because of her own firm belief in group-centered rather than individual-centered leadership.

SHARON HARLEY
University of Maryland

Ellen Cantarow and Susan Gushee O'Malley, *Moving the Mountain: Women Working for Social Change* (1980); Clayborne Carson, *In Struggle: SNCC and the Black Awakening of the 1960s* (1981); Joanne Grant, *Ella Baker: Freedom Bound* (1999); Barbara Ransby, *Ella Baker and the Black Freedom Movement: A Radical Democratic Vision* (2003).

The Birth of a Nation

D. W. Griffith's film *The Birth of a Nation* (Epoch, 1915) celebrates the Ku Klux Klan. This organization, according to the film's subtitles, saved the South from the anarchy of black rule by reuniting former wartime enemies "in defense of their Aryan birthright." Griffith based his film on two novels by Rev. Thomas Dixon Jr., *The Leopard's Spots* (1902) and *The Clansman* (1905).

One of the most controversial and profitable films ever made, the movie set many precedents. It was the first film to cost over $100,000 and charge a $2 admission, the first to have a full-scale premiere, and the first to be shown at the White House. President Woodrow Wilson reportedly declared, "It's like writing history with lightning. My only regret is that it is all so terribly true." African Americans protested the film's biased portrayal of Reconstruction.

Originally called *The Clansman* when it opened in Los Angeles on 8 February 1915, it was retitled *Birth*

Reconstruction violence against blacks portrayed in the film The Birth of a Nation, 1915
(Film Stills Archives, Museum of Modern Art, New York, N.Y.)

of a Nation just prior to its Broadway showing in March. Fully exploiting the motion picture as a propaganda vehicle, Griffith used every device he had developed in his years at Biograph studio—long shot, close-up, flashback, montage—to create excitement and tension. Provocative subtitles heightened his messages, and southern audiences acclaimed the film enthusiastically. Horsemen in Klan costumes often rode through towns prior to the film's showing to increase box-office receipts. In cities like New York, Chicago, and Boston, however, the film was greeted with pickets, demonstrations, and lawsuits.

For a time, Newark and Atlantic City, N.J., banned the film, as did St. Louis, Mo., and the states of Kansas, West Vir-

ginia, and Ohio. (In the 1950s, Atlanta banned the film, fearing that the violence of some scenes might provoke audience emulation.) As a result of the widespread interest in *Birth of a Nation*, newspapers began to review new films regularly, and motion picture advertising began to appear in the press. This film helped make moviegoing a middle-class activity, and its success led to the erection of ornate movie palaces in fashionable districts.

The two-part film centers on two families, the Camerons of South Carolina and the Stonemans of Pennsylvania, who are eventually joined in marriage. An idyllic, gracious, carefree antebellum South, based on the labor of happy slaves, is shattered by bloody battles and the devastation and defeat of the Confederacy. With the assassination of Lincoln, the South appears to be doomed to black control. Part two concerns the Reconstruction period and focuses on the Little Colonel, Ben Cameron (Henry B. Walthall), who is in love with Elsie Stoneman (Lillian Gish), daughter of a Negrophile congressman and his black mistress. One of the key scenes shows the Little Colonel's sister (Mae Marsh) hurling herself off a cliff, terrified by the black renegade Gus's lustful pursuit. "For her who had learned the stern lesson of honor we should not grieve that she found sweeter the opal gates of death," reads the subtitle.

Two kinds of blacks appear in the film: the sober, industrious slaves inspired by Uncle Tom, who stay on as loyal servants after the war, and the freedmen, portrayed as arrogant, lecherous, and bestial. Instead of working in the cotton fields, the former slaves make a mockery of legislative government, spend time carousing in saloons, lust after white women, and demand "equal rights, equal politics, equal marriage." The rise of the Ku Klux Klan led by the Little Colonel promises to restore the social order, disfranchise the blacks, protect southern womanhood, and reunite the nation.

The film is said to have inspired the revival of the Klan in November 1915 and to have promoted the passage of the prohibition amendment. Generally regarded as a masterpiece and the greatest American silent film, Birth of a Nation has never, because of its overt racism, received unequivocal praise.

JOAN L. SILVERMAN
New York University

Roy E. Aitken, *"The Birth of a Nation" Story* (1965); Michael R. Hurwitz, *D. W. Griffith's Film, "The Birth of a Nation": The Film That Transformed America* (2006); Fred Silva, ed., *Focus on "The Birth of a Nation"* (1971); Melvyn Stokes, *D. W. Griffith's "The Birth of a Nation": A History of the Most Controversial Motion Picture of All Time* (2007); Edward Wagenknecht and Anthony Slide, *The Films of D. W. Griffith* (1975).

Black Soldiers in Cuba and Puerto Rico

When the United States formally declared war on Spain and invaded Cuba and Puerto Rico in 1898, the Americans found themselves in the midst of a protracted revolution that was nearing the end of three phases: the Ten Years' War (1868–78), the *Guerra Chiquita*, or Little War (1879–80), and the final War of Independence (1895–98). The Americans made short shrift of the "splendid little war" in Puerto Rico but had to forge alliances with the Cuban revolutionaries who were unwilling to surrender to either the Spanish or the Americans. Cubans of all colors and social origins had created a formidable cross-racial, cross-class alliance and had forged a nationalist ideology in which all, regardless of race and social status, became equal members in the new nation.

The African Americans who fought in Cuba, Puerto Rico, and ultimately the Philippines included regulars (the Buffalo Soldiers), state-organized volunteers, and "immunes," federally organized regiments of volunteers who purportedly could withstand the diseases of the tropics. The Buffalo Soldiers were servicemen so named for their

African American soldiers who participated in the Spanish-American War, ca. 1899 (photographer unknown, Library of Congress Prints and Photographs Division [LC-USZ62-41594], Washington, D.C.)

work in the West suppressing American Indian tribes. The volunteers included 11 regiments of African American volunteers enlisted via state militias. And 4 of the 10 federally organized "immune regiments" were made up of African Americans largely from southern states. Moreover, scores of African American women, many of them yellow fever nurses from the southern states or former nurses from the Civil War, also flooded recruitment stations,

later serving in the medical hospitals in Cuba.

The immune regiments appeared to be an answer to the problem of fighting a war in the midst of malaria season. The discussion over the immunes divided African Americans as they debated whether this idea was scientifically legitimate and the best means to bring honor upon the race, particularly when McKinley decided that white men would fill all the officers' positions above the rank of lieutenant—captain, major, and colonel. Nevertheless, African American volunteers resolved the debate by enlisting en masse. Soldiers enlisted for a myriad of reasons: they wanted to take up the cause of Antonio Maceo, the slain mulatto Cuban revolutionary leader, prove their manhood, buttress their ongoing claims for full citizenship, and improve the economic lives of their families.

Charged with disarming the Cuban revolutionary forces and restoring peace, black soldiers found themselves at the center of a conflict over how to govern Cuba and protect American interests there. Environmental conditions and diseases proved to be the greatest challenge for the soldiers, however, and when the soldiers returned home, many of them were sick with disease and in no better position politically than when they had left.

SHERRI CHARLESTON
University of Wisconsin

Sherri Ann Charleston, "The Fruits of Citizenship: African Americans, Military Service, and the Cause of Cuba Libre, 1868–1920" (Ph.D. dissertation, University of Michigan at Ann Arbor, 2009); Ada Ferrer, *Insurgent Cuba: Race, Nation, and Revolution, 1868–1898* (1999); Willard B. Gatewood Jr., *Black Americans and the White Man's Burden, 1898–1903* (1975); Rebecca J. Scott, *Degrees of Freedom: Louisiana and Cuba after Slavery* (2005).

Blues

Nowhere is the aesthetic of the "changing same" of African American music more resonant than in the emergent sounds and styles of the blues.

From its foundations in the vernacular song of enslaved African peoples of the American South, the blues enunciated new black mobilities at the threshold of the 20th century. A legacy of blues poetics, aesthetics, styles of dress and dance, political discourses, performances of class and gender, and local inflections offers a self-authored genealogy of African American life. In its many variations, migrations, and transformations, the blues represents at once a multitude of authors, works, and narratives and a unified body of black aesthetic practices by which African Americans continue to articulate a living relationship to the agrarian American South.

Blues narratives often collect around particular personalities, historical eras, and geographic centers, most notably the extensive travels of the early 20th-century touring minstrel show singers Ma Rainey and Bessie Smith, the heavy sharecropping-era blues of Robert Johnson and John Lee Hooker of the Mississippi Delta and their contemporaries in the pre–World War II Deep South, the up-tempo 1930s Carolina Piedmont blues of Blind Boy Fuller and Rev. Gary Davis, the mid-century jump blues popular in New York dance clubs with incoming southerners, and the electrified Upsouth Chicago blues of the Great Migration's Muddy Waters and B. B. King. Wherever deployed, the blues maintains cultural routes to a common African American South, despite historical limitations on conventional mobility and communication, including binding sharecropping contracts, poverty, imposed illiteracy, and Jim Crow laws.

Popular discourses define particular blues recordings according to their adherence to common formal characteristics: verse form, musical scale, chord patterns, or lyrical themes, but these criteria are highly contested and offer a limited understanding of the broader spectrum of blues practices. Other conventional studies place certain blues styles along a timeline of evolutionary development, from what they may call "primitive," "authentic," or "country" blues to contemporary studio work, electric instrumentation, and urban orientation. Rather than attempt to authenticate the blues via a continuum of formal, historical, or stylistic criteria, contemporary critics suggest that the blues has taken on a series of complex forms at the confluences of two currents: first, a collection of Afro-diasporic musical and poetic practices interwoven by communities of enslaved African peoples and their descendants; and second, the historical conditions of the agrarian American South as they extend through contemporary African American life.

The notion that the blues is born simply of pathological reaction to oppressive social circumstances fails to account for the self- and community-motivated empowerment of blues performance. While articulating a private vocabulary of personal strength, forming safe space for otherwise dangerous discourses of social protest, and establishing alternative systems of community leadership and communication out of the reach of hostile officials, the blues represents a series of practices by which African Americans have actively authored themselves and their communities beyond the historical constraints of the southern plantation system. As both an inspiration and an aesthetic foundation, the blues finds continuity with a host of contemporary genres that draw direct familial and cultural lineage with blues communities; soul, hip-hop, and contemporary R&B each allows artists to reference blues themes, lyrics, and styles across new global contexts.

Early 20th-century folklorists, charged with collecting national vernacular traditions for the 1930s Works Progress Administration, sought to record individual blues players at their rural plantation homes or workplaces. These documentary recordings, often accomplished outdoors and under the watchful eye of overseers and sheriffs, stand in contrast to the lively community affairs that unfolded in private, often interior spaces—living rooms, juke joints, the Chitlin' Circuit of black-owned southern venues, and dance clubs. While many blues musicians have cultural origins in the agrarian South, blues performance modes reflect the remarkable cosmopolitanism of African American culture that converged at bustling southern centers for trade and transportation.

Another dimension of the blues is its function as a point of encounter between southern African Americans and the groups with which they have found historical proximity. Working-class white southerners Elvis Presley and Johnny Cash brought local traditions of minstrelsy into conversation with a sympathetic engagement with blues themes and styles in their germinal rock and roll recordings. Blues artists were presented to collegiate, curious, and mainstream audiences at the 1950s Newport Jazz Festival and stages across hip 1960s Western Europe. In its poetries of liberation and expressive style, the blues also appeals to a host of global minority groups, from American Indian blues players in Oklahoma to Jewish songwriters Leiber and Stoller, who helped to forge the rock and roll genre from the intersection of Tin Pan Alley and the 12-bar blues. These tributes serve as an index to the masterful skill and intensive community schooling manifest in African American musicianship and lyricism, as well as the powerful cross-cultural appeal of the blues.

While the academic folklorist's 78-rpm record captured a single song for the sake of archives and commercial sale to a variety of audiences, a full blues performance assembles multiple modes of black oral and musical creativity. These include hyperbolic boasts, the trading of stylized insults called the "dozens," dramatic tales of rogue "badmen," eloquent toasts, and the witty call-and-response between artists and various audience members. The music's community-based performative context also suggests the many important ways African American women have engaged the art form as vocalists, instrumentalists, dancers, interjecting speakers, and fans, although this work was rarely of interest to early songcatchers. African American thinkers, including W. C. Handy, W. E. B. Du Bois, Albert Murray, Amiri Baraka, and Eileen Southern, have drawn from the blues to write foundational texts in black cultural

theory. When writer Ralph Ellison describes the blues as a medium by which African Americans "finger [the] jagged grain" of the memories of plantation brutality, he invokes an important aspect of the blues that cannot be captured by conventional formal studies: that is, the importance of the blues as an embodied form of musical remembrance rooted in the shared experience of black Americans.

ALI COLLEEN NEFF
University of North Carolina at Chapel Hill

Angela Y. Davis, *Blues Legacies and Black Feminism* (1999); W. E. B. Du Bois, *The Souls of Black Folk* (1903); William R. Ferris, *Give My Poor Heart Ease: Voices of the Mississippi Blues* (2009); Robert Gordon and Bruce Nemerov, eds., *Lost Delta Found: Rediscovering the Fisk University–Library of Congress Coahoma County Study, 1941–1942* (1995); LeRoi Jones, *Blues People: Negro Music in White America* (1963); Charles Kiel, *Urban Blues* (1992); Jacqui Malone, *Stepping the Blues: The Visible Rhythms of African American Dance* (1996); Albert Murray, *Stomping the Blues* (1976); Mark Anthony Neal, *Songs in the Key of Black Life: A Rhythm and Blues Nation* (1993); Ali Colleen Neff, *Let the World Listen Right: The Mississippi Delta Hip-Hop Story* (2009); Robert Palmer, *Deep Blues* (1981); Eileen Southern, *The Music of Black Americans: A History* (1971).

Bontemps, Arna

(1902–1973) WRITER AND SCHOLAR. Arnaud Wendell Bontemps was three years old when his father decided to move his family from his son's birthplace in Alexandria, La., to California. The elder Bontemps hoped to escape the prejudice and intimidation that tormented his and other black families. Trying to protect his son, he later warned Arna never to act black.

Having read *Harlem Shadows*, a book of poems by black author Claude McKay, Arna Bontemps became aware of the emergence of black voices from Harlem. After he graduated from Union Pacific College in 1923 and with the first publication of one of his own poems, Bontemps moved from Los Angeles to Harlem, where he taught at the Harlem Academy. He continued to write and, subsequently, became identified with the Harlem Renaissance. In 1931, he published his first novel, *God Sends Sunday*, which was later adapted as *St. Louis Woman*, the musical in which Pearl Bailey made her Broadway acting debut.

A few years of teaching and writing in Alabama, a master's degree from the University of Chicago, and work with the Illinois Writers Project marked Bontemps's career until the beginning of his 22-year tenure as librarian at Fisk University in Nashville, Tenn. In 1968, he resumed teaching, first at the University of Illinois and then at Yale, where he also served as curator of the James Weldon Johnson Collection of Negro Arts and Letters. He had moved back to Nashville when he died of a heart attack in 1973.

Bontemps devoted much time to writing about black life, wanting, as he said in *Harper's*, "to write something about the changes I have seen in my lifetime, and about the Negro awakening and regeneration." Short stories portraying southern black life (*The Old*

South: "A Summer Tragedy" and Other Stories of the Thirties), historical novels about black uprisings (*Black Thunder*), children's literature about black leaders (*Free at Last: The Life of Frederick Douglass*), and anthologies of works by black authors (*American Negro Poetry*) represent the range of his writings. He also edited W. C. Handy's autobiography, *Father of the Blues*, and collaborated with fellow writers Langston Hughes, Jack Conroy, and Countee Cullen.

Arna Bontemps spent much of his life exploring the culture of his race and his southern black heritage. In doing so, he became a primary force in the development and promotion of black literature in America.

JESSICA FOY
*Cooperstown Graduate Program
Cooperstown, New York*

J. A. Alvarez, *African American Review* (Spring 1998); Robert A. Bone, *Down Home: A History of Afro-American Short Fiction from Its Beginnings to the End of the Harlem Renaissance* (1975); Arna Bontemps, *Harper's*, April 1965; Arthur P. Davis, *From the Dark Tower: Afro-American Writers, 1900–1960* (1974); V. Harris, *The Lion and the Unicorn* (1 June 1990); Daniel Reagan, *Studies in American Fiction* (Spring 1991).

Brown, Sterling Allen

(1901–1989) TEACHER, POET, LITERARY CRITIC.

*The strong men keep a-comin' on
The strong men git stronger.
—from "Strong Men"*

More a celebrant of southern culture than a child of its soil, Sterling Allen Brown exalted southern culture and examined the legacy of African Americans in the South through his poetry and essays and, perhaps most markedly, through his long teaching career at Howard University.

Brown was born on 1 May 1901, the youngest of six and the only son to former slave Sterling Nelson Brown and Adelaide Allen Brown. His father was a minister in the Congregational Church and a professor in the School of Religion at Howard University. An alumna of Fisk University, his mother was a former Fisk Jubilee Singer and a major influence on her children's appreciation for the arts.

Growing up on the Howard University campus, Brown established relationships with notable scholars of the time, including Jean Toomer, Alain Locke, and W. E. B. Du Bois, and had the benefit of Jessie Redmon Fauset as a high school teacher. Interaction with scholars and writers led to an early appreciation of poetry, history, and culture. Graduation with honors from prestigious Dunbar High School led to a scholarship at Williams College in eastern Massachusetts. There Brown earned an A.B. degree and his Phi Beta Kappa key. He then entered Harvard in 1922, where he earned the M.A. degree.

A prolific teaching career followed, started by an English faculty position at Virginia Seminary in Lynchburg, Va. In the three years he was there, he encountered two important influences that would change his life: Daisy Turnball, whom he married in 1927, and the southern culture that would become his inspiration and the foundation of his writing and teaching for the remainder of his career.

His teaching career included Lincoln University in Missouri (1926–28) and Fisk University (1928–29). In 1929, Brown stepped onto the path his father had walked and began teaching at Howard University. His tenure at Howard would span more than 40 years and included semesters spent as visiting faculty at Atlanta University, Vassar College, and New York University.

At Howard, Brown taught the first courses in black literature and became known for his intellectual support of African American culture. He was a "great man" in the community because of active community involvement, consistent patronage of African American businesses, and mentoring of young people. The hallmark of his Howard years is his work highlighting African American culture. According to literary critic Joanne Gabbien, "During the 1930s and 1940s, Brown's studies of the folk experience and culture were the fullest of any in the field." He was one of the first scholars to identify folklore as critical to the black aesthetic and to appreciate it as a form of literature and art. *The Negro in American Fiction* (1937) reveals parallels between the literary experience of African Americans and their real-life experiences. Although now familiar concepts, theories like these made Brown a pioneer in the field of African American criticism. He was able to "tie literature in with life, music, justice, and the struggle for existence."

As a poet, Brown blended the rhythms of black music and black southern culture. He championed the southern black community, creating folk heroes where caricatures had previously existed. His belief in the voice of the black community extended to his students, who included Ossie Davis, Stokely Carmichael, and Toni Morrison. He challenged them to have confidence in their own voices and to find strength in the experiences of their people.

Sterling Brown's influence is so far reaching that contemporary theorists believe that "all trails lead, at some point, to Sterling Brown," although Brown's acclaim did not extend far beyond Howard's walls until the Black Arts Movement of the 1960s. In 1979, the Washington, D.C., city council declared his birthday, 1 May, to be Sterling A. Brown Day. The next year, Brown published *The Collected Poems of Sterling Brown*, which won the 1980 Lenore Marshall Prize as the best book of poetry published. In 1984, he was named poet laureate of the District of Columbia. In 1991, Brown was honored in a way that illustrates the impact that he left on the Howard University community. Following a campus contest, "Sterling" was the name selected for Howard University libraries' online catalog. Brown's legacy comes alive every time Howard students access the libraries, and Sterling once again guides them to countless resources of research and literature.

JONI JOHNSON WILLIAMS
Georgia State University

Harold Bloom, *Black American Poets and Dramatists of the Harlem Renaissance* (1995); Arna Bontemps and Langston Hughes, *The Book of Negro Folklore* (1958); Sterling Brown, *Phylon* (1953); Joyce Camper, *African American Review* (Fall 1997); Joanne Gabbin, *African American Review* (Fall 1997); Ronald Palmer, *African American Review* (Fall 1997); Dudley Randall, *The Black Poets* (1972).

Chesnutt, Charles Waddell

(1858–1932) WRITER.

Charles Waddell Chesnutt, African American man of letters, was born in Cleveland, Ohio, on 20 June 1858, the son of free blacks who had emigrated from Fayetteville, N.C. When he was eight years old, Chesnutt's parents returned to Fayetteville, where Charles worked part time in the family grocery store and attended a school founded by the Freedmen's Bureau. In 1872, financial necessity forced him to begin a teaching career in Charlotte, N.C. He returned to Fayetteville in 1877, married a year later, and by 1880 had become principal of the Fayetteville State Normal School for Negroes. Meanwhile, he continued to pursue private studies of classic English literature, foreign languages, music, and stenography. Despite his successes, he longed for broader opportunities and a chance to develop the literary skills that by 1880 led him toward an author's life. In 1883, he moved his family to Cleveland. There he passed the state bar examination and established his own court-reporting firm. Financially prosperous and prominent in civic affairs, he resided in Cleveland for the remainder of his life.

"The Goophered Grapevine," an unusual dialect story that displayed intimate knowledge of black folk culture in the South, was Chesnutt's first nationally recognized work of fiction. Its publication in the August 1887 issue of *Atlantic Monthly* marked the first time that a short story by an African American had appeared in that prestigious magazine. After subsequent tales in this vein were accepted by other magazines, Chesnutt submitted to Houghton Mifflin a collection of these stories, which was published in 1899 as *The Conjure Woman*. His second collection of short fiction, *The Wife of His Youth and Other Stories of the Color Line* (1899), ranged over a broader area of southern and northern racial experience than any previous writer on African American life had attempted. These two volumes were popular enough to convince Houghton Mifflin to publish Chesnutt's first novel, *The House behind the Cedars*, in 1900. This story of two light-skinned African American siblings who pass for white in the postwar South revealed Chesnutt's sense of the psychological and social dilemmas facing persons of mixed blood in the region. In his second novel, *The Marrow of Tradition* (1901), Chesnutt confronted the causes and effects of the Wilmington, N.C., race riot of 1898. Hoping to write the *Uncle Tom's Cabin* of his generation, Chesnutt made a plea for racial justice that impressed the noted novelist and critic William Dean Howells, who reviewed *The Marrow of Tradition* as a work of "great power," though with "more justice than mercy in it." The failure of Chesnutt's second novel to sell widely forced its author to give up his dream of supporting his family as a professional author. In 1905, he published his final novel, *The Colonel's Dream*, a tragic story of an idealist's attempt to revive a depressed North Carolina town through a socioeconomic program

much akin to the New South creed of Henry W. Grady and Booker T. Washington. The novel received little critical notice.

In the twilight of his literary career, Chesnutt continued to write novels (some of which ultimately found publishers in the late 20th century) and published occasional short stories. His fiction was largely eclipsed in the 1920s by the writers of the Harlem Renaissance. Nevertheless, he was awarded the Spingarn Medal in 1928 by the NAACP for his pioneering literary work on behalf of African American civil rights and racial understanding. Today, Chesnutt is recognized as a major innovator in African American fiction, an important contributor to the deromanticizing trend in post–Civil War southern literature, and a singular voice among turn-of-the-century literary realists who probed the color line in American life.

WILLIAM L. ANDREWS
University of North Carolina at Chapel Hill

William L. Andrews, *The Literary Career of Charles W. Chesnutt* (1980); Frances Richardson Keller, *An American Crusade: The Life of Charles Waddell Chesnutt* (1978); Joseph R. McElrath Jr., ed., *Critical Essays on Charles Chesnutt* (1999); Henry B. Wonham, *Studies in American Fiction* (Fall 1998).

Chinese

Chinese first came to the South to work in cotton and sugarcane fields and in construction of Texas railroads. Young men from the artisan and peasant classes traveled as sojourners, and this is how they came to Texas, Mississippi, and Louisiana. These first arrivals were often from the Sze Yap (or Four Counties) district of Guangdong Province in southern China. Much like other Chinese who came to the United States in the 1800s, the Chinese in the South sent most of their money home to their families and planned to retire to their homeland. Their prosperity encouraged the immigration of family and friends.

Beginning during Reconstruction, planters and businessmen recruited Asians as a new source of labor to replace freed slaves. Most found employment in agricultural work, although some took railroad construction jobs. They soon realized that their new roles in the plantation system would not foster the wealth with which they had hoped to return to China, and many left farmwork in the late 19th century to work in laundries and restaurants in urban areas. In the rural Mississippi Delta, many opened small grocery and agricultural supply stores. There they found their economic niche supplying African Americans, who were often turned away or refused credit by white grocers but who had new cash purchasing power. Chinese men replaced slave labor at the sugar plantations in Jefferson Parish, La., where they often intermarried with African Americans or American Indians. Fewer than 1,000 Chinese had come to the South before the nationwide Chinese Exclusion Act of 1882.

Once the Exclusion Act was repealed by the 1943 Magnuson Act, the Chinese communities in Mississippi attracted new arrivals, and communities also began forming in Houston and San Antonio. By 1900, El Paso had a small Chinatown. In Texas, cultural distinctions still separate the "Old" and the "New" Chinese immigrants. The Cantonese-speaking, 19th-century immigrants were mostly from southern China, while 20th-century arrivals were from various other locations in China and are predominantly Mandarin-speaking. The older immigrants came mostly from peasant backgrounds, were upwardly mobile, and have succeeded in business. The newer immigrants were of China's elite and have focused on the professions. Descendants of the older immigrants long maintained a focus on clan or family association (defined by surname). Today, Chinese New Year may still be celebrated, and a Confucian emphasis on family obligations remains strong. Many are now Baptists.

Considered "colored," Chinese children attended African American schools. The Chinese established a few private schools in Texas and Mississippi with the assistance of Baptist missions, whose members sought to convert Chinese immigrants and to provide a vehicle for acculturation. Not until the 1950s and 1960s, when approximately 10,000 Chinese called the South home, did Chinese children attend white public schools.

Many in the Mississippi Delta came to see the Chinese as having a social identity "between black and white" in a biracial hierarchy. The Chinese grocery stores were almost entirely in African American neighborhoods, and this is also where the Chinese people lived. Neighborhood residents were the regular clientele for these "mom and

Chinese grocery, Vicksburg, Miss., 1975 (William R. Ferris Collection, Southern Folklife Collection, Wilson Library, University of North Carolina at Chapel Hill)

pop" establishments, although whites came to shop there on occasion. The lack of a Chinatown offered in larger, more urban areas did not prevent the Delta Chinese from forming a distinct community. Even though there has been some competition among family-owned businesses, extended families formed support networks. Store labor was shared, with the very young and the old taking their turns stocking shelves and bagging groceries. Meals would be in a traditional family style, usually with Chinese dishes, but those sitting at the table would rotate in shifts while the store was open. Regular mah jong nights (a gambling game for four players) have characterized evenings with families and neighbors, and tournaments even take place at Chinese Baptist church halls. Birthday and wedding celebrations have a distinctly Chinese style with traditional decorations (such as wall hangings of calligraphic characters), speeches given in Cantonese, and Chinese food. Holidays, such as Chinese New Year and the New Moon Festival, are recognized, typically with smaller, extended family gatherings. Cantonese, the dialect of Guangdong Province and of most of the Delta Chinese, is passed on to children in varying degrees in the home.

The number of Chinese families in the Mississippi Delta who continue to live this grocery-store lifestyle is shrinking, as many of the younger generation move away for other opportunities and to go into the professions. Waves of in-migration and out-migration continue. In the past few decades, Chinese businesses have diversified, with the opening of Chinese restaurants and fast-food takeouts. Retirees are frequently replaced not by their children but rather by new Chinese families looking to immigrate into the area. New immigrants are increasingly coming from large urban areas within the United States to escape the higher costs of living in cities like New York, Los Angeles, or Chicago.

MELINDA CHOW
University of Memphis

Lucy Cohen, *Chinese in the Post–Civil War South: A People without a History* (1984); James W. Loewen, *The Mississippi Chinese: Between Black and White* (1988); Robert Seto Quan, *Lotus among the Magnolias: The Mississippi Chinese* (1982); Ronald Takaki, *Strangers from a Different Shore: A History of Asian Americans* (1998).

Cooper, Anna Julia Haywood

(1858–1964) WRITER.
Anna Julia Cooper's extraordinary energy and long productive life propelled her from her beginnings as the daughter of a bondwoman to a place among the most educated and articulate voices in America. She devoted her 105 years in North Carolina, Ohio, and Washington, D.C., to education, language, and social change.

Cooper's education in rhetoric at St. Augustine's Normal and Collegiate Institute in Raleigh, N.C., at Oberlin College in Ohio, and in her faculty position as a teacher of Latin at the renowned M Street School in Washington, D.C., paved the way for her writings. Her education also created the subject and method she used to stand for asserting

rights in the educational and gender politics of African American women.

Cooper's father was reputed to be her mother's owner. After the Civil War, at age nine, Cooper attended a school founded as an outgrowth of the Freedmen's Bureau, St. Augustine's Normal School, and made it her "world." At St. Augustine's, she ignored school rules limiting Latin and Greek instruction to boys and finagled her way into classes. By the time she enrolled at Oberlin College in 1881, she had read a wide array of Greek and Latin texts. Oberlin stoked those interests in classical literature, and, beginning in 1887, Cooper taught Latin and Greek at the M Street School for nearly 40 years. Cooper used education to prepare students for societal leadership roles. Her focus on cultivating the minds of black children put her at odds with Booker T. Washington and those who believed that blacks were suited only for manual work, and she temporarily lost her job at the M Street School when she insisted on an intellectually based curriculum for her students.

Cooper had a command of argumentative skills at a time when American racial ideologies and educational institutions specifically excluded blacks from the power of oratory and rhetoric. Popular culture framed blacks as people incapable of delivering useful information or shaping the public discourse. Nevertheless, in *A Voice from the South* (1892), Cooper built tight deductive arguments using the skills of classical rhetoric she had learned in her youth. She quickly convinced her audience to agree with her on some point about general moral standards and, with a swift turn of phrase, hijacked their assumptions governing women's rights and even the definition of race. Cooper's collection of orations and essays demonstrates her command of argument and prose to rework the very foundations of race and gender in the United States.

While teaching at M Street, Cooper took a leave from her job and attended the University of Paris–Sorbonne, earning a Ph.D. in French with a 1925 dissertation on slavery and the French Revolution. Cooper served as the president of Frelinghuysen University in Washington, D.C., in her 70s. For 10 years she oversaw the school, which offered adult education at night to working people in the city. She remained committed to education and the power to speak throughout her long life.

TODD VOGEL
University of Washington

Anna Julia Cooper, *Slavery and the French Revolutionists, 1788–1805, Studies in French Civilization*, vol. 1 (1925; 1988), *The Voice of Anna Julia Cooper: Including "A Voice from the South" and Other Important Essays, Papers, and Letters*, ed. Esme Bhan and Charles Lemert (1998); Leona C. Gable, *From Slavery to the Sorbonne and Beyond: The Life and Writings of Anna J. Cooper* (1982); Todd Vogel, *Rewriting White: Race, Class, and Cultural Capital in Nineteenth-Century America* (2004).

Country Music

Country music has related to racial categories in two ways. On the one hand, it is an expression of white yeoman folk culture and took commercial form during the high point of Jim Crow segregation, when southern society enforced a legal racial separation and national recording companies divided popular music into white "hillbilly" music and black "race" music. Few African Americans have been successful as country music performers, and blacks traditionally were not often spectators at country music shows. On the other hand, country music has borrowed heavily from black musical culture, including blues, jazz, spirituals, ragtime, rhythm and blues, and rock and roll. In the contemporary era, even rap has produced country rappers. Instrumentation and instrumental techniques have crossed racial lines. Country music came out of a southern musical culture that had folk origins of biracial interchanges and produced a musical street culture of diverse sounds that could not be limited to groups classified at the time as "white" or "black." Country music influenced black performers, further promoting a biracial southern musical context.

Historian Bill Malone identifies British-Celtic music as one of the major musical streams shaping southern music, and country music grew out of that inheritance. British ballads and stringed instrumentation became a foundation for frontier southerners making music, with European dance styles popular in both the Upper South and the lowlands. British music was itself in transition among the settlers who came to early America, though, so it would be hard to identify pure strands of British music, which, in any event, included distinct traditions of English, Scots-Irish, Irish, Welsh, and Scottish music. Early on, British sounds mixed with those of other subcultures—Germans in the mountains, the Piedmont, and central Texas; Cajuns in south Louisiana; Mexicans in south Texas; and Spanish and French along the Gulf Coast. Malone identifies the other large musical stream flowing into southern music as coming from Africa. Black and white southerners began exchanging musical ideas from first encountering each other in colonial Virginia, with the common farm and plantation life providing a setting for slaves and indentured servants exchanging songs and musical instrumentation. Racial prejudice did not prevent whites from borrowing from blacks. Over centuries, a folk pool of music took deepest root among people who were rural, agricultural, working class, and southern, people with common experiences with poverty, isolation, and exploitation. Minstrelsy emerged in the antebellum years as a prime American entertainment form, which drew from stereotypical ideas of southern life and became popular among northern working-class audiences. White-faced performers mimicked blacks, but by the early 20th century, black and white performers were popular figures within the medicine show and traveling show circuit in the South itself.

The crossing of racial lines in country music was apparent in musical instrumentation. The first references to country music in North America go back to fiddling contests in the mid-1700s in Virginia. The instrument was associated with southern whites, and it was so compact that it easily fit into saddlebags as white farmers moved west. Many references can be found to fiddling slaves in advertisements for runaways, reflecting the popularity of slave fiddlers at plantation dances. The banjo also crossed racial lines as time went on in southern history. Originally, the instrument came from Africa, typical of that continent's stringed instrument traditions, but blacks abandoned it as whites took it up after the Civil War. It became crucial to mountain string bands, early country hillbilly groups, and, later, bluegrass entertainers. Guitars were found in the South going back to the 18th century, but only in the late 19th century did they become more popular than fiddles among rural musicians. Black southerners took up the instrument earlier than whites. Bluesmen used the slide guitar technique, while white country performers used the steel guitar, but both sounds had a common origin in late 19th-century Hawaiian guitar music. South Carolina country performer Jimmy Tarlton adopted the bottleneck style in the 1920s after seeing black guitarists use a steel bar.

Songs also reflected interchanges across racial boundaries. The ballad "Frankie and Johnny" originated among blacks in 1899, but it became a common song after that among black and white musicians. In the 1920s, blues singer Mississippi John Hurt recorded it, for example, but so did the "father of country music," Jimmie Rodgers.

Jimmie Rodgers, the "father of country music," 1929. His music was influenced by the blues, as was the music of countless other country musicians. (Jimmie Rodgers Museum, Meridian, Miss.)

and 1940s, including "Brain Cloudy Blues."

Country music influenced black performers as well. The Mississippi Sheiks, Charley Patton, Son House, and other Mississippi blues performers played often at white house parties in the early 20th century, expanding their repertoire to sing country songs to please their audiences. Western Virginia bluesman John Jackson admitted indebtedness to white country performers, absorbing and playing songs by Jimmie Rodgers, the Delmore Brothers, and Uncle Dave Macon. Furry Lewis sang Rodgers's "Waiting for a Train" under the title "The Dying Hobo" and yodeled on it. Examples of black musicians recording country songs range from the Memphis Sheiks doing Jimmie Rodgers's "He's in the Jailhouse Now" in the 1930s to Aaron Neville's version of the George Jones classic "The Grand Tour" in the 1990s.

Several black performers have become country music stars, contributing to its biracial heritage. DeFord Bailey, a harmonica player who was an early regular on Nashville's *Grand Ole Opry*, was one of the first country performers recorded. More recently, Charley Pride heard the *Grand Ole Opry* on clear channel WSM broadcasting into his Mississippi Delta tenant house, learned to sing not the blues but Hank Williams songs, and became one of modern country's greatest stars. Perhaps the more enduring contribution of blacks to country music, though, has been from amateurs who taught country stars, from the railroad workers who taught Jimmie Rodgers the blues to Tee-Tot

"Casey Jones" was identified with white folk music but was written by a black railroad worker, Wallace Saunders, and was recorded in the 1920s by both Fiddlin' John Carson and Furry Lewis. The blues form originated among blacks, but it became a durable genre among country performers as well. Dock Boggs's "Country Blues" and his "Old Rub Alcohol Blues" established him as one of the South's most compelling earlier country figures, but Gene Autry, Cliff Carlisle, Jimmie Davis, and the Delmore Brothers all became noted as white performers of the blues. Blind Lemon Jefferson's "Matchbox Blues" was recorded by at least a half dozen country performers from 1927 to 1958. Western swing was particularly attuned to African American blues in the 1930s

(Rufus Payne), the Alabama street musician whom Hank Williams singled out as a musical influence.

CHARLES REAGAN WILSON
University of Mississippi

John Cohen, *Sing Out! The Folk Song Magazine* (January 1964); Bill Malone and David Stricklin, *Southern Music/American Music* (1979; 2003); Tony Russell, *Blacks, Whites, and Blues* (1970); Nick Tosches, *Country: Living Legends and Dying Metaphors in America's Biggest Music* (1977; 1985).

Delta

The Yazoo Mississippi Delta is not the true delta of the Mississippi River but the fertile alluvial plain shared by the Mississippi and Yazoo rivers. Encompassing all of 10 Mississippi counties and parts of 8 more, it is 160 miles long and 50 miles wide at its widest. Distinguished by its flatness and its fertility, the Delta was even better defined by its late-developing plantation economy and the distinctive society that economy nurtured.

Destined to become the richest agricultural region in the South, the Delta was only sparsely settled in 1860 and still not far removed from the frontier in 1880. During the next two decades, a new network of levees and a modern railway system opened the plantation South's last frontier for full-scale settlement and development.

The fertile Delta drew not only ambitious whites but also blacks, who saw it as the best place to test their newly won freedom and climb the agricultural ladder to become independent landowners. For many whites, the Delta became a land of wildest fantasies fulfilled, but for thousands of blacks the Delta that had promised them the rural South's best chance for upward mobility became the burial ground for hopes and dreams. In reality, the Delta proved to be little more than a stopover for many southern blacks on their way (via the conveniently located Illinois Central Railroad, which bisected the area) to the North. The Delta experienced a massive out-migration of blacks in the years after World War I. During the same period, the region was emerging as a spawning ground for the blues. This new musical idiom explored the shared experiences of southern blacks, who had tested the economic, social, and political parameters of their freedom, as defined by a rigidly enforced system of caste, and discovered that, for them, the American Dream was little more than a cruel myth.

Meanwhile, despite their constant fears over labor shortages, Delta planters thrived on the annual gamble on the price of cotton, living lavishly and laughing at debts. Even the onslaught of the boll weevil did the Delta relatively little harm. Meanwhile, by channeling all of its acreage reduction and related payments through the planter and looking the other way as these same planters illegally evicted now-superfluous sharecroppers, the Agricultural Adjustment Administration (AAA) confirmed the dominance of the large landholder in the region. In 1934, 44 percent of all AAA payments in excess of $10,000 nationwide went to 10 counties in the Delta. This largesse facilitated mechanization and consolidation of agriculture, and as federal

Day laborers carrying sacks of cotton from the field to the cotton house to be weighed, Marcella Plantation, Mississippi Delta, Miss. (Marion Post Wolcott, photographer, Library of Congress Prints and Photographs Division [LC-USF33-030557-M5], Washington, D.C.)

farm programs continued, the money kept rolling in. In 1967, Delta planter and U.S. senator James Eastland received $167,000 in federal payments. The Delta's poor blacks were not nearly as fortunate, as a power structure dominated by lavishly subsidized planters declared war on the War on Poverty.

Many Delta planters finally met their day of reckoning in the farm crisis of the 1980s, and although the Delta was the birthplace of the Citizens' Council and a citadel of white resistance to racial equality, the black-majority area finally elected a black congressman, Mike Espy, in 1986. The region's history had been one of tension and struggle—between the races, against the poorer hill counties, against the impenetrable swampy wilderness and the ravages of flood, pestilence, and disease, and finally,

against the intrusions of civil rights activists and federal civil rights policies.

Out of this tangle of tension and paradox came a remarkable outpouring of creativity, one that made the Delta's artistic climate arguably as rich as its agricultural one. Greenville alone produced writers William Alexander Percy, Walker Percy, Shelby Foote, Ellen Douglas, Hodding Carter II, Hodding Carter III, David Cohn, and Beverly Lowry. Classical composer Kenneth Haxton is from the Greenville area, as are sculptor Leon Koury and artist Valerie Jaudon. The Delta has produced a host of entertainers, including Jim Henson, creator of the Muppets, country singers Charley Pride and Conway Twitty, and an especially large number of blues singers past and present, from the legendary Charley

Patton to contemporary artists like B. B. King and James "Son" Thomas. Sometimes appalling, always fascinating, the Delta's historical and cultural experience often seemed that of an entire region in microcosm. It richly deserved the title, accorded by writer Richard Ford, as "the South's South."

JAMES C. COBB
University of Georgia

Robert L. Brandfon, *Cotton Kingdom of the New South: A History of the Yazoo Mississippi Delta from Reconstruction to the Twentieth Century* (1967); James C. Cobb, *The Most Southern Place on Earth: The Mississippi Delta and the Roots of Regional Identity* (1992); David L. Cohn, *Where I Was Born and Raised* (1967); Tony Dunbar, *Delta Time* (1990); John C. Willis, *Forgotten Time: The Yazoo-Mississippi Delta after the Civil War* (2000).

Dixon, Thomas, Jr.

(1864–1946) WRITER.
Throughout Thomas Dixon's adult life, he fixated on the apocryphal notion that black men yearned to commit sexual violence against white women, while black temptresses lured white men into their embrace. In his mind, the mulatto children that resulted from white men and women's "forced" unions with black sexual predators spelled the death of American civilization and the Anglo-Saxon race. To Dixon, the decline of the United States rested upon the North's insistence on granting bestial black men political rights during Reconstruction, thereby unleashing their libidinous desires for white women and facilitating the transformation of the white nation into a "mongrelized" and vulnerable state.

While Dixon's notions were profoundly shaped by a rabid racism rooted in his southern heritage, he was piercingly attuned to the cultural beats of his time. Steeped in the moral intensity of his Baptist background and of Victorian America as a whole, he plied his cautionary tales about white and black men and women acting outside their gendered roles and racial hierarchies within the easily digested forms of popular romance and melodrama.

Dixon was born in 1864 in Cleveland County in the southwestern corner of North Carolina. His father was a minister and farmer who belonged to the Ku Klux Klan, as did his Confederate veteran brother. Thomas Dixon Sr. seems to have been the source of many of his son's psychosexual perceptions. Not only did his son decry his mother's ostensible rape as a child bride in his autobiography, but Dixon Sr. was rumored to have fathered a son with the family's African American cook.

Thomas Dixon Jr. embraced the principles of white superiority that rationalized Jim Crow disfranchisement, segregation, and brutality against African Americans in the turn-of-the-century South. He believed that thousands of years of development separated Aryans from Africans, and that African Americans believed they could bridge that gap through interracial marriage. White men, Dixon argued, must stop this black press for miscegenation at all costs. Dixon's beliefs reflected a wider culture in which white southern manhood seemed under siege. A developing market economy and interracial political alliances, combined with a changing population in which young single white women could move to the cities for employment and black men could become urban entrepreneurs and businessmen, challenged traditional white patriarchal authority and served as a crucible for the myth of the black beast rapist.

Dixon has played an unparalleled role in disseminating that myth throughout American culture. He portrayed black men as innate barbarians unable to restrain their lust for white virgins, a theme hammered home in his best-selling trilogy, *The Leopard's Spots* (1902), *The Clansman* (1905), and *The Traitor* (1907). He used his inflammatory scenes of black men skulking after unprotected white women to justify the resurrection of the chivalric Ku Klux Klan, charged with saving not only southern womanhood but the country as a whole. America's future, Dixon was suggesting, depended on the heroism of southern white men, a point literally writ large in the sensationalistic film he cowrote with D. W. Griffith, *The Birth of a Nation* (1915).

Dixon did not write exclusively about the South however. As an advocate of the Social Gospel Movement, he addressed the social problems of modernity. He condemned society's blind eye for poor working women's desperate lives and wished that they were honored as mothers of civilization instead. Interestingly, Dixon did not see white women as passive victims in all contexts. He celebrated women's strong leadership in church, even as he sought more exemplifiers of Christian manhood in his pews. He believed that strong women could prevent men from pursuing the twin dangers of radicalism and promiscuity, a theme he explored in several of his books, including his first best seller, *The One Woman* (1903). For Dixon, a white man and white woman's romantic love, made sacred by having a child, ensured a man's highest morality. Modern white women who pursued careers and independence must give up those aspirations to "save" their men. Black men and black women, by comparison, lacked the capacity for romantic love, and therefore the capacity for true piety.

Dixon's preoccupation with the dangers of black sexuality never waned. In his final book, *The Flaming Sword* (1939), he tied the rape of a white Piedmont wife by a savage black man to Communist efforts to overthrow the United States with the support of a black army. Throughout his long career, Dixon appealed to a national audience of white men and white women anxious about modernization and its impact on manliness, race, and white authority. In the end, it is important to recognize that Dixon's horrific stereotypes ultimately reflected the collective anxieties of white America as much or more than Dixon's own warped imagination.

MICHELE GILLESPIE
Wake Forest University

Michele K. Gillespie and Randal L. Hall, eds., *Thomas Dixon Jr. and the Birth of Modern America* (2006); Glenda Gilmore, *Gender and Jim Crow: Women and the Politics of White Supremacy in North Carolina, 1896–1920* (1996); Diane Miller Sommerville, *Rape and Race in the Nineteenth-Century South* (2004); Joel Williamson,

Crucible of Race: Black-White Relations in the American South since Emancipation (1984).

Douglass, Frederick

(1808–1895) BLACK LEADER.
Frederick Douglass was the most important black American leader of the 19th century. He was born Frederick Augustus Washington Bailey, in Talbot County, on Maryland's Eastern Shore, in 1808, the son of a slave woman and, in all likelihood, her white master. Upon his escape from slavery at age 20, Douglass adopted a new surname from the hero of Sir Walter Scott's *The Lady of the Lake*. Douglass immortalized his formative years as a slave in the first of three autobiographies, *Narrative of the Life of Frederick Douglass, an American Slave*, published in 1845. This and two subsequent autobiographies, *My Bondage and My Freedom* (1855) and *The Life and Times of Frederick Douglass* (1881), mark Douglass's greatest contributions to southern culture. Written both as antislavery propaganda and as personal revelation, they are universally regarded as the finest examples of the slave narrative tradition and as classics of American autobiography.

Douglass's public life ranged from his work as an abolitionist in the early 1840s to his attacks on Jim Crow segregation in the 1890s. Douglass spent the bulk of his career in Rochester, N.Y., where for 16 years he edited the most influential black newspaper of the mid-19th century, called successively *The North Star* (1847–51), *Frederick Douglass' Paper* (1851–58), and *Douglass' Monthly* (1859–63). Douglass achieved interna-

Frederick Douglass, abolitionist and black leader, date unknown (Sophia Smith Collection, Smith College, Northampton, Mass.)

tional fame as an orator with few peers and as a writer of persuasive power. In thousands of speeches and editorials, Douglass levied an irresistible indictment against slavery and racism, provided an indomitable voice of hope for his people, embraced antislavery politics, and preached his own brand of American ideals.

Douglass welcomed the Civil War in 1861 as a moral crusade to eradicate the evil of slavery. During the war, he labored as a fierce propagandist of the Union cause and emancipation, as a recruiter of black troops, and on two occasions as an adviser to President Abraham Lincoln. Douglass made a major contribution to the intellectual tradition of millennial nationalism, the outlook from which many Americans, North and South, interpreted the Civil War. During Reconstruction and the Gilded Age, Douglass's leadership became less activist and more emblematic. He traveled and lectured widely on racial issues, but his most popular topic was "Self-Made Men." By the 1870s, Douglass had moved to Washington, D.C., where he edited the newspaper the *New National Era* and became president of the ill-fated Freedmen's Bank. As a stalwart Republican, he was appointed marshal (1877–81) and recorder of deeds (1881–86) for the District of Columbia and chargé d'affaires for Santo Domingo and minister to Haiti (1889–91). Douglass had five children by his first wife, Anna Murray, a free black woman from Baltimore who followed him out of slavery in 1838. Less than two years after Anna died in 1882, the 63-year-old Douglass married Helen Pitts, his white former secretary, an event of considerable controversy. Thus, by birth and by his two marriages, Douglass is one of the South's most famous examples of the region's mixed racial heritage.

Douglass never lost a sense of attachment to the South. "Nothing but an intense love of personal freedom keeps us [fugitive slaves] from the South," Douglass wrote in 1848. He often referred to Maryland as his "own dear native soil." Brilliant, heroic, and complex, Douglass became a symbol of his age and a unique American voice for humanism and social justice. His life and thought will always speak profoundly to the dilemma of being black in America. Douglass died of heart failure in 1895, the year Booker T. Washington rose to national prominence with his Atlanta Exposition speech suggesting black accommodation to racial segregation.

DAVID W. BLIGHT
Yale University

John W. Blassingame et al., *The Frederick Douglass Papers*, 2 vols. (1979–82); David W. Blight, *Frederick Douglass' Civil War: Keeping Faith in Jubilee* (1989); Philip S. Foner, *Life and Writings of Frederick Douglass*, 4 vols. (1955); August Meier, *Negro Thought in America, 1800–1915* (1963); Benjamin Quarles, *Frederick Douglass* (1948).

Du Bois, W. E. B.

(1868–1963) HISTORIAN, SOCIOLOGIST, EDITOR, NOVELIST.
William Edward Burghardt Du Bois was born on 23 February 1868 in Great Barrington, Mass. A New Englander in thought and conduct, as he put it, he entered the South in 1885, after a promising high school career, to attend Fisk University in Nashville. He found the South deeply humiliating. "No one but a Negro," he wrote, "going into the South without previous experience of color caste can have any conception of its barbarism." Nevertheless, Fisk itself was challenging, even exhilarating, and summer teaching in rural counties sealed his attachment to the black masses and his determination to champion their cause. Graduating in 1888, he trained further at Harvard University (Ph.D., 1895) and the University of Berlin. His doctoral dissertation on the suppression of the slave trade was published in 1896. He held positions briefly with the University of Pennsylvania and Wilberforce in Ohio before returning

to the South in 1897 to teach sociology, economics, and history at Atlanta University.

His third book, *The Souls of Black Folk* (1903), was a collection of hauntingly beautiful essays on every important aspect of black culture in the South; perhaps its most famous insight concerned the "double-consciousness" of the black American: "One ever feels his twoness—an American, a Negro; two souls, two thoughts, two unreconciled strivings; two warring ideals in one dark body, whose dogged strength alone keeps it from being torn asunder." With this book, he secured preeminence among all African American intellectuals and became the leader of those opposed to the powerful and conservative Booker T. Washington of Tuskegee. His yearly (1897–1914) Atlanta University Studies of black social conditions and a biography of John Brown (1909) added to his reputation.

Increasingly controversial, he moved to New York in 1910 to found and edit *The Crisis*, the monthly magazine of the fledgling NAACP. For 24 years, he sustained an assault on all forms of racial injustice, especially in the South. In 1934, he published *Black Reconstruction in America*, a grand Marxist-framed reevaluation of the much-maligned role of blacks in the Civil War and its aftermath. That year, he returned to Atlanta University after grave disagreements with the NAACP leadership over strategies during the Depression; Du Bois favored a program of voluntary self-segregation stressing economics, which many people found similar to the old program of Booker T. Washington. At Atlanta University, he found little support for his projected scheme to organize the study of sociology among black colleges and other institutions in the South. In 1944, he rejoined the NAACP in New York but soon found himself again at odds with the leadership, this time over his growing interest in radical socialism. He left the NAACP finally in 1948. By this time, his attitude toward the South had changed somewhat. Influenced no doubt by the aims of the leftist Southern Negro Youth Congress, he declared in 1948 that "the future of American Negroes is in the South. . . . Here is the magnificent climate; here is the fruitful earth under the beauty of the southern sun; and here . . . is the need of the thinker, the worker, and the dreamer." His socialist activities culminated in his arrest and trial in 1951 as an unregistered agent of a foreign principal; the presiding judge heard the evidence and then directed his acquittal.

Unpopular and even shunned in some quarters, he turned to fiction to express his deepest feelings. In a trilogy set mainly in the South, *The Black Flame (The Ordeal of Mansart)* (1957), *Mansart Builds a School* (1959), and *Worlds of Color* (1961), he told the story of a black southerner, born at the end of Reconstruction, who rises slowly and patiently to the leadership of a small southern school, witnessing in his long lifetime the important events of modern American and world history. In October 1961, Du Bois was admitted to membership in the Communist Party of the United States; that month he left his country to live in Ghana at the invitation of Kwame Nkrumah. In February 1963, he renounced his American citizenship and became a Ghanaian. He had made little progress on the task for which Nkrumah had summoned him, the editing of an *Encyclopedia Africana*, when he died of natural causes on 27 August 1963.

ARNOLD RAMPERSAD
Stanford University

Herbert Aptheker, *Annotated Bibliography of the Published Writings of W. E. B. Du Bois* (1973); David Levering Lewis, *W. E. B. Du Bois: Biography of a Race, 1868–1919* (1993); Arnold Rampersad, *The Art and Imagination of W. E. B. Du Bois* (1976); Raymond Wolters, *Du Bois and His Rivals* (2002); Shamoon Zamir, *Dark Voices: W.E.B. Du Bois and American Thought, 1888–1903* (1995).

Faulkner, William

(1897–1962) WRITER.
William Cuthbert Faulkner was born on 25 September 1897, in New Albany, Miss. The great-grandson of William Clark Falkner, a southern novelist and Confederate officer, Faulkner was responsible for adding the *u* to his family name—just as he was responsible for transmogrifying his native South into a universal place of the imagination in brilliant novels and stories that have put him first among 20th-century American writers of prose fiction. He explored the psychology of race relations and made race itself the central feature of southern life, realistically showing the brutalities and complexities for southerners.

Faulkner came to maturity at a time when Mississippi and the South were changing. He grew up a part of post–Civil War southern culture, which was dominated by memories of the Old South and the war, and yet he also ex-perienced the modernizing forces of the early 20th century in the region. He had romantic instincts, expressed in his early poetry and prose and in his enlistment in the Royal Canadian Air Force in 1918, hoping to be a gallant fighter pilot. He went back to Oxford, Miss., in that same year, though, and pursued work as a writer. Lawyer Phil Stone encouraged him, financially and intellectually, introducing him to the work of modernists such as T. S. Eliot.

Faulkner spent several months in New Orleans in 1925, becoming friends with Sherwood Anderson and other creative talents there, and in July of that year he embarked on a walking tour through parts of Europe. With the exception of stints working as a screenwriter in California, he mostly lived thereafter in Mississippi. His first novel, *Soldiers' Pay*, appeared in 1926, followed by *Mosquitoes* in 1927.

All of Faulkner's major novels reflect his southern rootedness. Beginning with *Flags in the Dust* (published as *Sartoris* in 1929), he creates a mythical Mississippi county, Yoknapatawpha, in which his main characters and their families confront not only specifically southern subjects—such as a native Indian population, the Civil War, plantation life, and race relations—but also themes that transcend a regional focus. *Absalom, Absalom!* (1936), perhaps Faulkner's greatest achievement, explicitly conjoins his southernness and his universality in the partnership of the southerner, Quentin Compson, and the Canadian, Shreve McCannon, Harvard roommates, whose exploration of the southern past provokes questions about the meaning of history itself. Race is central here, with the ambitions of planter Thomas Sutpen leading to his refusal to accept his mixed-race son and the ultimate failure of his grand plans.

In *The Sound and the Fury* (1929), his first great novel, Faulkner depicts several generations of a southern family, the Compsons, with a sophisticated handling of point of view and human voice that is equal to the greatest work of his European contemporaries. In *As I Lay Dying* (1930), *Light in August* (1932), *The Hamlet* (1940), and *Go Down, Moses* (1942), Faulkner portrays many different kinds and classes of southerners, exemplified by the Bundrens, the Snopeses, and the McCaslins. He also conveys penetrating insights into southern Protestantism, miscegenation, and discrimination, which again point beyond themselves—especially in the figure of Joe Christmas—to fundamental concerns about the nature of human identity and how it is shaped, as well as the specific embodiments of racial identities in the South.

Other leading Faulkner novels include *Pylon* (1935), *The Unvanquished* (1938), *The Wild Palms* (1939), *A Fable* (1954), and his last major work, *The Reivers* (1962). *Sanctuary* (1931) was one of the few Faulkner novels to sell well, and he had abiding financial problems that led to his work in films and as a short story writer for popular magazines. His accomplished short fiction appears in *Collected Stories* (1950) and *Uncollected Stories* (1979). Despite his critical success, especially in Europe, all of Faulkner's novels were out of print when Malcolm Cowley's edited *Portable*

Faulkner appeared in 1946, which led to a steadily rising appreciation, and sale, of his work.

In the latter part of his career, Faulkner became increasingly aware that he had established his apocryphal county as a counterweight to the actual South, where he had spent most of his life. In *Requiem for a Nun* (1951), he juxtaposed the development of Yoknapatawpha and its town, Jefferson, with the history of Mississippi and its capital, Jackson. In this underrated experimental drama, as well as in his later Snopes novels, *The Town* (1957) and *The Mansion* (1959), he directly addressed the issue of the South's changing culture and political structure in the context of world history and national events—as he did at the same time in numerous public letters, speeches, and interviews, especially after receiving the Nobel Prize in 1950. He died in Oxford, Miss., on 6 July 1962.

CARL E. ROLLYSON JR.
Wayne State University

Ann Abadie and Doreen Fowler, eds., *Faulkner and the Short Story: Faulkner and Yoknapatawpha, 1990* (1992); John E. Bassett, *William Faulkner: An Annotated Checklist of Criticism* (1972), *William Faulkner: An Annotated Checklist of Recent Criticism* (1983); Joseph Blotner, *William Faulkner: A Biography*, 2 vols. (1974); Louis Daniel Brodsky and Robert W. Hamblin, eds., *Faulkner: A Comprehensive Guide to the Brodsky Collection*, 2 vols. (1982–84); Cleanth Brooks, *William Faulkner: The Yoknapatawpha Country* (1963), *William Faulkner: Toward Yoknapatawpha and Beyond* (1978); James Ferguson, *Faulkner's Short Fiction* (1991); Donald M. Kartiganer, *Modern Fiction Studies* (Fall 1998);

Thomas L. McHaney, *William Faulkner: A Reference Guide* (1976); Michael Millgate, *The Achievement of William Faulkner* (1965); Jay Parini, *One Matchless Time: A Life of William Faulkner* (2004); Daniel J. Singal, *William Faulkner: The Making of a Modernist* (1997); Joel Williamson, *William Faulkner and Southern History* (1993).

French

Francophone populations, though usually neglected in recounting the history and development of the South, have nonetheless played a prominent role, exemplifying ethnic-racial complexities. The first settlers in North America seeking refuge for religious reasons were not the Pilgrims at Plymouth Rock in 1620, but French Huguenots in 1562 at coastal Charlefort (sometimes also called Charlesfort), located in what is now South Carolina. Because of privation and Spanish aggression, the settlement at Charlefort did not last long, but toward the end of the 17th century hundreds more Huguenots became part of the founding population of South Carolina, especially in Charleston. Many of their progeny grew wealthy, and indeed for a time Charleston rivaled every other colonial city on the Atlantic Coast for affluence, because of the extensive development of slave-based rice plantations. Despite sporadic testimonies of the subsequent survival of French, it appears that these prominent Huguenots (the most famous among them being "Swamp Fox" Francis Marion) assimilated rather quickly to the English language that predominated in the surrounding colonial setting. Much more for the sake of tradition than for linguistic necessity, the Huguenot Church at the corner of Church and Queen streets in Charleston still conducts an occasional service in French according to the 18th-century liturgy of *les Eglises de la Principauté de Neuchâtel et Valangin*.

Though Charleston is unrivaled in Old South tradition, its French Quarter cannot contend with the French Quarter of New Orleans, La., as the leading French-related cultural icon of the South. Indeed, the best-known and longest-surviving Francophone population in the South—and, until recently, the largest—has been located in Louisiana and its environs since the early 18th century. Robert Cavelier de La Salle descended the Mississippi from New France to its mouth in 1682 and claimed the entire Mississippi Valley and its tributaries for Louis XIV of France (hence, *la Louisiane*). Soon after, French settlements, or posts, were founded at Biloxi (1699), Mobile (1701), Natchitoches (1714), and La Nouvelle Orléans (1718). The varieties of French from the founding of Louisiana up to the present time form a complex picture, much of which is still speculative. Records clearly attest that French was the language of the colonial administrators, and some form of "popular French" was certainly in wide use. However, French was probably not the first language of many early colonists, who would have spoken a regional patois of France or who were often recruited from Germany or Switzerland. Moreover, communication with early indigenous peoples took place through a regional lingua franca, Mobilian Jargon, which served as a trade language and the language of diplomacy rather than French. It is noteworthy that very few French borrowings penetrated into the indigenous languages of the Southeast, such as the language of the Choctaw, with whom the French had a strong and long-standing military alliance.

The largest single population of French speakers to arrive in Louisiana during the colonial period did not come directly from France. French colonists who left the west central provinces of France and arrived in the early 17th century in Acadia (modern Nova Scotia and New Brunswick) were expelled from there by the British in 1755. Between 1765 and 1785, approximately 3,000 of them migrated to Louisiana (under Spanish administration from 1763) and occupied arable land principally along the bayous of southeastern Louisiana and the prairies of south-central Louisiana. This prolific population was destined to become the standard-bearer for maintaining French in Louisiana to the present day.

During the Spanish administration, the plantation economy of Louisiana began to blossom, dramatically affecting the French language there. On the one hand, the massive importation of slaves, coming directly from West Africa for the most part, apparently led to the formation of a French-based Creole language. Theories vary as to the genesis of Louisiana Creole, as it is usually referred to by scholars. The debate surrounding the origin of creole languages is complex, but, at the risk of oversimplifying, the two poles of opposition can be summed up here. Some scholars contend that creole languages were spontaneously generated on (large) plantations where slaves were linguistically heterogeneous and did not share a common tongue. According to this view, the structural parallels among creole languages are because of either linguistic universals or the interaction of a particular set of African and European languages. Others contend that most creole languages are simply daughter dialects of a pidgin associated with the slave trade, and though the lexicon can vary from one site to another owing to different vocabulary replacement, their basic structure remains the same. Regardless, Louisiana Creole became the native mode of communication within the slave population of Louisiana. Very frequently it was also the first language of the slave masters' children, who were typically raised by domestic bondservants.

In tandem with this, the wealth of what was then known as the Creole society grew. Creole society is not to be confused with the entire population of Louisiana Creole speakers but is composed rather of the affluent European-origin planter class and also of mostly biracial Creoles of Color who held considerable social standing during the Spanish administration, sometimes being plantation owners themselves. Their considerable resources allowed for widespread schooling among Creoles and the resultant acquisition of the evolving prestige French of France, by virtue of boarding schools in France and Louisiana or by private tutoring. Referred to as Plantation Society French in recent scholarship, this brand of French has all but disappeared, in part because of the ruin of Creole society in the aftermath of the Civil War and the resultant severing of ties with France and in part because of the rather swift acquisition of English (even before the Civil War) by members of Creole society. English became economically and socially important under the new American administration, which brought a massive influx of Anglophones, both free and slave, into Louisiana after the Louisiana Purchase of 1803. Not all newcomers after 1803 were English speakers, however. Prior to the Civil War, the affluence of Louisiana attracted additional Francophone immigrants, often educated, whose ranks were swelled by defeated Bonapartistes banished from France and by planters (with their creolophone slaves in tow) fleeing the successful slave revolt in Saint-Domingue (modern Haiti). Not all of the 19th-century newcomers settled in Louisiana: a group of Bonapartiste exiles founded Demopolis (in Alabama) in 1817, just prior to statehood.

Dependent on wealth generated by the plantation system and vulnerable to competition with the English for maintaining socioeconomic standing, once-prestigious Plantation Society French disappeared from use rather quickly. The vast majority of the agrarian, lower-class Acadian (or "Cajun") population worked small farms and did not operate plantations (though some Acadians did gentrify and merge with creole society). Their autonomy and relative isolation led to a greater longevity for Cajun French. Significant numbers of immigrants (German, Irish, Italian, for example) in some places even assimilated to the use of Cajun French for a time. Meanwhile, Louisiana Creole was undergoing its demise, ultimately because of the breakup of the plantation system itself, but even before that because of the immense influx of Anglophone slaves during the 19th century when the importation of foreign slaves was prohibited, leading to massive importation of slaves from states farther east to meet the demand in booming Louisiana. Nevertheless, the social isolation of its speakers led Louisiana Creole to fare better than Plantation Society French, and today approximately 4,500 mostly elderly speakers remain, with the largest concentrations in Point Coupee and St. Martin parishes.

Acadiana, the 22-parish area where most Cajun French speakers still live, can be roughly described as a triangle whose apex is in Avoyelles Parish in the center of the state and whose base extends along the coast from eastern Texas to the Mississippi border. The Cajun French spoken there did not begin its demise until the 20th century, with the advent of compulsory schooling in English in 1916. This factor, coupled with better state infrastructure and accelerated exposure to mass media, eroded the social isolation of the Cajun population and led inexorably to assimilation to the English standard by younger ethnic Cajuns. Despite an important resurgence in Cajun pride since the late 1960s (the "Cajun Renaissance") and attempts to bolster French in Louisiana, only the smallest fraction of children are now acquiring fluency in any variety of French. The few thousand who do so are not acquiring it in natural linguistic communities but primarily in French immersion programs in the public schools (introduced in 1968 when the state created the Council for the Development of French in Louisiana, CODOFIL, to reclaim French and promote bilingualism). Nevertheless, the Cajun Renaissance has spawned preservationist tendencies in some households, has resulted in a modicum of literary production by Cajun poets, playwrights, and storytellers, and is linked to the resurgence in popularity of Cajun music. Authenticity demands that Cajun musicians perform pieces in French and that even young songsmiths compose a portion of their newest lyrics in Cajun French.

Census figures for 2000 indicate a Francophone population of 194,100 for Louisiana. Even adding the creolophone population (4,685 in 2000) to that figure, the total fell far short of the combined French-speaking and creolophone populations of Florida in 2000 (125,650 + 211,950 = 337,600). Though European immigrants must also be taken into consideration, Florida is the new front-runner in the South, primarily because of its large number of French Canadian "snowbirds" and recent Haitian refugees. The Canadians, though elderly, represent a sustainable population as long as Florida remains an attractive retirement location, whereas the mostly elderly Francophone population of Louisiana is not self-replacing, except in a very small minority of cases where grandchildren are being reintroduced to French in a conscious attempt to preserve a linguistic legacy.

A description of the salient features of Cajun French and Louisiana Creole must take into account archaisms harking back to the French of the colonizers as well as innovations resulting from isolation and contact with other languages, especially English. For example, in various vocabulary items such as *haut* 'high' and *happer* 'to seize', both Cajun French and Louisiana Creole preserve the archaic pronunciation of the initial *h*, whereas the initial *h* has fallen silent in the contemporary French of France. At the grammatical level, both Cajun French and Louisiana Creole preserve the progressive modal *après* (sometimes *apé* or *ap*) of western regional France, denoting an ongoing action—for example, *je sus après jongler* 'I'm thinking' (Cajun French) or *m'apé fatigué* 'I'm getting tired' (Louisiana Creole). This usage is entirely absent in the standard French of France. Concerning innovations, historic contact with indigenous languages has enriched the vocabularies of French dialects in Louisiana with words such as *chaoui* 'raccoon' and *bayou* (subsequently borrowed into English). Contact with dominant English has had a profound impact on both Cajun French and Louisiana Creole. Assimilated borrowings are easy to find (*récorder* 'to record'), but because of near-universal bilingualism among Cajun French speakers and creolophones in Louisiana, it is even more common to hear the insertion of English vocabulary items into French or creole conversation: *j'ai RIDE dessus le BIKE* 'I rode the bike.' Imitative calques of English phrasing are also common, as in the case of a Cajun radio announcer reciting the standard expression *apporté à vous-aut' par* 'brought to you by.'

Though overlapping vocabularies are extensive, Louisiana Creole is distinct from Cajun French in a variety of ways. Of particular note in Louisiana Creole are a different system of pronouns, more frequent use of nouns that have permanently incorporated part or all of what were once preceding French articles, placement of the definite article after its noun, absence of linking verbs, absence of inflection on main verbs, and use of various particles to indicate tense. Compare the Louisiana Creole sentence *yé té lave zonyon-yé* 'they washed the onions' with *ils ont lavé les oignons* in Cajun French.

English in Louisiana dethroned Plantation Society French as the most highly valued idiom and may have temporarily protected nonstandard Louisiana Creole and Cajun French from absorption by prestigious standard French (such was the demise of patois and regional French in France). However, today English has become a formidable competitor, with the imminent prospect of supplanting all traditional varieties of Louisiana French and Louisiana Creole in the region where both thrived for over two-and-a-half centuries. Yet despite the demise of French as a first language in Louisiana, its influence remains noticeable in the spoken English of the region. Even in New Orleans, where the transition from French to English as the language of everyday communication has long been complete, vestiges of French can be found in colloquial calques such as *get*

down 'get out' (of a vehicle) and borrowings such as *banquette* 'sidewalk,' *parrain* 'godfather,' and *beignet* (type of fried dough). This phenomenon is even more common in rural Cajun communities, where one hears French borrowings in remarks such as *we were so honte* (that is, 'embarrassed') and *I have the envie* (that is, 'the desire') *for rice and gravy*. Less common but still used are structural calques from French: *Your hair's too long. You need to cut 'em* (hair as plural, corresponding in use to *les cheveux*) or *That makes forty years we married* (calqued from *ça fait quarante ans qu'on est marié*).

English is not the only force arrayed against the survival of French in Louisiana. In Plaquemines Parish, Hurricane Katrina, in 2005, decimated one of the few remaining non-Cajun Francophone enclaves, and ecological degradation, such as that which augmented the devastating effects of the storm, is contributing to the breakup of some of the more isolated Francophone communities (who mostly self-identify as Houma Indians) in Terrebonne Parish, where French has been best preserved among younger speakers.

MICHAEL D. PICONE
University of Alabama

AMANDA LAFLEUR
Louisiana State University

Barry Jean Ancelet, *Cajun and Creole Folktales: The French Oral Tradition of South Louisiana* (1994); Carl A. Brasseaux, *French, Cajun, Creole, Houma: A Primer on Francophone Louisiana* (2005); Marilyn J. Conwell and Alphonse Juilland, *Louisiana French Grammar* (1963); Thomas A. Klingler, *If I Could Turn My Tongue Like That: The*

Creole Language of Pointe Coupee, Louisiana (2003); Kevin J. Rottet, *Language Shift in the Coastal Marshes of Louisiana* (2001); Albert Valdman, ed., *French and Creole in Louisiana* (1997).

Hurston, Zora Neale

(ca. 1901–1960) WRITER AND FOLKLORIST.

Born in either 1891 or 1901—the latter is normally given as the date of birth but recent studies suggest an earlier date—in the all-black town of Eatonville, Fla., Zora Neale Hurston became a distinguished novelist, folklorist, and anthropologist. She was next to the youngest of eight children, born the daughter of a Baptist minister who was mayor of Eatonville. Her mother died when Hurston was 9, and she left home at 14 to join a traveling show. She later attended Howard University, where she studied under Alain Locke and Lorenzo Dow Turner, and she earned an A.B. degree from Barnard College in 1928, working with Franz Boas. She became a well-known figure among the New York intellectuals of the Harlem Renaissance in the mid-1920s and then devoted the years 1927 to 1932 to field research in Florida, Alabama, Louisiana, and the Bahamas. *Mules and Men* (1935) was a collection of black music, games, oral lore, and religious practices. *Tell My Horse* (1938) was a similar collection of folklore from Jamaica and Haiti.

Hurston published four novels—*Jonah's Gourd Vine* (1934), *Their Eyes Were Watching God* (1937), *Moses, Man of the Mountain* (1939), and *Seraph on the Sewanee* (1948). Her autobiography,

Zora Neale Hurston, a distinguished novelist, folklorist, and anthropologist who was noteworthy for her portrayal of the strength of black life in the South. (Photo by Carl Van Vechten, 1938)

Dust Tracks on a Road, appeared in 1948. Married and divorced twice, she worked for the WPA Federal Theatre Project in New York (1935–36) and for the Federal Writers' Project in Florida (1938). She taught briefly at Bethune-Cookman College in Daytona Beach, Fla. (1934), and at North Carolina College in Durham (1939), and she received Rosenwald and Guggenheim fellowships (1934, 1936–37).

In her essay "The Pet Negro System," Hurston assured her readers that not all black southerners fit the illiterate sharecropper stereotype fostered by the northern media. She pointed to the seldom-noted black professionals who, like herself, remained in the South because they liked some things about it. Most educated blacks, Hurston insisted, preferred not to live up North because they came to realize that there was "segregation and discrimination up there, too, with none of the human touches of the South." One of the "human touches" to which Hurston referred was the "pet Negro system" itself, a southern practice that afforded special privileges to blacks who met standards set by their white benefactors. The system survived, she said, because it reinforced the white southerner's sense of superiority. Clearly, it was not a desirable substitute for social, economic, and political equality, but Hurston's portrayal of the system indicated her affirmative attitude toward the region, despite its dubious customs.

Hurston had faith in individual initiative, confidence in the strength of black culture, and strong trust in the ultimate goodwill of southern white people, all of which influenced her perceptions of significant racial issues. When she saw blacks suffering hardships, she refused to acknowledge that racism was a major contributing factor, probably because she never let racism stop her. Hurston's biographer, Robert E. Hemenway, notes that "in her later life she came to interpret all attempts to emphasize black suffering . . . as the politics of deprivation, implying a tragedy of color in Afro-American life."

After working for years as a maid in Miami, Hurston suffered a stroke in early 1959 and, alone and indigent, died in the Saint Lucie County Welfare

Home, Fort Pierce, Fla., on 28 January 1960. Alice Walker led a "rediscovery" of Hurston, whose works have become inspiration for black women writers.

ELVIN HOLT
University of Kentucky

Valerie Boyd, *Wrapped in Rainbows: The Life of Zora Neale Hurston* (2002); Robert E. Hemenway, *Zora Neale Hurston: A Literary Biography* (1977); Zora Neale Hurston, *I Love Myself*, ed. Alice Walker (1979); Carla Kaplan, ed., *Zora Neale Hurston: A Life in Letters* (2002); Alice Walker, *In Search of Our Mothers' Gardens* (1983).

Japanese American Incarceration during World War II

Following decades of racial prejudice, combined with economic envy and sexual anxiety over miscegenation and nationality, 120,000 Japanese Americans during World War II were indiscriminately subjected to eviction from their homes, expulsion from the West Coast, detention in 16 makeshift compounds, and then concentration into 10 longer-term camps. Empowered by President Franklin Roosevelt's Executive Order 9066 of 19 February 1942, military and civilian officials carried out these constitutionally dubious procedures with guns and euphemism. The forced migrations were called, in turn, "evacuation," implying rescue; "removal," suggesting it was voluntary; "assembly," a purported freedom; and "relocation," a mere transfer.

However, after a grueling four-day train journey, blinds down, Americans of Japanese descent arriving at the two camps in southeast Arkansas expected no relief. Disembarking, they saw guard towers, barbed wire fencing, and—at both camps—nearly a square mile of barracks. Previously referred to by their dehumanizing family numbers, attached to clothing and suitcases, they now would be known by their three-part address: block and building number and the letter of their one-room apartment, none more than 20 by 24 feet. Ever after, Japanese Americans would remember where they or their ancestors had been incarcerated during the war. Here, near the banks of the Mississippi, in rural Chicot and Desha counties, respectively, it was the Jerome and Rohwer camps.

With peak populations of 8,500 each, Jerome and Rohwer brought together captives from southern California and the Central Valley, along with white staffers, mostly Arkansans. They worked side by side in similar jobs, as teachers and legal professionals, for example, but at a fraction of the pay for the former. Still, Japanese American women, less tied to onerous domestic duties, worked at the same rates as Japanese American men, enjoying unexpected autonomy. Most jobs were voluntary, though boys and men were forced into hazardous logging and woodcutting operations for winter fuel, resulting in dozens of injuries and at least three deaths. Labor unrest was characterized by strikes and harsh administration crackdowns, especially at Jerome. Inmates were targeted for indoctrination, through so-called Americanization campaigns in the schools and adult classes. The largely Buddhist population endured aggressive Protestant revivals.

English-speaking Christians gained special privileges, including greater freedom of movement. Leave was selectively granted for temporary work contracts outside the camps and for college education. Japanese Americans enrolled at otherwise segregated southern campuses, including elite private universities such as Emory, Rice, Tulane, and Vanderbilt and flagship state universities in Florida, North Carolina, and Texas, among others. From all 10 camps and from the Territory of Hawaii, thousands volunteered—more were later drafted—for military service in the 442nd Regimental Combat Team, which trained at Camp Shelby in Mississippi. Though segregated into their own units and barracks, the 442nd competed in "white" rather than "colored" sports leagues, at Shelby and across the South. Generally under local biracial structures of Jim Crow, authorities encouraged soldiers, students, contract laborers, and day-pass holders to use white facilities and to frequent white establishments. Many of these establishments turned them away.

At the same time, officials conspired to delimit Japanese American interaction with whites and with blacks. Interracial dating and marriage were particularly proscribed, and given the segregation of USO clubs around Camp Shelby, Japanese American women at Jerome and Rohwer were regularly bussed 250 miles for dances with the 442nd. Leave was denied to inmates with job offers from black schools and businesses. When black agricultural workers took collective action against local planters, these labor hotspots were declared off-limits to Japanese Americans. Though sometimes joining African Americans, as a matter of principle, in the back of the bus, Japanese Americans more commonly sought and occasionally secured the benefits of higher status, even blacking up with their white captors for camp minstrel shows.

When government agencies finally attempted to ascertain individual allegiance, rather than assuming collective guilt, Japanese American discontent hardened. Across all 10 camps in the West and the South, an ill-conceived, ill-administered loyalty questionnaire both confounded and enraged prisoners. And at higher percentages than at any other camp, Jerome protesters were reassigned to the Tule Lake camp in California, reconfigured as an isolation center. Among them was Tokio Yamane, who in sworn testimony to Congress described officers torturing him and others there. Yamane and hundreds more renounced their American citizenship and moved to Japan. No Japanese American was ever convicted of espionage.

Though resilient and productive, growing almost all their own food and sourcing other essentials through an innovative system of cooperative stores, Japanese Americans in Arkansas experienced yet another wrenching upheaval. Called "resettlement" by authorities, the closing of the camps involved a calculated dispersal of Japanese Americans in order to break up prewar ethnic enclaves: a massive population redistribution from west to east. Arkansas inmates proposed converting Jerome and Rohwer into agrarian cooperative colonies, given their marked improvements to local infrastructure. Instead, the government sold it all and kicked them out. Just as early in the incarceration a despairing John Yoshida committed suicide at the railroad tracks near Jerome—haunting photos of his decapitated body lingering in the archives—so too in the wake of Hiroshima, ancestral prefecture to the largest number of Japanese Americans, did Julia Dakuzaku take her life after release from Arkansas.

The most cynical euphemism of all, persisting to this day, "internment" is a concept recognized in international law for the wartime detention of "enemy aliens," citizens of combatant nations. The vast majority—over 70 percent—of the 120,000 people imprisoned in American concentration camps were birthright U.S. citizens; the remaining 30 percent were decades-long residents who were forbidden naturalization. Though these Americans of Japanese descent advocated for and eventually won restitution as partial recompense for loss of income and property, the United States has never accepted responsibility for loss of life.

JOHN HOWARD
King's College London

Roger Daniels, in *Nikkei in the Pacific Northwest: Japanese Americans and Japanese Canadians in the Twentieth Century*, ed. Louis Fiset and Gail M. Nomura (2005); John Howard, *Concentration Camps on the Home Front: Japanese Americans in the House of Jim Crow* (2008); Emily Roxworthy and Amit Chourasia, *Drama in the Delta: Digitally Reenacting Civil Rights Performances at Arkansas' Wartime Camps for Japanese Americans*, www.dramainthedelta .com; Jason Morgan Ward, *Journal of Southern History* (February 2007).

JAPANESE AMERICAN INCARCERATION DURING WORLD WAR II   223

Jazz

Jazz can be defined by its musical elements, such as improvisation, syncopation, blue notes, cyclical forms, and rhythmic contrasts, but also through its place in the social, economic, and cultural history of the United States. The subject of its racial identity has proved particularly thorny for musicians, critics, and audiences, for despite the diversity of jazz styles and performers, it is rooted in African American musical traditions at the turn of the 20th century. The tension between its aesthetic breadth and racial specificity has long animated debates regarding ownership, politics, and history. Rather than simplifying matters, its New Orleans origins demonstrate that the birth of jazz was enmeshed in the historical development of modern African American identity and culture.

Among the most prosperous and populous cities in the antebellum South—central to both international commerce and the domestic slave trade—19th-century New Orleans was musically and culturally rich. Contemporaries noted with wonder the proliferation of opera houses, orchestras, parades, and carnivals, as well as the slaves and free blacks who gathered at Congo Square on Sundays to dance and perform. With the end of American slavery, waves of freedpeople left the rural South. They brought with them African-influenced musical traditions, including spirituals and field songs as well as instrumental bands and arrangements formed in the lower Mississippi Delta. By the end of the 19th century, the city was an amalgam of English, French, and Spanish cultures, but its structure was soon transformed in the wake of Jim Crow racial codes spreading throughout the South. Caribbean Creoles, or *gens de couleur*, had previously held significant political and economic power as an intermediate group between white Europeans and blacks. However, with the Supreme Court's 1896 *Plessy* decision to uphold the separate-but-equal statute, the situation changed. Longtime Creole residents and recent black migrants, who continued to enter the city in ever-greater numbers seeking employment, found themselves on the same side of a stricter color line.

While Jim Crow was racially redefining many of its pioneers and performers, the musical components of jazz came together in New Orleans. It is difficult to know what early jazz sounded like without recorded documentation, but scholars believe that fundamental transformations in the form and instrumentation of popular music occurred between 1900 and 1910. Hoping to fill a dance hall, attract a crowd, or enliven a march, Uptown blacks and Downtown Creole musicians crossed previous social and geographic divides. They found new techniques and instrumentations in the various quarters of New Orleans and transformed well-known arrangements and popular songs by syncopating instrumental parts, improvising melodies over marchlike rhythms, and adding melodic strains and blue notes. Musicians drew on a diverse repertory, which included ragtime, marches, blues, popular songs, dance music, Spanish Caribbean music, and spirituals. They played in brass bands and in smaller ensembles made up of a rhythm section—drums, piano, banjo, bass, tuba—and a lead section, which could include a clarinet, trumpet, cornet, or trombone. While this new sound was associated with saloons in the red-light district of Storyville, groups like the Golden Rule and the Eagle played at store openings, parades, picnics, funerals, and balls. Bandleaders such as Buddy Bolden, Manuel Perez, Nick LaRocca, and Kid Ory cultivated a dense and competitive musical environment that circulated new rhythmic and melodic styles. Many of the soloists known for the New Orleans jazz style, like Joe "King" Oliver, Bunk Johnson, Louis Armstrong, Jelly Roll Morton, and Sidney Bechet, trained within an all-male environment that valued individual technique as well as ensemble arrangements and fraternal support.

Through itinerant musicians and expanding transportation networks, many of the identifiable musical precedents of jazz continued to develop on their own beyond New Orleans. In St. Louis, ragtime and blues formed the root of a distinctive boogie-woogie piano-playing style. Meanwhile, the Kansas City style achieved national recognition through musicians like Count Basie and Mary Lou Williams. The development of jazz was further aided by the large-scale migration of African Americans that began at the turn of the century. Like other black Americans who left the South, jazz musicians sought work in Chicago, New York, and California, where they found new audiences but maintained southern professional

networks. The migration was accompanied by major advances in radio and recording technology that in turn made jazz a national and international music. White New Orleans musicians in the Original Dixieland Jazz Band made the first jazz recordings, but soon black southerners, including Oliver and Armstrong, were putting out records and touring Europe. As jazz gained global recognition, the American South remained an important cultural symbol. Jazz enthusiasts in the 1920s flocked to New York's Cotton Club and Chicago's Plantation Club, where racial stereotypes of the South were reproduced for urban audiences in the North. In the 1930s, the revival of the Dixieland style represented authenticity in the face of the rising popularity of big band arrangements. The South also remained politically important for many musicians. A wide range of performers supported the southern civil rights movement by fund-raising for the Congress of Racial Equality (CORE), speaking out against civil rights abuses, and creating music, like Max Roach's 1960 *We Insist! The Freedom Now Suite*. From its origins to contemporary efforts at preservation, the South has been a site of opportunity and struggle for jazz musicians, shaping the roots of this racially defined yet culturally cosmopolitan music.

CELESTE DAY MOORE
University of Chicago

David Ake, *Jazz Cultures* (2002); Sidney Bechet, *Treat It Gentle* (1960); Charles B. Hersch, *Subversive Sounds: Race and the Birth of Jazz in New Orleans* (2007); William H. Kenney, *Chicago Jazz: A Cultural History, 1904–1930* (1993); Ingrid

Monson, *Freedom Sounds: Civil Rights Call Out to Jazz and Africa* (2007); Jelly Roll Morton, *Jelly Roll Morton: The Complete Library of Congress Recordings by Alan Lomax* (1938); Burton Peretti, *The Creation of Jazz: Music, Race, and Culture in Urban America* (1992); Eric Porter, *What Is This Thing Called Jazz? African American Musicians as Artists, Critics, and Activists* (2002).

King, Martin Luther, Jr.

(1929–1968) CIVIL RIGHTS LEADER. Born into a middle-class black family in Atlanta, Ga., on 15 January 1929, Martin Luther King Jr. emerged as the key figure in the civil rights crusade that transformed the American South in the 1950s and 1960s. As a student at Atlanta's Morehouse College (1944–48), he majored in sociology and developed an intense interest in the behavior of social groups and the economic and cultural arrangements of southern society. King's education continued at Crozer Theological Seminary (1948–51) and Boston University (1951–55), where he studied trends in liberal Christian theology, philosophy, and ethics, while also engaging in an intellectual quest for a method to eliminate social evil. With a seminary degree and a Ph.D. from Boston, King lived remarkably free of material concerns and personified the intellectual-activist type that constituted the principal model for W. E. B. Du Bois's talented-tenth leadership theory.

Although mindful of how poverty and economic injustice victimized both races in the South in his time, King understood the social stratification of the region largely in terms of the basic distinctions between powerful whites and powerless Negroes. Framing the struggle as essentially a clash between loveless power and powerless love, King rose to prominence in the Montgomery Bus Boycott in 1955–56, and he and his Southern Christian Leadership Conference (SCLC) later led nonviolent direct-action campaigns for equal rights and social justice in Albany, Birmingham, St. Augustine, Selma, and other southern towns. King's celebrated "I Have a Dream" speech during the March on Washington on 28 August 1963 firmly established him as the most powerful leader of the black freedom struggle.

After receiving the Nobel Peace Prize in 1964, King moved toward a more enlightened and explicit globalism. Convinced that the struggle for basic civil and/or constitutional rights had been won with the Civil Rights Act of 1964 and the Voting Rights Act of 1965, he turned more consciously toward economic justice and international peace issues. He saw the interconnectedness of racial oppression, class exploitation, and militarism and moved beyond integrated buses, lunch counters, and schools for blacks to highlight the need for basic structural changes within the capitalistic system. He recognized that economic justice was a more complex and costlier matter than civil rights and that poverty and economic powerlessness afflicted both people of color and whites. He prophetically critiqued the wealth and power of the white American elites and chided the black middle class for its neglect of and indifference toward what he labeled "the least of these." King also fought for

Martin Luther King Jr. (in hat) and Stokely Carmichael (right) during civil rights march in
Coldwater, Miss., 1966 (Ernest C. Withers, photographer, Memphis, Tenn.)

the elimination of slum conditions in Chicago in 1965–66, launched a Poor People's Campaign in 1967, and participated in the Memphis Sanitation Workers' Strike in early 1968. His attacks on capitalism, his call for a radical redistribution of economic power, his assault on poverty and economic injustice in the so-called Third World, and his cry against his nation's misadventure in Vietnam were all aimed at the same structures of systemic social evil. King framed his vision in terms of the metaphors of "New South," "American Dream," and "World House," all of which embodied what he considered the highest human and ethical ideal, namely, the beloved community, or a completely integrated society and world based on love, justice, human dignity, and peace.

King's broadened social vision can be understood in terms of democratic socialism and the tactics of massive civil disobedience and nonviolent sabotage that he thought would be required to achieve this ideal. While traveling to Oslo, Norway, to receive the Nobel Prize, he saw democratic socialism at work in the Scandinavian countries. In King's estimation, democratic socialism, which he considered more consistent with the Christian ethic than either capitalism or communism, would allow for the nationalization of basic industries, massive federal expenditures to enhance city centers and to provide employment for residents, a guaranteed income for every adult citizen, and universal education and health care, thus amounting to the kind of sweeping economic and structural changes essential for the creation of a more just, inclusive, and peaceful society.

King was assassinated in Memphis, Tenn., on 4 April 1968, weeks before his planned Poor People's Campaign was launched. Economic justice and international peace remain as the core issues in his unfinished holy crusade. In the half century since his death, some conservative forces have increasingly sought to use him as a kind of sacred aura for their own political ends, particularly in their attacks on affirmative action, immigration, reparations, and government spending for social programs.

LEWIS V. BALDWIN
Vanderbilt University

Lewis V. Baldwin, *The Voice of Conscience: The Church in the Mind of Martin Luther King, Jr.* (2010); Clayborne Carson, ed., *The Autobiography of Martin Luther King, Jr.* (1998); Kenneth L. Smith, *Journal of Ecumenical Studies* (Spring 1989); William D. Watley, *Roots of Resistance: The Nonviolent Ethic of Martin Luther King, Jr.* (1985).

Ku Klux Klan, Civil Rights Era to the Present

The Ku Klux Klan (KKK) is the oldest documented white supremacist group in the United States. Historically, the KKK precipitated, engaged in, and supported numerous acts of intimidation and violence in the South. Bombings, murders, assaults, and other violent acts were sanctioned by the social norms of southern culture during a time in which KKK members were also employed in positions of power (for example, as sheriffs and judges). Their place in society contributed to the dispropor-

tionate enforcement, prosecution, and sentencing of whites who antagonized and victimized blacks and others in the South. Although the first two waves of KKK members benefited from a cohesive unit of organization, members of the third wave arose from dozens of independent groups that utilized the KKK moniker during the 1960s in resistance to the civil rights movement.

The rise of black freedom struggles in the 1950s provoked a massive resistance on the part of southern whites. The KKK reemerged as the most violent expression of this resistance. KKK members were implicated in a series of incidents, including the 1963 church bombing that killed four young girls, the 1963 assassination of NAACP organizer Medgar Evers, and the 1964 murder of three civil rights workers in Neshoba County, Miss. The nationwide media coverage of the aftermath of these violent incidents contributed to the KKK's increasingly unfavorable image outside the South.

During the 1970s and 1980s, racially motivated acts of violence perpetrated by KKK members did not cease entirely. For instance, in 1979, in what came to be known as the Greensboro Massacre, KKK members (in collaboration with Nazi Party members) murdered five protesters at an anti-Klan rally in Greensboro, N.C. In 1980, four older black women were shot after a KKK initiation rally in Chattanooga, Tenn. In 1981, Michael Donald became the last documented lynching in Alabama. Unlike earlier incidences in which cases were dismissed or offenders were ac-

quitted by all-white juries, the perpetrators of these acts were criminally
prosecuted for their crimes. In some
instances, KKK organizations faced
civil opposition, resulting in their financial collapse (for example, United
Klans of America and Imperial Klans
of America). The Southern Poverty Law
Center's founder, Morris Dees, led civil
cases against these groups, and the U.S.
government increased its oversight.
These factors made it increasingly unacceptable for the KKK to resort to violence as a means to further its political
agenda.

Today the Southern Poverty Law
Center estimates that thousands of KKK
members are split among at least 186
KKK chapters. These fragmented fac-
tions have been weakened by "internal
conflicts, court cases, and government
infiltration." However, they still disseminate hate against blacks, Jews,
Latinos, immigrants, homosexuals, and
Catholics. Instead of violence, some of
today's KKK organizations focus on collective political action by participating
in and restructuring the government.
Others focus on marketing strategies in
order to appeal to mainstream America,
with the intention of increasing recruitment and disseminating their ideology
to a wider audience. Although violent
acts, like the 2008 murder of a woman
in Louisiana after a failed KKK initiation, do still randomly occur, violence is
no longer considered a socially accepted
means to achieving white hegemony in
the South.

STACIA GILLIARD-MATTHEWS
West Virginia University

Josh Adams and Vincent Roscigno, *Social
Forces* (December 2005); Chip Berlet and
Stanislav Vysotsky, *Journal of Political and
Military Sociology* (Summer 2006); David
Chalmers, *Backfire: How the Ku Klux Klan
Helped the Civil Rights Movement* (2005),
*Hooded Americanism: The History of the
Ku Klux Klan* (1987); David Holthouse, *The
Year in Hate* (2009); Diane McWhorter,
*Carry Me Home: Birmingham, Alabama:
The Climactic Battle of the Civil Rights Revo-
lution* (2001); Pete Simi and Robert Futrell,
*American Swastika: Inside the White Power
Movement's Hidden Spaces of Hate* (2010).

Ku Klux Klan, Reconstruction-Era

The Ku Klux Klan was the name popularly given to hundreds of loosely connected vigilante groups that emerged
in the early Reconstruction era in locations throughout the South. These
groups used violence and threats, primarily against freedpeople, local white
Republicans, immigrants from the
North, and agents of the federal government, to gain political, social, cultural, and economic benefits in the wake
of the war. Although some prominent
figures attempted to organize the Klan
and use it as political tool, the Klan was
never effectively centralized. Klan
groups proliferated rapidly in 1868 and
saw a second peak in 1870–71. The Klan
movement was in decline by late 1871
and had almost disappeared by the end
of 1872.

The first group to call itself the Ku
Klux Klan began in Pulaski, Tenn.,
probably in summer 1866. The six
original members were young, small-
town professionals and Confederate veterans. This group was at first fundamen-

tally a social club. Members performed music and organized entertainments. Significantly, they also introduced a particularly elaborate version of the rituals and costumes common to fraternal associations.

As the Pulaski Klan spread, local elites became interested in its potential as a political organization in opposition to the government of Gov. William Gannaway Brownlow. In an April 1867 meeting in nearby Nashville, they produced a governing document called the Prescript. The Prescript described the Klan as a political organization opposed to black enfranchisement and in favor of southern autonomy and the strengthening of white political power. It also detailed a complex and rigidly hierarchical organization. At this time, Nathan Bedford Forrest was probably chosen as the Klan's first Grand Wizard. Other prominent men like Albert Pike, Matthew Galloway, and John B. Gordon joined around this time and used their influence to spread the organization.

The tightly organized, politically focused regional Klan envisioned by the Prescript never materialized. Each state faced substantially different political situations, making coordination difficult; Klan groups had few effective ways to organize or communicate; and the federal government soon became aware of the Klan and worked to suppress it. The Tennessee leaders disbanded the group in 1869. Klan activity persisted, and even increased, after this disbandment, but the disbandment spelled the end of the attempt to centralize the Klan.

The Klan, instead, became an amor-phous movement that included a range of clandestine groups in many parts of the South that exploited postwar political, social, and economic disorganization for various ends. Each group had its own composition, goals, and tactics. Some had political goals, such as intimidating Republican voters, politicians, and local government officials. Others hoped to prevent the establishment of schools for freedpeople. Some styled themselves after western lynch mobs and portrayed themselves as protecting the weak and punishing crime and immorality. Some were conventional criminal gangs using a Klan identity to escape detection or punishment for theft, illegal distilling, rape, or other violent and sadistic acts. Others apparently had economic goals, such as driving away freedpeople competing with them as laborers or tenants, terrifying workers into compliance, or forcing tenants to abandon their crops, animals, or improvements. Still others engaged in Klan violence to settle personal disputes involving land use, social status, feuds, or sexual competition.

Perpetrators of Klan violence varied from place to place. Some Klan groups consisted largely of privileged, though temporarily dispossessed, southern elites, who rode horses and wore extravagant costumes. Other, probably most, Klan groups consisted of poor whites. Many Klan groups, for instance, too poor to own horses, committed their attacks while riding mules or going on foot and either did not disguise themselves or simply covered their faces with cheap materials like painted burlap sacks or squirrel skins.

Klan tactics differed as much as did membership and apparent motives. Some Klan groups were largely performative, parading through the streets and leaving cryptic messages about town. Most, however, brought intimidation and/or violence against specific targets. Even when they were pursuing goals that were not primarily political, their victims were almost always Republicans and were usually freedpeople. By targeting these groups, Klansmen frequently gained broad support among local Democratic whites. The most common form that intimidation and violence took was the nighttime visit, in which a group of Klansmen would descend upon the home of their victim and either force their way in or demand that their victim come outside. Klan visits frequently involved property theft from victims, whether the Klansmen were "confiscating" firearms or simply stealing money, food, or household goods. Some Klansmen threatened their targets, requiring that they renounce a political party, leave town, or otherwise change their behavior. Other Klan groups whipped their victims. A number of Klan attacks were sexual in nature: Klansmen raped victims, whipped them while naked, forced them to perform humiliating sexual acts, or castrated them.

Klansmen sometimes killed their victims. Because of the weak and disorganized nature of local government at the time and because of the difficulty in defining which attacks should count as Klan attacks, it is impossible to get reliable numbers on how many people the Klan killed, but the number is at least several hundred. In most cases, Klansmen killed victims execution style, by either shooting or hanging them. Klansmen shot others while they were attempting to escape. Klan groups killed some victims, particularly those who were politically connected, through ambush. Additionally, Klan groups committed some larger collective murders, such as the abduction and killing of ten freedmen in Union County, S.C., in spring 1871.

Freedpeople and white Republicans often attempted, sometimes with success, to prevent or resist Klan threats and violence. Those anticipating attack fled to nearby cities for safety or "laid out," spending the night out of doors in their fields. Others gathered friends and family, or, in South Carolina, black militiamen, to stand guard for them. At the same time, Republican leaders and local agents of the federal government gathered information about Klan activity and plans and sent it urgently to state and federal officials, in the hope of gaining protection. Klan survivors and witnesses often agreed to testify to state or federal committees, even at grave personal risk. In the face of threatened violence at election time, Republicans tried various strategies, such as approaching the polls in groups. Faced with an attack, some who had managed to arm themselves met approaching Klansmen with gunfire. Unarmed victims sometimes used household implements as weapons. Others attempted to reason or plea with their captors; frequently, they recognized some of their attackers and directly called upon their protection.

The federal government, convinced that local and state efforts were ineffective, took several steps to suppress the Klan but could intervene only when Klan violence had a political nature. Congress passed a series of bills popularly referred to as the Enforcement Acts, intended to enforce the voting rights granted to freedmen under the Fifteenth Amendment. The first, passed on 31 May 1870, then strengthened and supplemented by another act passed on 28 February 1871, made it a federal crime for individuals to conspire or wear disguise to deprive citizens of their constitutional rights and set up federal mechanisms for the arrest, prosecution, and trials of accused offenders. The most controversial, popularly called the Ku Klux Force Act, which was passed on 20 April 1871, gave the president the authority to suspend the writ of habeas corpus and to send federal troops to areas incapable of controlling Klan violence, even without the invitation of a governor. It also made punishable by federal law several common forms of political Klan behavior and forbade Klansmen from serving on juries. President Ulysses S. Grant took limited advantage of this legislation, sending small numbers of troops to some of the hardest-hit areas. South Carolina became the focus of federal Klan enforcement: Grant suspended habeas corpus briefly in nine counties, federal marshals and troops made hundreds of arrests, and the federal district court began a high-profile series of trials of accused Klan leaders in fall 1871.

The Ku Klux Klan was significant in federal politics, particularly during the Johnson impeachment and in the federal elections of 1868 and 1872. The Klan first emerged to national notice during the impeachment trials, as Johnson's opponents attempted to associate him with the Klan. In the election of 1868, supporters of Ulysses S. Grant, the Republican candidate, labeled supporters of Democrat Horatio Seymour as the "Ku-Klux Democracy." Though the election of 1872 occurred after the Klan's decline, the Klan was even more central to it than to the election of 1868. Grant's supporters attempted to tie Horace Greeley, the Liberal Republican and Democratic candidate, to the Klan, claiming that a vote for Greeley was a vote for Klan resurgence. Greeley's supporters claimed that Grant was using the Klan as a "bugbear" and that Klan suppression was a pretext for unconstitutionally increasing the reach of federal power.

In the months after winning reelection, Grant stopped federal Klan arrests and trials and quietly released those dozens of men who had been committed to federal prison as Klansmen. Besides some interest surrounding the publication of Albion Tourgée's 1879 Klan-themed novel, *A Fool's Errand*, the Ku Klux Klan would not be significant in American social and political life, or even in cultural representation, until its 20th-century revival.

ELAINE FRANTZ PARSONS
Duquesne University

Steven Hahn, *A Nation under Our Feet: Black Political Struggles in the Rural South from Slavery to the Great Migration* (2003); Kwando Kinshasa, *Black Resistance to the Ku Klux Klan in the Wake of the Civil War*

(2006); Scott Reynolds Nelson, *Iron Confederacies: Southern Railways, Klan Violence, and Reconstruction* (1999); Mitchell Snay, *Fenians, Freedmen, and Southern Whites* (2007); Allen Trelease, *White Terror: The Ku Klux Klan Conspiracy and Southern Reconstruction* (1971); Xi Wang, *The Trial of Democracy: Black Suffrage and Northern Republicans, 1860–1910* (1997); Lou Faulkner Williams, *The Great South Carolina Ku Klux Klan Trials, 1871–1872* (1996).

Ku Klux Klan, Second (1915–1944)

The Ku Klux Klan was never more powerful than it was in the 1920s. At that time, it thrived as a nativist and racist organization, championing the rights and superiority of white Protestant Americans. Unlike the first Klan of the Reconstruction era, the second Klan was a nationwide movement. At its height, it boasted 5 million members in 4,000 local chapters across the country, although some historians contend that it never had more than 1.5 million active members at any one time. The Klan's main appeal was its promise to restore what it deemed traditional values in the face of the transformations of modern society, and it was most popular in communities where it acted in support of moral reform. Klansmen opposed the social and political advancement of blacks, Jews, and Catholics, but they also virulently attacked bootleggers, drinkers, gamblers, adulterers, fornicators, and others who they believed had flouted Protestant moral codes.

Although the Klan was strongest in the Midwest, in states like Indiana and Illinois, where it peddled its slogan of "100% Americanism" to great effect, it was still in many ways a distinctly southern organization. William Simmons, a former Methodist preacher from Alabama, reestablished the Klan in an elaborate ceremony atop Stone Mountain, just outside of Atlanta, Ga., on Thanksgiving Day in 1915. Even as the organization spread across the country, its leadership and base of operations remained in Atlanta. Moreover, Klansmen regularly engaged in rituals and rhetoric that drew upon southern traditions from the Reconstruction Klan and Lost Cause mythology to enact their nationalistic agenda.

Klans throughout the country held public rallies, staged parades, and engaged in various political activities, mostly attempting to influence political leaders to adopt Klan positions. Klansmen tended to be solid, churchgoing middle- and working-class men who were concerned about the loss of traditional white, patriarchal power in the face of urbanization, immigration, black migration, feminism, and the cracking of Victorian morality. As much as they expressed contempt toward those at the bottom of the social ladder, they railed against the excesses of Wall Street and Hollywood, leading one historian to characterize their politics as a kind of "reactionary populism."

In wanting to present itself as a mainstream movement that stood for law and order, the Klan, as an organization, prohibited and disavowed acts of violence. That did not stop individual Klansmen, in full Klan regalia, from committing numerous acts of terror and violence, especially in southern states. Klansmen whipped and tortured

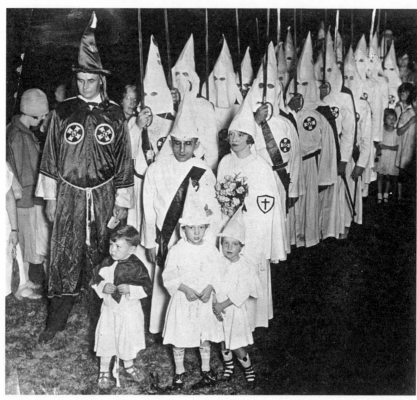

Ku Klux Klan members with children, ca. 1912–30 (Library of Congress [LC-DIG-npcc-27617], Washington, D.C.)

blacks who transgressed Jim Crow racial codes, but they also targeted whites who had violated moral codes. They engaged in threats, beatings, and tarring and featherings to humiliate their victims. During the 1920s, probably over 1,000 violent assaults took place in Texas and Oklahoma alone, and over 100 assaults each in Florida, Georgia, and Alabama. In 1921, the *New York World* published a three-week serial exposé on the Klan, highlighting its moneymaking scams, its radical propaganda, and its violence. The articles led to a congressional hearing on the organization, which ended abruptly with no conclusion.

Although the Klan supported tra-

ditional gender roles, white women received their own recognition in the formation of the Women's Ku Klux Klan in 1915. Implemented as a separate organization, the Women's Ku Klux Klan bound itself to the Klan's ideals but remained independent of the men's organization. As Klanswomen, members marched in parades, organized community events, and recruited new Klan members—primarily children. As it grew in numbers and visibility, the Klan expanded to include its youth. In 1923, the Klan voted to create two auxiliaries, the Junior Ku Klux Klan for adolescent boys and the Tri-K-Klub for teenage girls. The Junior Klan sought to promote the principles of the Ku Klux Klan in preparation for adult male membership. The Tri-K-Klub, under the umbrella of the Women's Ku Klux Klan, taught girls the ideals the Klan desired in wives and mothers, such as racial purity, cheerfulness, and determination.

In the late 1920s, the Klan's power began to wane and its membership declined. After the 1921 hearings, mainstream newspapers and the black press increased their reportage of Klan violence, and the NAACP began its own documentation of Klan terror. In addition, a number of prominent Klan leaders were caught in embarrassing scandals, exposing the hypocrisy of the organization. Finally, the Klan's insistence that its movement was democratic and patriotic began to appear contradictory. For some, the Klan in America began to resemble the rising fascism in Europe, a perception only furthered by the increasing radicalism of Klan leaders. By 1930, the national Klan movement had gradually retreated into the South, where the economic crises of the Great Depression further weakened the organization. In that year, it claimed barely 50,000 members. In 1944, the Internal Revenue Service presented the Second Ku Klux Klan with a bill for $685,000 in unpaid taxes. Unable to pay, the Imperial Wizard on 23 April 1944 revoked the charters and disbanded all Klaverns of the Klan.

KRIS DUROCHER
Morehead State University

AMY LOUISE WOOD
Illinois State University

Charles C. Alexander, *The Ku Klux Klan in the Southwest* (1965); Kathleen M. Blee, *Women of the Klan: Racism and Gender in the 1920s* (1991); David Chalmers, *Backfire: How the Ku Klux Klan Helped the Civil Rights Movement* (2003); Kenneth T. Jackson, *The Ku Klux Klan in the City, 1915–1930* (1967); Nancy K. MacLean, *Behind the Mask of Chivalry: The Making of the Second Ku Klux Klan* (1995); Wyn Craig Wade, *The Fiery Cross: The Ku Klux Klan in America* (1997).

Mardi Gras Indians

The Black Mardi Gras Indians are African Americans (some of whom claim American Indian ancestry) who perform a colorful, elaborate, and symbol-laden ritual drama on the streets of New Orleans. Their dynamic street performances feature characters that play specific roles, polyrhythmic percussion and creolized music texts, and artistic suit assemblages that reflect ritual influences from both Indian America and West Africa. With roots stretching back to the 18th century, this unique tradition has given rise to a rich array of customs and artistic forms and continues to testify to the historical affinity of the region's Indians and African Americans.

New Orleans hosts two Mardi Gras every year. One is the highly commercialized celebration planned for the aristocratic krews, with their carnival balls and float parades. The other is the walking and masking festival that includes Baby Dolls, Skeleton Men, and the Mardi Gras Indians. Each celebration features unique traditions that are deeply rooted in a distinctive culture and environment.

The Black Mardi Gras Indians draw upon American Indian, West African, and Caribbean motifs and theatrics to create a unique creolized folk ritual. In Louisiana, these three cultural groups came together during the French and Spanish colonial periods. Indians were African Americans' first allies in resisting European enslavement and general labor oppression; and they too were often enslaved. The shared experience of bondage led to many intermarriages between West Africans and Indians, yielding a legacy of mixed ancestry that is still evident among many Mardi Gras Indians hundreds of years later. Such ancestry, however, has never been a criteria for joining the Indian "tribes" or "gangs." Wearing and performing the Indian mask has instead long served as a means of escape and a way to resist and protest the white hegemony that has so long defined Jim Crow New Orleans.

No one knows exactly when the Mardi Gras Indian tradition started, but it was first documented in the late 1700s. Its early years were marked by fierce rivalries between African American "tribes" from New Orleans's Uptown and Downtown districts, with the masked marchers carrying weapons and attacking their "tribal" adversaries. In recent decades, the resolution of these territorial rivalries has shifted from a physical to an aesthetic plane.

In today's New Orleans, neighborhood tribes—dressed in elaborately beaded and feather-laden costumes—display their dazzling artistry every year on Mardi Gras Day, St. Joseph's Day (March 19), and Super Sunday (the third Sunday in March). The colorfully costumed Indians parade from house to house and bar to bar, singing call-and-response songs and boasting chants to the exuberant accompaniment of drums, tambourines, and ad hoc instruments. Alongside of and behind the procession, "second liners"—relatives, friends, and neighborhood supporters—strut, dance, and sing along. When the group meets an opposing tribe, the street is filled with dancing and general "showing off," as the costumed participants proudly display their masques, hand signals, and tribal gestures, exhibiting a shared pride in "suiting up as Indian." This street theater—with its percussive rhythms, creolized song texts, boasting chants, and colorful feather and bead explosions—reflects Indianness through an African-based lens of celebration and ritual.

The most obviously "Indian" element of these performances is the full-body masque worn by tribe members, replete with a feather crown and detailed beadwork that typically depicts Native American themes. Though clearly a tribute to Native American culture, these elaborate costumes also show an overt connection to West African assemblage styles and beading techniques. Most of the patchwork scenes depicting Native Americans are flat and show warriors in battle or other stereotypically "Indian" scenes. Among Downtown tribes, however, the beaded images are more varied and often break into sculptural relief. Rather than conveying Native American themes, they offer Japanese pagodas, aquatic scenes, Egyp-

The Wild Tchoupitoulas in Les Blank's film Always for Pleasure, 1978
(Michael P. Smith, photographer, Brazos Films/Arhoolie Records, Los Cerrito, Calif.)

tian regalia, and whatever other images their creators can imagine and then craft. Constructed anew each year, each suit testifies to countless painstaking hours on the part of the Indian who wears it in Mardi Gras.

The Mardi Gras Indians' lavish outfits and spirited performances also reveal a distinct social hierarchy within each tribe, with different positions—chief, spy boy, flag boy, and wild man, in descending order of status—presenting themselves differently and filling particular roles in the unfolding performance. Many tribes now also crown their own queens, reprising and reinvigorating a role that was less prominent in the early, more violent years.

The unique tradition of the Mardi Gras Indians has given rise to an array of distinctive artistic forms and shared customs. At the same time, this tradi-

tion displays strong ancestral ties to West Africa and testifies to the historical affinity of Indians and Africans, two groups that played leading roles in the creolization of New Orleans. In essence, the Mardi Gras Indians' ritual performances speak to the need to celebrate life and death in all of their splendor and to address power and enact resistance through masking and dramatic street theater.

JOYCE MARIE JACKSON
Louisiana State University

Joyce Marie Jackson and Fehintola Mosa-domi, in *Orisha: Yoruba Gods and Spiritual Identity*, ed. Toyin Falola (2005); Maurice M. Martinez and James E. Hinton, *The Black Indians of New Orleans* (film, 1976); Michael P. Smith, *Mardi Gras Indians* (1994).

Martin Luther King Jr. Day

Celebrated on the third Monday in January, the Martin Luther King Jr. federal holiday honors the civil rights leader and has special meaning in the South where he was born and where his triumphs and the tragedy of his assassination took place. Michigan congressman John Conyers introduced the legislation to support the holiday shortly after King's death, but Congress did not pass it until over a decade later, after a national promotional campaign led by Atlanta's King Center, which overcame opposition led by North Carolina senators John East and Jesse Helms. President Ronald Reagan signed the King Holiday law in 1983. President Bill Clinton signed the King Holiday and Service Act in 1994, which honored King's legacy by encouraging public service work on his holiday. Some southern states did not officially recognize the holiday as a paid one for state employees at first, and some combined it with commemoration of Confederate heroes, especially Robert E. Lee, whose 19 January birthday was near King's actual birthday of 15 January. Some southern whites still use the holiday ironically to honor Civil War heroes, but in 2000 South Carolina became the last southern state to officially recognize the King Holiday as a paid state holiday for employees, giving it official legitimacy.

The King Holiday has had spiritual, political, and commercial significance. Martin Dennison notes that "this holiday reverentially recalls 'St. Martin Luther King.'" King led a social movement, with profound political impact in the South, but he was a religious figure as well. While leading the Montgomery Bus Boycott in the mid-1950s, he became known as Alabama's Modern Moses, and his assassination in April 1968, shortly after Palm Sunday, evoked the religious language of martyrdom. King Holiday commemorations often occur in black churches, with homilies, prayers, and religious music making the day one on the South's sacred calendar.

The holiday has also had political meanings. On 17 January 1998, in the 30th year after King's death, 50 Indiana Klansmen staged a rally in Memphis, the site of King's assassination. A crowd of 12,000 black and white civil rights supporters gathered in response, with a few young gang members resorting to violence, tarnishing King's nonviolent legacy. More important, peaceful rallies occurred throughout the city, affirming King's contributions. In January 2000, the King Holiday became the focus for advocates of the Confederate battle flag atop the South Carolina state capitol, but counter demonstrators rallied to remove the flag, which state legislators authorized later that year.

The King Holiday is widely honored now, partly as a day of rest and commercialization. King Holiday sales market much American produce far removed from civil rights, but this represents a normalization of the day in typical American fashion and its wide acceptance. Critics suggest its commercialization trivializes the holiday's meaning. The day continues, though, to include projects celebrating social justice, racial reconciliation, tolerance, nonviolence, and the special place of African Americans in the nation's democratic heritage. Southern churches, community centers, arts centers, public schools, town halls, and other public facilities host these activities, recognizing the centrality of African Americans to the region's historical memory. On 19 January 2009, the King Holiday included more than 13,000 service projects.

CHARLES REAGAN WILSON
University of Mississippi

Martin Dennison, *Red, White, and Blue Letter Days: An American Calendar* (2002).

Mason-Dixon Line

"An artificial line . . . and yet more unalterable than if nature had made it for it limits the sovereignty of four states, each of whom is tenacious of its particular systems of law as of its soil. It is the boundary of empire."

Writing his history of the Mason-Dixon Line in 1857, James Veech reflected the well-founded anxieties of the day—the fear that the horizontal fault between slave and free territory was about to become an open breach. Although the Mason-Dixon Line was long associated with the division between free and slave states, slavery existed on both its sides when it was first drawn. To settle a long-standing boundary dispute arising from ambiguous colonial charters, the Calvert and Penn families chose English astronomers Charles Mason and Jeremiah Dixon to survey the territory. After four years of work (1763–67), they fixed the common boundary of Maryland and Pennsylvania at 39°43′17.6″ north latitude, marking their line at every fifth

mile with stones bearing the arms of the Penn family on one side and the Calvert crest on the other. Halted in their westward survey by the presence of hostile Indians, their work was concluded in 1784 by a new team, which included David Rittenhouse, Andrew Ellicott, and Benjamin Banneker.

In 1820, the Missouri Compromise temporarily readjusted the fragile tacit balance between slave and free territory and extended the Mason-Dixon Line to include the 36th parallel. By that date, all states north of the line had abolished slavery, and the acceptance of the line as the symbolic division both politically and socially between North and South was firmly established.

The Mason-Dixon Line has been a source of many idiomatic expressions and popular images. Slogans ("Hang your wash to dry on the Mason-Dixon Line") originated with early antislavery agitation; variations on the theme (Smith and Wesson line) and novel applications (the logo for a cross-country trucking firm) are contemporary phenomena. A popular shorthand for a sometimes mythic, sometimes very real regional distinction, the term "Mason-Dixon Line" continues to be used, and its meaning is immediately comprehended.

ELIZABETH M. MAKOWSKI
University of Mississippi

Journals of Charles Mason and Jeremiah Dixon (1969); John H. B. Latrobe, *History of Mason and Dixon's Line* (1855); James Veech, ed., *Mason and Dixon's Line: A History* (1857).

Memphis Sanitation Workers' Strike

The subject of two award-winning documentary films—*At the River I Stand* and *I Am a Man: From Memphis, a Lesson in Life*—at least one play, and several books, the 1968 Memphis Sanitation Workers' Strike has become emblematic of the universal struggle for dignity and respect by downtrodden people. Its iconic slogan—"I AM a Man!"—has been appropriated by labor struggles in the United States and internationally. And its memory is renewed every year on 4 April—the eve of a planned march in support of the sanitation workers and the date of Dr. Martin Luther King Jr.'s assassination.

In February 1968, nearly 1,300 sanitation workers walked off their jobs in a strike for collective bargaining rights that would ultimately represent a pivotal moment in which the labor movement, the antipoverty movement, and the black freedom movement coalesced. The quest for union recognition could hardly have been more dramatic. African American workers with wages so low that their families qualified for food stamps, with neither sick pay nor disability insurance, whose families lived in the very poorest neighborhoods in the city, confronted a segregationist mayor and city administration determined to deny them union recognition. The garbage men had been attempting to win union recognition since 1960, but their dramatic walkout on 12 February was precipitated by the deaths of two coworkers who were crushed inside a garbage truck while waiting out a rainstorm (an electrical malfunction tripped the mashing mechanism). The striking sanitation workers, who had joined Local 1733 of the American Federation of State, County, and Municipal Employees, risked instant dismissal; federal law did not accord municipal employees the protections it extended to private-sector workers.

What began as a strike transformed into a mass community movement two weeks later after city police officers sprayed the workers and their supporters, including African American ministers, with mace. Even the most well-heeled among them determined that the struggle for dignity and respect was not only for the poorest and most maligned but for all African Americans. Although the gendered slogan may seem relevant only to men, women—especially the factory workers and welfare rights activists who became the backbone of the support movement—saw in it a struggle against not only the racist indignities suffered by the men but also those confronted by black women.

When King arrived on 18 March to address a mass meeting, he was stunned at the turnout of 15,000. "Now, you are doing something else here!" he declared. "You are highlighting the economic issue. You are going beyond purely civil rights to the question of human rights." For King, the struggle for human rights was about power: "Let it be known everywhere that along with wages and all of the other securities that you are struggling for, you're also struggling for the right to organize and be recognized. This is the way to gain power—power is the ability to achieve purpose. Power is the ability to effect change."

That struggle for power, born out of a quest for justice among black workers earning starvation wages and facing racist indignities on a daily basis, continues to have meaning today.

LAURIE B. GREEN
University of Texas at Austin

Laurie B. Green, *Battling the Plantation Mentality: Memphis and the Black Freedom Struggle* (2007); Martin Luther King Jr., in *All Labor Has Dignity*, ed. Michael K. Honey (2011).

Migrant Workers

Migrant workers for agriculture, forestry, and fisheries emerged as distinct social classes during the period following the Civil War, when migrant crews seasonally supplemented the work of sharecroppers, tenant farmers, and debt peons. During the first decades of the 20th century, the demand for migrant workers grew with the increase in fruit and vegetable production along the Eastern Seaboard to supply urban markets, resulting in the development of southern- and Caribbean-based crews of African Americans, Mexican Americans, and Puerto Ricans. African Americans and Puerto Ricans, based primarily in Florida and Puerto Rico, supplied labor to farms, forests, and seafood plants as far north as Maine, while Mexican Americans, based in south Texas, supplied labor across the Midwest and Great Plains. World War II drew many of these migrant workers out of agriculture, forestry, and fisheries and into the defense industry, stimulating the U.S. federal government to develop a class of migrant workers that could supply wartime food needs. By constructing labor camps

and creating guest-worker programs to access foreign labor, federal officials assisted with recruiting and transporting migrant labor. Following the war, the U.S. government relinquished control of the migrant labor supply to grower associations and labor contractors.

Southern migrant labor began shifting from primarily domestic to primarily international supply regions during the 1960s and 1970s, creating an underclass of largely undocumented migrant workers from Mexico and Central America, which continues today. Within the migrant labor force, upward mobility is limited to workers who can become labor contractors or supervisors, and the majority remain confined to class positions that provide relatively low annual incomes—30 percent of all farmworkers have family incomes below federally established poverty levels. When undocumented, paid by the piece rather than hourly, and working for labor contractors rather than directly for companies, migrant labor's relationship to capital has been stripped of worker protections in the form of guaranteed minimum wages, unemployment insurance, and health and safety standards. These conditions lead to high annual labor turnover rates, with 16 percent of all those surveyed in the National Agricultural Worker Survey reporting that they plan to work in agriculture for fewer than two or three years. High labor turnover has also led many southern employers of seasonal workers to embrace guest-worker programs. From 1943 to 1992, Florida sugar producers brought over 8,000 workers from the Caribbean an-

Mexican carrot worker, Edinburg (vicinity), Tex., 1939 (Russell Lee, photographer,
USDA Historic Photos Collection [LC-USF33-011974-M3 (P&P)], Washington, D.C.)

nually, and today mid-Atlantic tobacco growers, forestry companies, and seafood processors utilize several thousand guest workers from Mexico under temporary contracts.

In response to conditions of economic hardship facing migrant workers, several federal programs and networks of advocacy organizations have developed to provide migrant workers with legal services, food and medical assistance, education, job training, and other services. For many years, these organizations acted on behalf of migrant workers in lieu of collective bargaining. In North Carolina, the Farm Labor Organizing Committee, after a prolonged boycott of Mt. Olive Pickles, signed a union agreement with the North Carolina Growers' Association, while the Coalition of Immokalee Workers forced a piece-rate increase in Florida's tomato fields by organizing farmworkers and boycotting Taco Bell and other large buyers of Florida tomatoes. Similar collective bargaining successes have not been achieved by migrant forestry or seafood workers, most of whom are temporary foreign guest workers carrying H-2B visas.

Migrant workers have occupied the lowest strata of the southern working class since the end of the Civil War. Every year, as migrant-crew buses arrive throughout the South and as workers crowd into low-quality labor camps and other temporary housing, local newspapers print exposés about conditions in the fields, factories, forests, and labor camps and life on the road. Popular and scholarly books and documentaries, focusing on the plights of migrant workers, often lead to congressional investigations. Presidential commissions on migrant labor have been established to hold public hearings, fund research, and present information about the lives of migrant workers. None of these efforts, unfortunately, have improved the lot of the migrant.

DAVID GRIFFITH
East Carolina University

Pete Daniel, *In the Shadow of Slavery: Debt Peonage in the U.S. South* (1972); David Griffith, *American Guestworkers: Jamaicans and Mexicans in the U.S. Labor Market* (2006); David Griffith, Ed Kissam, et al., *Working Poor: Farmworkers in the United States* (1995); Cindy Hahamovitch, *The Fruits of Their Labor: Atlantic Coast Farmworkers and the Making of Migrant Poverty, 1870–1945* (1997); U.S. Department of Labor, National Agricultural Worker Survey, Research Report 9 (2005).

Muscle Shoals

The quad cities of Florence, Tuscumbia, Sheffield, and Muscle Shoals, Ala., known collectively as Muscle Shoals, are located in the state's northwest corner nearly halfway between Nashville and Memphis. Muscle Shoals assimilated the sounds of country music, blues, and rhythm and blues, becoming influential in the creation and popularity of soul music. "The Shoals" developed as an important center of popular music, becoming the self-titled Hit Recording Capitol of the World during the 1970s and requesting musical amalgamation across rigid lines in the decades after the end of Jim Crow segregation.

All four cities sit along the Tennessee River. Before the arrival of white settlers in the 1700s, Euchee, Cherokee, Chickasaw, and Shawnee Indian tribes inhabited the area. Some cite the legend of "The Singing River"—the river sounding like a female chorus—as the source of the region's modern musical prosperity.

Florence was the birthplace and childhood home of W. C. Handy and Sam Phillips. The sounds of secular and sacred music by the area's black population influenced their careers. The modern music industry of the Shoals began in 1951 when local musician Dexter Johnson opened the first recording studio. Florence businessmen and musicians James Joiner and Kelso Herston produced the area's first commercial recording: Bobby Denton's 1956 regional hit "A Fallen Star." In 1958, partners Rick Hall, Billy Sherrill, and Tom Stafford formed Florence Alabama Musical Enterprises (FAME). Spar Records, their recording studio, attracted Alabama musicians, including Donnie Fritts, Spooner Oldham, David Briggs, Norbert Putnam, Terry Thompson, Earl "Peanut" Montgomery, Jerry Carrigan, and Dan Penn. The partnership dissolved, and Hall retained the rights to FAME, opening his own studio. Hall, working with local white musicians, recorded the R&B track "You Better Move On" in 1961, by Sheffield native Arthur Alexander, a black teenager who befriended the aspiring musicians. Dan Penn recalled, "We didn't really consider Arthur as black."

The crossroads where black culture and white culture meet is often a musical one. Alexander remembered, "We were trying to bridge the gap. We wanted it all, the country, the R&B, the pop. We only had this one thing in common: we all liked all types of music." Alexander's success provided FAME with industry recognition, allowing Hall the impetus to record Tommy Roe, the Tams, Jimmy Hughes, and Joe Tex. Quin Ivy, a DJ at WLAY in Muscle Shoals, opened Norala studios in Sheffield. Ivy recorded "When a Man Loves a Woman" by Sheffield native Percy Sledge, which reached number one on the R&B and pop charts in 1966.

Atlantic Records producer Jerry Wexler brought Wilson Pickett to FAME in 1966. Upon arriving in Muscle Shoals, Pickett recalled, "I couldn't believe it. I looked out the plane window, and there's these [black] people picking cotton." Pickett's first sessions, utilizing FAME's house band, produced "Mustang Sally" and "Land of 1000 Dances." Aretha Franklin recorded "I Never Loved a Man (The Way I Loved You)" at FAME in 1967. This recording, also using white studio musicians, launched Franklin's reign as the Queen of Soul. Franklin's subsequent soul hits utilized Muscle Shoals musical talent, although the recordings took place in New York.

FAME rhythm section—Jimmy Johnson, Roger Hawkins, David Hood, and Barry Beckett—backed King Curtis, Arthur Conley, Etta James, Clarence Carter, and others. This rhythm section left Hall in 1969, christened themselves the Muscle Shoals Rhythm Section (MSRS), later dubbed "the Swampers," and opened Muscle Shoals Sound (MSS) in Sheffield. Many R&B artists recorded at MSS. According to Hood, the Staples Singers, who recorded "I'll Take You

There" and "Respect Yourself" at MSS, could not believe that the MSRS musicians were white. In the early 1970s, "The Muscle Shoals Sound," heard on recordings by black artists, attracted interest from white pop/rock artists such as Paul Simon, Traffic, and Rod Stewart, because these artists thought that the MSRS musicians were black.

During the 1970s, FAME produced recordings for diverse artists, including Candi Staton, the Osmonds, Mac Davis, and Paul Anka. Many country acts, including Shenandoah, scored hits recording at FAME in the 1980s.

The annual W. C. Handy Music Festival began in 1982 and highlighted the region's diverse music culture. In 1985, Malaco Records bought MSS, producing R&B, gospel, and blues hits from the studio.

Even as violence between whites and blacks often broke out in areas of Alabama during the civil rights struggle, the Shoals remained peaceful. The music produced in the Shoals by black and white musicians remains one of the greatest cultural testaments to racial equality.

CHRISTOPHER M. REALI
University of North Carolina at Chapel Hill

Matt Dobkin, *I Never Loved a Man the Way I Loved You* (2004); Christopher S. Fuqua, *Music Fell on Alabama: The Muscle Shoals Sound That Shook the World* (2006); Peter Guralnick, *Sweet Soul Music: Rhythm and Blues and the Southern Dream of Freedom* (1986; rev. ed., 1999); Vron Ware and Les Back, *Out of Whiteness* (2002); Richard Younger, *Get a Shot of Rhythm and Blues: The Arthur Alexander Story* (2000).

Police Brutality in the Urban South

Although some of the most painful images of the civil rights movement involve police dogs attacking black teenagers in Birmingham and sheriff deputies assaulting black marchers in Selma, police brutality is not commonly associated with black life in the South. However, in the postwar migration of African Americans out of the rural South into the region's urban centers, they came into contact with the most visible arm of the state: the police. African Americans throughout the South confronted repressive police departments that were threatened by black demands for equality after World War II.

In the urban South, police departments adhered to a strict policy of segregation and its ideological pattern of white supremacy that controlled black Americans in their relations with whites. While white supremacist organizations such as the Ku Klux Klan and the White Citizens' Council used racial violence to maintain white control in rural areas, the local police department, with the support of politicians, segregationists, district attorneys, and judges, carried out this form of domestic terrorism. Consequently, the term "police brutality" was all-encompassing to African Americans. It included police homicides; unlawful arrests; assaults; threatening and abusive language; the use of racial slurs; sexual exploitation of black women; the beating of prisoners in police custody; racial profiling; police complicity in drug dealing, prostitution, burglaries, protection schemes, and gun smuggling; and the lack of justice available to black defendants in the courts.

A cursory examination of black newspapers reveals, almost on a weekly basis, graphic descriptions of police brutality and misconduct. Likewise, the archives of local and national civil rights organizations are filled with thousands of affidavits and letters relaying first-person experiences of police brutality. But African Americans in the urban South did not quietly tolerate wanton police misconduct. They utilized a variety of tactics in their response: sit-ins, boycotts, picketing, close supervision of police activity, armed confrontations, and, at times, killing and assaulting police officers. Further, they demanded major police reforms, including more black officers, more black officers in management positions, integrated patrols, a civilian review board, only-black-police-in-black-neighborhoods policies, and federal intervention.

Ironically, police brutality actually served as a tool to unify the community, since it was an issue that transcended class divisions, and in many cities an incident of police brutality was the catalyst for larger civil rights protest.

LEONARD N. MOORE
University of Texas at Austin

Glenn Eskew, *But for Birmingham: The Local and National Movements in the Civil Rights Struggle* (1997); Laurie Green, *Battling the Plantation Mentality: Memphis and the Black Freedom Struggle* (2007); Leonard Moore, *Black Rage in New Orleans: Police Brutality and African American Activism from World War II to Hurricane Katrina* (2010).

Rodgers, Jimmie

(1897–1933) COUNTRY MUSIC SINGER. Generally acknowledged as the "father of country music," James Charles "Jimmie" Rodgers, who was born on 8 September 1897 in Meridian, Miss., was a major influence on the emerging "hillbilly" recording industry almost from the time of his first records in 1927. Although Rodgers initially conceived of himself in broader terms, singing Tin Pan Alley hits and popular standards, his intrinsic musical talent was deeply rooted in the rural southern environment out of which he came, as seen in the titles of many of his songs: "My Carolina Sunshine Girl," "My Little Old Home Down in New Orleans," "Dear Old Sunny South by the Sea," "Mississippi River Blues," "Peach Pickin' Time Down in Georgia," "Memphis Yodel," "In the Hills of Tennessee," the original "Blue Yodel" ("T for Texas"), and others.

In adapting the black country blues of his native South to the nascent patterns of commercial hillbilly music of the day, Rodgers created a unique new form—the famous "blue yodel"—which led the way to further innovations in style and subject matter and exerted a lasting influence on country music as both art form and industry. Through the force of his magnetic personality and showmanship, Rodgers almost single-handedly established the role of the singing star, influencing such later performers as Gene Autry, Hank Williams, Ernest Tubb, George Jones, and Willie Nelson.

The son of a track foreman for the Mobile & Ohio Railroad, Rodgers in his twenties worked as a brakeman for many railroads in the South and West. Stricken by tuberculosis in 1924, he left the rails soon after to pursue his childhood dream of becoming a professional entertainer. After several years of hard knocks and failure, he gained an audition with Ralph Peer, an independent producer who had set up a temporary recording studio in Bristol, Tenn., for the Victor Talking Machine Company (later RCA Victor). There, on 4 August 1927, Rodgers made his first recordings. Within a year, he reached national popularity and received billing as "The Singing Brakeman" and "America's Blue Yodeler." In 1929, he built a home in the resort town of Kerrville, Tex., and moved there in an effort to restore his failing health. The onset of the Depression and increasing illness further slowed the progress of his career, but throughout the early 1930s he continued to record and perform with touring stage shows. By the time of his death in New York City at age 35 in May 1933, he had recorded 110 titles, representing a diverse repertoire that included almost every type of song now identified with country music: love ballads, honky-tonk tunes, railroad and hobo songs, cowboy songs, novelty numbers, and the series of 13 blue yodels. In November 1961, Rodgers became the first performer elected to Nashville's Country Music Hall of Fame, immortalized as "the man who started it all." The Jimmie Rodgers Memorial Museum in Meridian, Miss., hosts the annual Jimmie Rodgers Memorial Festival, which began in May 1953.

NOLAN PORTERFIELD
Cape Girardeau, Missouri

Bill C. Malone, *Country Music, U.S.A.: A Fifty-Year History* (1968); Nolan Porterfield, *Jimmie Rodgers: The Life and Times of America's Blue Yodeler* (1979); Mrs. Jimmie Rodgers, *My Husband, Jimmie Rodgers* (1975).

Segregation and Train Travel

Nothing made more clear the lie of segregation in the late 19th-century South than train travel. Now that southern people were moving—taking the train from small towns to other towns and cities, walking even from a farm to a crossing, flagging down the engine, and ending up far away—strangers became more common even in the smallest places. Trains took traveling pockets of anonymous urban social relations wherever the tracks went. Traveling forced passengers to deal with a world in which other people were not known, in which their identity could only be determined from their outward appearance, and in which lines of division and order, other than who could afford first class and who had to ride coach, became hopelessly confused.

From the 1880s to the 1950s, in magazine articles, essays, court cases, and novels, southerners referred again and again to this figure, the middle-class black, made visible through clothing, educated speech, and often a lightness of skin color, and made increasingly visible too beyond their numbers by this new ability to travel. In fact, the 1896 Supreme Court decision that upheld the constitutionality of segregation and made "separate-but-equal" the law of the land, *Plessy v. Ferguson*, turned on a man who perfectly embodied this confusion, Homer Adolph Plessy. Light-skinned and racially mixed, Plessy made a planned challenge to Louisiana's 1890 law requiring segregated streetcars. His lawyer, Albion Tourgée, a northern white Reconstruction official and popular novelist, argued that the government did not have the right to determine the racial identities of its citizens.

Who but Plessy himself should say where the almost-white Plessy belonged? The Court, of course, disagreed, reasoning that racial differences lay before and outside the law, in human nature itself. Plessy would have to be placed on one side or the other, would have to be either black or white. The *Plessy* decision fully denied what African American writer Albert Murray later called the "incontestable mulatto" nature of American culture and set this lie at the very center of modern society. The Court simply added its voice to the increasingly racialist and white supremacist thinking that permeated late 19th-century American society, an attempt in part to ground Plessy-like people's mutable identities in a concreteness of blood, bodies, science, and the law.

The middle-class, racially ambiguous person on the train made visible white southerners' fear of making a mistake in identifying strangers. In 1889, a Tennessee newspaper turned this anxiety into humor. When "a bright and good-looking colored girl (or rather an almost white colored girl)" got on board a train in Nashville, a "flashily dressed white gentleman," usually known as the "car masher," began a flirtation. Wooing his "lady friend" with lunch and witty con-

versation, he did not realize his mistake until after she got off the train, and the other ladies still aboard laughed at him. The joke (and the incident would not have been at all funny to whites if the genders had been reversed) served as a warning about the dangers inherent in the first-class train car's world of anonymous yet intimate social relations. For whites, the middle-class African American, now able and willing to travel—not the ragged riders in second-class cars—made segregation a necessity.

For African Americans, however, people who identified themselves or were identified by others as black, nothing demonstrated the lie of segregation's premise of absolute racial difference, of white supremacy and black inferiority, like the figure on the train. Activists and writers Mary Church Terrell and Anna Julia Cooper describe their own encounters with travel in the South, what Cooper called America's "out-of-the-way jungles of barbarism," where young black girls and dignified colored ladies were routinely ejected from first-class cars by tobacco-stained, stinking white men in the years before *Plessy*. In 1885, white southern writer George Washington Cable took the figure to *Century Magazine*, describing a middle-class mother and child trapped in a car with chained convicts in his passionate plea for African American civil rights. In his 1901 novel *The Marrow of Tradition*, Charles Chesnutt brought his readers along on a train ride from New York to North Carolina, exploring the experience of being "branded and tagged and set apart from the rest of mankind upon the public highways like an unclean thing."

Writer, intellectual, and activist W. E. B. Du Bois referred often to the figure on the train and to his own travels: "I am in the hot, crowded, and dirty Jim Crow car where I belong. . . . I am not comfortable." But he also went further, shaping the figure into an image that defined racial identity even as it pointed to the very impossibility of any "natural" racial categories. Asked how blacks could be both superior and the salvation of humanity if race was unreal, segregation a lie, he answered: "I recognize it [racial identity] easily and with full legal sanction: the black man is a person who must ride 'Jim Crow' in Georgia." For African Americans and a few dissident whites, the middle-class person on the train made it clear that segregation created the very racial categories it was supposedly enacted to uphold.

GRACE ELIZABETH HALE
University of Virginia

Edward L. Ayers, *The Promise of the New South: Life after Reconstruction* (1992); Grace Elizabeth Hale, *Making Whiteness: The Culture of Segregation in the South, 1890–1940* (1998); David Levering Lewis, ed., *W. E. B. Du Bois: A Reader* (1995); Eric Sundquist, *To Wake the Nations: Race in the Making of American Literature* (1993).

Soul Music

The cultural division between R&B and pop music manifested itself most directly in the association of soul music with the Black Power Movement in the late 1960s. While the term "soul" always invoked connotations of black power

and cultural pride, musical developments in the later 1960s helped to bond the Black Power Movement and black popular music more closely. The 1967 release of "Respect" by Aretha Franklin (originally written and recorded by Otis Redding) and "Say It Loud (I'm Black and I'm Proud)" by James Brown in 1968 signaled to the American public a heightened sense of political and social awareness in black popular music and among some of its most popular purveyors. The term "soul," then, came to represent a musical style, and, further, for many black Americans soul embodied an African mystique that became increasingly widespread as the 1960s progressed.

The modern elements of soul music coalesced in the mid-1950s, yet the fundamentals of this black American popular music style are traceable to the antebellum American South and West African traditions. The term "soul" often refers to a style and subgenre of secular music commonly associated with black Americans, particularly from the South. Musicians and audiences had used the word in connection with gospel music since the late 1920s. The term gained wider recognition for its musical associations when a famous black gospel quartet, the Soul Stirrers, used it in their name. The crossover appeal of the group's lead singer, Sam Cooke, revealed a musical and aesthetic connection between the group and the genesis of the soul music style of the 1960s.

A shift away from integrationist rhetoric and the growing popularity of the Nation of Islam and Malcolm X helped give rise to the Black Arts Movement and its efforts to create an Afro-centric aesthetic. Starting with inner-city uprisings in 1964, "soul" became a household word in black communities. Black businessmen used the phrase "soul brother" posted in store windows to prevent destruction and looting. In the mid-1960s, black DJs identified their stations as "soul radio." As Portia Maultsby noted, "Soul became associated with all forms of black cultural production."

The mass media and music trade publications embraced the term around 1967. *Time* magazine and the *Saturday Evening Post* featured stories about soul music, which brought the term to a broader audience while revealing its cultural association with black America. *Time* featured Franklin on the cover in June 1968. The article quoted LeRoi Jones as saying, "Soul music is music coming out of the black spirit." The 1969 *Post* article stated, "Across the country, 'soul' has become synonymous with 'black'—as in 'soul brother.'"

In June 1967, *Billboard* magazine issued its first annual feature titled "The World of Soul," documenting "the impact of blues and R&B upon our musical culture." On 23 August 1969, *Billboard* replaced the term "rhythm and blues" with "soul" to chart sales of music recorded by black artists. Writing in 1983, Maultsby commented that *Billboard*'s decision was "motivated by the fact that the term *soul* more properly embraces the broad range of song and instrumental material which derives from the musical genius of the black American." *Billboard* used the term until 1982, when "black music" replaced it.

Authors contemporaneous with soul music's national ascent reinforced the association between soul music and black America. In 1969, Phyl Garland wrote, "Soul music in all of its forms is the aesthetic property of a race of people who were brought to this country against their will." Arnold Shaw, writing in 1971, stated, "Soul is black, not blue, sass, anger, and rage. Soul is black nationalism in pop."

Seemingly contradictory to the idea that soul music expressed the views of black nationalism is the fact that soul's three main production centers—Stax (Memphis), FAME (Muscle Shoals, Ala.), and Motown (Detroit)—utilized racially integrated groups of musicians in the creation of the music. Unaware of the accompanying musicians' racial diversity, the listening public and those in the media directly associated the soul singer, who was black, with the song and its lyrics. White vocalists employing techniques similar to those used by black soul artists in the 1960s were categorized as "Blue-eyed Soul." These artists included the Righteous Brothers, Bobbie Gentry, Tom Jones, Dusty Springfield, and others.

Soul Train, a weekly television program, began broadcasting nationwide in October 1971, giving many black soul artists broad exposure. During the 1970s, several major concert events, both nationally and internationally, furthered the globalization of soul music. In March 1971, many black American musicians performed at the Soul to Soul concert in Accra, Ghana, which directly linked African American and African culture. Stax Records produced Wattstax in 1972 as a "community-based" event commemorating the anniversary of the Watts riots. James Brown, B. B. King, Bill Withers, and others performed at the Zaire '74 festival. Film crews documented the concerts, and the resulting movies were released publicly.

From the early 1960s through the early 1970s, independent labels such as Atlantic, Stax, Motown, King, and others led the soul music market. With the broadening appeal of soul music in the mid-1970s, major labels signed black artists as an attempt to cross over to a white market. According to Nelson George, "In the [crossover] process, much of what made the R&B world work was lost, perhaps some of it forever." By the end of the 1970s, soul artists from the 1960s had disappeared from the charts, and disco replaced the soul aesthetic.

CHRISTOPHER M. REALI
University of North Carolina at Chapel Hill

Stanley Booth, *Saturday Evening Post*, 8 February 1969; Mellonee V. Burnim and Portia Maultsby, *African American Music* (2006); Samuel A. Floyd, *The Power of Black Music: Interpreting Its History from Africa to the United States* (1995); Phyl Garland, *The Sound of Soul* (1969); Nelson George, *The Death of Rhythm and Blues* (1991); Portia K. Maultsby, *Journal of Popular Culture* (Fall 1983); Arnold Shaw, *The World of Soul* (1971).

Southern Regional Council

Founded in 1944, the Southern Regional Council (SRC) sought to ameliorate racial injustice in the American South through expanded dialogue and cooperation between the races. Unlike the NAACP, the SRC did not pursue litigation aimed at dismantling segregation, nor did it organize grassroots protest in favor of civil rights. Rather, it focused on bringing white leaders and black leaders together across the South to focus on issues that could ameliorate racial injustice without fundamentally challenging the segregated, social structure of southern society. Such an approach hinged less on "human relations," noted Leslie Dunbar, than on "human resources," meaning that the SRC focused less on explicitly racial issues like integration than it did on structural issues contributing to racial injustice, issues like jobs, social services, and education.

Because of its early focus on leadership elites, the SRC began as a distinctly upper-class institution, aimed at attracting predominantly white members of "commanding regional stature and authority." However, the organization lost a sizable segment of its membership in 1951, when it took a public stance against racial segregation. From that point onward, the SRC assumed a slightly less elite, but decidedly more inclusive, academic, and arguably middle-class status, including many more black members than originally envisioned. For much of the 1940s and 1950s, the SRC became the voice of many southern liberals, particularly white liberals who sought to improve race relations in the region without enlisting the help of the federal government.

Foremost among the SRC's declared goals were research, information, and interracial dialogue, a project that the council pursued by sponsoring a series of studies on the South, including George McMillan's *Racial Violence and Law Enforcement* (1960), Howard Zinn's *Albany: A Study in National Responsibility*, and James McBridde Dabbs's *Who Speaks for the South?* (1964). In 1962, the SRC mounted the massive Voter Education Project, aimed at facilitating the registration of black voters across the South—a project that dovetailed nicely with voter registration campaigns mounted by more grassroots civil rights organizations like the Student Non-Violent Coordinating Committee in places like the Mississippi Delta in 1964 and Selma, Ala., in 1965.

ANDERS WALKER
Saint Louis University

Leslie W. Dunbar, *Annals of the American Academy of Political and Social Science* (January 1965).

State Sovereignty Commissions

During the civil rights years of the 1950s and 1960s, a number of administrative commissions and legislative committees were created by southern states' governments to resist the civil rights crusades in the region. Though their names varied, these official agencies were bound together by common interests and purposes—defending the region's cherished "segregated southern way of life," devising both legal and extralegal means to circumvent the U.S. Supreme Court's desegregation rulings, propagandizing the vindication of states' rights ideology and racial separation, and suffocating any dissenters and deviators from the South's racial norms.

In the early 1950s, reflective of the Dixiecrat revolt during the 1948 presidential election and in anticipation of the Supreme Court's impending school desegregation ruling, some Deep South states began to create legislative committees to protect their public schools from racial integration. The first such strategy-mapping segregationist committee was created by South Carolina in April 1951 when the state legislature established the South Carolina School Committee, or the Gressette Committee—named after its chair, state senator L. Marion Gressette. Georgia then followed its neighboring state to organize the Georgia Commission on Education in December 1953.

Meanwhile, during the 1952 regular session, the Mississippi state legislature appointed a study committee officially called the Mississippi Legislative Recess Education Committee. The committee's whole responsibility was to equalize the physical standards for black pupils with those for whites in the state's elementary and secondary educational systems in the hope that this equalization movement would influence the expected Supreme Court's school desegregation decision and would, if possible, circumvent any federal court rulings unfavorable to the continuation of racial segregation in Mississippi's public schools. While reorganizing this study committee as the new State Education Finance Commission to have it supervise the construction of new public schools for black pupils and the consolidation of school districts in the state, the Mississippi legislature established the Legal Educational Advisory Committee in April 1954. In the name of pre-serving and promoting the best interests of both black and white Mississippians, the advisory committee, in substance, was vested with authority to draft segre-gationist laws to maintain racially sepa-rate schools in the state. The Legal Edu-cational Advisory Committee would soon be converted into a tax-supported "permanent authority for maintenance of racial segregation" in Mississippi.

In the immediate aftermath of the Supreme Court's *Brown v. Board of Edu-cation* ruling in May 1954, Louisiana joined other Deep South states by creating the Louisiana Joint Legisla-tive Committee on Segregation, better known as the Rainach Committee—after an all-powerful state senator, Willie M. Rainach. A year later, the Supreme Court announced the imple-mentation order of *Brown*, propelling southern states to organize "massive re-sistance"—an all-out resistance move-ment to what they termed "judicial tyranny" and to the ever-intensifying civil rights movement in the region. An overwhelming mood of defiance to the federal government dominated southern states' legislative sessions in 1956. Virginia, Alabama, South Caro-lina, and Mississippi adopted the so-called interposition resolutions by the end of February, in which these states' legislatures expressed their strongest de-termination to defend the South against the "illegal encroachment" of the federal government.

In Mississippi, with the defiance of the federal government at its most ex-treme and inspired by the issuance of its own interposition resolution, the state lawmakers then turned to cre-ating a tax-supported implementation agency of the resolves expressed in the resolution. On 29 March 1956, with the blessing of Gov. James P. Coleman, Mis-sissippi—the citadel of racial injustice in the South—created the Mississippi State Sovereignty Commission as part of the executive branch of its govern-ment, "to do and perform any and all acts . . . to protect the sovereignty of the State of Mississippi . . . from encroach-ment thereon by the Federal Govern-ment." Though the State Sovereignty Commission in Mississippi was soon to be identified as the state's "segrega-tion watchdog agency," neither the word "segregation" nor the word "integration" appeared in the carefully crafted bill that created the new agency. To be sure, however, federal "encroachment" was a periphrasis implying "forced racial integration," and "to protect the sov-ereignty" of Mississippi from that "en-croachment" was a sophisticated round-about expression of the state's resolve "to preserve and protect racial segrega-tion" in Mississippi.

Mississippi thus became the very first southern state to reinstate the word "sovereignty" of states' rights ideology in naming its anti-*Brown* and anti–civil rights state agency. With the aura of sophistication and respectability ema-nating from the word, the State Sov-ereignty Commission, for all practical purposes, was expected to maintain segregation at all costs and to wreck the NAACP and other civil rights orga-nizations in both Mississippi and her southern sister states. From its incep-tion in 1956 to its practical demise in the late 1960s, the Mississippi State Sovereignty Commission, maintaining both public relations and investigative departments, was the most emphatic prosegregation and pro–states' rights governmental agency in the South. The Mississippi commission's heyday came under the chairmanship of Gov. Ross R. Barnett.

After the September 1957 Little Rock, Ark., school desegregation crisis, though it brought wretched consequences to southern segregationists, "massive resistance" attained its height. Virginia created the Virginia Commission on Constitutional Government in 1958 as an official vehicle to carry on the state's "respectable" resistance to the civil rights movement. Then in June 1960, Louisiana established its own state sovereignty commission and the Louisiana Joint Legislative Committee on Un-American Activities. While the grand missions of the Louisiana State Sovereignty Commission were to paint the state's race relations in a rosy color and to alert the rest of the nation to the gradual encroachment on states' rights by the centralized federal government, the Un-American Activities Committee, indicative of its name, took up the broadly defined "subversive hunt" in Louisiana. After all, the civil rights leaders, activists, and their sympathizers in the South could all be categorized as "subversives" in the sense that they willfully defied the region's white establishment and its long-cherished "segregated way of life."

In September 1962, the entire South witnessed the first dramatic and physical confrontation between a Deep South state and the federal government over the University of Mississippi desegregation crisis. Soon thereafter, at the behest of Gov. George C. Wallace, Alabama belatedly organized its state sovereignty commission as well as the Alabama Legislative Commission to Preserve the Peace, in 1963. As in the case of Louisiana, the Alabama State Sovereignty Commission devoted its time and energy mainly to public relations schemes, and the "Peace Commission" spied on civil rights activists.

Abominable racial incidents and irresponsible actions of die-hard segregationists occurred during the first half of the 1960s, and fatal blows were rendered to the white South's resistance movement with the passage of the Civil Rights Act of 1964 and the Voting Rights Act of 1965. Combined, these facts resulted in robbing both the legality and the respectability of the South's "massive resistance." Having virtually outlived its usefulness by 1968 to defend the state's racial status quo, the Mississippi State Sovereignty Commission, in its dying days, spent its resources on investigating anti–Vietnam War demonstrators, black nationalists, and campus radicals in the state, reflecting the transformation of the nation's political and social trends in the late 1960s. For the purpose of cracking down on these "new subversives," the state sovereignty commissions of Mississippi, Louisiana, and Alabama formed the Interstate Sovereignty Association in May 1968, but this cooperative scheme did not enjoy any longevity.

In June 1969, Louisiana's state sovereignty commission and its Un-

American Activities Committee were terminated. Having outlived the one in Louisiana, both the Mississippi State Sovereignty Commission and the Alabama State Sovereignty Commission faded away in 1973. By the time its death knell rang, Mississippi's "segregation watchdog agency" had ended up spending over $1,542,000 to "protect the sovereignty" of the state.

YASUHIRO KATAGIRI
Tokai University (Japan)

Numan V. Bartley, *The Rise of Massive Resistance: Race and Politics in the South during the 1950s* (1969); Dan T. Carter, *The Politics of Rage: George Wallace, the Origins of the New Conservatism, and the Transformation of American Politics* (1995); Adam Fairclough, *Race and Democracy: The Civil Rights Struggle in Louisiana, 1915–1972* (1995); Erle Johnston, *Mississippi's Defiant Years, 1953–1973: An Interpretive Documentary with Personal Experiences* (1990); Yasuhiro Katagiri, *The Mississippi State Sovereignty Commission: Civil Rights and States' Rights* (2001); Steven F. Lawson, in *An Uncertain Tradition: Constitutionalism and the History of the South*, ed. Kermit L. Hall and James W. Ely Jr. (1989); Neil R. McMillen, *The Citizens' Council: Organized Resistance to the Second Reconstruction, 1954–64* (1971); Jeff Roche, *Restructured Resistance: The Sibley Commission and the Politics of Desegregation in Georgia* (1995); William M. Stowe Jr., "Willie Rainach and the Defense of Segregation in Louisiana, 1954–1959" (Ph.D. dissertation, Southern Methodist University, 1989).

Stax Records

From a meager and tentative start in 1959 as Satellite Records, by the mid-1960s Stax had become the record label most responsible for defining the commercially successful and widely influential "Memphis Sound." Memphis, as one of the most significant cultural crossroads in the South, had supported a number of vibrant live music scenes throughout the earlier part of the 20th century, and the city's hybrid sounds had received their first major national exposure when artists initially recorded by Sam Phillips left Memphis for greener pastures. But it was Stax and its alumnus Chips Moman and his American Sound Studio that sent Memphis-recorded music to the top of the national pop charts. Stax, with its gritty, muscular "southern soul" or "deep soul" sound, provided an uncompromising rootsy counterpoint to northern urban black pop crossover attempts by Motown and soul crooners such as Sam Cooke and Ben E. King. Its sound and success also shaped the trajectory of the Muscle Shoals–area recorded music, an equally successful and influential southern sound. Booker T. & the MG's, Sam and Dave, Otis Redding, and Wilson Pickett became and have remained household names, and Stax's 1960s sound was famously commemorated for later generations in the 1981 movie *The Blues Brothers* and its sequel *Blues Brothers 2000*.

Although Stax struggled to stay afloat in racially torn Memphis after Martin Luther King's assassination and finally folded in 1976, it was not before hitting a second stylistic and commercial peak with psychedelic soul and funk. The premier exponent of that sound, Isaac Hayes, won multiple Grammies and an Oscar in 1972 for his

Booker T. & the MGs (courtesy Stax Museum of American Soul Music, Memphis)

score of the classic blaxploitation movie *Shaft* and set the tone for black popular music for at least the next decade.

In 1957, Jim Stewart, a banker and an erstwhile country fiddler, started the Satellite record label in his wife's uncle's garage in Memphis. Next, convincing his elder sister, Estelle Axton, to invest in a recording venture by mortgaging her house, he bought an Ampex monaural recorder and moved to a deserted grocery store in Brunswick, 30 miles east of Memphis. Finding little talent in the small community, Satellite rented the closed Capitol movie theater at 924 E. McLemore Ave. in Memphis and rechristened it Soulsville U.S.A. White guitarist, songwriter, and producer Lincoln Wayne "Chips" Moman, from LaGrange, Ga., helped in securing that

deal and proved integral to the fledgling operation before leaving to work at FAME studios in Muscle Shoals and later at his own American Studios back in Memphis.

Satellite did not have a focus on black music until the company's first break came with WDIA DJ Rufus Thomas recording "'Cause I Love You" with his daughter Carla. The regional popularity of the record led New York's Atlantic Records head Jerry Wexler to offer Satellite a purportedly distribution-only deal. Carla Thomas next scored the studio's first national hit with her self-composed "Gee Whiz." Wexler signed the teenaged Thomas to his own Atlantic label, on which he also released the song, thus starting an arrangement through which important

Atlantic-signed artists, many from the North, would record at Stax and later also at Muscle Shoals–area studios and at Chips Moman's Memphis-based American Sound Studio. Such arrangements became a significant route for southern sounds to enter the popular mainstream.

Satellite's next hit came in July 1961 with the Mar-Keys' instrumental "Last Night." Released initially on Satellite, the record shot to number two on the national pop charts. Threats of litigation by another company with the same name prompted the renaming, to Stax, a title that borrowed the initial letters from Stewart and Axton's last names. Controversy surrounds the details of which musicians were featured on the spliced-together record, but the band that toured in the wake of its popularity was all white and featured seven members, two of whom, guitarist Steve Cropper and bassist Donald "Duck" Dunn, would soon constitute half of the most famous studio house band in American popular music, Booker T. & the MG's. Booker T. Jones and Al Jackson Jr., organist and drummer, respectively, were the earliest African American musicians to play sessions at Stax, and they formed the other half of that legendary combo. The Mar-Keys' Wayne Jackson partnered with Andrew Love to form the Memphis Horns. Over the next six years, both in the studio and on the road, Booker T. & the MG's and the Memphis Horns—and often the reconstituted Mar-Keys and the Bar-Kays—backed numerous Stax and Atlantic acts that featured on regional and national pop charts with in-creasing frequency. Among these were Carla Thomas, Rufus Thomas, William Bell, Otis Redding, Wilson Pickett, Sam and Dave, Eddie Floyd, Johnnie Taylor, and Albert King. Additionally, the exceptional success of the MG's as an individual recording act inspired many studio backup bands, including the Bar-Kays, War, and MFSB (Mother Father Sister Brother), to launch individual careers and encouraged studio musicians to form "supergroups," such as Stuff and Fourplay. Keyboardist, composer, and arranger Isaac Hayes and lyricist David Porter constituted a major songwriting and production team at Stax during this period, especially for Sam and Dave.

The year 1968 proved to be a landmark in Stax's history. In February, Otis Redding's "Sittin' on the Dock of the Bay," overdubbed and released posthumously after Redding's plane crash in December 1967, became Stax's first pop chart topper. The racial tensions resulting from the April assassination of Martin Luther King Jr. in Memphis and Atlantic Records' decision to end its partnership with Stax, taking with it all the recorded masters, sent the company into a tailspin. Stax was eventually sold for over 2 million dollars to the Paramount Pictures subsidiary of Gulf-Western. Estelle Axton exited the picture, and African American executive vice president Al Bell, who had been hired in 1965, took increasing charge of the reins.

Bell and Stewart borrowed money from Deutsche Grammophon to buy back Stax in 1970 and negotiated a distribution deal with Columbia. While the 1964 to 1967 period is remembered as Stax's creative zenith, Isaac Hayes and the Staples Singers found artistic and exceptional commercial success with their updated sounds during the post-1968 period. It must be noted, however, that Stax often sent its artists down to Muscle Shoals to record—among others, the Staples' hit "I'll Take You There" was recorded at the Muscle Shoals Sound studio for Stax. Other successful Stax acts from this period include Mel and Tim, Little Milton, the Soul Children, the Emotions, the reconstituted Bar-Kays, the Dramatics, Shirley Brown, and gospel singer Rance Allen. In 1972, Al Bell bought Stewart's share in the company; Stewart continued as chief executive, however. Under Bell, Stax attempted to diversify, investing in a Broadway play, signing black comedian Richard Pryor to the new Partee subsidiary, and even recording an album by Rev. Jesse Jackson on the Respect subsidiary label. One of the company's most ambitious projects was August 1972's WattStax concert at the Los Angeles Memorial Coliseum during the Watts Summer Festival; the multiagency benefit event featured all the main artists on Stax's roster, was attended by an audience of over 100,000, and comparisons to Woodstock were put forth.

Al Bell and Johnny Baylor, a black New York record executive Bell had hired in 1968, had drastically different and not always above-board approaches to running the now multimillion-dollar empire, contrasting with the amicable family-business environment of the early years. Even through increasing legal problems and multiple federal investigations, starting in 1973, the label continued recording, albeit with decreasing commercial success; only the Staples Singers charted in the Top 20 in its last three years. Based on petitions filed by creditors, a bankruptcy court shut down the Stax operation in January 1976. Although an environment of rapidly changing musical tastes precluded any subsequent historic landmarks for its remaining alumni—except perhaps for actor Richard Pryor, Steve Cropper, and, later, Isaac Hayes—Stax's place in American popular music had long been secured.

AJAY KALRA
University of Texas at Austin

Rob Bowman, *Soulsville U.S.A.: The Story of Stax Records* (1997); James Dickerson, *Goin' Back to Memphis: A Century of Blues, Rock 'n' Roll, and Glorious Soul* (1996); Peter Guralnick, *Sweet Soul Music: Rhythm and Blues and the Southern Dream of Freedom* (1986; rev. ed., 1999).

Till, Emmett

(1941–1955) CIVIL RIGHTS MARTYR. Emmett Till's brutal murder and the heinous acquittal of his assailants ignited the civil rights movement in America. In mid-August 1955, 14-year-old Till, called "Bo," traveled from his home in Chicago to the Mississippi Delta to visit relatives. Goaded by cousins to address a white woman flirtatiously, on 24 August Till went inside Bryant's Grocery and Meat market in Money, Miss., to buy bubble gum. Here, allegedly, he wolf whistled at 27-year-old Carolyn Bryant, the owner's wife, who accused him of indecent advances. On the evening of 28 August 1955, Roy Bryant, with his half-brother J. W. Milam and possibly others, kidnapped Till from his great-uncle Mose Wright's house, savagely pistol whipped him, gouged out one of his eyes, ripped his tongue from his mouth, knocked the back of his head off, and then threw his body into the Tallahatchie River, where he was found three days later on 31 August with a 70-pound cotton-gin fan barb-wired around his neck.

On 10 September, after Till's mother, Mamie Bradley Till, insisted her son's body be returned to Chicago, she made the historic and brave decision to show what had happened to her son by leaving his coffin open. Photos of Till's mangled face first appeared in the *Chicago Defender* and then nationally in *Jet* magazine and finally around the world, outraging readers, who demanded justice for this horrific crime. But the trial of Till's murderers, 19–23 September, presided over by Judge Curtis Swango, only added to the injustice. The jury of 12 white men, some of whom contributed to a fund for the defense, found Bryant and Milam not guilty after only 67 minutes of deliberation. Till's murder was one of the very early civil rights atrocities to win national media attention. It was also the first time a black man—Mose Wright—testified against a white person in Mississippi. Moreover, by unquestioningly identifying her son's mutilated, rotting corpse, Mamie Bradley Till challenged the defense's claim that since the body was unrecognizable there was no corpus delicti to prove Bryant and Milam's guilt.

Exactly what Till said to Carolyn Bryant may never be known, but Mamie Till declared in court and in speeches over the next 35 years that she had told her son to blow a sound out like a whistle to stop his stuttering. In January 1956, William Bradford Huie published an interview with Bryant and Milam in *Life* magazine in which they shockingly admitted that they had murdered Till and reveled in how they had punished the alleged sexual aggressor. An investigation by the FBI would have been the only way to indict the two on federal kidnapping charges, but President Eisenhower, wary of offending southern states, and FBI director J. Edgar Hoover refused. However, in November 2004, the Justice Department reopened the case and then turned it over to the district attorney of Leflore County, Miss.

Till's murder, the photo of his mangled corpse, and the trial are iconic images and events in civil rights history. Symbolically, Till was immortalized as a Christlike sacrificial lamb slaughtered for his people's freedom. Politically, the NAACP characterized his murder as a lynching and demanded justice, as did notable figures around the world, including Eleanor Roosevelt. Claiming that she was inspired by Till's murder, Rosa Parks refused to move to the back of a Montgomery, Ala., bus just three months after the trial. The Montgomery Bus Boycott was thus directly tied to the outrage over Till's murder. Young people around the country went on Freedom Marches for Emmett Till as he became an inspiration for civil rights protests and sit-ins, even as his gruesome death terrified blacks that the same fate might await them. Till's photo made a powerful impression on a new generation of African Americans who would fight for civil rights. Eldridge Cleaver, Stokely Carmichael, and Julian Bond maintained that Till's brutal murder captured in the *Jet* photo profoundly influenced their lives. Till was enshrined along with Martin Luther King and Medgar Evers in the civil rights memorial in Montgomery as martyrs in the fight for justice and freedom.

Till's legacy endures in music, literature, film, and memoirs. Songs about him were written by Aaron Kramer and Clyde Appleton, Bob Dylan, and Joan Baez. Till was the subject of poems by Langston Hughes, Audre Lorde, Gwendolyn Brooks, Sam Cornish, and Shirley Nelson. Lewis Nordan's *Wolf Whistle* and Bebe Campbell's *Your Blues Ain't Like Mine* have fictionalized Till's story. His life and death have also been dramatized by Toni Morrison, James Baldwin, and his mother, with David Bar III, in *The Face of Emmett Till* (1999). In 2005, Keith A. Beauchamp directed the documentary film *The Untold Story of Emmett Till*. The title of Mamie Bradley Till-Mobley's memoir—*The Hate Crime That Changed America*— aptly expresses her son's crucial role in the civil rights movement.

PHILIP C. KOLIN
University of Southern Mississippi

Adam Green, *Selling the Race: Culture, Community, and Black Chicago, 1940–1955* (2007); Philip Kolin, ed., *Southern Quarterly* (Summer 2008); Christopher Metress, *The Lynching of Emmett Till* (2002); Harriet Pollock and Christopher Metress, eds., *Emmett Till in Literary Memory and Imagination* (2007); Mamie Till-Mobley, *The Hate Crime That Changed America* (2002); Stephen J. Whitfield, *A Death in the Delta: The Story of Emmett Till* (1986).

Tuskegee Syphilis Study

The United States Public Health Service Study of Untreated Syphilis (USPHSS) in the Negro male in Macon County, Ala., is the original name of the longest nontherapeutic study conducted in the United States and one that showed how race influenced medical science in the 20th century. This study is more popularly known as the Tuskegee Syphilis Study because the U.S. Public Health Service originally conducted it with cooperation from Tuskegee Institute (now Tuskegee University). The study continued from 1932 to 1972. Since its founding in 1881, Tuskegee Institute worked with members of the black community in Macon County and the surrounding Black Belt counties to improve the well-being and standard of living for black people who resided in those counties. The institute designed several extension programs centered on education, farming, animal husbandry, housing improvements, nutrition, and health. Prior to the opening of the Macon County Public Health Department in 1946, all public health functions by the state of Alabama for black people in Macon County and several surrounding counties were conducted at the John A. Andrews Memorial Hospital, a private hospital operated by Tuskegee Institute. The proposed research study of syphilis was originally sponsored by the Rosenwald Health Fund, as a diagnostic and treatment program in six southern states, including Alabama, to address the national concerns about the syphilis epidemic that was expanding throughout the country.

The stock market crash forced the Rosenwald Fund to reevaluate its program funding, and the original study was dropped. In an effort to salvage the program, the U.S. Public Health Service proposed a more limited study of untreated syphilis, as a comparison study to the retrospective study conducted in Oslo, Norway, in 1925. The USPHSS began with approximately 600 men, 400 diagnosed with syphilis and 200 without the disease. When the study began, arsenic and mercury were used to treat those people infected with the disease. The men with syphilis were not treated. A concerted effort by the U.S. Public Health Service, the Alabama State Health Department, and local physicians was coordinated to ensure that even those men without the disease, who were later presented with syphilis, were not dropped from the study but were switched and included with the infected population.

The USPHSS did not stop in 1943, even when the U.S. Public Health Service determined that penicillin was the most effective method for treating venereal diseases, particularly syphilis and gonorrhea. And the Nuremburg Trial and the declaration against human experimentation without the consent of the subject did not end the study. Nor did the scientific community raise any concerns about unethical behavior by the research team or plausible bioethical violations by the U.S. Public Health Service or the Centers for Disease Control

(CDC) until the 1950s. Over the 40-year period (1932–72), several articles were published in the scientific literature about findings from the study. Additionally, information gathered from the study was included in the curriculum of many medical schools throughout the country.

By the late 1960s, several employees at the CDC had expressed grave concerns regarding the study. Nonetheless, the study continued until 1972, when an Associated Press article, written by Jean Heller, was published in the *New York Times*. The revelation resulted in a class-action suit filed in July 1973 by noted civil rights attorney Fred D. Gray and, among other study participants, Charlie W. Pollard. A settlement of approximately 10 million dollars was reached in 1974.

On 16 May 1997, President Bill Clinton apologized to the surviving men and their families, the Tuskegee community, and the African American population on behalf of the country for the study. At a White House ceremony in Washington, D.C., Clinton said the government did something that was "wrong, gravely and morally wrong." Five of the remaining seven study survivors, including Charlie Pollard, were present. As a part of the apology, Clinton mandated that the Department of Health and Human Services support the establishment of the Tuskegee University National Center for Bioethics in Research and Health Care on the campus of Tuskegee University and that a legacy museum be launched. In 1999, the Bioethics Center opened on the campus of Tuskegee University to conduct research, education, and community engagement activities related to bioethics, public health ethics, health disparities, and health equity. After more than a decade, the Bioethics Center continues its mission.

RUEBEN WARREN
Tuskegee University

Fred Grey, *The Tuskegee Syphilis Study* (1998); James H. Jones, *Bad Blood: The Tuskegee Syphilis Experiment* (1993); Ralph V. Katz et al., *American Journal of Public Health* (June 2008); Susan M. Reverby, *Examining Tuskegee: The Infamous Syphilis Study and Its Legacy* (2009), ed., *Tuskegee's Truths: Rethinking the Tuskegee Syphilis Study* (2000).

Vietnamese

The U.S. Gulf Coast is home to approximately 200,000 Southeast Asian Americans, those who fled their homelands in the aftermath of the Vietnam War and surrounding conflicts in Cambodia and Laos. Vietnamese Americans represent the vast majority of Southeast Asian Americans (and Asian Americans in general) within the Gulf Coast states of Texas, Louisiana, Mississippi, and Alabama. Their arrival and resettlement in the region began shortly after the surrender of South Vietnam to North Vietnamese Communist forces in late April 1975. In the lead-up to the Communist takeover of the South, the United States orchestrated a massive evacuation of South Vietnamese elites, particularly military officials and others who had served the U.S. occupation. These evacuees are known as "first wave" refugees, and they were taken to government bases in Guam, Thailand,

Wake Island, Hawaii, and the Philippines as part of Operation New Life and then transferred to emergency relocation centers in the United States: Camp Pendleton in California, Camp Chafee in Arkansas, Elgin Air Force Base in Florida, and Fort Indiantown Gap in Pennsylvania. From there, refugees would be dispersed to various U.S. cities for permanent resettlement, including the Gulf Coast cities of New Orleans and Houston.

Not all first-wave refugees were among the elite. In 1975, tens of thousands of devout Vietnamese Catholics—many of them farmers and fishermen—were also evacuated. Vietnamese Catholics considered themselves particularly susceptible to acts of Communist reprisal as a result of the Catholic Church's support of the U.S. occupation (and for its soft stance on the previous French colonial rule). The Catholic Church coordinated efforts with U.S. forces to ensure that many of its most devout members were evacuated from South Vietnam. Among them was the Catholic community from the northern Vietnamese villages of Bui Chu and Phat Diem. These parishioners had originally fled together from North Vietnam in 1954, following the final defeat of French colonists by the Communist-led national liberation effort. Together, they resettled to the southern Vietnamese villages of Haing Tau and Phuc Thinh, located southeast of Saigon, where for the time being Communist forces held little sway. But with the complete Communist victory of 1975, there was no future safe haven within Vietnam. And so they evacuated and resettled together once more—this time to the United States. Many were taken to Elgin Air Force Base and Camp Chafee. They were paid a visit by Archbishop Philip Hannan, then head of the New Orleans archdiocese, who was intrigued by the story of the devout Catholic refugees who had traveled together since 1954. The archbishop extended an open invitation to the refugees to resettle in New Orleans. New Orleans was a Catholic city, and it also possessed a tropical climate and seafaring opportunities, for which the Vietnamese were well suited. In the decades following resettlement, the refugees would indeed find steady work as Gulf Coast shrimpers.

The epicenter of the New Orleans Vietnamese American community is in New Orleans East, in a neighborhood known as Versailles, located approximately 20 miles east of downtown. Lacking the density of other parts of the city and surrounded by wetlands, Versailles has allowed the Vietnamese Americans to reestablish cultural and religious institutions, as well as create what some describe as a distinct Vietnamese American landscape. Over the years, the Vietnamese Americans would emerge as an economically diverse community. Many found steady work as shrimpers, but others would languish in working poverty in manufacturing firms. Others would subsist on welfare for multiple generations. The poverty rate among Vietnamese Americans in New Orleans is 31.7 percent, compared to 27.9 percent for the city as a whole. Those who were able to save and pool together resources began

purchasing small businesses during the 1980s. As such, Vietnamese American–owned lunch counters, grocery stores, and butcher shops are now common throughout the city.

After Hurricane Katrina flooded New Orleans in 2005, the residents of Versailles were among the first communities to return and rebuild their neighborhood. Some attribute their remarkable rate of return to a history of resilience that dates back to their original displacement from North Vietnam in 1954; others attribute it to the strong networks developed through the Catholic Church; and still others point to the way in which the Versailles community developed strong multiracial alliances, particularly with their African American neighbors, who represented nearly 80 percent of New Orleans East prior to the arrival of the refugees. Indeed, in the post-Katrina moment, the Vietnamese Americans seemed to defy their image as a quiescent and conservative immigrant community. Their leader excoriated the Bush administration for its mishandling of the rescue and recovery efforts. Meanwhile, its residents—both young and old—engaged in a bold civil disobedience action to close a toxic landfill in Versailles that city officials had opened in order to dump one-third of the Katrina debris.

The establishment of a Vietnamese American community in New Orleans provided a gateway to the settlement of other Southeast Asian American communities along the Gulf Coast, most notably Gulfport-Biloxi, Miss., and Bayou La Batre, Ala. Together with New

Orleans, these two cities constitute what some scholars refer to as the manufacturing periphery of the "Deep South triad," once booming port cities that in recent decades have been left in the shadow of the New South. While cities such as Houston, Atlanta, and Charlottesville became destinations for industries abandoning the Rust Belt, the manufacturing periphery did not attract large corporations that could offer new opportunities for the upwardly mobile while also attracting new waves of immigration from throughout the world. In Louisiana, Mississippi, and Alabama, the foreign-born population has remained at approximately 2 percent or less since the 1990s. As such, the arrival of Vietnamese Americans can be considered the lone "new immigration" event in the Deep South triad over the past three decades. The combined Vietnamese American population in Mississippi and Alabama is smaller than that of New Orleans, at approximately 10,000. It is made up of many second-wave refugees: those who arrived in the United States after the passage of the Refugee Act of 1980, through which Congress authorized the resettlement of tens of thousands of Vietnamese, Cambodians, and Laotians, who for years had been surviving in United Nations refugee camps. Second-wave refugees tended to be from poorer backgrounds than their first-wave counterparts, and many of them had witnessed atrocities and experienced harrowing journeys of escape before reaching UN camps. There are significant, if subtle, indicators of second-wave refugee presence in Biloxi/Gulfport and Bayou La Batre,

including the arrival of many non-Catholic (mostly Buddhist) Vietnamese Americans, as well as Cambodian and Laotian populations of approximately 1,700. Still, these communities have much in common with the Vietnamese Americans of New Orleans. The fishing industry is central to livelihoods of Southeast Asian Americans in both Mississippi and Alabama. Vietnamese Americans account for one-third of all commercial seafood workers in the Gulf Coast, and at least 80 percent of the Southeast Asian community is tied to the seafood industry. So too, poverty is a reality for many Southeast Asians; the poverty rate among Vietnamese Americans is 25 percent in Mississippi and 19 percent in Alabama. The average poverty rate among Cambodian Americans in both states is approximately 20 percent.

Hurricane Katrina caused significant damage to the Southeast Asian communities of Gulf Port/Biloxi and Bayou La Batre. Some have argued that the damage was actually far worse in these cities than in New Orleans. But unlike the case in New Orleans, the Vietnamese Americans in these cities were not backed by a powerful archdiocese that could coordinate relief efforts and hold accountable those in power. These cities did not draw the same post-Katrina national attention that was showered upon New Orleans.

In 2010, on the eve of the fifth anniversary of Katrina, the Deep Water Horizon oil spill would significantly impact Southeast Asian Americans of Louisiana, Mississippi, and Alabama who are employed by the fishing industry. These include commercial fishermen, as well as those who harvest and process shrimp, crabs, and oysters. Not only does the fishing industry provide employment, but the daily catch is also a means of sustenance, as many workers eat what they catch. Vietnamese Americans consume more Gulf seafood than average southerners, making them even more susceptible to high levels of contaminants. Residents have complained of respiratory and dermatological problems. Moreover, studies have shown that the mental health of oil-spill victims has deteriorated. Relief efforts, including promises of monetary compensation, have been difficult or ineffective because of language barriers that have prevented some Southeast Asians from navigating compensation programs. Meanwhile, finding employment in other industries is difficult because of language barriers and a skills mismatch. Fortunately, many local community groups have organized to demand justice for Southeast Asian Americans' lost income and altered lives. Efforts include translation services and advocacy for governmental recognition of the full impact of the spill on Southeast Asian communities.

The Houston area also has a significant Southeast Asian American population. But unlike the cities of the Deep South triad, Houston is a major center of commercial activity in the New South. Vietnamese resettlement to the area has therefore followed a different trajectory. Most Vietnamese who live in Houston and its surrounding suburbs are employed in a variety of industries, mainly manufacturing and retail

and other services. Yet those who live in nearby coastal cities such as Galveston Bay and Rockport have historically made a living in the fishing industry, much like their counterparts in the Deep South triad. Indeed, Vietnamese American fishermen made national headlines in the early 1980s when they came under attack by white shrimpers who saw the newcomers as a threat to their livelihoods. Before long, the Ku Klux Klan was brought into the fray, initiating a campaign of intimidation that included burning Vietnamese American–owned boats. The Klan's efforts were ultimately undone by a federal lawsuit filed by the Southern Poverty Law Center, arguing that its actions not only violated the civil rights of Vietnamese Americans but also the state's arcane antitrust laws.

ERIC TANG
University of Texas at Austin

Harvey Arden, *National Geographic*, September 1981; Jean Shiraki, *Asian American Policy Review* 21 (2011); U.S. Census Bureau, Census 2000.

Voting Rights Act (1965)

Two things above all others have changed the modern South: air-conditioning and the Voting Rights Act. Unfortunately, Americans have a better understanding of how air-conditioning functions than they do the Voting Rights Act.

Because discriminatory administration of state laws and constitutional amendments undermined federal protection of the rights of minority voters, Congress passed the Voting Rights Act in 1965, changing the landscape of electoral politics in America and over-throwing three generations of disfran-chisement. After the Civil War and emancipation, Reconstruction brought to formerly enslaved African Americans freedom, citizenship, and the right to vote under the Thirteenth, Fourteenth, and Fifteenth Amendments. Yet, when Reconstruction ended, these constitu-tional amendments did not assure a fair and equal vote. Recalcitrant whites, in-cluding members of organizations such as the Ku Klux Klan, used terrorist and fraudulent antisuffrage activities to deny African Americans the right to vote. A series of court cases systematically dismantled the civil and voting rights legislation of the first Reconstruction. Legal methods of disfranchising African Americans included gerrymandering, at-large elections, registration and secret ballot laws, the poll tax, literacy tests, and the white primary. By the early 20th century, these methods had effec-tively disfranchised millions of African Americans. In 1958, the Civil Rights Commission reported that there were 44 counties in the Deep South where there was not a single black voter regis-tered. Many of these counties had large African American populations; some had black American majorities.

The 1965 Voting Rights Act banned literacy tests, facilitated lawsuits to prohibit discriminatory laws or prac-tices, and sent federal voting registrars into intractable areas. In addition, sec-tion 5 of the Voting Rights Act required "covered jurisdictions," all initially in the South, to obtain "preclearance" from the Department of Justice for any change in their electoral procedures. An immediate effect of more minority voters was the replacement of blatant bigotry in electioneering with more subtle racial appeals. A longer-term effect has been the election of minority citizens to almost every level of govern-ment.

South Carolina, joined by other southern states, challenged the Voting Rights Act in 1966 in *South Carolina v. Katzenbach*, claiming that the act vio-lated its right to control and implement elections. After the Supreme Court re-jected this challenge, Mississippi and Virginia filed *Allen v. Board of Elections* (1969), contending, again unsuccess-fully, that the act protected only the right to cast a ballot, not the right to have nondiscriminatory election struc-tures, such as district elections. Con-gress renewed all the provisions of the Voting Rights Act in 1970 and 1975, amending it in 1975 to include, in sec-tion 203, provisions to protect language minorities, such as Asian, Hispanic, and Native American voters.

After its initial victories in court, the Voting Rights Act began to suffer de-feats. In *Beer v. U.S.* (1976), the Supreme Court ruled that section 5 of the act did not prevent discriminatory election laws generally but only those that resulted in a "retrogression" of minority influence. For instance, after African Americans were enfranchised by the act, a local jurisdiction could shift district lines in order to ensure a continuation of all-white government, and the Department of Justice had to allow the change to go into effect. Even more significant, the

U.S. Supreme Court ruled in *Mobile v. Bolden* (1980) that no election law violated section 2 of the act or the Fifteenth Amendment to the U.S. Constitution unless it could be shown that the law had been adopted with a racially discriminatory intent. During the First Reconstruction, in 1874, Mobile, Ala., had instituted at-large elections; after the passage of the act in 1965, many other southern localities switched from district to at-large elections. In such elections, because whites who outnumber minorities generally vote for whites (that is, racial bloc voting), minorities had a much more difficult time getting elected, and under *Bolden*, minority plaintiffs had a much more difficult time winning lawsuits.

In 1982, Congress not only renewed the preclearance provision of section 5 for 25 years, it also effectively overturned *Bolden* by making clear that a proof of intent was unnecessary to win a section 2 case. Moreover, it weakened *Beer* by instructing the Justice Department to not preclear state or local laws that were discriminatory in either intent or effect. Ironically, in view of the heated two-year struggle in Congress, this strongest version of the act passed by much more overwhelming congressional majorities than ever before. Even more surprising, within two days of the signing of the renewed act, the Supreme Court in *Rogers v. Lodge* announced an effect standard for the act that was nearly identical to that just passed by Congress and that implicitly repudiated the *Bolden* decision of 1980.

Along with the one-person, one-vote ruling of the Supreme Court in *Reynolds v. Sims* (1964), the Voting Rights Act has added another dimension to the politics of redistricting following each decadal census. Once a secretive, unchallengeable practice, redistricting is now played out in courtrooms as well as in backrooms, often ending up before the U.S. Supreme Court. The most startling Supreme Court decision was *Shaw v. Reno* (1993). Disfranchisement had prevented African Americans from electing a single member of Congress from North Carolina from 1898 to 1965; after 1965, the state's leaders had repeatedly redrawn district boundaries to keep the 11-member delegation all white in a 23 percent black state. But after the 1982 amendments strengthened the Voting Rights Act, a newer generation of North Carolina leaders, under pressure from the Department of Justice, drew two districts in which 54 percent of the voters were African American. In order to preserve the seats of white Democratic incumbents, North Carolina legislators drew new black-majority districts in even stranger shapes than the districts they replaced. Ignoring previous prowhite racial gerrymandering in the state, five members of the Supreme Court denounced the most integrated congressional districts in North Carolina's history as "segregated" and declared them unconstitutional. White-majority districts could take any shape, the same five justices wrote in a later case from Texas (*Bush v. Vera*, 1996), but black-majority districts could not look "bizarre" to judges. And in a

Georgia case, *Miller v. Johnson* (1995), the Supreme Court by the same 5–4 vote announced that black-majority districts could not be drawn with a predominantly racial intent and that white-majority districts could not be challenged under this standard. Finally, in two cases from Bossier Parish, La., the five-person Supreme Court majority ruled that the Justice Department under section 5 of the act had to pre-clear any election law change, unless it made minorities worse off than before the change. Bossier's school board could thus remain all white.

The Voting Rights Act rid the country of the most outrageous forms of voter disfranchisement. Equal voting rights has meant representation for a large minority of citizens and has brought a tremendous increase in minority elected officials, particularly Native Americans in the West and Hispanics in California and Texas and the election of literally thousands of African Americans to offices across the old Confederacy. The Voting Rights Act is a success story. Designed to increase minority voter registration, it has done so. It has also reduced election-related violence, increased responsiveness and the provision of services to minorities, made the political talents of the minority community, especially African Americans in the South, more available to society as a whole, made it possible for southern solons to support civil rights, made racial politics unfashionable, and opened opportunities for minorities to pursue careers in politics. Despite its significant weakening by a 5–4 majority of the U.S. Supreme Court

in the 1990s, the Voting Rights Act continues to have a tremendous influence on American, and especially southern, political life.

ORVILLE VERNON BURTON
University of Illinois at Urbana-Champaign

Chandler Davidson and Bernard Grofman, eds., *Quiet Revolution in the South: The Impact of the Voting Rights Act, 1965–1990* (1994); David Garrow, *Protest at Selma: Martin Luther King Jr. and the Voting Rights Act of 1965* (1978); Nick Kotz, *Judgment Days: Lyndon Baines Johnson, Martin Luther King Jr., and the Laws That Changed America* (2005); J. Morgan Kousser, *Colorblind Injustice: Minority Voting Rights and the Undoing of the Second Reconstruction* (1999); Steven F. Lawson, *Black Ballots: Voting Rights in the South, 1944–1969* (1976).

Walker, Alice

(b. 1944) WRITER.

Alice Walker's *The Color Purple* is saturated with the atmosphere of the South, the rural Georgia farmland of her childhood. Walker, who has written more than 29 books of poetry, fiction, biography, and essays, finds strength and inspiration in the land and the people: "You look at old photographs of Southern blacks and you see it—a fearlessness, a real determination and proof of a moral center that is absolutely bedrock to the land. I think there's hope in the South, not in the North," she says. In her work, the human spirit conquers racism.

Alice Walker was born in 1944 in Eatonton, Ga., the youngest of eight children. Her parents were poor sharecroppers. As a child, she read what books she could get, kept notebooks, and listened to the stories her relatives told. She attended Spelman College in Atlanta and graduated from Sarah Lawrence College in Bronxville, N.Y., where her writing was discovered by her teacher Muriel Rukeyser, who admired the manuscript that Alice had slipped under her door. Rukeyser sent the poems to her own editor at Harcourt Brace, and this first collection of Walker's poetry, *Once*, was published in 1965. From 1966 through 1974, Walker lived in Georgia and Mississippi and devoted herself to voter registration, Project Head Start, and writing. She married Mel Leventhal, a Brooklyn attorney who shared her dedication to civil rights in his work on school desegregation cases. Their daughter, Rebecca, was born in 1969. After they left the South, Walker and Leventhal lived for a while in a Brooklyn brownstone, and then they separated. Alice Walker now lives in rural northern California, which she chose primarily for the silence that would allow her to "hear" her fictional characters.

Alice Walker is the literary heir of Zora Neale Hurston and Flannery O'Connor. Walker has visited O'Connor's home in Milledgeville, Ga., and Hurston's grave in Eatonville, Fla., to pay homage. Walker's novels *The Third Life of Grange Copeland* (1977), *Meridian* (1976), and *The Color Purple* (1982) and short stories "In Love and Trouble" (1973) and "You Can't Keep a Good Woman Down" (1980) capture and explore her experiences of the South. She draws on her memories and her family's tales of Georgia

ancestors in creating the portraits of rural black women in *The Color Purple*. Their speech is pure dialect—colloquial, poetic, and moving. Walker's poems too are filled with the rich landscape and atmosphere of the South.

Consciousness of the South has always been central to Alice Walker. The flowers and fruits in her California garden recall her mother's garden back in Georgia, a place so important to Walker that it became the inspiration for her collection of essays entitled *In Search of Our Mothers' Gardens: Womanist Prose* (1983). Her mother's creativity was a compelling example to Alice Walker as well as a constant source of beauty amid the poverty of rural Georgia. Her mother died in 1993 at the age of 80. Her headstone reads "Loving Soul, Great Spirit."

Among her many accomplishments and honors, Alice Walker has been Fannie Hurst Professor of Literature at Brandeis University and a contributing editor to *Ms.* magazine. In her writing and teaching she continually stresses the importance of black women writers. She edited a Zora Neale Hurston reader and wrote a biography of Langston Hughes for children. In 1984, Walker launched Wild Trees Press in Navarro, Calif., publishing the work of unknown writers until 1988. The film version of *The Color Purple* was released in 1985 to much acclaim. In 2004, the musical version of *The Color Purple* premiered in Chicago, and it opened on Broadway in 2005. Alice Walker continues to champion vital issues such as female genital mutilation, which is central in her 1992 novel *Possessing the Secret of Joy*. Alice

Walker's literary awards include the Rosenthal Award of the National Institute of Arts and Letters, the Lillian Smith Award for her second book of poems, *Revolutionary Petunias* (1972), and the American Book Award and the Pulitzer Prize for fiction for *The Color Purple* (1983).

ELIZABETH GAFFNEY
Westchester Community College, SUNY

David Bradley, *New York Times Magazine*, January 1984; Robert Towers, *New York Review of Books*, 12 August 1982; Alice Walker, *Atlanta Constitution*, 19 April 1983; Evelyn C. White, *Alice Walker: A Life* (2004).

Walker, Margaret

(1913–1998) AUTHOR.

Margaret Walker, who was born in Birmingham, Ala., played an active role in American arts and letters for at least seven decades. She was a distinguished poet, respected essayist, groundbreaking novelist, and award-winning educator. Her final collection of poetry, *This Is My Century*, accurately describes the wide range of themes and issues encompassed in her work, with racial concerns inevitably central. The 20th century became Margaret Walker's century, as she "saw it grow from darkness into dawn" ("This Is My Century"). Her writings demonstrate vestiges of the Harlem Renaissance of the 1920s and 1930s, traces of the Black Arts Movement of the 1960s and 1970s, and markings of what some might call the Womanist Renaissance of the 1980s.

Walker wrote across literary genres, but she is most accomplished as a poet.

She began publishing poetry in local vehicles at the age of 12 and gained her first appearance in a national publication by age 19 when "I Want to Write" appeared in *Crisis*, under the editorship of W. E. B. Du Bois. Just a few years later, at age 22, "For My People" was printed in the November 1937 issue of *Poetry: A Magazine of Verse*, which launched her career as a poet. In 1940, Walker collected 26 poems under the title *For My People* as her master's thesis, and it was published as a collection in 1942. She produced four other significant collections of poetry: *The Ballad of the Free* (1966), *Prophets for a New Day* (1970), *October Journey* (1973), and *This is My Century: New and Collected Poems* (1989). *Prophets for a New Day* celebrates the civil rights movement; *October Journey* (1973) takes its name from a piece written in honor of her husband, whom she met in the month of October and who died in the month of October after 37 years of marriage. *This Is My Century: New and Collected Poems* (1989) was her last collection of poetry, and it presents 100 poems—37 of which had never appeared in print.

Walker chose to write in only three forms: (1) narratives as stories or ballads, (2) lyrical songs and sonnets, and (3) the long line of free verse punctuated with a short line. Within these three forms, she pays attention to an assortment of issues and themes. At times, she elegizes the South, as in "Southern Songs," in which she writes that she longs to have her "body bathed again by southern souls" and to "rest unbroken in the fields of southern earth." In other pieces, she memorializes the acts of cultural heroes, such as Paul Lawrence Dunbar, Harriet Tubman, Mary McCleod Bethune, and Owen Dodson, and she struggles to place her own life and work within a collective black American experience in pieces such as the legendary "For My People," "A Litany of Black History for Black People," "A Litany from the Dark People," and "They Have Put Us on Hold." What remains constant throughout is Walker's ability to capture everyday experiences of the common and the legendary with effective cadences and striking imagery.

Many of these same characteristics are visible in her one novel, *Jubilee* (1966). Walker labored over *Jubilee* from 1934 to 1966, constructing it as a fictional tribute to the life of her maternal grandmother, Margaret Duggans Ware Brown, who was born into enslavement. Readers are able to follow the biracial protagonist, Vyry, through enslavement and Reconstruction and closely follow her ascent out of the pit of slavery. *Jubilee* won the 1966 Houghton Mifflin Literary Fellowship Award, and she saw the novel go through 40 printings, sell over 2 million copies, be published in 7 foreign countries, and be adapted as an opera. Walker unsuccessfully sued Alex Haley for copyright infringement of *Jubilee* with his publication of *Roots*.

All of Walker's writing is geographically and ideologically grounded in the South. She taught at Jackson State University for 30 years (1949–79), where she established a Black Studies program and retired as professor emeritus. She acknowledges the South as a critical part of her artistic aesthetic, claiming that "my adjustment or accommodation to this South—whether real or imagined (mythic and legendary), violent or nonviolent—is the subject and source of all my poetry. It is also my life." Even though Walker maintained a love for the South throughout her life, she credits Langston Hughes for telling her parents to get her out of the South, so that she could develop as a writer. Partially because of Hughes's urgings, Walker's parents sent her to Northwestern University where she earned a B.A. in English in 1935.

Margaret Walker was successful in gaining publishing opportunities for diverse forms of writing, and in 1988 she published a psychobiography of Richard Wright, *Daemonic Genius*, which grew out of their long and tumultuous friendship. In 1990, she published *How I Wrote "Jubilee" and Other Essays on Life and Literature*. And, in 1997, with the help of Maryemma Graham, she published a final collection of speeches and essays, *On Being Female, Black, and Free*. In the last decade of her life, she won countless Mississippi and national awards honoring her work, including the National Book Award for Lifetime Achievement (1993).

ETHEL YOUNG-MINOR
University of Mississippi

Amiri Baraka, *Nation* (4 January 1999); Maryemma Graham, ed., *Conversations with Margaret Walker* (2002); Margaret Walker, *This Is My Century* (1989).

Washington, Booker T.
(1856–1915) EDUCATOR.
Booker Taliaferro Washington was the foremost black educator of the late 19th

Booker T. Washington, black educator, ca. 1900 (photographer and number unavailable, Library of Congress, Washington, D.C.)

and early 20th centuries. He also had a major influence on southern race relations and was the dominant figure in black public affairs from 1895 until his death in 1915. Born a slave on a small farm in the Virginia backcountry, he moved with his family after emancipation to work in the salt furnaces and coal mines of West Virginia. After a secondary education at Hampton Institute, he taught in an upgraded school and experimented briefly with the study of law and the ministry, but a teaching position at Hampton decided his future career. In 1881, he founded Tuskegee Normal and Industrial Institute on the Hampton model in the Black Belt of Alabama.

Though Washington offered little

that was innovative in industrial education, which both northern philanthropic foundations and southern leaders were already promoting, he became its chief black exemplar and spokesman. In his advocacy of Tuskegee Institute and its educational method, Washington revealed the political adroitness and accommodationist philosophy that were to characterize his career in the wider arena of race leadership. He convinced southern white employers and governors that Tuskegee offered an education that would keep blacks "down on the farm" and in the trades. To prospective northern donors and particularly the new self-made millionaires such as Rockefeller and Carnegie, he promised the inculcation of the Protestant work ethic. To blacks living within the limited horizons of the post-Reconstruction South, Washington held out industrial education as the means of escape from the web of sharecropping and debt and the achievement of attainable, petit bourgeois goals of self-employment, landownership, and small business. Washington cultivated local white approval and secured a small state appropriation, but it was northern donations that made Tuskegee Institute by 1900 the best-supported black educational institution in the country.

The Atlanta Compromise Address, delivered before the Cotton States Exposition in 1895, widened Washington's influence into the arena of race relations and black leadership. Washington offered black acquiescence in disfranchisement and social segregation if whites would encourage black progress in economic and educational opportunity. Hailed as a sage by whites of both sections, Washington further consolidated his influence with his widely read autobiography, *Up from Slavery* (1901), the founding of the National Negro Business League in 1900, his celebrated dinner at the White House in 1901, and control of patronage politics as chief black adviser to presidents Theodore Roosevelt and William Howard Taft.

Washington kept his white following by conservative policies and moderate utterances, but he faced growing black and white liberal opposition in the Niagara Movement (1905–9) and the NAACP (1909–), groups demanding civil rights and encouraging protest in response to white aggressions such as lynchings, disfranchisement, and seg-regation laws. Washington successfully fended off these critics, often by underhanded means. At the same time, however, he tried to translate his own personal success into black advancement through secret sponsorship of civil rights suits, serving on the boards of Fisk and Howard universities, and directing philanthropic aid to these and other black colleges. His speaking tours and private persuasion tried to equalize public educational opportunities and to reduce racial violence. These efforts were generally unsuccessful, and the year of Washington's death marked the beginning of the Great Migration from the rural South to the urban North. Washington's racial philosophy, pragmatically adjusted to the limiting conditions of his own era, did not survive the change.

LOUIS R. HARLAN
University of Maryland

W. Fitzhugh Brundage, ed., *Booker T. Washington and Black Progress: "Up from Slavery" 100 Years Later* (2003); Louis R. Harlan, *Booker T. Washington*, 2 vols. (1972, 1983); David H. Jackson Jr., *Booker T. Washington and the Struggle against White Supremacy: The Southern Educational Tours, 1908–1912* (2008); August Meyer, *Negro Thought in America, 1880–1915* (1963); Robert J. Norrell, *Up from History: The Life of Booker T. Washington* (2009); Raymond W. Smock, ed., *Booker T. Washington in Perspective: Essays of Louis R. Harlan* (2006).

WDIA

In fall 1948, WDIA in Memphis, Tenn., became the first radio station in the South to adopt an all-black programming format. The station was owned by two white businessmen, but the man most responsible for the format change at WDIA was Nat D. Williams, a local black high school history teacher. Williams was brought into the station to do his own show on an experimental basis; it proved to be an overnight sensation. He was the first black radio announcer in the South to play the popular rhythm-and-blues records of the day over the airways. His show was so successful that within six months of its debut WDIA had changed its format from a classical music station to one appealing solely to black listeners and advertisers.

In addition to initiating an entirely new music format, Williams launched a wide variety of programming innovations at WDIA and recruited other talented blacks onto the airways. His first recruits were fellow high school teachers A. C. Williams and Maurice Hulbert. Both men went on to have long and distinguished careers in black radio. Nat Williams's most famous recruit was a youthful B. B. King, who used the exposure on WDIA to initiate his career as the country's premier urban blues artist. Rufus Thomas became one of the station's most popular on-air disc jockeys. In addition to these black males, Nat D. Williams also recruited the South's first black female announcers to WDIA's airways; two of the best known were Willa Monroe and Starr McKinney, both of whom did programs oriented toward black women.

Gospel music, religious programs, and black news and public affairs shows were also prominent on WDIA. The most acclaimed public affairs program was called *Brown America Speaks*, which was created and hosted by Nat D. Williams. The program addressed race issues from a black perspective and won an award for excellence from the prestigious Ohio State Institute for Education in radio in 1949. With the success of WDIA, other radio stations around the country also began to adopt black-oriented formats, and black radio became a fixture in commercial broadcasting nationwide. WDIA still programs for a black audience in Memphis, making it the oldest black-oriented radio station in the country.

BILL BARLOW
Howard University

Bill Barlow, *Voice Over: The Making of Black Radio* (1999); Louis Cantor, *Wheelin' on Beale: How WDIA-Memphis Became the Nation's First All-Black Radio Station and Created the Sound That Changed America* (1992); Robert Gordon, *It Came from Memphis* (1995); Margaret McKee and Fred Chisenhall, *Beale Black and Blue: Life and Music on Black America's Main Street* (1981); Charles Sawyer, *The Arrival of B. B. King: The Authorized Biography* (1980).

Wells-Barnett, Ida B.

(1862–1931) JOURNALIST AND SOCIAL ACTIVIST.

For Ida B. Wells-Barnett, "southern culture" was an embattled site of identification. She was a native of Holly Springs, Miss., born a slave in 1862. There she attended Rust College, run by the American Missionary Association, and was strongly influenced by its "Yankee" teachers. Wells-Barnett was baptized in the Methodist Episcopal Church. After her parents' death in the yellow fever epidemic of 1878, she moved to Memphis, Tenn., around 1880 and lived there until 1892. That year, she published her most important writing, a pamphlet entitled "Southern Horrors: Lynch Law in All Its Phases." This essay placed southern codes of honor in the context of the horror of the lynching-for-rape scenario, part of a violent, morally hypocritical, crassly economic system of white supremacy. White men justified the murder of "bestial" black men by claiming the role of protectors of "weak" white women; Wells-Barnett proved that, statistically, the rape charge was rarely in play during actual, documented lynchings. Instead, the cry of rape was often a cover to punish black men who in any way challenged the social, political, or economic status quo of the South. She also pointed out that white women sometimes participated in both mob activity and consensual sex with black men. When a death threat appeared in print in 1893 because of Wells-Barnett's newspaper criticism of lynching and southern honor, the region became off-limits for her and she left for the North. She returned only once, in 1917, to investigate the plight of 16 Arkansas farmers imprisoned for labor-organizing activity and sentenced to die in Helena, and then she went in disguise.

Ida B. Wells-Barnett became famous—to opponents, infamous—for her critique of the South, but she accomplished the work largely outside of it. In 1895, she settled in Chicago, married lawyer Ferdinand L. Barnett, and raised four children. She died there in 1931. She arguably achieved greatest prominence outside the United States during the years 1893 and 1894, when she traveled to England and Scotland to mobilize opposition to lynching in the United States. At strategic points, however, she referred to herself as a "southern girl, born and bred," or by the pen name "Exiled." Such identifications established her credibility as a native witness to history, especially since a black woman's moral authority was by definition suspect in U.S. society. After a difficult period of political retrenchment in Chicago and the brutal race riot of July 1919, Wells-Barnett again accented her southern roots and reached out to the progressive elements of the white South in renewed efforts toward interracial understanding in the region, but this offer likely did not even reach the ears that had long since tuned her out.

Ironically, some of the best evidence of Ida B. Wells-Barnett's sparsely documented personal life dates from the 1880s, when she lived in Memphis and participated in a wide array of activities that mark her as a product of the post-Reconstruction New South. She left a diary dating from December 1885 to September 1887, which provides vivid details of her life during this dynamic period. Entries describe a context not, perhaps, stereotypically "southern" or dominated by folkways. She studied Shakespeare and elocution, attended lectures by national figures like Dwight Moody, and was present at gender- and racially inclusive meetings of the Knights of Labor. The diary further documents her anger at injustice and violence directed at African Americans, some of which touched Wells-Barnett directly, as in her forced removal from a railroad "ladies" car. She was also the godmother of a child whose father was murdered, along with two business associates, during a conflict in spring 1892. This triple lynching in Memphis was a life-changing event that directed her attention to full-time anti–mob violence protest.

Ida B. Wells-Barnett organized against southern violence outside of the region, resulting in scores of local anti-lynching committees and the founding of the National Association of Colored Women (1896) and the NAACP (1909). Her efforts successfully positioned anti-lynching as a legitimate focus of national reform, but based in the urban North. In that context, individuals and groups more securely positioned than she by academic credentials, social status, or political connections in publishing, philanthropy, and government assumed leadership of the issue in the World War I era. Although Ida B. Wells-Barnett's southernness enabled her powerful voice to emerge in the 1890s, she was eclipsed by the competitive, money-driven, and consolidating trends that came to characterize social reform in the United States over her lifetime.

PATRICIA A. SCHECHTER
Portland State University

Miriam DeCosta-Willis, ed., *The Memphis Diary of Ida B. Wells: An Intimate Portrait of the Activist as a Young Woman* (1995); Trudier Harris, ed., *Selected Works of Ida B. Wells-Barnett* (1991); Patricia A. Schechter, *Ida B. Wells-Barnett and American Reform, 1880–1930* (2001); Ida B. Wells-Barnett, *Crusade for Justice: The Autobiography of Ida B. Wells* (1970).

Williams, Hank

(1923–1953) COUNTRY MUSIC SINGER. Widely acclaimed as country music's greatest singer and composer, Hiram Hank Williams was born on 17 October 1923 at Olive Hill, near Georgiana, Ala., the son of a sawmill and railroad worker. He was introduced to music in the Baptist Church where he was faithfully taken by his mother. According to popular legend, he learned both songs and guitar chords from a black street singer in Georgiana, Rufus Payne ("Teetot"). Williams often recorded country blues and is a prime example of the influence of African American music on country music.

Williams's evolution as a professional performer and composer began at the age of 14 when he won a talent show in a Montgomery theater singing his own composition, "WPA Blues." He obtained his first radio job in the same year, 1937, at WSFA in Montgomery. When World War II—that crucible that integrated country music's disparate regional styles and ultimately nationalized it—came, Williams worked in the Mobile ship-yards and sang regularly in the honky-tonks of south Alabama. By the time the war ended, Williams had experienced eight hard years of performing and had built a style that reflected the composite musical influences of his youth: gospel, blues, and old-time country. Professionally, he acknowledged a debt to the Texas honky-tonk singer Ernest Tubb and to the Tennessee mountain singer Roy Acuff, whose styles Williams fused in a way that reflected a similar synthesis in the larger country field during the war and immediate postwar years.

Hank Williams, country music star, ca. 1950
(Country Music Foundation, Library and Media
Center, Nashville)

Williams's ascendance to fame began shortly after the war when he became associated with Fred Rose, the famous Nashville songwriter and publisher. Rose encouraged Williams's natural songwriting abilities and published his songs; helped him obtain recording contracts with Sterling and MGM Records; persuaded Molly O'Day, one of the greatest singers of the time, to record some of Williams's compositions; and helped him get a position on KWKH's *Louisiana Hayride* in Shreveport. The *Hayride*, which was then second only to the *Grand Ole Opry* as a successful country radio show, was the vehicle that launched Williams on the road to performing fame.

Hank Williams's national ascendancy came in 1949 when he recorded an old pop tune, "Lovesick Blues," which featured the yodeling he had learned from another Alabama singer,

Rex Griffin. Williams soon moved to the *Grand Ole Opry*, where he became the most popular country singer since Jimmie Rodgers. In the brief span from 1949 to 1953, Williams dominated the country charts with songs that are still considered classics of country music: "I'm So Lonesome I Could Cry," "Cold Cold Heart," "Your Cheating Heart," "Honky Tonk Blues," "Jambalaya," and many others. With his band, the Drifting Cowboys, Williams played a major role in making country music a national phenomenon. With a remarkably expressive voice that moved with equal facility from the strident yodeling of "Long Gone Lonesome Blues" to the gentle lyricism of "I Just Told Mama Goodbye," Williams communicated with his listeners in a fashion that has only rarely been equaled by other country singers. The word "sincerity" has no doubt been overused in describing the styles of country musicians, but in the case of Williams it means simply that he as a singer convincingly articulated in song a feeling that he and his listeners shared.

As a songwriter—not as a singer—Williams played a most important role in breaking down the fragile barriers between country and pop music. Williams's singing was quintessentially rural, and his own records never "crossed over" into the lucrative pop market. His songs, though, moved into the larger sphere of American popular music and from there, perhaps, into the permanent consciousness of the American people. Like no earlier country writer's works, Williams's songs appeared with great frequency in the repertoires of such pop musicians as Tony Bennett, Frankie Laine, and Mitch Miller. For good or ill, this popularization in pop music continues.

Commercial and professional success did not bring peace of mind to the Alabama country boy. A chronic back ailment, a troubled marriage, and a subsequent divorce and remarriage accentuated a penchant for alcohol, which he had acquired when only a small boy. After being fired by the *Grand Ole Opry* for drunkenness and erratic behavior, he returned to the scene of his first triumphs—the *Louisiana Hayride*. He died of a heart attack on 1 January 1953, but his legacy lives on in his songs and in the scores of singers, including his immensely talented son, Hank Jr., who still bear his influence.

BILL C. MALONE
Madison, Wisconsin

Colin Escott, *Hank Williams: The Biography* (1995); Chet Flippo, *Your Cheatin' Heart: A Biography of Hank Williams* (1981); Paul Hemphill, *Lovesick Blues: The Life of Hank Williams* (2005); George William Koon and Bill Koon, *Hank Williams, So Lonesome* (2002); Bill C. Malone, *Country Music, U.S.A.: A Fifty-Year History* (1968; rev. eds., 1985, 2002); Roger M. Williams, *Sing a Sad Song: The Life of Hank Williams* (1981).

Wright, Richard

(1908–1960) WRITER.
Born near Natchez, Miss., on 4 September 1908, Richard Wright, like the famous protagonist of his first novel, was a native son in a region obsessed with race. The child of a sharecropper who deserted the family in 1914, young Richard moved with his mother during his early years from one to another of the extended family's homes in Arkansas and Jackson, Miss., living in Memphis after he completed the ninth grade. Poverty and the fear and hate typifying post-Reconstruction racial relations in the Lower South, more than the sustaining power of black culture or education in segregated schools, prepared him to be an author. If he omitted from his autobiographical record his experience with middle-class values in his mother's family, or the effect of the motions and rituals of the black world, there was psychological truth in his record of nativity as written in *Black Boy* (1945). He was surely a product of the older South and of the great black migration to the cities; his distinction lay in his refusal to be simply a product.

In "The Ethics of Living Jim Crow," published in a WPA writer's anthology, *American Stuff* (1937), which first appeared in the year he moved from Chicago to New York City, Wright revealed the dynamics of his life's work as an author. Caste, he wrote, prescribed his public behavior; but though he knew its requirements, he would not accede. Terror could not induce him to adopt the pretense that he knew his place. Conflict was unavoidable and its only resolution was violence.

Uncle Tom's Children (1938, and expanded 1940), the collection of novellas with which Wright won his first literary success, indicates by an irony of its title the goal southern whites had for southern blacks. The stories are united by the theme of collective response to racist terror, as the children of Uncle Tom refuse to accept the popular stereotype.

Lawd Today was the first example of Wright's extension of southern learning to life in the migrant black communities of the North, but this apprentice novel was not published until 1963. *Native Son* (1940) first carried his insights to a large and appreciative audience. A Guggenheim Fellowship to complete the novel, its selection by the Book-of-the-Month Club, and its arrival within weeks at the top of the best-seller list attested to the appearance of a major American author. In the compelling character of Bigger Thomas, Wright created a complex symbol of a rising awareness that no risk is too great in order to become master of one's own life. Through creating sympathy for Bigger's violent actions, Wright carried the tradition of protest to new lengths.

His insider's view of Jim Crow earned Wright acclaim for his use of literary naturalism. His projection of violence and rebellion against social conditions led to his emergence as a major literary voice of black America.

Wright's next book, *12 Million Black Voices* (1941), presented a folk history extending from slavery's middle passage through the development of an Afro-American culture in the South and the hope of a black nation as a result of migration north. On the other hand, *Black Boy*, an ostensible autobiography representing the birth of the artist, necessarily suppressed the importance of group experience in order to focus on the power of the individual sensibility.

Wright forged his identity among his people on southern ground but sought room to write by passage into modern life, symbolized by northern cities. This strategy becomes even clearer in the second part of the autobiography, published as *American Hunger* in 1977.

In time, Wright found that Jim Crow knew no regional boundaries. Chicago and then New York constrained him as much as had Mississippi. So in 1946 he moved with his wife, Ellen Poplar, whom he had married in 1941, and their daughter to Paris. Suggestions have been made that the self-imposed exile, which was to last until Wright's death in 1960, sapped his creativity. To be sure, distance prevented intimate knowledge of contemporary changes in his native region and the black migrant communities, yet he created two novels concerning American racial relations and politics even after his exile. *The Outsider*, presenting an existentialist antihero living in Chicago and New York, appeared in 1953, and *The Long Dream*, a comprehensive reimagining of coming-of-age in Mississippi, appeared in 1958. Other fiction from the exile years includes *Savage Holiday* (1954), an experiment in raceless fiction, and the collection of stories, old and new, posthumously published as *Eight Men* (1961). This record of production hardly suggests flagging creativity.

Even more important to Wright's career, however, was the energy he found in exile to undertake four studies on a global scale. *Black Power* (1954) relates observations on his travels in the Gold Coast shortly before it became the nation of Ghana; *The Color Curtain* (1956) reports on the anticolonial positions developed at the conference in Bandung; *Pagan Spain* (1957) records a trip into a culture Wright viewed as a survival of premodern Europe; and *White Man, Listen!* (1957) collects essays on race in America and the European colonies.

Despite the apparent departure from the experience of the American South in these later works, continuity exists between the original treatments of Jim Crow and the commentary on historical change in Africa and Asia. The prevailing subject remains race relations between whites and blacks, but beyond that is the more profound connection Wright saw in the special history of "colored" peoples. To be black in America, he believed, was to be marched forcibly into the pain of the modern world. As a representative black American, Wright already had lived the historical experience that awaited the Third World. By the power of literary imagination, Wright, with unmatched skill, drew forth the significance of his southern education for world citizenship.

JOHN M. REILLY
State University of New York at Albany

Charles T. Davis and Michel Fabre, *Richard Wright: A Primary Bibliography* (1982); Michel Fabre, *The Unfinished Quest of Richard Wright* (1973); Eugene E. Miller, *Voice of a Native Son: The Poetics of Richard Wright* (1990); John M. Reilly, in *Black American Writers: Bibliographical Essays*, ed. M. Thomas Inge and Maurice Duke (1978); Hazel Rowley, *Richard Wright: The Life and Times* (2002).

INDEX OF CONTRIBUTORS

Page numbers in boldface refer to articles.

Guangdong Province, China, 30
Guatemala, 137
Guinn v. United States, 169
Gullah, 65, 182
Gutiérrez, José Angel, 48
Guy, James Harris, 86

H-2A temporary worker program, 24, 105
Hahamovitch, Cindy, 24
Hahn, Steven, 158
Haiti, 19–20, 36–37, 39
Haley, Alex, 271
Hall, Rick, 244
Hall, Stuart, 62
Hamlet, The (Faulkner), 214
Hampton Indian Program, 118–20
Hampton Institute, 118–20
Hanan, Philip, 263
Handman, Max, 25–27
Handy, W. C., 195, 196
Harkins, George Washington, 113
Harlan County, Ky., 179
Harlem, N.Y., 196
Harlem Shadows (Bontemps), 196
Harper's Magazine, 154
Harris, Joel Chandler, 19, 83
Harris, J. William, 59–60
Hate Crime that Changed America, The (Till-Mobley), 260
Havana, Cuba, 37
Hawkins, Benjamin, 117
Hawkins, Roger, 244
Haxton, Kenneth, 207
Hayes, Isaac, 255–56, 257–58
Helena, Ark., 275
Heller, Jean, 261
Helms, Jesse, 104–5, 156, 238
Hemenway, Robert E., 221
Hemmings, Sally, 64
Henry, John, 72–73
Henson, Jim, 207
Hernández, Mario, 47
Herskovits, Melville J., 18
Hill, Darryl, 176–77
Hill-Burton Act, 96

HIV, 28
Holiness Church, 133
Holway, John, 175
Homestead Grays, 174
Homosexuals, 229
Honduras, 38, 108
Hood, David, 244
Hood, James, 151
Hooker, John Lee, 193
Hoover, J. Edgar, 269
Hopewell Plantation, 117
Hose, Sam, 90
Houma Indians, 219
House, Son, 205
House behind the Cedars, The (Chesnutt), 84, 199
Houston, Charles Hamilton, 40, 169
Houston, Tex., 6, 262–65
Howard, Elston, 176
Howard University, 197
Howard University Medical School, 94, 96
Howe, LeAnne, 86
Howells, William Dean, 199
How I Wrote "Jubilee" and Other Essays on Life and Literature (M. Walker), 271
Hucksters, 64–65
Hughes, Jimmy, 244
Hughes, Langston, 196, 260, 269, 271
Huguenots, 215
Huie, William Bradford, 259
Hulbert, Maurice, 274
Hurston, Kelso, 244
Hurston, Zora Neale, 85, **220–21**, 269
Hurt, Mississippi John, 204

I Am a Fugitive from a Chain Gang (Bontemps), 56
I Am a Man: From Memphis, a Lesson in Life (Bontemps), 240
Iglesia de Cristo Ministerios Elim, 137
Illinois, 108
Immigration, 21–23, 30–34, 37–39, 75, 80–81, 101, 147, 229
Immigration and Naturalization Service (INS), 33

84; removal, 1, **112–14**; migration, 5, 107–8; folktales, 19; racial classification, **162–66**; religion, 62, **138–42**; African Americans and, **114–19**; military service, 192; labor, 200; Voting Rights Act of 1965, 266, 268. *See also individual tribes*

Negro in American Fiction, The (S. Brown), 197

Negro Leagues, 174–76

Negro National News, 188

Nelson, George, 251

Nelson, Scott Reynolds, 72–73

Nelson, Shirley, 260

Nelson, Willie, 246

Neshoba County, Miss., 228

Neville, Aaron, 205

Newark, N.J., 190

Newark Eagles, 175

Newman, Ga., 90

New Mexico, 108

New National Era, 211

New Orleans, 21–22, 35–39, 111, 120–21, 124, 126, 187, 215, 224–25, 235–37

New Orleans Times Picayune, 154

New Orleans Tribune, 37

New Republic, 18

New York, N.Y., 21–22, 35, 102–3, 108–10, 189–90

New York Herald Tribune, 155

New York Times, 261

Nonviolent Resistance to Segregation Leadership Conference, 189

Nordan, Lewis, 260

North American Free Trade Agreement, 105

North Carolina, 17, 52, 99–101, 108, 136, 151, 156, 163–66, 243

North Carolina A&T College for Negroes, 41

North Carolina Growers' Association, 243

North Carolina State University, 176

Northington, Nat, 177

North Star, 210

Notes on the State of Virginia (Jefferson), 64, 82

Nott, Josiah, 67

Oblates of Mary Immaculate, 134

O'Connor, Flannery, 269

O'Connor, Sandra Day, 172

October Journey (M. Walker), 270

O'Day, Molly, 277

O'Donovan, Susan, 2

Office of Indian Affairs (OIA), 165–66

Ogeechee, 65

Oklahoma, 101–2, 141, 163, 182, 234

Oklahoma State University, 177

Oldham, Spooner, 244

Old South, The: "A Summer Tragedy" and Other Stories of the Thirties (Bontemps), 196

Ole Miss. *See* University of Mississippi

Oliver, Joseph "King," 187, 225

On Being Female, Black, and Free (M. Walker), 271

Once (A. Walker), 269

One Woman, The (Dixon), 209

Original Dixieland Jazz Band, 225

Ortiz, Fernando, 181

Ory, Edward "Kid," 187, 225

Oslo, Norway, 261

Osmonds, 245

Our Lady of Charity, 136

Outsider, The (Wright), 279

Oxford, Miss., 213–14

Oxford USA, 155

Pacific worlds and the South, **120–25**

Page, Greg, 177

Page, Thomas Nelson, 83

Paige, Satchel, 174, 176

Pan-Africanism, 72

Panic of 1893, 52

Paper industry, 80

Parchman Farm, Miss., 51

Parents Involved in Community Schools v. Seattle School District No. 1 et al., 152

U.S. Bureau of Refugees, Freedmen, and Abandoned Lands, 125
U.S. Department of Health and Human Services, 261
U.S. Marine Hospital Service (USMHS), 185–86
U.S. Naval Academy, 176
U.S. News and World Report, 154
U.S. Public Health Service, 96; Study of Untreated Syphilis (USPHSS), 260–61
United States v. Cruikshank et al., 127
Universal Negro Improvement Association, 72
University of Alabama, 151, 177
University of Kentucky, 177
University of Maryland, 176
University of Mississippi, 155, 157, 174, 176, 177, 254
University of Missouri Law School, 150
University of North Carolina, 164
Untold Story of Emmett Till, 260
Unvanquished, The (Faulkner), 157–58, 214
Up from Slavery (Washington), 273

Vagrancy codes, 71, 100
Vaughan, Stevie Ray, 111
Veech, James, 239
Vengeance and Justice (Ayers), 57
Verghese, Abraham, 28–29
Vesey, Denmark, 36
Vietnamese, **262–65**
Village de L'Est (New Orleans, La.), 124–25
Vincent, Michel, 36–37
Violence, 125–27, 128, 160, 228–35, 245, 268, 273, 275–76
Virginia, 17, 54, 74, 81–82, 108, 141, 143, 150, 151
Virginia Commission on Constitutional Government, 254
Virginia's Defenders of State Sovereignty, 156–57
Voice from the South, A (Cooper), 84, 202
Voodoo, 131
Voter Education Project, 252

Voting Rights Act of 1965, 42–43, 171, 226, 254, **265–68**

Wake Forest University, 177
Wallace, George, 151, 254
Walker, Alice, 85, 221, **268–70**
Walker, David, 3
Walker, Dorcus, 74–75
Walker, Edwin A., 157
Walker, Margaret, 270–71
War, 257
Waring, Thomas R., 154
Washington, Booker T., 51, 53, 130, 148, 186, 199, 202, 211, 212, **271–73**
Washington, D.C., 150, 156, 170
Washington, Kenny, 176
Watts Riot, 44
WDIA, **273–74**
Weiss, Julie, 22–23
Wells-Barnett, Ida B., 84, **275–76**
West, Nancy, 74
Westover's Secret Diary, 1709-1712 (Byrd), 82
West Virginia, 179
Wetumpka, Ala., 50
Wewoka, Okla., 183
Wexler, Jerry, 244, 256
Whippings, 92–93, 126, 231
White Citizens' Council (WCC), 151, 170
White Man (Wright), 280
White supremacy, 147, 159–60, 248; in religion, **142–46**
Who Speaks for the South? (Dobbs), 252
Wife of His Youth and Other Stories of the Color Line, The (Chesnutt), 199
Wildcat, 118
Wild Palms, The (Faulkner), 214
Willard, Jess, 174
Williams, A. C., 274
Williams, Hank, 205, 246, **276–78**
Williams, Hank, Jr., 278
Williams, Hosea, 43
Williams, John Bell, 156
Williams, Mary Lou, 225